D1155912

Space, Style and Structure

Volume Two

An American Revolution Bicentennial Commemorative Project

This cooperative study was financed in part through grants from the Junior League of Portland, Oregon, the National Society of the Colonial Dames of America in Oregon, the Oregon Committee for the Humanities (National Endowment for the Humanities, Washington, D.C.), the Oregon Historical Society, Portland, and the Louis W. and Maud Hill Family Foundation, St. Paul, Minnesota.

Thomas Vaughan, Editor
Virginia Guest Ferriday, Associate Editor

Space, Style and Structure

Building in Northwest America

Oregon Historical Society   Portland, Oregon, 1974

1230 S. W. Park Ave., Portland 97205

First Edition

Library of Congress Catalog Number 74–17267

SBN 87595 – 047 – 7

Designed by Corinna Campbell Cioeta

Typeset by
Modern Typographers, Inc.,
Clearwater, Florida

Printed by
Glass-Dahlstrom Printers and Lithographers
Portland, Oregon U.S.A.

Contents

III Railroad Era

Buildings and Gardens

Spas, Coastal Resorts, and Mountain Retreats

Elisabeth Walton

Railroads generated the first real surge of popular tourism in the Northwest. Hotels on the major railroad lines were designed to attract and accommodate great numbers of travelers, and the most noted were financed by railroad companies. They were promoted along with a cornucopia of promising characteristics of the newly developing region, ranging from commercial and agricultural prospects to climate and natural scenery. Railroad promotional literature of the period was designed to encourage newcomers to settle and, significantly enough, it advertised an impressive variety of recreational opportunities.

One of the landmarks of the period in the Columbia Gorge was the Mount Hood Hotel erected in Hood River in 1882 by Peter Hosford. The long, rectangular three and a half-story frame structure had a large patronage while the Oregon Railway and Navigation Company line was being completed along the south bank of the river early in the decade. It became a headquarters for excursions to resorts associated with lakes and glaciers of nearby Mt. Hood which could be reached by wagon road. A red letter day in the history of such hotels was created by the visit of an exceptional dignitary. In the spring of 1891, new management of the Mt. Hood Hotel hosted U.S. President Benjamin Harrison and several of his cabinet members, who were greeted by local citizens and school children at the Oregon Railway and Navigation Company station a stone's throw away. Afterwards, Company D, Third Regiment of the Oregon National Guard escorted the party to the gaily decorated dining room of the hotel for further ceremonies.[1]

In its original form, the Mt. Hood Hotel had a modified H-shaped plan in which two square observation towers with bell-cast hipped roofs flanked a small recessed court which sheltered an entrance at the second story. Brick piers supported slender, tapered columns of the Ionic order which extended fully two stories to carry an entablature and deck. Railings with elaborately turned spindles, lighter in mass at the second and

---

1. Unidentified clipping with dateline of Hood River, Oregon, July 31, 1915, Oregon Historical Society Scrapbook 53, p. 141.

Fig. III–334. "Water Lines to the Seaside and San Francisco," 1899. Illustrated advertisement of the Oregon Railway and Navigation Company passenger department.

third stories than at the first, made an impressive display of open, wraparound verandas which were the *sine qua non* of vernacular hotels of the period. The long hipped roof and belt cornices and roofs of the twin towers were carried by brackets in the Italianate tradition.

In larger cities on the long-distance railroad network, railroad hotels were big ventures conceived in the most up-to-date styles by architects recruited from the East.

It was Henry Villard, based in New York, whose interests extended the Oregon and California Railroad from Portland to California and built the Oregon Railway and Navigation Company line from Portland up the Columbia. He organized the Northern Pacific Terminal Company to build a station in Portland, then the center of transportation and commerce in the region and the proposed terminus of the transcontinental Northern Pacific Railroad. The scheme also called for a railroad bridge across the Willamette River, docks and machine shops, and a monumental hotel.[2]

In 1882 Villard commissioned the eminent New York firm of McKim, Mead and White to design the Portland Hotel. A design in the Queen Anne Revival Style then fashionable on the East Coast was provided, and construction of the foundation was underway before the collapse of Villard's fortunes in 1883.[3] In time, the commission was completed with local financing. Construction was supervised by William M. Whidden, formerly associated with McKim, Mead and White, and Ion Lewis, formerly of the Boston firm of Peabody and Stearns. Opened for use in 1890, the seven-story Portland Hotel occupied a full block west of the Pioneer Courthouse on Southwest Sixth Avenue. North and south wings of its U-shaped plan formed an interior court. Vertical and horizontal bandings of red brick marking off bays and stories made a pleasing contrast with stuccoed wall surfaces and a high two-story basement of dressed stone. The exterior plane was varied by oriel windows and corner bays extending from the top of the basement to eaves of a steeply pitched roof. Interest at the roof line was created by turrets over large bays in the interior corners, gable-roofed and shed-roofed dormers and bold brick chimneys which projected above all. Regrettably, the hotel was razed in 1951, and the site cleared for parking.

In 1885 a second commission in the region by the firm of McKim, Mead and White was completed in the deepwater port of Tacoma on Puget Sound. With new backing, the Northern Pacific Railroad Company was driving to completion its line directly to the Sound over the Cascade Range, and Tacoma was burgeoning at the prospect. The Tacoma Hotel, no longer extant, was carried out in the Queen Anne Style similar to that of the Portland Hotel, though the plan and roof line

2. Glenn Chesney Quiett, *They Built the West: An Epic of Rails and Cities* (New York, 1934), 368.

3. Willard B. Robinson, "Northwest Architecture, 1843–1893" (Master of Architecture thesis, Rice Institute, Houston, Texas, 1960), 93–94.

Fig. III–335. Mt. Hood Hotel, Hood River, Oregon, 1882.

Fig. III–336. Northeast view, Portland Hotel, 1882–89.

Fig. III–337. Tacoma Hotel, Tacoma, 1885.

were somewhat more complex, including wings crossing the main axis, recessed spaces, and corner towers with conical roofs. Tall chimney stacks and brick belt courses and vertical bandings in the form of quoining heightened the polychromatic effect here also. Many of the openings were round-arched, and darker colored brick was used to emphasize arch heads and outline decorative arches on a taut surface. Characteristic of this style was the use of many small panes in the upper window sashes. To give tourists every opportunity to take the air and enjoy the view, a one-story veranda extended across the front of the hotel which overlooked Commencement Bay. The hotel was destroyed by fire in the 1930s.

As the Northern Pacific line through the Cascades was completed, boom psychology prevailed in Tacoma, and at the height of this mood a scheme for a new tourist hotel on the bluffs overlooking the bay and with an unobstructed view of Mt. Rainier was developed. The original design for the Tourist Hotel is attributed to the Philadelphia firm of G. W. and W. D. Hewitt. The scheme was carried out in 1893.[4] It was conceived in an early French Renaissance Revival Style which was to be employed by the Canadian Pacific Railway as an institutional style from the time of completion, also in 1893, of Château Frontenac in Quebec, gateway to the Canadian transcontinental route. Typically, buildings of this historic style were immense and multi-storied. They were normally constructed of brick masonry with stone trim, and they commanded imposing sites on promontories or fronting harbors. Based upon a romantic concept of medieval castles, the most characteristic features of these buildings were steeply-pitched hipped roofs bristling with pointed dormer windows with compound openings, elongated chimney stacks, turrets, spires and iron roof ridge decoration. This Loire Valley Château mode introduced to Canada by the Canadian Pacific Railway's Boston architect, Bruce Price, was used steadfastly for CPR resort hotels in the West through the 1920s.[5] The Empress Hotel on the harbor in Victoria, British Columbia, designed by Francis Mawson Rattenbury and executed 1904–1908, is a well-known example of the "Chateauesque" Style integrated into a formal urban setting.

When financial panic occurred later in 1893, construction was halted on the Tourist Hotel in Tacoma, a project on which half a million dollars had been expended. A fire destroyed the interior subsequently, and in 1906 the shell was taken over by the city and converted for use as a public school. Adjacent to it in a natural gulch along the waterfront was constructed a concrete stadium with seating capacity of 30,000.[6] The

4. Robinson, "Northwest Architecture, 1843–1893," 95. The original design of the Tourist Hotel was attributed to Frederick Heath in *The New Washington: A Guide to the Evergreen State* (Portland, 1950), 158.

5. Harold D. Kalman, *The Railway Hotels and the Development of the Château Style in Canada* (Victoria, B.C., 1968), 30.

6. Quiett, *They Built the West*, 429.

Fig. III–338. Tourist Hotel, Tacoma, 1893. Water color rendering signed "J. Anderson, Washington, 1892."

Fig. III–339. Idanha Hotel, Boise, 1901.

property is still in use as Stadium High School.

In the hands of provincial architects and builders, the Chateauesque Style was vastly simplified in scale and plan, but the surface detail was unmistakable. The Idanha Hotel in Boise, designed by Walter S. Campbell, still stands at the northeast corner of 10th and Main Streets.[7] The six-story brick masonry hotel with its shallow mansard roof, turreted outside corner bays and oriel windows with crenellated parapets symmetrically placed on the principal facade, was the grandest hotel the city had ever had when it was completed in 1901.

The style was not very successfully translated into the vernacular, but as in the Idanha Hotel at Soda Springs, Idaho, variegated surface patterns of wood and jig-saw work achieved contrasting textural and polychromatic effects not unlike those obtained with brick and limestone. In frame structures further reduced to plain and angular forms, such as the Hotel Linkville in Klamath Falls, gable-roofed dormers, polygonal corner towers, and wood trim painted in contrasting colors amounted to an unpretentious nod to the high style.

A taste for the picturesque and rustic, which ran as a continuous thread through resort architecture in the West well into the 20th century, emerged at seaside resorts in the 1890s. The original Hotel Gearhart at Gearhart Park a few miles north of Seaside on Clatsop Beach on the northern Oregon coast, was built around 1894. It burned down some 20 years later. A good example of the Stick Style of the Queen Anne Revival, the three and a half-story hotel was sheltered from the wind in a grove of evergreens behind the foredune. In her article published

7. "Architecturally Significant and Historic Buildings of Boise, Idaho" (Idaho State Historical Society *Information Sheet No. 7*, 1971).

Fig. III–340. Idanha Hotel, Soda Springs, Idaho.

Fig. III–341. Hotel Linkville, Klamath Falls, Oregon.

in *The Overland* magazine in 1894, Frances Fuller Victor explained that Gearhart Park was modeled after the plan of Pacific Grove in California. It had "a large hotel in the modern style in connection with an extensive tract of woodland, which is sold in lots to those who prefer cottage homes of their own, or who annually encamp for a few weeks at this

Fig. III–342. West elevation, Hotel Gearhart, Gearhart, Oregon, circa 1894.

Fig. III–343. Footbridge west of Hotel Gearhart. Photograph circa 1896.

place." As at Pacific Grove, the Chautauqua Association erected an auditorium at the popular Clatsop Beach retreat.[8] Distinctive features of the west face of the hotel were a small central balcony at the attic story, and a two-story veranda with highly decorated railings and posts and a grand staircase with a double flight of steps joining in access to the second, or main story. On the ocean side of the hotel a rustic footbridge carried by braced, unfinished poles crossed a swale formed by parallel ridges. In imitation of the stylized decoration of the hotel's porches, bent wood members, uprights and cross pieces were assembled to form the bridge railings.

A whimsical expression of the rustic craze was the turn-of-the-century Driftwood Cottage at Long Beach, one of several sea beaches on the peninsula in southwestern Washington which rose to favor during this period as passenger trains were provided from the steamer landing at Ilwaco. The gable roof and dormers of the two-story log cottage were outlined with oblong wooden fishnet floats strung end-to-end, and driftwood formed twig-like facia boards of the porch and decorated the railings of the deck and open observation tower. Window openings were trimmed with unfinished tree branches appliquéd to simulate pediments. The interior was similarly embellished. Whole logs stripped of bark were used as beams, and between them driftwood pieces laid in contrasting patterns decorated the ceilings. Driftwood Cottage represented an idiosyncratic use of the "found object" in architecture of the region,

---

8. Frances Fuller Victor, "Northern Seaside Resorts," *The Overland*, Vol. 23 (February, 1894), 144.

Fig. III–344. Driftwood Cottage, Long Beach, Washington.

Fig. III–345. Camping en route to mineral springs, Grant County, Oregon, circa 1886.

Fig. III–346. Dore's Soda Springs, Grant County, Oregon. Photograph, 1888.

but its tradition is rooted in the grottoes and novel rustic elements of 17th century French gardens.

"General healthfulness" was an attribute of the Pacific Northwest assigned and promoted by the Bureau of Immigration and the Northern Pacific Railroad. The region's record of good health was attributed to temperate and "genial" climate and to an astonishing number of mineral springs which were beginning to attract great attention.[9] Those early hot springs developments remote from settlements and public transportation were somewhat primitive and informal.

The Wilhoit Springs resort, occupying a 20-acre site south of Molalla in Clackamas County, was noted for its camp-like atmosphere, but it also offered a wide variety of facilities and amusements at the height of its popularity in this period. John Wilhoit settled the area in 1866 and sold his interest in the springs in the 1870s. By the 1890s regular stage service was provided to the watering place from Salem, 32 miles away. The development begun by Frank W. McLeran consisted of a two-story clapboarded frame hotel with veranda, a store, bathhouse with board and batten siding, a bowling alley, a large octagonal dance pavilion surmounted by a bandstand, and later a clubhouse. In the small, octagonal conversation pavilions which dotted the hotel grounds, and in the novel verge board effects on the gable ends of the log cottages, the rustic mode was in tune with its wooded setting. Guests paid $10 to $12 for a

9. Bureau of Immigration and Northern Pacific Railroad, *The Pacific Northwest: Facts Relating to the History, Topography, Climate, Soil, Agriculture, Forests, Fisheries, Mineral Resources, Commerce, Industry, Lands, Means of Communication, of Oregon and Washington Territory* (New York, 1882), 21–22.

Fig. III–347. Hotel, Wilhoit Springs, Oregon, 1886.

week's board and lodging at the hotel and all the restorative mineral water they required. Those who stayed in the cabins paid $1.50 to $3.00 a week, and those who camped paid a token weekly rate of $.50.[10] Such facilities put resorts within reach of the average man.

On the Washington shore of the Columbia River, Collins Hot Mineral Springs Hotel was a somewhat more elegant resort with grounds laid out along similar lines. Portlanders took the Spokane Flyer of the Oregon Railway and Navigation Company to Collins Station, and proceeded by launch across the river. One of the features of F. A. Young's large, frame establishment with double wrap-around veranda, was a well-lighted dining room with seating capacity for 146 guests. As at Wilhoit Springs, there were provided on extensive grounds a dance hall, general store and bathhouse. Facilities for "tenters" were located in a

Fig. III–348. Springhouse and grounds, Wilhoit Springs.

grove of oak and fir trees east of the hotel. Another popular spa in the Columbia Gorge was the Saint Martins' Mineral Springs Hotel near Carson, Washington, on the west bank of the Wind River.

Shortly after the turn of the century the southern Oregon community of Ashland, in Jackson County, on the Southern Pacific Company line, became widely known as a health resort. Passengers alighting at the station could conveniently avail themselves of a drink of effervescent

10. Carl Schmeiser, "Wilhoit Hotel Famous for Good Food," *The Bulletin* (Dec. 19, 1973), 3; "Rest and Rejuvenation Secrets of Wilhoit," *The Bulletin* (Jan. 16, 1974), 3.

Fig. III–349. Log cottages, Wilhoit Springs.

Fig. III–350. Collins Hot Springs Hotel, Collins, Washington.

Fig. III–351. Lithia Fountain and Southern Pacific Railroad Station, Ashland, Oregon.

lithia water from a fountain in the nearby plaza. Those who intended to spend some time stayed at the tourist camp in Lithia Park or at the Southern Pacific's Hotel Oregon, a sizeable brick masonry structure in the Queen Anne Revival Style which was remodeled in later years and is no longer extant. Among early tourist attractions in Ashland were the Chautauqua series and sulphur baths, including Helman's Natatorium. Over a period of years, various marketing schemes were proposed to capitalize on the 40 or more lithia, soda and sulphur springs under the city's jurisdiction. As various civic improvements aimed at developing a major resort were voted by the people, Ashland for a time fully expected to become the Saratoga Springs of the West, and the Southern Pacific Railroad gave its full cooperation in promoting the concept.[11]

The Lewis and Clark Centennial Exposition of 1905 inspired a further spate of advertising by railroad companies. The Oregon Railway and Navigation Company promoted the new $150,000 sanatorium at Hot Lake near La Grande in Union County in eastern Oregon. Hot Lake, the "remarkable fountain of healing" reportedly used by aboriginals since ancient times, was an eight-acre lake replenished by a "large geyser of volcanic-heated water" with a temperature measured at 198 degrees where it spouted from the earth. The lake let out through a creek into the Grande Ronde River. It maintained a temperature of 70 to 80 degrees throughout the winter. Typically, it was claimed that the water improved "all ordinary forms of rheumatism, rheumatic gout, stomach and liver troubles, nervous ailments and other disorders."[12]

It was so efficiently arranged that thermal water heated the elegant 100-room hotel, a long, three-story building with three transverse wings in the Shingle Style tradition of the Queen Anne Revival. The complex was sited on the south side of the lake against the foot of barren hills. The railroad passed directly in front on the north side of the lake. A promenade porch with deck extended across the lake side of the hotel, and on the south side was a large enclosed sun porch. In the lobby guests enjoyed pianola or orchestrelle concerts, conversation and parlor games. A detached brick and concrete bathhouse was said to have been patterned after the "leading and most modern" bathhouses at Hot Springs, Arkansas.[13] Around the time of the Exposition, a hospital addition was added to the east end.

Among a number of other spas in the Northwest which emphasized luxury were the St. Alice Hotel (1885) at Harrison Hot Springs at the edge of Harrison Lake in southern British Columbia, and the Sol Duc Hot Springs Hotel (1910–12) near Lake Crescent on the Olympic Penin-

11. "Ashland Undertakes New Role as the Spa of Southern Oregon," *Oregon Journal* (Portland), June 27, 1915, sec. 1, p. 15.

12. Rinaldo Hall, *Oregon, Washington, Idaho and Their Resources* (OR&N and SP, 1904), 78.

13. Rinaldo M. Hall, *Restful Recreation Resorts of the Pacific Northwest* (OR&N, Portland, 1905), 36–37.

Fig. III–352. Hotel Oregon, Ashland.

Fig. III–353. Interior of Helman's Natatorium, Ashland.

Fig. III–354. North elevation, Hot Lake Sanatorium, Hot Lake, Oregon.

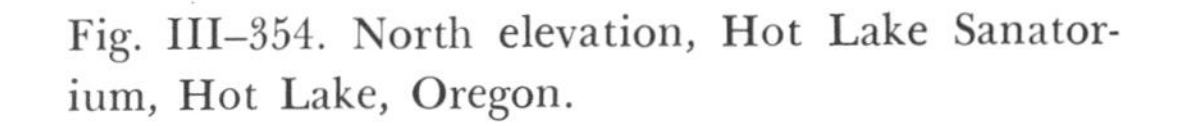

Fig. III–355. Interior view of porch, Hot Lake Sanatorium.

sula in Washington. One more nearly approaching the architectural pretensions of the Hotel Del Monte (1880) in Monterey, California, the Antlers Hotel (1883) at Colorado Springs, Colorado, or the Montezuma Hot Springs Hotel (1885) in New Mexico during this period, was the Boise Natatorium in Boise, Idaho (Fig. 24). Soon after a marsh close to the city was discovered to be the surface evidence of hot springs, the

Fig. III–356. Boise Natatorium, Boise, 1892.

Boise Water Works Company reorganized as the Artesian Hot and Cold Water Company and commenced construction of a natatorium which was to be regarded a "credit to the state."[14] Opened to the public in 1892, the Boise Natatorium contained reception rooms, parlors, a grand ballroom, reading room, dining room, billiard room and gentlemen's clubroom. The great interior space taken up by the plunge bath measured 122 by 62 feet, and the water ranged in depth from four to twelve feet. At the south end of the semi-circular wooden arch-spanned bath was a grotto, or "hollow pyramid of stones" 20 feet in height. In a dramatic visual effect, hot water discharged from a pipe at its apex was dispelled in clouds of steam as it dripped from stone to stone.[15]

Stylistic eclecticism, a keynote of architecture of the period, reached a high expression in the Natatorium. The celebrated baths, destroyed in 1934 as a result of a storm damage, were the work of John C. Paulsen, a leading architect of the intermountain district of Idaho and Montana. The Spanish Saracenic motif, recognizable in the horseshoe arch used repeatedly for openings, was exotic and appropriately festive for a recreation palace. Paulsen had experimented with the motif several years earlier as a collaborator in the Broadwater Hotel and natatorium projects in Helena, Montana.[16]

---

14. *A Description of the Western Resorts for Health and Pleasure Reached Via Union Pacific System, the Overland Route* (UP, Omaha, 1893), 78.

15. *Description of the Western Resorts for Health and Pleasure,* 78.

16. Robinson, "Northwest Architecture, 1843–1893," 97. Paulsen appears to have been among the first in the region to employ Saracenic, or "Moorish" stylistic features. A widely-known and more pronounced example of the style, with its great dome, onion-domed kiosks and vivid coloration, was the Saltair pleasure pavilion on the Great Salt Lake at Salt Lake City, Utah. Designed by Richard A. Kletting, it was not begun until 1893.

In form, the Natatorium was reminiscent of medieval church architecture. Observation towers flanked a semi-circular arched portal, and the "nave" or major axis was lighted by a clerestory. In this case, however, the transepts, which are the arms of a conventional cruciform plan, projected from either tower at the entrance to extend the principal facade. The ends of these two-story "transepts" were rounded in a manner associated with the Shingle Style and were actually bayed loggias or open verandas. The entire surface of the Natatorium was richly detailed with leaded and colored glass, various shingle patterns, tessellated spandrels, iron decoration and other applied ornament.

The Saracenic motif, which seems to have been specially favored in Idaho, cropped up later in the Dewey Palace Hotel in Nampa. In this nonchalant mixture of styles, the motif took the form of East Indian kiosks on the corner towers of an otherwise stately example of architecture in the Colonial Revival Style, which first evolved on the East Coast at the turn of the century.

Though a few hardy souls had pioneered mountain climbing as

Fig. III–357. Dewey Palace Hotel, Nampa, Idaho.

recreation in the Northwest in the 1860s and 1870s, it was not until the later 1880s that mountaineering emerged as a popular sport among the leisured class. Women, just then beginning to free themselves from certain staid conventions, were enthusiastic participants in climbing activities. In such garb as voluminous culottes tucked into leggings, the serious feminine hiker managed maximum freedom of stride.

As usual, the development of roads was crucial to the development of resorts on the mountainside. In 1884 and 1885 the Mt. Hood Trail and Wagon Company constructed a stage road from Hood River to the base of Mt. Hood, the highest peak in the Cascade Range in Oregon. Prominent Portlanders William M. Ladd and Charles Erskine Scott Wood acquired the transportation company in 1888, commissioned the clearing of additional right-of-way, which was done by Chinese laborers, and proceeded with construction of a mountain retreat at timberline

Fig. III–358. Return from a climb to the summit of Mt. Hood, July, 1896. Dora Moody, daughter of mountain enthusiast Malcolm A. Moody of The Dalles, a frequent guest at Cloud Cap Inn.

Fig. III–359. Cloud Cap Inn, 1889, Mt. Hood.

off the toe of Cooper Spur on the northeast slope of the mountain. East Coast architect William M. Whidden, freshly arrived on the scene to complete construction of the Portland Hotel, was engaged to design Cloud Cap Inn. Work was carried out in the spring and summer of 1889.[17] Patronage in the first season was limited but nonetheless enthusiastic, and in 1891 management of the inn and stages was turned over to the Langille family.

The Rev. Arthur J. Brown of the First Presbyterian Church of Portland, an early visitor to Cloud Cap, described "a long, irregular, one-story building, constructed of logs, with great, open fireplaces." The building was "securely anchored to the edge of a precipice by heavy wire cables." The pastor remarked that despite its rusticity, "it was a thoroughly homelike and hospitable place, a veritable olden time inn."[18] Accommodations included reception room or lobby in the central block, and kitchen and dining room and guest rooms in wings on either end. The resulting modified V-shaped plan conformed snugly to the site. Rough logs had square-cut lap joints. Stone chimneys and shingles of hipped and gable roofs united equally well with the natural setting. Clustered sash windows lighted the interior. The whole was restricted to a single level to minimize wind resistance at the high altitude. There was no observation tower, which would have toppled in the gusts, but guests could enjoy a spectacular view of Eliot Glacier and distant peaks from a platform with railing which straddled the ridge of the central

17. W. A. Langille, "Recollections of Old Cloud Inn," Mt. Hood, Oregon, April 10, 1927. (Copy at OHS).

18. "Summer Vacation Spent on Mount Hood this Year," undated clipping (1890s), in OHS Scrapbook 59, p. 44.

Fig. III–360. Cabins at Cloud Cap Inn. Photograph taken looking southeast to Cooper Spur and Eliot Glacier.

block and was reached by a ladder-like stair leading up the slope of the roof. Visitors could also rent one of a number of smaller cabins on the site. Cloud Cap Inn is intact and in private use by the Crag Rats as a base for rescue missions and surveys. The building has been extensively repaired over the years as the wind and scouring action of freezing and thawing have taken toll of some of the original material.

Another famous staging point for mountain climbers was Glacier House (1886), constructed by the Canadian Pacific Railway at Glacier in the Selkirk Mountains in British Columbia. No settings for mountain resorts in the region equalled the majesty of the Rocky Mountains in Canada. The deluxe Banff Springs Hotel at Banff, Alberta, on the east slope of the Rockies, was built by the Canadian Pacific Railway between 1886 and 1888 and was based upon an emergent Châteauesque design by Bruce Price.[19] Here vacationers and invalids revived in a rarefied atmosphere dominated by the Rockies. The five-story frame hotel had tiered verandas facing onto the mountains on the west. A rotunda pavilion was erected on the east side to provide a prospect over the Bow River. This prototypal resort was destroyed in 1925.

The picturesque and rustic style associated with U.S. National Parks in the West is rooted in the less classical modes of the Queen Anne Revival and the European chalet. Specifically, the pattern was set in Yellowstone Park in the northwest corner of Wyoming, the first in the national system, established in 1872. Tourists traveled long distances by rail and stage to Yellowstone National Park to see the famous geysers. In the original section of the Old Faithful Inn, built in 1903 from designs by Robert C. Reamer, and in the large wings added in 1913, liberal use was made of native stone for foundations and colossal chimneys; unfinished logs for posts and beams; and branches and poles for trusses, rafters, ridgepoles, brackets and surface decoration of imaginative variety.

Crater Lake National Park in Klamath County in southern Oregon, was created in 1902 to preserve the natural wonder of a lake-filled crater of an extinct volcano. First discovered in 1853, the spectacular lake attracted intrepid sightseers since the 1860s. In 1885 William Gladstone Steel, champion of Oregon's mountain scenery, began his campaign to have the entire area around the lake set aside as a national park. Steel became the park's first superintendent.[20] Initial development at the rim of the crater, on the south slope, was a primitive camp. A frame messhall apparently was the most substantial facility before improvements of a more permanent nature got underway in 1909. Laborers were recruited from Medford to speed work in the short dry season limited to the summer months.[21] Construction of Crater Lake Lodge was carried out

19. Kalman, *The Railway Hotels and the Development of the Château Style in Canada*, 9–10.

20. *Oregon: End of the Trail* (Portland, 1940), 504.

21. Interview with Park Naturalist Jim Holcomb, via telephone from Crater

Fig. III–361. North elevation, Crater Lake Lodge, Crater Lake National Park, Oregon, 1914.

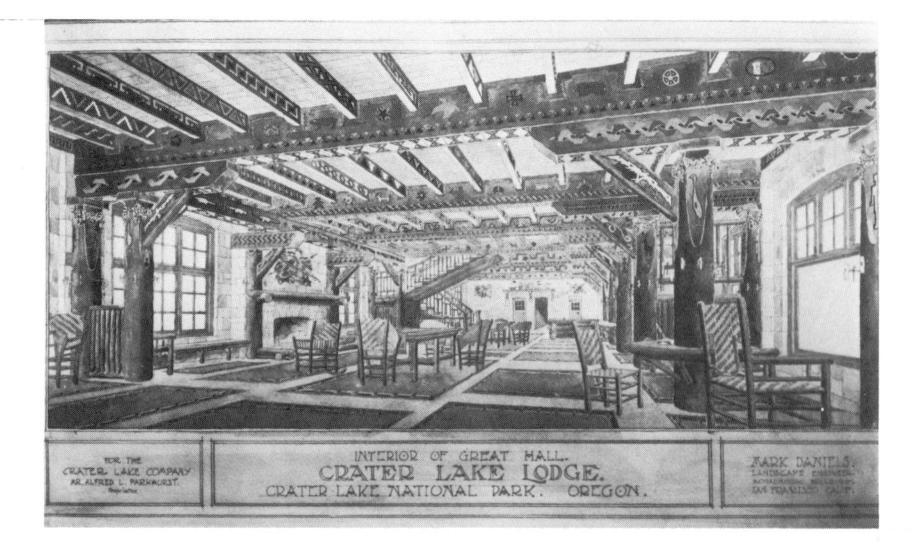

Fig. III–362. Interior design for Great Hall, Crater Lake Lodge, by Mark Daniels, landscape engineer, San Francisco.

between 1911 and 1914. Plans for the original building have been attributed to R. L. Hockenberry and Company, Architects, of Portland. Reportedly, the plans called for the exterior above the stone masonry ground story to be "half timbered" and stuccoed.[22] The result was more akin to the Shingle Style. Projecting from either end of a four-story central block were three-story wings with outside end chimneys. Tiers of shed-roofed dormers, shadow-casting overhanging eaves of the hipped roofs, rows of window openings, and the contrasting strata of stone and shingles created horizontal lines which tapered into the landscape through the wings and helped to anchor the Lodge, visually, to its rimside site.

A scheme for decoration of the great hall in the central block submitted to lodge proprietor Alfred L. Parkhurst by a San Francisco landscape engineer called for traditional rustic elements and geometric native symbols which perhaps were more suggestive of the American Southwest than the iconography of Northwest Indians. Between 1922 and 1924 a four-story annex matching the original building in style was added to the west end. In response to the wear and tear caused by the rising rate of visitor traffic, there is a move in the National Parks today to deflect a certain amount of use away from the landmark facilities. At Crater Lake a detached dormitory for park employees is under construction, and a moratorium on all new development is in effect until the master plan is fully reviewed and updated where necessary to protect

Fig. III–363. National Park Inn, Mt. Rainier National Park, Washington.

Lake National Park, March 13, 1974. According to a clipping in Park files, the Medford *Mail Tribune* of July 25, 1910, reported that construction foreman Frank Keyes was in town recruiting workers.

22. Laurin C. Huffman, Architect, National Park Service Pacific Northwest Region, Seattle, Washington. National Register nomination form for Crater Lake Lodge prepared 1973.

Fig. III–364. East elevation, Paradise Inn, Mt. Rainier National Park, 1917.

Fig. III–365. Interior view of lobby, Paradise Inn.

the fragile environment of the crater rim.

Majestic Mt. Rainier, 40 miles southeast of Tacoma in the Cascade Range in Washington, is one of the best-known alpine playgrounds in the region. Among the first points made accessible at the base of the mountain was Longmire mineral springs. The trail blazed to that point by pioneer James Longmire in 1884 became a rough wagon road used by hikers and climbers through the 1890s. Mount Rainier National Park was created by Act of Congress in 1899.

Concerted efforts of boosters in Seattle and Tacoma brought forth appropriations for further road improvements. Some 20 miles of government road from the park entrance to the Camp of the Clouds in Paradise Valley on the south slope was opened for travel late in the summer of 1910.[23] The National Park Inn was constructed at Longmire at about the same time. It was a three-story frame building, rectangular in plan, measuring 125 by 32 feet. The long gable roof and the gable roofs of

23. Robert A. Reid, *Puget Sound and Western Washington* (Seattle, 1912), 50.

large dormers containing coupled sash windows were steeply pitched to encourage snow run-off. Shingle siding was used throughout.

Paradise Inn, opened for use in Paradise Valley on the first of July, 1917, is admirably suited to its sloping site, which is in view of the summit and overlooks the Tatoosh Range. A long, two-story stem forms the main part of the inn, and a three-story wing telescopes at right angles from it on the downhill side. The dominant feature is the expansive, chalet-like roof, its steeply angled planes broken by rows of dormer windows. The building has a shallow water course of rubble masonry. Exterior walls are shingled and decorated by half-rounds of logs marking off stories and bays and creating a half-timbered effect in the gable ends. Paradise Inn was not a substantial departure from the more conventional form of the earlier National Park Inn, but through its use of varied materials, surface planes and elevations, or levels, it produced a genuinely picturesque and harmonious result. The two-story lobby space of the interior, with its complex framing and roof-truss system created of weathered logs, was conceived in the tradition of the Old Faithful Inn at Yellowstone.

The era of the railroad was the heyday of the mineral spring resort. It was also an era of architectural eclecticism, and the spas, seaside developments and grand railroad hotels in urban centers were reflected images of a variety of historic styles, notably the several modes of the Queen Anne Revival and the Loire Valley Château, or Châteauesque Style. In the mountains, resort architecture in the Northwest reached some of its purest expressions of regional style. In the best examples, historicism and quaint rusticity were subordinated to considerations of the wilderness setting, climate and appropriate use of native materials. The approach was an enduring legacy passed on to the age of the automobile.

Industrial Building

Lewis L. McArthur

The Railroad ushered in a new era based on improved transportation which also exercised a pronounced effect upon industrial construction. Prior to the 1870s there was little local manufacturing or heavy machinery. Demand did not justify large-scale mechanized methods, and the lack of rail transportation limited movement of large or heavy objects to main watercourses. The coming of the railroad provided the two-way transportation necessary for commerce and industry and in addition furnished a pool of trained builders. The construction of the American railroad network required civil engineers in vast numbers and their professional knowledge of road, bridge and building construction soon passed beyond the railroads into all sorts of industrial work. In the Pacific Northwest the still uncut virgin forests of prime saw timber served as an effective barrier to the large use of wrought iron and Portland cement, then coming into favor in the Eastern United States. Clay brick, more readily available from local sources, made an appearance where fire resistance or more substantial exterior walls were required.

Railroad construction in the Pacific Northwest started with short, local runs. One of the earliest was the four-mile portage built at the Cascades of the Columbia by J. S. Ruckel in 1861. This was followed by a 13-mile railroad around the Dalles of the Columbia, completed in 1863 by the Oregon Steam Navigation Company. Transportation above and below both these portages was by river steamer so transfer facilities were required. The historian is indebted to C. E. Watkins for his series of excellent photographs recording this scene in 1867. The large view of Celilo at the east end of the portage shows a steamer at the main warehouse. As the entire complex was wood and the eastern part completely surrounded by water, it is difficult to see how the structures withstood the periodic floods. This operation was phased out just before the completion of the transcontinental railroad to Portland in 1883, and any construction then remaining, in all probability was removed by the memorable flood of 1894.

An examination of the picture shows a small steam locomotive near the center of the warehouse but almost completely hidden by a huge pile of the cordwood that was then used locally as fuel. The detail illustra-

Fig. III–366. Celilo, Oregon. C. E. Watkins photo, 1867.

Fig. III–367. Interior of main portage warehouse, Celilo, Oregon. Notice the roof framing and knee bracing. Freight hand-trucks have changed little in 100 years. The author is unable to explain what appear to be practice rings for some amateur trapeze artist. C. E. Watkins photo, 1867.

tion also shows that while the lumber was all rough sawn, design and construction was efficient and exact. The machine shop at The Dalles was in an important populated area, which undoubtedly accounted for the additional attention to appearance.

Sheep came with the earliest Oregon immigrants. At first, the animals were brought for food, but the Hudson's Bay Company began their cultivation for wool in the 1830s. Joshua Shaw brought a small flock across the plains in the emigration of 1844, and with this party came young Joseph Watt who had a long family background with both textiles and livestock. Watt was so impressed with the possibilities of the Oregon Country that he returned to Missouri in 1847 and the following year, after considerable preparation, brought his family and a flock of 300 high grade Merino sheep to the Willamette Valley. These animals were the nucleus of the early wool industry. In 1856, Watt, along with A. H. Reynolds, Daniel Waldo and John Minto, organized the Willamette Woolen Manufacturing Company in Salem. This was the first full textile plant on the Pacific Coast and it operated from 1857 until 1875, when it was destroyed by fire. (Woolen mills burned fast and often.) The building was a three-story frame structure of sawn lumber 190 feet by 47 feet located at the mouth of Mill Creek. The machinery was in charge of L. E. Pratt who came to Oregon from Worcester, Massachusetts in 1857 for this express purpose. After a period of tribulation, Pratt took over control of the operation and made it the dominant factor of the Pacific Coast textile business during the 1860s.

In 1861 the first Brownsville mill was opened in a wooden building covered with hand-split cedar shakes, and in 1865 the original building of

Fig. III–368. Oregon Steam Navigation Company machine shop, The Dalles, Oregon. Notice the elaborate design of the large openings and the swing doors with vertical interior and diagonal exterior boarding for stiffness. The strap hinges are at least three feet long. C. E. Watkins photo, 1867.

Fig. III–369. Oregon City Woolen Mills building, Oregon City, Oregon, with the original roof line before the fire. C. E. Watkins photo, 1867.

Fig. III–370. Oregon City Woolen Mills, Oregon City, Oregon, Grand arch where the mill race entered the basement. The top of this arch is just visible on the left end of the front foundation in the 1867 picture.

Fig. III–371. Oregon City Woolen Mills, Oregon City, Oregon, with tower stairs framed around wood centerpost. Notice the iron handrail to force traffic out away from waster end of treads, for a tumble near the centerpost where the treads are only an inch or two wide would mean a near vertical fall. The vertical and horizontal corner framing are new concrete posts and beams added recently to preserve the structure.

the Oregon City Woolen Mill was completed. This was damaged by fire in 1872, but was rebuilt and added to the following year. While there have been many minor alterations, the original building still stands in 1974. The illustrations show three important features of its construction. The grand arch where the mill race entered the building is of massive native basalt masonry with a minimum amount of fine fitting in critical areas; above the foundations there is brick; and supporting the floors and framing the whole structure are the typical heavy timbers with extensive use of through bolts, probably of wrought iron.

In 1863 Thomas Kay, who was born in Yorkshire, England in 1837, came to Brownsville, Oregon where he began as foreman of the Brownsville Woolen Mills weave room. By 1875 he was superintendent and part owner. In 1889 along with his son-in-law, Charles P. Bishop, and others, he founded the Thomas Kay Woolen Mill in Salem. The original mill building was frame, on a foundation of native basalt. It was destroyed by fire in 1895 and construction of the existing building began almost immediately thereafter. When first completed in 1896 the new building was roughly 60 x 147 feet, two-and-a-half stories above a partial basement, built of masonry walls with heavy timber frame and timber roof trusses, and utilizing the original foundations. The large view shows the building circa 1910. The basement has since been excavated under the entire structure and the 1889 poured concrete foundations for the original masonry have been exposed. Brick has been added from the new foundation up to the old concrete which is still in excellent condition. The roof trusses have 1″ and 1½″ round vertical tension rods of rolled steel, which in 1895 was just beginning to replace wrought iron in this area. With one exception, all the truss members and floor beams are unspliced lengths the full width of the building. Trusses are secured to the masonry at each end with substantial through bolts and washers. All the main roof truss connections have vertical through bolts with suitable bevelled cast washers. The doors and casings, sash and frames, interior trim, cornice and gutters were locally milled. Sprinklers were installed in the building about 1900, certainly one of the earlier Oregon installations. The sprinkler system is substantially the same as today's, but the Grinnell brass heads have the early direct in-line fusible links. Walter D. Pugh, just then becoming prominent in Salem, was the architect, and contractors were John Gray and Henry Lukers. The Thomas Kay mill was an important enterprise in Salem, and the 1890s were a highly successful period in its operation. The selection of an architect of Pugh's reputation shows the importance attached to the rebuilding project. The building was expanded in 1898, 1904 and 1925 and there are several ancillary buildings, including the wood frame dye house which antedates the present mill, surrounding the main structure. Some of the original machinery is still in place, and in 1965 title was passed to the Mission and Mill Museum Association, which intends to pursue a course of restoration including rehabilitation of sufficient machinery to demonstrate the early methods.

Mining continued after the Civil War but it decreased in impor-

Fig. III–372. Thomas Kay Woolen Mill, Salem, Oregon. Cronise photo, circa 1910.

Fig. III–373. Coal Bunker on South Prairie Creek near Burnett, Washington. This elaborate structure appears to be made entirely of sawn timber. Photo circa 1881.

tance in both Oregon and Washington as the end of the century approached. There were rich but limited strikes in many areas but not enough to make the mining industry a serious competitor to lumbering and agriculture. There was an interesting development near Cle Elum, Washington where coal was produced on a large scale for the Northern Pacific Railway. The railroad continued to use this fuel source until the advent of the diesel locomotive.

However, there were substantial mining operations in northern Idaho. In 1886 silver was discovered in the Coeur d'Alene district. This was accompanied by large amounts of lead with some copper and zinc.

Fig. III–374. Interior of the Superior Coal Company mine, Coos Bay area, Oregon. The bulk of this timber shoring is hand-hewn. The display of tools also shows that mechanization had made little headway.

The Northern Pacific Railway bisected the area and this made for simple access for personnel and machinery. The mines were developed with modern methods and the more successful have continued to the present day. The illustrations show how building here sacrificed esthetics for practicality, for the engineer-builder was faced with many problems, including heavy cribbed foundations to compensate for steep sidehill sites and the mountain country's everpresent snow load and avalanche hazard.

Iron was in short supply in the Pacific Northwest. After the Civil War wrought iron began to be used as structural material and cast iron became commonplace for building facades, columns and architectural features as well as for machinery and industrial castings. The first pig iron west of the Rocky Mountains was poured near Salt Lake City on September 30, 1852. The first pour on the Pacific Coast was at Lake Oswego, Oregon on August 24, 1867. The Oregon Iron Company was organized in 1865 and two-and-one-half years later had completed an eight-ton per day plant at a cost of $126,000. The original furnace was built of locally quarried basalt and is still standing in 1974 as a historic attraction. The furnace was lined with brick, some of which remain, and also had a forty-foot-high brick chimney above the stone to provide the hot blast.

Fig. III–375. Gold Hill, Idaho, an early development east of Coeur d'Alene. While the buildings are all made of wood, little material was used to brace the flume supports. M. M. Hazeltine photo, circa 1890.

Fig. III–376. Hecla Mine, Burke, Idaho, a fine example of cribbed timber foundations.

Watkins' picture of the Oregon Iron Works was taken in 1867 from a point on what is now the playing field of George Rogers Park, not far from the highway bridge over Oswego Creek. The creek is just visible on the right. The various new buildings are all of wood frame construction with vertical siding. Most appear to have wood shingle roofs, although the open shed in the small picture has a full length board-on-board roof somewhat resembling the corrugated or ribbed steel roofing of today. The shed also illustrates use of "Y" and diagonal bracing. It sits on top

Fig. III–377. Granite Hill mine near Grants Pass, Oregon. Ore was raised by winch from the mine to the top of the mill building. From here gravity did most of the material moving. Notice the corrugated steel roofing. While this substantial installation was a gold mine, Granite Hill took its name from a vast deposit of decomposed granite that was used to ballast hundreds of miles of the Southern Pacific Company lines in the first decade of the century.

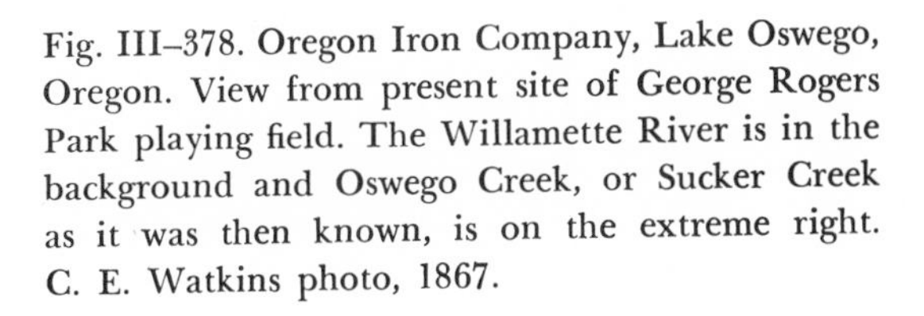

Fig. III–378. Oregon Iron Company, Lake Oswego, Oregon. View from present site of George Rogers Park playing field. The Willamette River is in the background and Oswego Creek, or Sucker Creek as it was then known, is on the extreme right. C. E. Watkins photo, 1867.

Fig. III–379. Oregon Iron Company, Lake Oswego, Oregon. Storage shed with board-on-board roof. C. E. Watkins photo, 1867.

Fig. III–380. Oregon Iron Company, Lake Oswego, Oregon. Stone chimney as it appeared in 1973. Notice the wedged tie bars in the original stonework.

of a log and plank crib used, probably, for coke or some other bulk material. The eaves are covered with vertical plank applied without battens, as there would be no need to make a structure of this nature watertight. In 1879 the stone stack was raised several feet. The line of demarcation is visible in the current picture. The older, lower part has substantial iron bars either all or part way through each side to contain the masonry. The projecting ends of the bars are slotted and each has an iron wedge bearing against a plate washer. The upper addition is tied by round rods or bolts with more conventional washers and nuts.

This operation was never a complete financial success. It took two-and-a-half tons of limonite ore to produce one ton of pig iron. The ore came first by ox cart and later by narrow gauge railroad from nearby Iron Mountain. Charcoal was made locally and water power was provided by Oswego, or as it was then known, Sucker Creek. Numerous alterations were made or proposed over the years but low volume and low grade ore combined to keep costs above competing imports. This plant ceased operations in 1885 and a new company was organized that built a large, new furnace several hundred yards away slightly north of the present Oregon Portland Cement Company plant. The second company encountered the same economic problems and in turn closed in 1894. This plant remained vacant until 1929 when it was torn down.

The Indians started the fishing industry in the Pacific Northwest in prehistoric times. The fish-eaters caught and cured for their own use as well as some limited barter with nomadic groups. The Hudson's Bay Company did not overlook this resource, and in 1830 they were smoking and salting salmon along the Columbia River both for local consumption and for trade. The early pioneers also preserved their fish by one of several curing processes. The tin can was being developed, and the invention of the Bessemer steel making process coupled with new mills for hot rolling steel sheets, made the new material, tin plate, available to this market.

Fig. III–381. Sketch of Kinney's Salmon Cannery, Astoria, Oregon.

William and George Hume along with Andrew Hapgood came to the Columbia River in 1866 and in 1867 packed the first canned salmon in a small cannery on the Washington bank not far from Cathlamet.

Another brother, Robert D. Hume, who later headed the famous Rogue River operation, came in 1871. John West probably packed the first salmon in Oregon at Westport prior to 1870. Marshall Kinney built his salmon cannery at Astoria in the 1870s and shipped his first pack in 1876. When the fish business slowed in the early 1880s Kinney along with several competitors had a try at canned beef and mutton. The demand for canned mutton was far from spirited, and the product was abandoned. Astoria continued as a major packing center, and included such substantial installations as the Union Fisherman's Cooperative Packing Company and members of the Alaska Packers Association. Fishing was pursued all along the Oregon and Washington coast, where clams and crabs were taken as well as salmon.

On the upper Columbia canners were extremely active. The Seufert brothers set up a fish wheel near The Dalles in 1884, and a few years later bought the recently completed Everding & Farrell Cannery. The large wood frame building is still standing, although fish packing ended

Fig. III–382. Warren's Salmon Cannery, Warrendale, Oregon. Benj. Gifford photo.

Fig. III–383. Seufert Brothers Cannery, The Dalles, Oregon. Photo circa 1900.

Fig. III–384. Seufert Brothers Cannery, The Dalles, Oregon. Fish room with butcher tables in background. The wood post and truss construction is typical of buildings of this vintage.

Fig. III–385. Main line of Union Pacific Railroad and Seufert Brothers buildings at Celilo, Oregon. Photo circa 1899.

before World War II with the outlawing of the fish wheel. The small illustration shows the Seuferts' ancillary fishing and shipping facility at Celilo. The light building in the foreground is the horse barn and apparently has a board and batten roof while the mess hall and fish house to the rear have conventional shingles. The railroad in the center is the main line of the Union Pacific. The picture was taken about 1899, obviously prior to the rebuilding of the line on the south bank of the Columbia.

Brick was used extensively in the post-Civil War period, but usually for commercial buildings and expensive residences. Until the turn of the century, the early pattern of numerous small brickyards persisted, each close to the point of consumption and utilizing existing deposits of ordinary quality clay to turn out common brick. Brick of a dun color were made at the Oregon State Penitentiary in Salem in the 1870s and were used to construct cell blocks and for sale. The Pacific Face Brick Company established a plant near good clay in Newberg in the 1890s, and in 1907 moved to a better location in Willamina where they soon became the Willamina Clay Products Company. Here raw material was available to make tan and white brick as well as various grades of fire brick. By World War I, this product found an extensive market in fireboxes for steam locomotives.

The Willamina brick of varied colors were also much admired by Belluschi and other architects, and were heavily used until 1974, when internal pressures of modern safety demands forced closure of the immediately missed production lines. The new home office of Evans Products in Portland is their last major job. Another interesting contemporary use is in the court, ground and first floors of the Oregon Historical Center.

Another brickyard of exceptional interest is the (Robert) Hidden Brothers Brick Company in Vancouver, Washington. For longevity this modern company may have achieved a record. We know that its brick was floated to Sauvie Island for use in construction of the Bybee-Howell house. When the house was restored 110 years later, brick from the Hidden works was again used.

The Columbia Brickworks began operations near Gresham in the early 1900s and for a time combined with the Standard Brick and Tile Company at Sylvan. These three large brickworks supplied much of the brick used in the innumerable brick and brick-faced buildings built in Portland in the first 30 years of this century. While masonry appeared in commercial and warehouse structures, buildings such as the Thomas Kay Woolen Mill, the Oregon City Woolen Mill and the early paper mill building were the exception, and most industrial masonry appeared in chimneys and furnace or heating installations. The same pattern persisted throughout the Pacific Northwest where brick was made as near as possible to the point of consumption. An historically interesting exception is Vancouver, British Columbia where three of the first settlers anywhere near present-day downtown picked a site on False Creek as their claim because of deposits of excellent clay. They began to manu-

Fig. III–386. Willamina Brick plant, Willamina, Oregon, photographed during the peak of its operations shortly after World War I.

Fig. III–387. Night view of sugar beet refinery, Nampa, Idaho. By the turn of the century, brick was a prime building material in many areas. Sugar refining involved heat, moisture and moving machinery, and masonry made for a low maintenance building. Even for such an austere, formidable structure, the builder has provided some small ornamentation, something readily obtainable at low cost in brick masonry.

facture brick and the community literally grew up around them.

Hollow clay tile came into use prior to World War I. It had much of the fire resistance of brick and less than one half the weight for an 8″ wall. It was also able to satisfy the sanitary codes that were beginning to govern the dairy industry's milk processing plants, creameries and cheese factories. The Warrenton Clay Products Company opened its large plant with much fanfare and a speech by Governor Withycombe on April 7, 1917, although this interesting display of local economic enthusiasm took a backseat to the big news of the previous day, the Declaration of War against Germany. The building was a handsome structure of four stories with a monitor vent. The interior was wood post and beam construction. As there was a grid of steam pipes below

Fig. III–388. The two-story brick warehouse built by John McCraken in 1895 at what is now 907 N. W. Irving Street in Portland. The basement walls are poured concrete and the first story brick walls are 21 inches thick with arches forming what were originally drive-through openings for heavy drays. First floor joists are 4″ x 16″ fir, 12″ on center. The thick plank floor still has hitching rings for the dray horses. The building is separated into two 50′ by 100′ sections by a brick bearing wall with openings protected by metal clad fire doors. The wood roof trusses have sloping top chords but the ends are built up with falsework to support a roof with only a nominal slope.

Fig. III–389. Detail of masonry at first floor sash. This is original construction. A similar opening on the opposite side did extend to the sidewalk grade. Note the use of stucco plaster above the arch.

the first floor to provide heat, the heavy floor planks were spaced far enough apart to permit a general circulation of air throughout. Tile and other clay products were pressed from the wet clay mix, and racked and air dried in the main building before being sent to the two round kilns for firing.

The most profitable phase of the operation was the sale of common stock, for the clay supply from the Lewis and Clark River was not of the best quality and the tile business soon failed. The plant was then taken over by a pottery concern making assorted bowls, jugs and the like. This also was found wanting and a desultory effort was made to produce clay-based coloring materials for the then common kalsomines, but the product was too gritty. Mr. Clarence Sigurdson of Warrenton, who provided much of this information in 1974, also added one other item. He says that the foundation soil was suspect and he well remembers a temporary wood frame tower some 12 feet high loaded with brick that stood for

Fig. III–390. Warrenton Clay Products Company plant, Warrenton, Oregon.

several months while the soil bearing values were being determined.

The Railroad Era of building, while 50 to 100 years old, is still new enough that much remains. A number of notable structures are being kept by public bodies or for the public benefit, and the current interest in historic preservation along with existing and proposed legislation to assist and encourage such preservation will no doubt be a further stimulant. However, much more could be done along the lines of documentation. Few plans are available of old industrial buildings and there will continue to be losses due to fire and unintentional destruction as well as for economic reasons. Hopefully, a file of photographs, sketches, dimensions and notes can be built up to cover the important buildings even if drawings are not produced to the current high standards of the Historic American Building Survey.

Parks and Gardens of Western Oregon

Wallace Kay Huntington

The 19th century was the great age of botanical exploration. Scientific curiosity had stimulated the founding of geographic and botanical societies that sponsored exploration into then remote areas of the globe in search of flora and fauna unknown to Western civilization. Still unknown in the early 1800s, when Lewis and Clark made botanical observations as part of their expedition duties, was the western part of the American continent. Other botanists followed, working there and elsewhere in "exotic" areas. The result of the early expeditions was never meant to be of financial benefit to the sponsors; novelty and knowledge were sufficient justification. Through the years, the American West continued to be botanically and otherwise explored, but even though the conservatories and lawns of Kew and other English arboretums contained samples from the American West (obtained by David Douglas and others), Victorian gardeners in western Oregon preferred to look to remote areas for their curiosities.

The changing seasons of the temperate zones impose a discipline on plants that only varies within limits; following the forced dormancy caused by cooler temperatures, trees, flowers and shrubs respond by going into a period of active growth with the sole purpose of reproduction. The sequence of flower formation and fertilization, followed by maturing and dissemination of the fruit or seed, is variable only within a relative time span, and with few exceptions the blooming period is finished by late spring and the summer and fall months are devoted to growth and maturity. As a result, 18th and early 19th century gardens of England, the Continent, and North America might be splendid with color in the spring and possibly have a final blaze of autumnal color, but flowers were a seasonal luxury that only supplemented the design of the permanent garden. Versailles no less than Hampton Court or Williamsburg depended for color—both summer and winter—on lawns and gravel, crushed brick or oystershell.

The Victorian era saw an end to the discipline imposed by seasons. Sub-tropical, tropical, jungle and desert plants will grow in temperate zones for a summer season at least or if wintered over under glass, for an indefinite period. These plants, with a life cycle not keyed to periodic dormancy, can flower in midsummer or fall or continuously without expectation of killing frost. Also, many plants with milleniums of evolution under specialized conditions have developed unusual foliage colors—bronzes or reds, blue-greens, or striking variegations. These were the plants that the Victorians learned to love; now, instead of the muted colors of gravel and lawn, the summer scene could be enlivened with vivid displays of rich color: the blue of lobelia and ageratum, the red of begonias and salvia, the white of allysum and candytuft; cannas, coleus, the sempervivums added exotic foliage colors and striking form.

The obsession with color and novelty that evoked visions of foreign lands and climates was one of the factors that led to the disintegration of form in gardens. Like children with a new box of toys, the Victorians reveled in the luxury of their new acquisitions but lacked a tradition to guide them in their use. Sometimes grouping the colors in close array, as though challenging nature to a game, they created scrolls and volutes, circles and stars, scallops and hearts. The Victorian eye was more attuned to brilliant color displays of annuals and succulents and to plants of evocative form than to subtleties of space and proportion. Portraits could be "painted" in flowers; clocks with underground mechanisms were feasible; and in parks and along carriageways, verses, names and dates could be bedded out for special occasions.

In the Western world the bedding-out infatuation extended from St. Petersburg to San Francisco and, as would be expected, the newly affluent families of the Pacific Northwest exhibited their "taste" in conspicuous displays. City Park (later renamed Washington Park) was an object of special civic pride. Surviving photographs from the early 20th century illustrate the elaborate flower parterres and lawns adorned with tubs of semi-hardy greenhouse specimens. The arbitrary forms of the flower beds with their fabric-like patterns are scattered randomly

Fig. III–391. "City Park" (Washington Park). Exotic floral displays rather than space or form characterized 19th century park scenes.

over an informal lawn with complete disregard to any all encompassing plan. By the end of the century a zoological society had been formed and the animals in the City Park Zoo were displayed in the same spirit as the yuccas on the lawn. Downing's legacy—the placid sweep of lawn, the bold massing of the trees along a drive or walkway—had become a victim of popular taste. The wonderfully contrived arrangements of flowers displayed in Portland's Exhibition Hall suggest—as do all flower shows—ideas that could be utilized on the home grounds. Almost no identifiable plant in the photograph is hardy and the planting schemes were as transient as the summer days.

Civic responsibility and pride were gratifying products of the late Victorian and Edwardian eras. Portland had acquired several major

Fig. III–392. Portland Garden Show in Exhibition Hall. Such Victorian garden schemes used annuals and succulents accented by palms to create "carpet bedding" of intricate designs.

parks by donation: Lownsdale and Chapman squares, the Park Blocks, Holladay Park, Macleay and Terwilliger parks. The commercial district had been given a focal point by the donation of a handsome bronze fountain; commissioned by the will of druggist Stephen Skidmore, it had been designed and cast by a major American sculptor, Olin Warner, and was an enviable work of art for a Western city.

The generosity of the many donors and benefactors to civic betterment in an age dedicated to the pursuit of wealth seems ironic, but the diligence expended on the game of making money did not preclude a munificence of civic spirit. The Skidmore Fountain was exceptional only in its quality, for other cities enjoyed lesser monuments from a magnanimous citizenry; the Breyman Fountain in Willson Park in Salem is possibly a more typical example—startling though it is with its alarming proportions. Ashland had a near duplicate that flowed with Lithia water. Portland's Thompson Fountain, dedicated in 1900, was a standard sentimental symbol that the Victorians loved: the "majesty of God's creation" epitomized by the elk in unequivocal terms!

Cemeteries were held in especial esteem by the Victorians. The cultivation of "sweet melancholy" was considered so enobling that no beauty was more poignantly expressive than that of a languid young woman expressing her grief for loved ones amidst the monuments and yews of the graveyard; hence, cemeteries were visited in a ritual display of carefully constrained public emotion. No less than parks, cemeteries

Fig. III–393. Skidmore Fountain, Portland, 1888, by Olin Warner. Civic pride and generosity account for donations of park land and monuments.

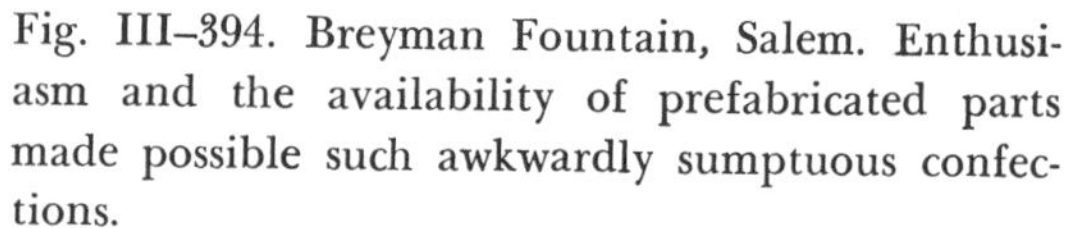

Fig. III–394. Breyman Fountain, Salem. Enthusiasm and the availability of prefabricated parts made possible such awkwardly sumptuous confections.

Fig. III–395. Thompson Fountain, Portland, 1900. The Elk was a standard sentimental symbol which the Victorians felt epitomized "the majesty of God's creation."

gave status to a city and Lone Fir and Riverview cemeteries are pictured in *The West Shore* as legitimate objects of civic pride and as an appropriate place for a family outing.

Popular taste, though not so fickle as the taste of the Haute Monde, evolves inexorably, and in the final years of the 19th century the impact of the Colonial Revival was asserting itself in gardens as well as houses, making the public aware that gardens had been designed at one time with structure, form, and space. Though unwilling to relinquish the wondrous array of colors and shapes now available, the progressive homeowner conceded a compromise with formality was not unseemly, since even the undisciplined eye could detect the incongruity of palms and bamboo in the context of a "colonial" house of New England ancestry. Though no arbiter of taste such as Downing appeared in the late century to formulate the taste of the nation, the earnest writings and restrained designs of an English landscape designer, Gertrude Jekyll, slowly began to assert themselves. With an empathy for plants that made the Victorian craze for novelty seem crass, Jekyll created orderly formal gardens and then loosely structured the geometric beds with casual drifts of harmonius plants chosen on the basis of form and texture as well as color. Thus the "perennial border" was born and this, plus the impact of the World's Columbian Exposition in Chicago would ultimately re-establish gardens as formulated outdoor space rather than plant "zoos" without form or structure.

The Columbian Exposition of 1893, like all the major 19th century expositions, was to affect many aspects of taste, but it was particularly influential in the fields of architecture and city planning. The assem-

Fig. III–396. Riverview Cemetery, Portland, 1886. View from *The West Shore.* As an object of civic pride, the cemetery ranked with boulevard and park.

blage of artists who contributed to the White City on the shores of Lake Michigan was impressive indeed: America's most famous sculptors, painters and architects were involved in a communal effort to an extent that was unique in America's cultural history. Planned by America's most famous landscape architect, Frederick Law Olmsted, the buildings were designed by such eminent architects as Burnham and Root, McKim, Mead and White, Richard Morris Hunt, etc.

Our retrospective view from the 20th century tempers the almost unanimous opinion of the day as to its unqualified esthetic achievement. Writing in 1958, John A. Kowenhoven sums up 20th century hindsight:

It has often been said that the Chicago Fair set back American architecture thirty years; and in a sense it did . . . But in another sense the fair was a significant achievement. Never before had Americans seen a group of buildings so skillfully harmonized; nowhere else had they been able to wander down one apparently endless vista of beautifully correlated facades, then turn a corner and face another, and never encounter a discordant detail. It was this over-all planning, this total effect, which made the borrowed academic style so impressive to the thousands who visited the fair.[1]

Olmsted's legacy to the United States would be assured without his involvement in the Columbian Exposition. As a social critic and theorist, as a humanitarian no less than as an artist, Olmsted was a man of stature. Though his design for Central Park was his most famous achievement, city, park, and university plans throughout the United

1. John A. Kouwenhoven, *Made in America* (Newton Centre, Mass., 1948), 94.

States in the late 19th century reflect his thinking. The design for the Columbian Exposition was almost the antithesis of the design for Central Park; Central Park was human in the scale of its parts and the landscape vignettes were in the romantic natural tradition. The Columbian Exposition was monumental in scale, formal in its planning, and dominated by man-made construction. Though it might be said that the design for the White City was progressive in that it set a pattern for more orderly urban growth, the humanism that Olmsted strove to express in his writings and designs, was too fragile to survive the marathon collaboration in Chicago.

The wonder and admiration that fair inspired was of particular significance due to its timing. America was rapidly changing from a rural republic into an urban democracy and the penalty exacted had become obvious: squalid, crime-infested cities peopled by a destitute working class. The White City offered hope; it was the physical expression of urban idealism. Here at last was a city—an American city—so beautiful that it established a definitive standard for the 20th century to emulate!

Though the financial recession of 1893 delayed the impact of the Exposition, by the end of the century the "City Beautiful" movement had begun and classical Beaux Arts achitecture was as securely in favor as the formal plan.

The Lewis and Clark expedition's epic achievement, culminating on the Pacific shore in 1805, demanded an anniversary celebration in Oregon as lavish as the state could produce. Portland's population at the turn of the century was approximately 161,000, and undertaking an international fair was a major decision. There was significant dissent in the incipient planning; possibly the enthusiasm generated by the plans for the St. Louis Fair of 1904 was sufficient to dissipate the pessimism of the unconvinced; planning for the Lewis and Clark Centennial Exposition began in earnest in 1902.

Frederick L. Olmsted died in 1903, but his office continued to function with unabated prestige, and one of his sons, John C. Olmsted, arrived that year for the dual purpose of inspecting the Guild's Lake site and discussing a park program for the city. Reportedly Olmsted was pleased with the site. The report and preliminary plans that he later submitted were well received by the Lewis and Clark Exposition board.

The plan for the Lewis and Clark Exposition was patterned after the Columbian Exposition, and considering the Mediterranean style of architecture that had been selected as the official mode of building, much of the pretentiousness of the Chicago fair would be repeated on a smaller scale in Portland.

The initial plan submitted by the Olmsted Brothers was an eminently practical and comparatively modest formal design that expanded from an entrance plaza in a cross-axial arrangement. The main axis, at right angles to the entrance plaza, was formalized in a sunken garden

Fig. III–397. Lewis and Clark Exposition, Portland. The Olmsted Brothers' plan of 1903 brought professional design to Oregon's biggest social event in its history.

flanked by balustrades and urns and passed between the two major fair buildings to a broad terrace that commanded a view of the lake and mountains beyond. A grand staircase continued down the hill along the axis and terminated with the bandstand at lakeside. Perhaps sensing the potential weakness of the eclectic architecture, the landscape architects avoided using any of the structures as the terminus of an axis. Passing from the enclosed spaces of the formal core of the exposition to the suddenly expanding panoramic view over the lake (originally intended to have "decorative" islands), the natural beauty of the site was featured at the expense of possible grandiose achitectural effects.

Olmsted's report to the Board made certain specific recommendations: he felt that all wiring should be put temporarily underground in wooden channels; he recommended that public transportation should be provided—electric trains on land and boat transportation on the lake. The more obstreperous concessions such as the Wild West show, water games and the Indian village were to be isolated across the bridge that led across the lake to a peninsula called "the Neck."

Olmsted's plan was adhered to with considerable faithfulness, though the interior electrical train system of transportation didn't materialize. The major change was in the location of the U. S. Government Building. It was considered doubtful that the federal government could act with sufficient speed to construct a major display building, and the site allotted to the hypothetical structure was of secondary importance. The Government Building, which did materialize, was of unanticipated size, and its site was shifted across the bridge to the "Neck" where its

Fig. III–398. Lewis and Clark Exposition. Eclectic architecture and formal planning are reminiscent of the World's Columbian Exposition in Chicago of 1893.

Fig. III–399. Lewis and Clark Exposition. Formal planting schemes with accessory urns and balustrades set the stage in Oregon for the "City Beautiful" movement.

twin towers terminated the formal axis and dominated Guild's Lake and the view of the mountains. The concessions, which Olmsted had used peripherally, were in actuality integrated into the plan more closely, with the probable result of the fair being less static than the preliminary

Fig. III–400. Lewis and Clark Exposition, the Grand Staircase. Such lavish planning created a spectacular show that both Seattle and San Francisco would emulate.

Fig. III–401. Lewis and Clark Exposition. Electric lighting was new in Portland at the beginning of the 20th century, and imaginative fixtures lent magic to evening scenes.

plan suggested.

There was no doubt that the Lewis and Clark Exposition was intended to illustrate an ideal in planning, as the Columbian Exposition had done, and serve as a model for the city of the future—a city more beautiful than had previously been thought possible in democratic America. In one of the illustrated souvenir pamphlets sold on the grounds, there is an illustration of the main plaza flanked by the Hall of Agriculture and the European Exhibition Building, and the notation below: "The sunken gardens, simple and beautiful, are an object lesson. Why should not every new American town and city have such in its center?"[2]

With the exception of the Forestry Building, the architecture of the fair seems bland to 20th century critics, but the photographs testify to some of the excitement that the fair generated. The view across the sunken garden to the lake and mountains was impressive in the same way that the Columbian Exposition had been impressive: it was a totally manipulated view that incorporated all the "Arts" in a grandiose assemblage of sculpture, architecture and planting. The grand staircase extending down the hill and flanked by singularly dramatic light standards conceived as great "bouquets" of light bulbs, communicates some of the drama and gaiety of the occasion. The view from the Neck of land occupied by the Government Building back across the bridge toward the grand staircase and the monumental buildings aligned on the brow of the hill is undoubtedly more impressive than the sum total of its architectural parts. Particularly at night, with the novelty of total outdoor electrical illumination, Oregon's answer to the White City was a rather splendid statement of Western pride and optimism.

The conceptual plan for Portland's park system, which resulted from Olmsted's dual engagement in 1903, might have come to naught except for the abilities of a talented landscape architect, E. T. Mische, who had been recommended by the Olmsted Brothers for the position of park superintendent. Mische, who accepted the job in 1908, was park designer during the formative period in the development of Peninsula Park, Laurelhurst Park, and Terwilliger Boulevard; much credit is due him for bringing a technical knowledge and sophisticated taste to Portland so early in the 20th century. Though leaving the position in 1914 due to a row with Commissioner Brewster over who should be conductor of the Park Band, Mische left a legacy of inspired work in the manner of Olmsted.

Peninsula Park and Laurelhurst Park are diametric opposites in their design; one is a rigidly formal manipulation of land to a preconceived geometric ideal; the other, utilizing existing land forms and trees, uses a flexible circulatory system that heightens the sense of flow and the feeling for expansive, moving space. In the age of eclecticism

2. *Sights and Scenes at the Lewis and Clark Centennial Exposition, Portland, Oregon* (Portland, 1905), 6.

Fig. III–402. Laurelhurst Park, Portland. Park Superintendent E. T. Mische implemented the Olmsted park plan by converting Ladd Lake into this English landscape scene.

Fig. III–403. Peninsula Park, Portland. E. T. Mische, using a geometric scheme, converted a level tract of land into a formal sunken garden.

Mische was no doubt equally versatile in the traditional formal European style of applying geometric forms to the landscape and the English naturalistic style that had evolved during the 18th century. Letting himself be guided by the difference in character of the two sites, he conceived one as broad in scale and grandly organized, the other intimate, informal and dominated by vegetation. But both were done with a sense of style and a bigness of scale that are a credit to both Mische and his profession.

Terwilliger Boulevard which reflects the English landscape school, was donated by the Terwilliger heirs, who stipulated a 200′ landscaped right-of-way. Mische was able to keep a screen of foliage between the roadway and nearby houses and at the same time alternately constrict and expand the space formed by the vegetation. Periodically highlighted by expansive city and mountain views, the winding boulevard narrows dramatically into the enclosing folds of constrictive forest.

Other Oregon parks in the early 20th century for the most part were either undesigned or had the arbitrary forms of Victorian flower beds imposed on lawns in random fashion, though formal walkways did begin to appear as the result of the Lewis and Clark Exposition and its object lesson in formal planning. Lithia Park in Ashland is an exception, designed by John McLaren, who also created that tour de force of landscape design, Golden Gate Park in San Francisco. McLaren manipulated the natural advantages of the Ashland site, enclosed as it was by flanking hills, to give a feeling of great space through which the circulatory system meanders and surprises with gushing water, pools,

Fig. III–404. Peninsula Park, the most European and one of the most interesting early 20th century parks.

Fig. III–405. Terwilliger Boulevard in 1920s. Visualized in Olmsted's plan as a residential boulevard, Terwilliger was to become the handsomest of the hillside drives.

meadows and deep woods. Carriageways and the occasional incidence of an automobile, which were hardly conceived of as disruptive elements in the first decades of the century, added to the human interest and excitement of a park outing. Only the "colonial" design of the light standard on the lookout suggests the period of construction in Lithia Park. Architectural features, cars and costumes can indicate dates of photographs, but without such clues the immutability of landscape design done in the naturalistic style gives no suggestion as to the decade of its origin.

Distinctively different parks were developing simultaneously with the genteel residential neighborhood parks in the early 20th century; the privately owned Oaks Park offered the excitement of carnival events and entertainment of which the closing of the Lewis and Clark Exposition had deprived the citizens of Portland. Salvaging the electrical fixtures from the Exposition and duplicating the esplanades that had once edged Guild's Lake, Oaks Park recreated on the Willamette the appeal of crowds, light, color and sporting events. Council Crest, with its splendid view and access by cable car, also developed concessions: a scenic railway for the young and daring; the White Owl Tea Room

Fig. III–406. Lithia Park, Ashland, Oregon, by John McLaren. An extensive manipulation of nature, Lithia Park lent Ashland an ambience few Northwest cities could match.

Fig. III–407. Lithia Park. The Edwardian park was more cultural and social than recreational. The automobile was a welcome novelty.

Fig. III–408. Oaks Park, Portland, view of 1920s. Deprived of "sporting events" by the closure of the Lewis and Clark Exposition, young Portlanders sought entertainment in amusement parks.

a short distance away for the more sedate. Complaints that it was a public nuisance and eyesore and attracted a rowdy element were heard from the developing residential areas nearby, though surviving photographs showing the boardwalks, clipped lawns and fanciful standards for containers of flowers lend an air of innocence and order to a late 20th century observer.

Fig. III–409. Council Crest, Portland. Carnival events combined with observatories and landscape displays made the trolley ride to Council Crest an exciting event.

Fig. III–410. Kerr garden, Elk Rock, 1916. An Olmsted design that capitalized on existing trees and views of the river, the Kerr garden was generous in scale and restrained in plan.

Fig. III–411. Mrs. Peter Kerr with *Lilium giganteum*. A Scot gentleman's garden recreated in the Northwest, Elk Rock served as a point of introduction for many rare botanical specimens.

One of the remarkable gardens of the era was that at Elk Rock, built by Peter Kerr and reputedly designed by the Olmsted Brothers. Though the site had already been developed in the late Victorian decades and Cliff Cottage overlooked the Willamette across from Milwaukie, Mr. Kerr built in 1916, as nearly as his architects could interpret, a Scottish Baronial Style house as replacement for the cottage, and expanded the site with great lawns, terraced hillsides, a swimming pool, and a woodland walk that led to an overlook.

Gardeners in the Northwest fall into two basic categories: to one group, the plants are of prime importance; basically collectors, they try

Fig. III–412. Kerr garden. Gracious living involved lavish outdoor entertainments necessitating such musical accompaniments as this orchestra provided.

Fig. III–413. Wilcox estate, Portland. The first decades of the 20th century saw a developing nostalgia for America's past and the Colonial Revival was a fashionable mode.

to provide optimum growing conditions for their collection with little regard to how the plants relate to the garden as a whole. The other category of gardener considers the garden of prime importance and plants as important only as "structural" materials which always remain subservient to the overall design. The disparity between these views of the garden as either botanical collection or art form has muddied the conception of landscape architecture since the 19th century and is manifested more acutely in temperate zones where the widest possible

Fig. III–414. Wilcox estate. Landscape architect L. M. Thielan created an impressive axial plan for an enclosed garden.

range of plant material can be accomodated.

Mr. Kerr was a special breed of gardener. Though a collector and plantsman with a sophisticated taste for magnolias, hamamelis, coreopsis and Japanese varieties of flowering cherry, he never lost sight of the overall plans and never allowed an inconsequential interruption of the lawns which extended as a broad swath beneath oaks and firs to the edge of the cliff above the river. As in 18th century English gardens, "nature" was improved upon and though to the casual observer the stands of trees and the vistas to the river appear natural, in actuality the groupings were contrived by thinning and pruning to more effectively create space and movement, light and shade. The flowers and shrubs were contained in the hillside terraces, or beds specifically devoted to their culture, and ample walks in flowing curves meandered gracefully from lawn to woodland, skirting the bank of the cliff, and leading back to the terrace. The scale and unity of the design, supplemented by the rich assortment of plant materials, was unique in Oregon

Fig. III–415. Hirsch garden, Portland. Planting schemes become more relaxed under the influence of Gertrude Jekyll and perennials replace carpet bedding.

at the time. In an era when Department of Agriculture regulations for plant importation were nonexistent, Mr. Kerr was able to import directly from the British Isles the rarities that he thirsted for. With a staff of gardeners, his meticulously maintained estate was a splendid and personal creation.

The Neo-Colonial Style of the Wilcox estate with its formal garden was a more typical and more academic design of the early 20th century; landscape architect L. M. Thielan used a central axis and a large panel of lawn flanked by bold balustrades to lead the eye toward the twin pavilions and connecting arcade that terminated the view. It was singled out in the 1919 issue of *Architect and Engineer,* a San Francisco publication, as one of Portland's most notable landscape designs. Whereas the Kerr garden was an "open" design, incorporating the river, woods, and mountains as essential parts of the garden, the Wilcox estate was finite; it respected property lines and was self-contained. An artificial sense of order was imposed on nature and in a statement that had almost become a litany in the Western world, man demonstrated again his feeling of supremacy in the hierarchy of God's world.

The compromise between the formal plan and the informal planting that had been the innovative direction explored by Gertrude Jekyll can be seen in a view of the Hirsch garden in Portland, with a placid West Burnside Street in the background. Though the formality of the design predominates, the rigidity of line is leavened by the spritely variation of textures and forms in the bulbs and perennials.

Fig. III–416. Street scene, Portland, circa 1920. The rose is the fashionable flower and the homeowner feels an obligation to ornament the front yard.

Fig. III–417. Henry Hahn garden, circa 1920. Design and style are less important than earnest zeal.

The character of streets in the Northwest underwent a metamorphosis during the "City Beautiful" movement inspired by the fairs. The protective walls and fences that so definitively declared the right of ownership in the 1870s and 1880s became unfashionable by the first decades of the 20th century; streets and sidewalks were now paved and curbs protected the street trees from swerving carriages. Roses held a mystique for homeowners in the early 20th century and particularly that new and wondrous rose, Caroline Testout, which bloomed continuously through summer and fall; Willson Park, in Salem, was completely surrounded by Caroline Testout at the curb line. In 1912, Mrs. Pittock held a rose display in her yard in Portland. It was the beginning of a tradition.

The residential streets of Western cities suggested both affluence and comfort prior to World War I; wooden two-story houses, built centrally on the lot (and often clumsily unstylish) observed a common setback and displayed a mutual concern for plantings that "enhanced" the street landscape. Though the incidence of overhead electric wiring becomes painfully disruptive as electricity becomes a standard utility, the uncrowded streets and the generous scale of the homes lend to these streets of middle income families an air of well-being. The house is unequivocably the status symbol and though the stable may have been converted to a garage in some instances, as yet the automobile has not caused the shattering physical disruption of the city and the emotional disruption of family ties and traditional values.

Parks and Gardens in the Puget Sound Area

Thomas Allsopp*

The state of Washington is favored with some of the most beautiful natural scenery and dramatic landscapes in the United States. Within its boundaries can be found almost every variation on nature's climatic, geologic, and topographic themes. Moving inland from the Pacific Ocean, which bounds us on the west with its rugged coastline, the Hoh River Rain Forest is a jungle of giant trees dripping with moss and lichens. It nestles at the feet of the state's most dramatic mountain range, the Olympics. These peaks are snow-capped all year long and form a backdrop for many of the cities located on Puget Sound. The basin between the Olympics and the Cascade Mountains enjoys a mild, protected climate. The landscape is always green. Douglas fir, cedar, and hemlock are all native evergreens. These are complemented during the summer with various hues of green supplied by native deciduous trees such as the big leaf maple and vine maple, cottonwood and alder. Though at lower elevations these trees provide a minimum of fall color, at higher elevations the aspens turn a blazing yellow. The Cascade Mountains are not as rugged as the Olympics, yet they contain some of the most majestic single peaks in the state. Mount Rainier and Mount Baker are included in beautiful National Parks. East of these mountains the scene changes. On the eastern slopes, pines replace the firs and finally green foliage gives way to barren hills which are brown in the summer showing little sign of life. Here, however, are some of the state's most colorful wildflowers which cover the hills in spring. The climate is severe. Winters are cold and usually bring more snow than in the western half of the state; summers are hot and dry.

The richest region for investigating parks and gardens is the western half of the state along the Puget Sound Basin. The cities of Seattle and

---

*The author would like to acknowledge the assistance of the following people in researching his essay: Don Sherwood, Seattle park historian; David Streatfield, professor of landscape architecture, University of Washington; Norman Johnston, professor of architectural and landscape architectural history, University of Washington; Mrs. David L. Stone, daughter of the Thornes of Thornewood.

Tacoma were early towns which developed at about the same time. Both were major ports of north and southbound trade, and became centers of wealth, influence, and culture in the late 19th and early 20th centuries.

When culture (in the Victorian sense) begins to blossom, so do parks and gardens. The first park created by a city ordinance, the 5.22-acre Seattle Cemetery, was donated to the City of Seattle by one of its founding fathers, David Denny. Little by little Seattle acquired additional parkland. The Park Commissioners purchased land such as the Phinney estate, which has become the Woodland Park Zoo and Greenlake Park. Others, like Mr. Denny, were generous enough to donate their land to the city, stipulating perpetual park use. Still other parcels of land were set up as parks as part of real estate ventures. Leschi Park, for example,

Fig. III–418. The original pavilion at Leschi Park, Seattle.

was established on the shores of Lake Washington below land which had been platted for home sites. Often these parks were developed as places where buyers and their families might relax after their trip from the city and viewing the lots. The developers of Leschi were a bit more aggressive, however, and in their park they constructed a seven-story beerhall.[1] Entertainment here included everything from respectable plays and concerts to not so respectable dancehall shows and gambling. Along with whatever it took to attract buyers came the inevitable sales pitch which was probably delivered on "just a slight detour" on the drive from the city. Madison was another real estate venture which grew into an amusement center with caged animals, rides and other exhibits. It was called White City.

1. Don Sherwood, "History of Seattle's Parks" (unpublished manuscript).

In 1903 the Seattle Park Commissioners engaged the Olmsted brothers, landscape architects from Brookline, Massachusetts, to make a survey of the Seattle park system. Most of the city's major parks had already been acquired at that time. The few improvements which had been made in these parks before the survey, had been done without any planning. The Olmsteds supplied the needed direction; improvements were begun that complied with their recommendations. As shown on their plan, the Olmsteds suggested a series of boulevards to link the various parks in a cohesive system. Though this portion of the plan was never fully executed, Ravenna and Lake Washington boulevards were improved with tree plantings and are still two of the city's most beautiful drives.

In 1884, shortly after Denny Park was donated to Seattle, the city asked the next of kin of persons buried there to move the bodies to some other cemetery. Because many of those buried were early settlers or Indians, relatives could not be found. The city had to take the responsibility for moving these bodies to Lakeview Cemetery.

The city limits did not extend as far as the park in 1884 and only minimal improvements were made including paths and benches. In 1887 the city named the park for its donor. But by 1903 Seattle's expanding residential district had surrounded the park and demands were being made for further improvements. That same year the Olmsteds submitted their report to the Park Commissioners on the state of the Seattle park system. In it they referred to Denny Park:

> It is unlikely that fir trees will be permanently successful in this locality as there will be more and more smoke from factories and from the numerous dwellings of the dense population likely to occupy the surrounding land; hence, the fir trees, in fact all coniferous evergreens, would better be removed at once.
>
> The shrubbery plantations, in general, are too miscellaneous in composition and too much like, in selection, many of the private grounds of the city. . . . A distinctly informal style of design having been chosen, all rows of plants should be avoided.[2]

As changes were being made in the park to comply with the Olmsted directives, Denny Park was being threatened by Seattle's most ambitious undertaking.

In 1898, Reginald H. Thomson, then director of the Seattle Engineering Department, decided that the city had too many hills and their steep grades were a great inconvenience. His solution to the problem was to wash the hills away. Applying the hydraulic mining techniques then used in the mining fields of Alaska, he began a program of sluicing earth down to the tideflats. Water carried the mud down huge conveyor belts to the shore where it was used to fill and extend the city into Puget Sound. According to advocates of the plan, this land extension would provide a better harbor. When there was enough fill for this purpose,

2. The Annual Report of the Seattle Park Commissioners (Seattle, 1903), 80.

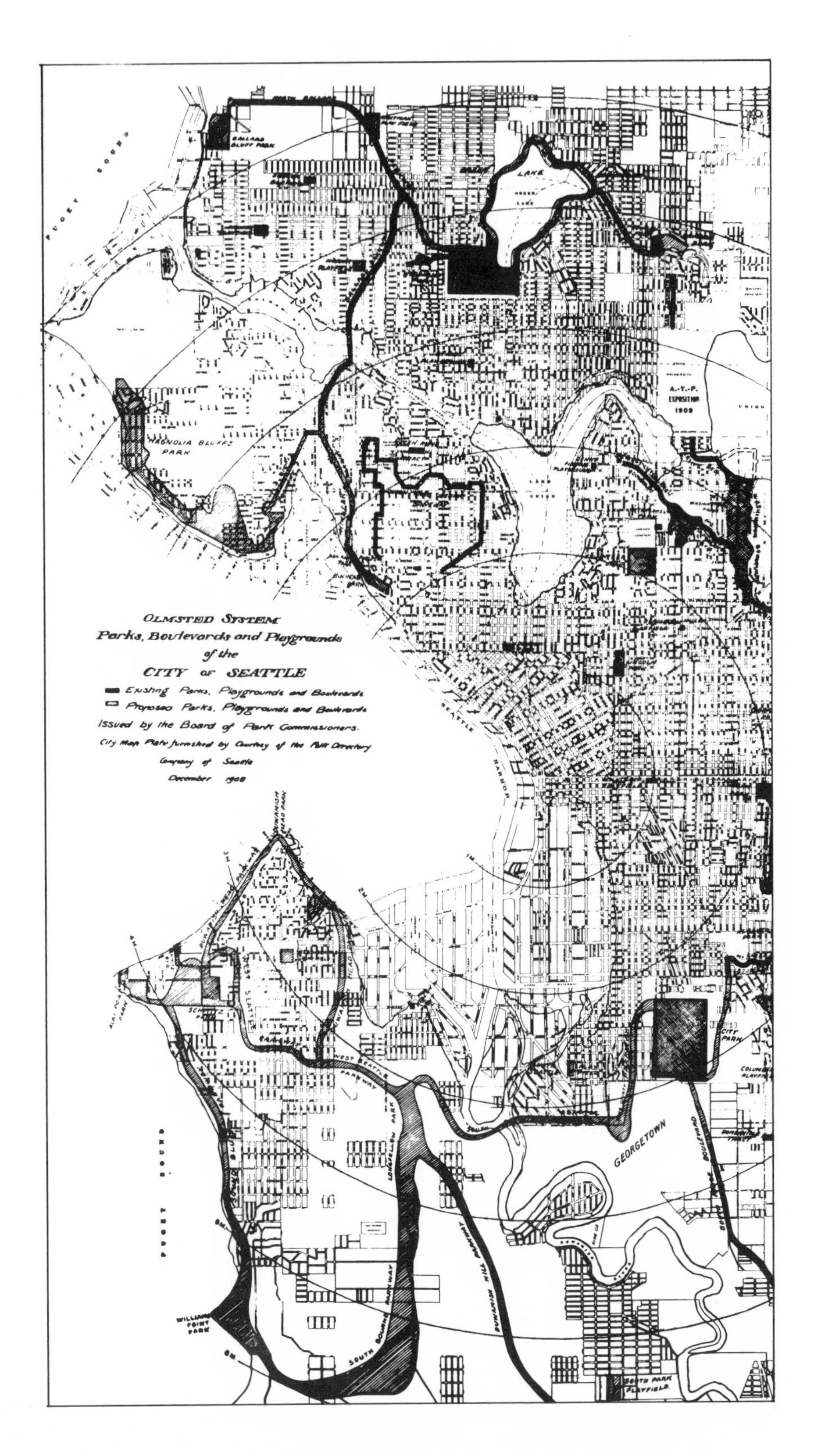

Fig. III–419. The Olmsted Plan for the Seattle Park System showing existing and proposed parks, boulevards, and playgrounds.

there were still hills to be conquered. The conveyors then carried the earth to specially built barges waiting in the harbor, which were towed into Elliot Bay and dumped by flooding a side compartment so the whole barge would roll over.

Denny Hill was the first area to be removed. The city was pressing at the hill's southern flank in its attempt to expand northward to Lake Union. Oddly enough, Denny Park was left standing. It must have been a strange sight when C. B. Bagley wrote in 1916 that the park was "forty to ninety feet above the grade contemplated by the regrade."[3] Seattle's pioneers rallied in an attempt to save the park, saying that it had historic value. They pointed out that it was Seattle's first park and that it still retained some virgin timber, of which there was little left so close to the city. And because it was originally a cemetery, there might still be bodies buried there which should not be disturbed. When these arguments received little attention, the group presented figures estimating the cost of the regrading project and how much the city might save by leaving Denny Park undisturbed. Thomson was unimpressed and work proceeded. By 1930 Denny Park had been flattened to its present grade.

When a new design was called for, the old informality which the Olmsteds had mentioned in their report was scrapped for the more popular formal plan. Paths radiate out to the four corners of the park from a central focal point. The park was replanted with a mixture of deciduous and evergreen trees and a palette of plant shrubs which the Olmsteds would have deplored. During the summer, the Park Department, whose offices have been located within the park, maintains a floral display reminiscent of its ancestors. Maturing after a tumultuous past, Denny Park provides a green oasis in what many residents consider one of the most visually blighted sections of Seattle.

In 1876 Seattle purchased what would become its most popular park. The 40-acre site crowns Capitol Hill and was sold to the city by J. M. Colman. A city ordinance created Washelli Cemetery there and graves from Seattle Cemetery (Denny Park) were transferred to Washelli to make way for Denny Park improvements. The city soon realized that the new cemetery was a valuable property and the graves were moved again to Lakeview Cemetery. Here they were allowed to remain and the grounds are still maintained as Seattle's Pioneer Cemetery. In 1887 Washelli was renamed Lakeview Park, and in 1901 the name was changed again to Volunteer Park in honor of Seattle's volunteers in the Spanish American War. The park commands a panoramic view from all sides. The city, Puget Sound, and the mountains are to the west; Mount Rainier looms to the south. The Cascades and Lake Washington can be seen to the east and Mount Baker to the north.

Volunteer Park developed slowly and haphazardly at first. In 1903 the Olmsteds recommended that the city purchase the remaining prop-

3. C. B. Bagley, *History of King County, Washington* (Chicago, 1929), 678–85.

erty on the south end of the site. That would ensure that the park faced on a street rather than on the back gardens of residences which would eventually be built there. With their usual foresight, the Olmsteds warned that

> trees to be planted on the (adjoining) properties and streets will in time completely shut out distant views. Thus, almost all of the advantages of having this park located on the top of a hill will be lost. It may be worthwhile, therefore, in time, to erect an observation tower at the summit, sufficiently high to enable visitors to overlook all surrounding trees and large enough to accommodate considerable numbers without discomfort.[4]

A most interesting answer to the observation tower suggestion came in 1906. In 1901 the city water department had constructed a reservoir in the park. The water tower was built in 1906. The tower was unsightly, so it was sheathed in brick to make it fit into its surroundings. Two sets of stairs spiral between the brick and the tank and lead to the top of the tower. There visitors find a spacious observation platform and legends to explain the most breathtaking view in Seattle.

The problem of an observation point was temporarily solved in the Olmsted plan with the construction of a rustic arcade and bandstand on the highest point in the park. Even after the tower was built, the arcade remained a favorite place for visitors to sit and enjoy the view, listen to a concert, or to stroll through one of the displays which were regularly scheduled there. Impressive Easter sunrise services were conducted there each year and were always well attended.

The only other building in the park was the Park Department's greenhouse, which the Olmsteds described as "ugly and much too prominent. The residence of the superintendent and the park barn and administration buildings and yards together with the greenhouse nursery should be grouped together in some less valuable part of the park, probably near the cemetery."[5] The ugly greenhouse was replaced and the whole operation was re-sited on the northern boundary of the park near the cemetery fence. The Park Department grows plants for the park system there and takes pride in the continuing floral displays in the miniature Victorian conservatory.

The Olmsteds thought that the park plantings were too fragmented. They saw a need for at least one large open area for games and large gatherings. They had the same criticism here as at Denny Park concerning the display: "It seems to be the intention to make a feature of the flowers . . . it should be done in a formal or informal manner but not mixed, formal beds in an informal setting."[6] They suggested that a formal garden be laid out just below the arcade. Sets of stairs lead down

4. *The Annual Report of the Seattle Park Commissioners,* 1903, 76–78.

5. *The Annual Report of the Seattle Park Commissioners,* 1903.

6. *The Annual Report of the Seattle Park Commissioners,* 1903.

Fig. III–420. Volunteer Park from the water tower showing Olmsted improvements. The museum is now located where the bandstand and arcade appear in the photograph.

Fig. III–421. The Orchid Room at the Volunteer Park Conservatory.

from the arcade level to a small parterre. Here box-lined beds accommodate summer displays of colorful annuals, and two matching circular ponds hold water plants and goldfish. The design of these ponds had to be revised slightly because parents were concerned about children falling in, and dogs had to be deterred from eating the goldfish. The Olmsteds also advised that "many firs should be removed. Crowded firs look good as a distant mass but weak and crowded close up. Wild undergrowth should be gradually replaced with exotic shrubbery." Subsequently many fir trees were removed and replaced with specimens of exotic shrubbery which now dot the lawns in the park.

In the Olmsted view, the neighboring cemetery was both an asset and a detriment. They felt that its openness supplied the park with a feeling of amplitude missing in parks surrounded by houses. However, they also reasoned that the monuments were not pleasant to see and that the vines growing on the fence between the park and the cemetery were preferable to trees which would have to be pruned.

Volunteer Park seems to be constantly involved in controversy. In 1910 there was a proposal to have the state art museum located there. The Olmsteds were consulted and they replied that a museum was not in keeping with the activities of the park. This attitude was consistent with John Olmsted's reaction to the buildings in Balboa Park in San Diego. In 1915 an exposition was planned for Balboa Park which was to include a number of structures. The Olmsteds, wishing to preserve the natural ravine in the park, suggested that the buildings be placed on large terraces near the edge of the site. Here they would relate to the city and do no damage to the park. An architect made a proposal which located the buildings in the center of the park, to be reached by a monumental bridge over the center of the ravine. Because of the insensitivity of that design, the Olmsteds resigned from the project. Seattle followed the Olmsteds' advice, however, and the museum proposal was discarded.

In 1932 Mrs. Eugene Fuller and her son, Dr. Richard Fuller, donated an art museum to the city and it was decided that it should be placed in Volunteer Park. The arcade was torn down and the museum designed by Carl Gould was built in its place. Currently, plans to enlarge the museum are meeting with opposition. With the museum came a proliferation of art in the park. Directly opposite the museum entrance is the newest addition to the outdoor collection, titled "Black Sun." This sculpture by Nogouchi is executed in black Brazilian granite and is the sister piece of Yale's "White Sun." It is the third major work of art to be commissioned by the Foundation for the Arts and Humanities. Monuments in the park include a statue of Seward which was brought from the Alaska-Yukon-Pacific Exposition, and a memorial to Judge Thomas Burke, Seattle pioneer.

Another current controversy revolves around the directive of the State Board of Health that Seattle should cover all its open reservoirs, including that at Volunteer Park. Though designs have already been proposed for the cover, no work has begun. The city council is opposing the plan and health officials are undecided as to its necessity. Many visitors to the park feel that it would lose one of its most pleasant features if this large open body of water were covered. Because Volunteer Park offers so many choices for restful recreation, and is so accessible, it remains one of Seattle's favorite parks.

Earlier, the Olmsteds were asked to come to Seattle to draw a plan for the Alaska-Yukon-Pacific Exposition which was being held on the grounds of the University of Washington in Seattle. This magnificent fair, with all of its plaster buildings, was erected to celebrate the re-

Fig. III–422. The Alaska-Yukon-Pacific Exposition, Seattle.

source-rich Yukon Territory. Neighboring states participated as well as foreign countries such as Japan. Though most of the buildings were not intended as permanent structures, the Fine Arts Palace from that fair is still in use as the University College of Architecture. The main axis along which the fair buildings were located has been preserved, as well as a pond and fountain which was called the Arctic circle. Mount Rainier is the focal point of this vista. In the foreground of the view can be seen another of the Olmsteds' accomplishments: the University of Washington Arboretum. Laid out in the later more informal manner, it appears to be a large park. The designers carefully preserved existing land forms as well as vegetation. The many micro-environments located in this 200-acre laboratory are variable enough to encourage and nurture over 500 species of trees, 1,800 species of shrubs,[7] and an abundance of herbaceous material. The contribution of the Olmsteds to park development in the Northwest is obvious. We are indebted to those in municipal government who were farsighted enough to engage such a renowned firm.

The Olmsted influence is also seen in the gardens of private citizens. The dates of the Olmsted activity in the state seem to coincide with the beginnings of a movement toward the establishment of many of the great estates of the area. John Olmsted complained to the Seattle Parks Commissioners that whenever he or a representative of the office visited the Puget Sound area, they were immediately petitioned by wealthy fashion-conscious homeowners, who would demand that the most fashionable landscape architects help design their gardens.

Because of its age, Tacoma can boast of having some of the earliest large gardens. The most ambitious of these are spotted around Gravelly and American lakes which lie in a group just south of the city. The location is perfect for gardening. The lakes provide plenty of moist air and water. The Olympic Mountains form a backdrop for some of the gardens while others use majestic Mount Rainier as a snow-capped focal point throughout the year. One of these gardens is Thornewood, finished in 1911 by Chester Thorne, according to a carved inscription on one of the brick walls. This estate on the shores of the larger American Lake was at the height of its development in 1930 when it was visited by the members of the Garden Club of America, then holding a meeting in Seattle. The garden was laid out by the Olmsted Brothers and has been attributed by some to Frederick Law Olmsted personally, along with a much earlier date for development. Though this is possible, it is unlikely; his achievements usually show a more Reptonian Picturesque influence. To quote the 1930 Garden Club description: "To those of us who had not happened to hear of Thornewood, it came as a thunderclap of astounding beauty. To those who had long known of the renowned garden, it came as the perfect consummation of the ideal garden . . . not

7. Friends of the Arboretum, *University of Washington Arboretum; A Showcase for All Seasons* (Seattle, 1969).

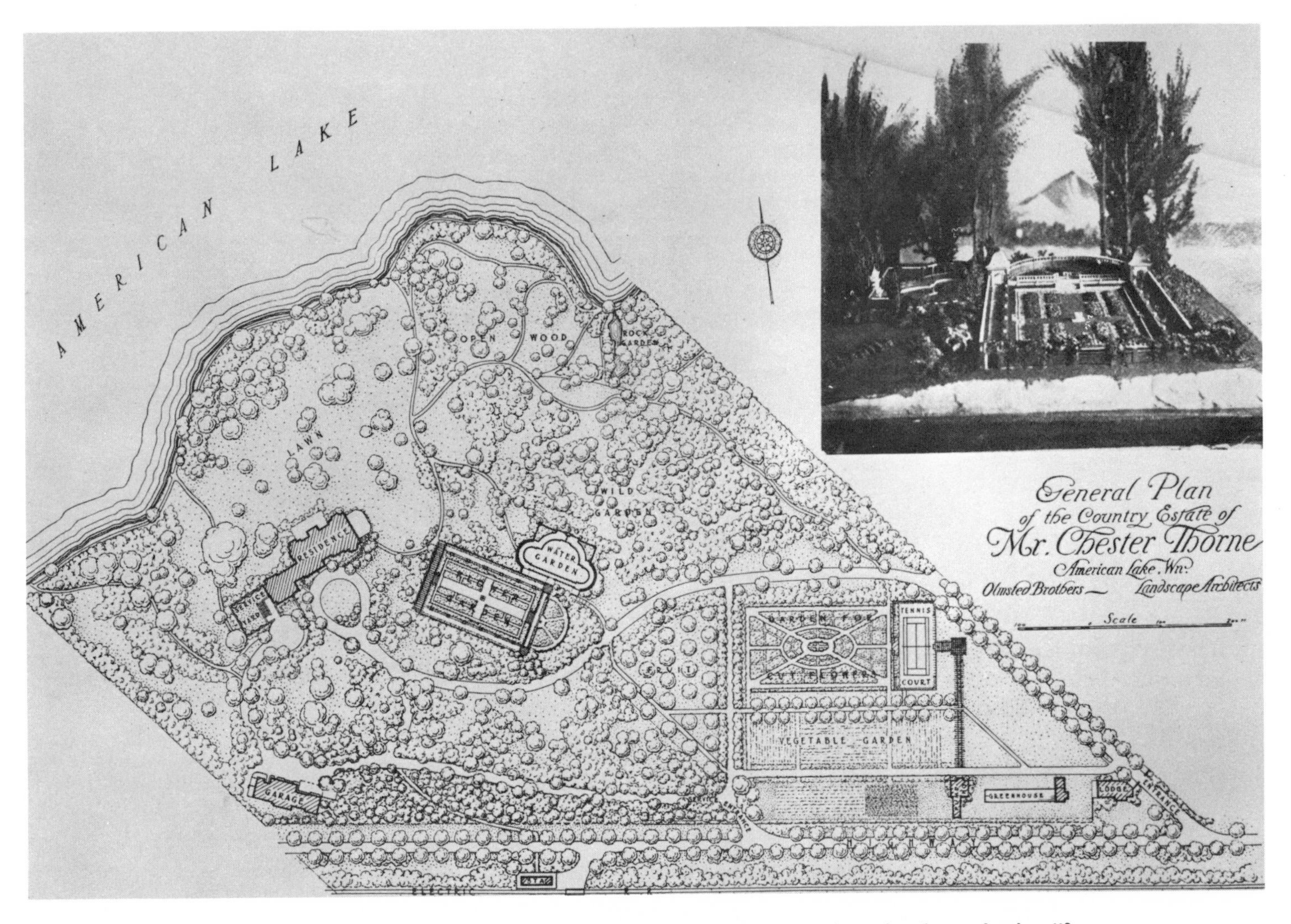

Fig. III–423. The Olmsted plan for the gardens of Thornewood.

too large, not too elaborate, just simple perfection."[8]

What were components of this perfect garden? The house itself must have had something to do with first impressions. Its heavy neo-Elizabethan lines, relieved by an almost continuous mantle of ivy and soaring chimneys, would have seemed appropriate in its surroundings of massive Douglas firs. In England, 18th and early 19th century landscape critics had deplored the use of evergreen trees in the popular clumps of landscape gardener "Capability" Brown, preferring the softer forms of the deciduous species. At Thornewood, the magnificent firs, in combination with the sweeps of lawn beneath them, create a West Coast Picturesque. This, then, was the first impression one received when driving the entrance road of Thornewood.

The house was built well back from the road and near the water's

8. *The Garden Club of America Yearbook*, 1930.

Fig. III–424. The Tudor Garden with the Thornewood house in the background.

Fig. III–425. The wall of the Tudor Garden today.

edge. The entrance faced east and the lake was to the west. The Tudor Garden was to the right of the entry behind a seven-foot brick wall which enclosed it on three sides. A favorite of Mrs. Thorne, who enjoyed working with her gardener in charge of color, the Tudor Garden displayed an array of hues and flower forms during the summer. It is rectangular and is entered from the west end where the wall is vine-covered and an arbor is supported the width of the garden on brick columns. In the center of the wall is a small shell fountain; the focal point for the garden to the east is Mount Rainier. The garden is sunk about three feet in the center and the beds around the raised sides were loosely planted with perennials and small shrubs. The central beds were the most defined with boxwood hedges. The panel of lawn which ran the length of the garden was interrupted in its center by a small tile-lined pond and fountain. It culminated in a short flight of stairs at the top of which the sundial was located. This little garden had much of the grace of its ancestors: it is sunken, it had a pond, sundial, clipped boxwood, vine-covered walls, a lush display of flowers and two pergolas. The mountain and the coniferous forests beyond are variations never found in the original Tudor gardens.

The two garden pergolas were on either side of the east end. One was just for sitting; the other to the north was the entrance for the Pond Garden. Viewed from this entrance the large pond is about six feet below. It is reached by two ramps which lead off to the right and the left. Directly across from this entrance is a lion's head fountain and basin with flanking topiary trees and seats. Huge urns of flowers sat on the balustrades and around the pond. The pool itself, which takes up

Fig. III–426. The pergola at the Pond Garden, Thornewood.

most of the space, was turned into a horticultural challenge by the owner. Rather than a clean uninterrupted reflecting surface, it held a display of aquatic plants such as iris, cattails, rushes, and water lilies. To complement the plants in the pool, beds were cut out of the lawn which surrounded it. The whole of this garden was ringed with a rustic arbor supported by brick columns on a low wall. Vines were trained up the columns and across the arbor to soften the effect of this architectural element and facilitate the transition between garden and woodlands beyond.

The strangest and most uncomfortable room in this series of garden rooms was the Spanish Garden. In photographs taken in 1931 and published in *Horticulture Magazine*, the garden appears immature. The only thing linking it to any known Spanish garden is the ornamental well in the center of the scene with a wrought iron arch and detailed pulley mechanism. The tiny boxwood squares, planted apart from one another, appear as a dotted line around the strictly geometric beds and have an arid quality. The center beds hold severely clipped roses which are the only color relief. This garden looks like a museum exhibit—interesting, but only a display, and unrelated to the woods beyond.

Today this 100-acre estate has become a housing development. The main house has been converted into apartments and the gardens are in ruins. The walls of the Tudor Garden are in fairly good condition. At the Pond Garden one finds a perfect example of insensitive design: a house has been built over the pond! Thornewood used to be "one of the three most beautiful gardens in America."[9] One wonders what has be-

9. "The Gardens of Thornewood," *Horticulture* (March, 1931), 94–95.

Fig. III–427. Scene of Schmitz Park in the early 1900s.

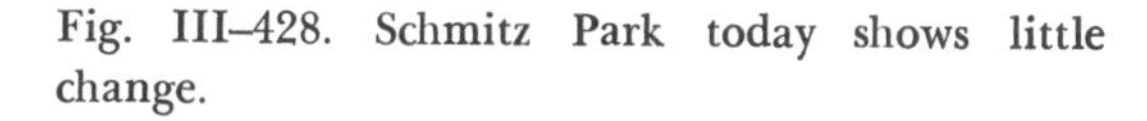

Fig. III–428. Schmitz Park today shows little change.

come of the other two.

Few cities have availed themselves of the luxury of having a virgin forest park within the city limits. In Seattle, however, the foresight of Ferdinand Schmitz and city officials have preserved a living museum of the Northwest's past. From 1908 to 1912 Schmitz donated the greater part of this 50.4 acres; the remainder was purchased in 1947. The ordinance which created the park specified it as "virgin forest preserved by pioneers as a reminder . . . to be preserved perpetually . . . for park purposes in order that certain natural features might be preserved."[10]

The park is located in a ravine. It used to be a cool retreat for picnickers, who would take a ferry trip to Alki Beach for sun and swimming. Then there was a half-mile walk to Schmitz Park for lunch and cooling off. A cable car ride back to Seattle completed the day. At the park entrance was a rustic arch made from large timbers and a matching shelter house. To reach the highest point in the park at its southern boundary, one passes through thickets of salmonberry, elderberry, Indian plum, and pockets of colorful skunk cabbage, deer fern, sword fern and heuchera. Moss and lichens climb the stately trunks of towering Douglas firs and hemlocks which form a year-round canopy, filled out in the summer by maples and other deciduous trees.

In the very bottom of the ravine runs a creek. In places it runs as a single force; elsewhere it is split into ribbons as it falls over rocks and fallen trees. Some of these fallen trees have become nurse logs for new trees. Some have fallen high over the creek forming natural bridges for

10. Sherwood, "Seattle's Parks."

the adventurous who would dare to cross on their slippery bark. For the not so adventurous, the park department has built rustic bridges of hand-split timbers.

Except for the missing arch and shelter and a lack of benches, the park looks very much like it did in old photographs. It probably looks much like it did when David Denny first landed in this area looking for a place to start a city. There are no roads through the park, though they have been suggested. To see the delicate balance of natural beauty here you must be willing to see it as its first visitors did, on foot. Seattle-ites and other city dwellers will travel miles to one of our national or state parks. The gasoline shortage may lead citizens to discover Schmitz Park, which has been "conceded to be the most remarkable natural park within the limits of any city in the United States."

IV Motor Age

OFFICIAL AAA ROAD MAP

WESTERN STATES

PUBLISHED AND COPYRIGHTED BY
AMERICAN AUTOMOBILE ASSOCIATION
WASHINGTON, D. C.

SCALE OF MILES

0 20 40 60 80 100

ONE INCH EQUALS APPROXIMATELY 48 MILES

LEGEND

HEAVY LINES INDICATE THROUGH ROUTES

PAVEMENT: *All Types.*

IMPROVEMENT: *Such as Gravel, Stone, Shell and good Sand Clay. (All weather roads.)*

GRADED EARTH:

EARTH:

U. S. ROUTE NUMBERS SHOWN IN SHIELD, THUS: 25
STATE ROUTE NUMBERS SHOWN IN CIRCLE, THUS: 19
PLAIN NUMERALS INDICATE MILEAGE BETWEEN OUTLINED POINTS OR INTERSECTIONS INDICATED BY THIS SYMBOL, THUS:

52 31 40 26 34

Fig. IV–1. Portion of American Automobile Association official road map of the western states, 1936. Early highway construction tended to equalize access to various areas of the Northwest.

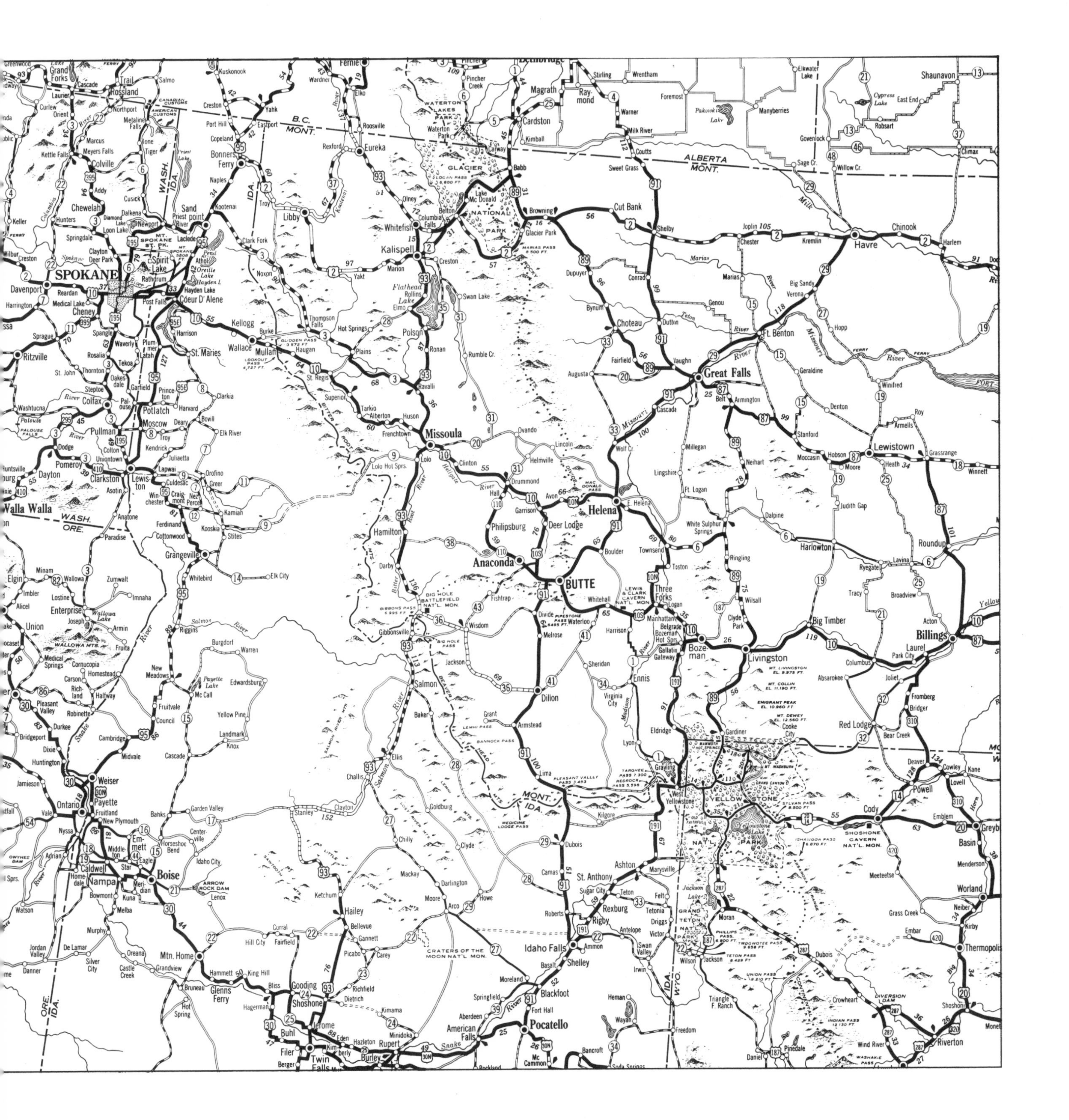
Grand Forks
Cascade
Trail
Rossland
Salmo
Kuskonook
Fernie
Elko
Pincher Creek
Stirling
Wrentham
Elkwater Lake
Shaunavon
Magrath
Raymond
Foremost
Pakowki Lake
Manyberries
Cypress Lake
East End
Robsart
Govenlock
Climax
Laurier
Curlew
Orient
Northport
Metaline Falls
CANADIAN CUSTOMS
AMERICAN CUSTOMS
Creston
Yahk
Port Hill
Eastport
B.C.
MONT.
Roosville
WATERTON LAKES PARK
Waterton Park
Cardston
Kimball
Carway
Warner
Milk River
Coutts
ALBERTA
MONT.
Sage Cr.
Willow Cr.
Marcus
Meyers Falls
Kettle Falls
Colville
Ione
Tiger
Copeland
Bonners Ferry
Naples
WASH.
IDA.
Rexford
Eureka
GLACIER
LOGAN PASS
Lake Mc Donald
NATIONAL
PARK
Babb
Sweet Grass
Addy
Cusick
Chewelah
Dalkena
Newport
Diamond Lake
Loon Lake
Sand Point
Priest River
Kootenai
Troy
Libby
Olney
Whitefish
Columbia Falls
Belton
Browning
Glacier Park
Cut Bank
Shelby
Joplin
Chester
Kremlin
Havre
Chinook
Harlem
Keller
Hunters
Springdale
Clayton
Deer Park
MT. SPOKANE ST. PK.
Laclede
Clark Fork
Kalispell
Creston
MARIAS PASS
Wilbur
Creston
Spokane
Spirit Lake
Athol
Rathdrum
Oreille Lake
Hayden L.
Hayden Lake
Noxon
Marion
Yakt
Dupuyer
Conrad
Marias
Big Sandy
Verona
SPOKANE
Davenport
Reardan
Medical Lake
Cheney
Post Falls
Coeur D'Alene
Flathead Lake
Rollins
Elmo
Swan Lake
Harrington
Sprague
Spangle
Waverly
Plummer
Latah
Harrison
Kellogg
Wallace
Mullan
GLIDDEN PASS
Thompson Falls
Hot Springs
Polson
Bynum
Genou
Teton
Choteau
Dutton
Ft. Benton
Hopp
Ritzville
Rosalia
Tekoa
St. John
Thornton
Oakesdale
St. Maries
LOOKOUT PASS
Haugan
St. Regis
Plains
Ronan
Rumble Cr.
Augusta
Fairfield
Vaughn
Great Falls
Belt
Armington
Geraldine
Winifred
Steptoe
Colfax
Garfield
Palouse
Potlatch
Princeton
Clarkia
Superior
Tarkio
Alberton
Huson
Ravalli
Cascade
Denton
Roy
Armells
Washtucna
Palouse
Pullman
Moscow
Deary
Harvard
Bovill
Elk River
Frenchtown
Missoula
Ovando
Lincoln
Wolf Cr.
Millegan
Stanford
Moccasin
Hobson
Lewistown
Grassrange
Palouse Falls
Dodge
Pomeroy
Colton
Uniontown
Kendrick
Juliaetta
Lolo
Lolo Hot Sprs.
Clinton
Helmville
Neihart
Moore
Heath
Winnett
Dayton
Clarkston
Lewiston
Lapwai
Culdesac
Orofino
Greer
Drummond
Hall
MAC DONALD PASS
Avon
Helena
E. Helena
Lingshire
Ft. Logan
Judith Gap
Walla Walla
WASH.
ORE.
Asotin
Winchester
Craigmont
Nez Perce
Kamiah
Anatone
Ferdinand
Cottonwood
Kooskia
Stites
Garrison
Philipsburg
Deer Lodge
White Sulphur Springs
Dalpine
Harlowton
Roundup
Paradise
Grangeville
Hamilton
Anaconda
Boulder
Townsend
Toston
Ringling
Lavina
Ryegate
Elgin
Minam
Wallowa
Zumwalt
Imnaha
Imbler
Lostine
Alicel
Enterprise
Wallowa Lake
Joseph
Armin
Union
WALLOWA MTS.
Whitebird
Elk City
Darby
BIG HOLE BATTLEFIELD NAT'L. MON.
GIBBONS PASS
Fishtrap
BUTTE
Divide
Whitehall
LEWIS & CLARK CAVERN NAT'L. MON.
Three Forks
Logan
Wilsall
Tracy
Broadview
Riggins
Gibbonsville
Wisdom
PIPESTONE PASS
Waterloo
Manhattan
Belgrade
Bozeman Hot Sprs.
Clyde Park
Big Timber
Acton
Billings
Fruita
Medical Springs
Homestead
Carson
Richland
Halfway
Burgdorf
Warren
BIG HOLE PASS
Melrose
Harrison
Gallatin Gateway
Bozeman
Livingston
Laurel
Park City
Columbus
Joliet
Cornucopia
New Meadows
Payette Lake
Mc Call
Edwardsburg
Jackson
Sheridan
Ennis
MT. LIVINGSTON
MT. COLLIN
Absarokee
Pleasant Valley
Robinette
Durkee
Fruitvale
Council
Yellow Pine
Salmon
Dillon
Virginia City
EMIGRANT PEAK
Fromberg
Bridger
Red Lodge
Bear Creek
Bridgeport
Dixie
Huntington
Cambridge
Midvale
Cascade
Landmark
Knox
Baker
Grant
LEMHI PASS
Armstead
BANNOCK PASS
Eldridge
Gardiner
MT. DEWEY
Cooke City
Lyon
Jamieson
Weiser
Payette
Ontario
Fruitland
Vale
Nyssa
Ellis
Challis
Lima
PLEASANT VALLEY PASS
TARGHEE PASS
REDROCK PASS
Grayling
MT. WASHBURN
Deaver
Cowley
Kane
Lovell
Powell
MONT.
IDA.
West Yellowstone
YELLOWSTONE
SYLVAN PASS
Cody
Emblem
Greybull
Basin
Bahks
Garden Valley
Stanley
Clayton
New Plymouth
Emmett
Horseshoe Bend
Centerville
Idaho City
Goldburg
Kilgore
MEDICINE LODGE PASS
Dubois
Chilly
Clyde
Yellowstone Lake
ISHAWOOA PASS
SHOSHONE CAVERN NAT'L. MON.
Middleton
Star
Eagle
Caldwell
Adrian
Homedale
Nampa
Meridian
Boise
Kuna
Bowmont
Melba
ARROW ROCK DAM
Lenox
Ketchum
Mackay
Darlington
Howe
Moore
Arco
Camas
Ashton
Marysville
St. Anthony
Sugar City
Teton
Rexburg
Felt
Tetonia
Driggs
Victor
Swan Valley
Jackson Lake
GRAND TETON NAT'L. PARK
Moran
TWOGWOTEE PASS
TETON PASS
PHILLIPS PASS
Meeteetse
Menderson
Worland
Neiber
Kirby
Grass Creek
Embar
Thermopolis
Watson
Murphy
Jordan Valley
De Lamar
Silver City
Oreana
Castle Creek
Grandview
Mtn. Home
Hammett
King Hill
Hill City
Corral
Fairfield
Hailey
Bellevue
Gannett
Picabo
Carey
CRATERS OF THE MOON NAT'L. MON.
Roberts
Rigby
Idaho Falls
Ammon
Shelley
Antelope
Irwin
Wilson
Jackson
UNION PASS
Dubois
CONTINENTAL DIVIDE
DIVERSION DAM
Crowheart
Shoshoni
Bruneau
Glenns Ferry
Hot Spring
Hagerman
Bliss
Gooding
Shoshone
Richfield
Dietrich
Kimama
Minidoka
Moreland
Basalt
Blackfoot
Springfield
Aberdeen
Fort Hall
Pocatello
American Falls
Heman
Wayan
Triangle F. Ranch
INDIAN PASS
Freedom
Buhl
Jerome
Eden
Hazleton
Rupert
Filer
Kimberly
Twin Falls
Berger
Burley
Rockland
Mc Cammon
Bancroft
Soda Springs
Daniel
Pinedale
Wind River
WASHAKIE PASS
Riverton
ORE.
IDA.
IDA.
WYO.
Snake
Salmon River
Missouri
Columbia
Milk

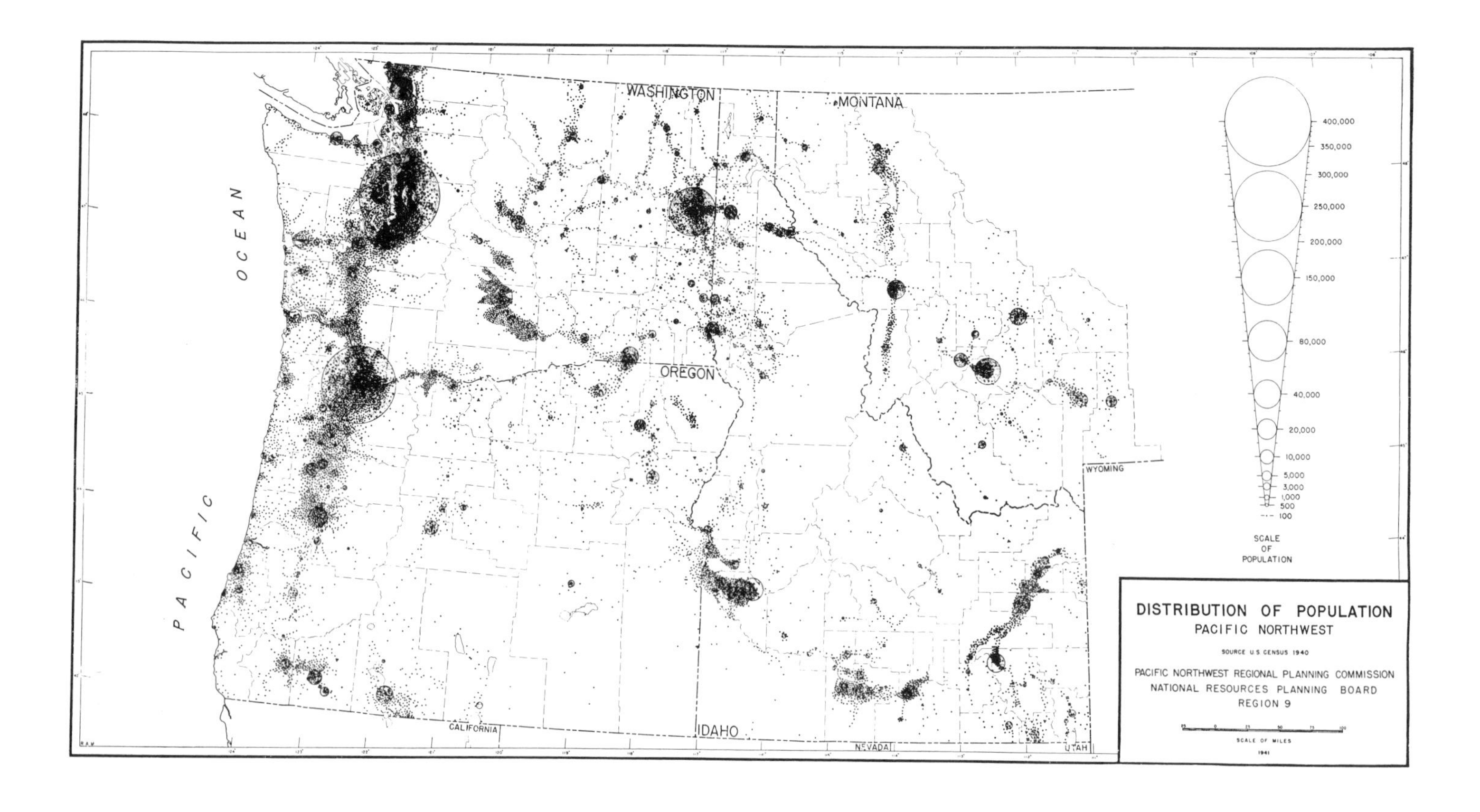

Fig. IV–2. Population distribution map from *Economic Atlas of the Pacific Northwest* published by the Northwest Regional Council, 1942. In 1940 the portion west of the Cascades accounted for three-fifths of the region's population although representing only one-fifth of the Northwest's area.

Population Pacific Northwest 1940

Idaho	524,873
Oregon	1,089,684
Washington	1,736,191
	3,350,748

Regional Setting

Virginia Guest Ferriday

Even as the railroads were built in the American West, resentment toward their monopolistic control of rates and their large land holdings was spreading throughout the United States. The last Congressional land grant was authorized in 1871. By 1892 the Populist Party in Oregon was calling for improved navigation and for a government-owned railroad along the Columbia as a means of establishing some degree of competition. Looking back, it seems inevitable that the next major transportation system receiving widespread public support would be one built by governmental bodies and one which, at the same time, allowed for some degree of individual control. The combination of privately-owned vehicles run on a system of state and federal highways answered both requirements.

The Good Roads Movement had its beginnings on the East Coast with the efforts of bicycling enthusiasts to obtain better facilities for their sport. Following introduction of the Model T in 1907 automobile ownership increased rapidly and by the time the campaign reached the West Coast the automobile interests, including both car owners and automobile sales agents, had taken over leadership. Because the automobile remained for some time a play-toy for the rich rather than a serious means of transportation, the movement was in its early stages characterized by a spirit of adventure and camaraderie, in marked contrast to the intense competition which had accompanied the building of the railroads.

Good roads promotional tactics were, ironically, similar to those used in the 1970s by the anti-freeway groups. Publicity-drawing events such as conventions, "good road days" and "good road tours," widespread distribution of literature, letter-writing campaigns, and legislative proposals were all part of the repertoire. Proponents claimed better roads would provide both cultural and economic advantages. Increased tourism was an oft-mentioned benefit. Sam Hill, of Washington, believed good roads would "ameliorate the condition of mankind."[1] Typical of the

1. As quoted in Ronald J. Fahl, "S. C. Lancaster and the Columbia River Highway: Engineer as Conservationist," footnote 25, in *Oregon Historical Quarterly*,

Fig. IV–3. "Ford Sociability Drive," Dayton, Washington.

rhetoric accompanying the movement is this excerpt from a 1912 address given by Frank Branch Riley, vice president for Oregon of the Pacific Highway Association:

> . . . all roads lead to Portland . . . and if they are fine roads we shall grow; if they are rotten roads we shall shrivel up. For this is the age of the highway, not the railroad; the age of the motor car, not the locomotive. The motor car is both feeding and in competition with, the railroad. Connecting up with the empire that lies at our back door is just as important as developing our commerce upon the ocean that lies at our front door.[2]

Railroad interests were at first supportive of the movement. Better roads were seen as a means of facilitating the transport of farm goods to the railroad shipping points. It was only after the increase in the number of trucks following World War I and the realization that roads could be used for long-distance hauling that their interest waned.

The relation of farmers to the movement was from the first ambivalent. The question from their viewpoint was not whether the road system should be improved, but rather which roads would be given priority and how the work would be financed. Farmers wanted inexpensive "farm to market roads," financed by state or federal governments and remaining under local control. Urban interests, which tended to domi-

---

LXXIV (June, 1973), 101–44.

2. "Stenographic Report of an Address by Frank Branch Riley . . . ," in *The Pacific Coast Architect—A Monthly Journal for the Architectural Interests of the Pacific Coast*, IV, no. 2, p. 84.

Fig. IV–4. WPA Wolf Creek highway project, Oregon, 1936.

nate the Good Roads Movement, favored development of a primary road system specifically designed for automobiles. This conflict was finally resolved through establishment of a hierarchy of roads: primary roads, to be built and maintained by state highway departments; and secondary roads, to remain primarily the responsibility of the counties, with some added state support.

By 1915 Idaho, Oregon, and Washington had all established state highway departments. These departments were able to provide the coordination and technical know-how required for the construction of a system able to accommodate the growing number of cars and trucks and their rapidly increasing speeds. In 1916 the federal government entered the picture with the Federal Road Act which provided $75 million to be spent through the state highway departments.

The Northwest, which had up to this time lagged behind the rest of the country in development of transportation systems, took the lead when Oregon became both the first state to institute a gasoline tax and the first state west of the Mississippi to have a paved highway running its entire length (the Pacific Highway in the Willamette Valley completed in 1922). By 1936 the combination of state and federal financing had produced in the Northwest the extensive network of paved roads shown on the AAA map.

The shifting of responsibility from the private to the public sector and from the smaller to the larger governmental unit was characteristic for many services during the Motor Age. The process was, of course, accelerated during the depression years. Roosevelt's New Deal Program resulted in a galaxy of new federal and state agencies—the Soil Conservation Service, the Farm Security Administration, WPA and PWA, the Grazing Division, the Water Conservation Board of Idaho, the Conservation Department at Olympia, the Unemployment Compensation commissions, and many others—operating in the Northwest.

Of particular concern to this region during the thirties were the refugees who came from the dust bowl. A 1940 publication states that in 1938 several hundred thousand migrants were "seeking opportunity in a region already troubled with unemployment and lack of immediately available cheap land."[3] The U.S. Resettlement Administration was charged with solving this problem. Rexford G. Tugwell, Administrator, stated its goal in 1935:

> The fundamental problem is the re-adjustment of people to the land resources of the Nation. Land must be adapted to its best economic use. Our pioneering policies of exploitation and careless use of the land are no longer possible or feasible and can no longer be continued. Millions of American citizens in rural areas require assistance to enable them to become self-sustaining and to enjoy a decent American standard of living.[4]

3. "Discovering Anew the Pacific Northwest, Two Year Report of the Northwest Regional Council (Portland, Ore. 1940), 1.

4. Foreword for pamphlet, "The Resettlement Administration" (Washington, D.C., 1935).

As a first step toward finding its best economic use, land was classified according to its suitability for grazing and various types of agriculture. This information was made available to prospective emigrants to the Northwest. But the best land had already been taken; what remained was marginal or sub-marginal and, in a time of low agricultural prices, was not capable of providing a decent living. An increase in farm employment opportunities required either an increase in the amount of productive land or an increase in the intensity of cultivation on existing farmland. "Reclamation" would accomplish both.

Reclamation, in the form of irrigation, was by no means new to the Northwest. Twenty inches of precipitation a year is accepted as the minimum requirement for diversified agriculture. Very few areas east of the Cascades with land suitable for plowing receive this amount. Only grain could be grown successfully without supplementary water. Missionaries at Waiilatpu and Lapwai diverted streams into their vegetable gardens. Individual ranchers early had constructed projects in small valleys for raising winter feed for livestock. The Mormons, who built canals as early as 1849, were the first to undertake large-scale projects. During the latter part of the 19th century irrigation companies were founded, sometimes under the auspices of the railroads, which stood to profit from increased productivity of land along their tracks.

Private capital developed those areas which, because of terrain and easy access to water, could be most easily irrigated. More difficult areas

Fig. IV–5. Wenatchee Valley, Washington, where in 1943 there were 24,100 acres under irrigation. The first large project had been finished in 1903. There were no federal irrigation projects.

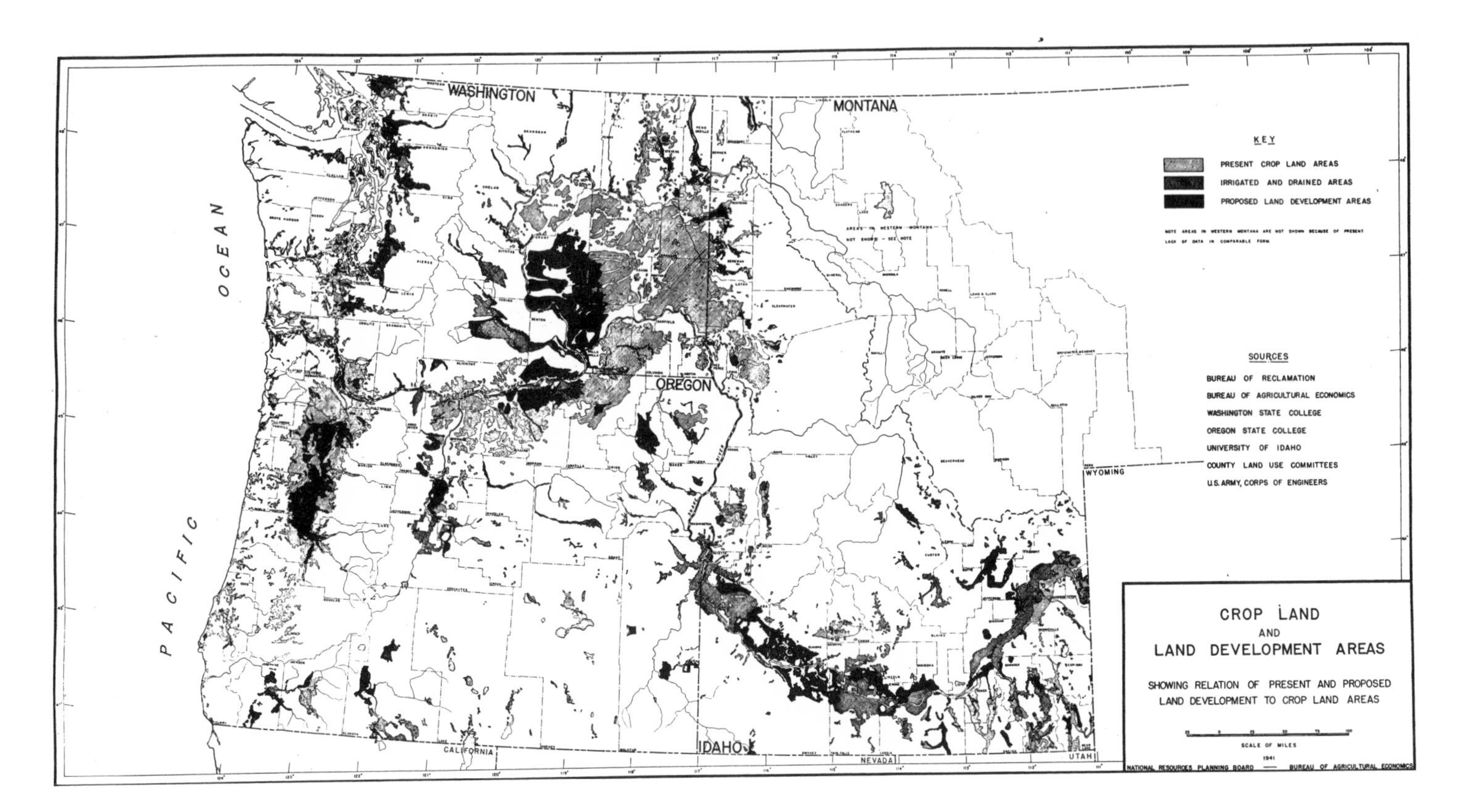

Fig. IV–6. Crop land and land development areas in the Northwest. Note the extent of irrigated land along the Snake River in southern Idaho. This map is from the *Economic Atlas of the Pacific Northwest* published by the Northwest Regional Council, a non-profit organization funded by the Rockefeller Foundation.

required state or federal help. Under provisions of the Carey Act of 1894 the U.S. donated arid land to the states with the understanding that the states would cause lands to be irrigated, settled, and cultivated. Projects requiring very large outlays of capital over long periods of time and involving rivers interstate and international in character became, of necessity, the responsibility of the federal government. In 1902 the National Reclamation Act made a fund available for surveys, and the construction and maintenance of irrigation projects.

This combination of private, state and federal effort produced dramatic transformations of the landscape in certain sections of the Northwest. The Snake River Basin, described by an 1852 emigrant over the Oregon Trail as "poor, mean miserable good for nothing country,"[5] by 1942 could, with good reason, be referred to as the "Fertile Crescent." In fact, Idaho was in 1947 exceeded only by California and Colorado in number of acres under irrigation.

In 1933, as an effort to stimulate economic activity, construction began on a series of dams in the Columbia Basin designed both to provide water for irrigation and to generate hydro-electricity. The Columbia River drops 1,288 feet from the Canadian border to its mouth and plans

5. E. Ruth Rockwood, ed. "Letters of Charles Stevens, II," in *Oregon Historical Quarterly*, XXXVII (Sept., 1936), 241–261, 253.

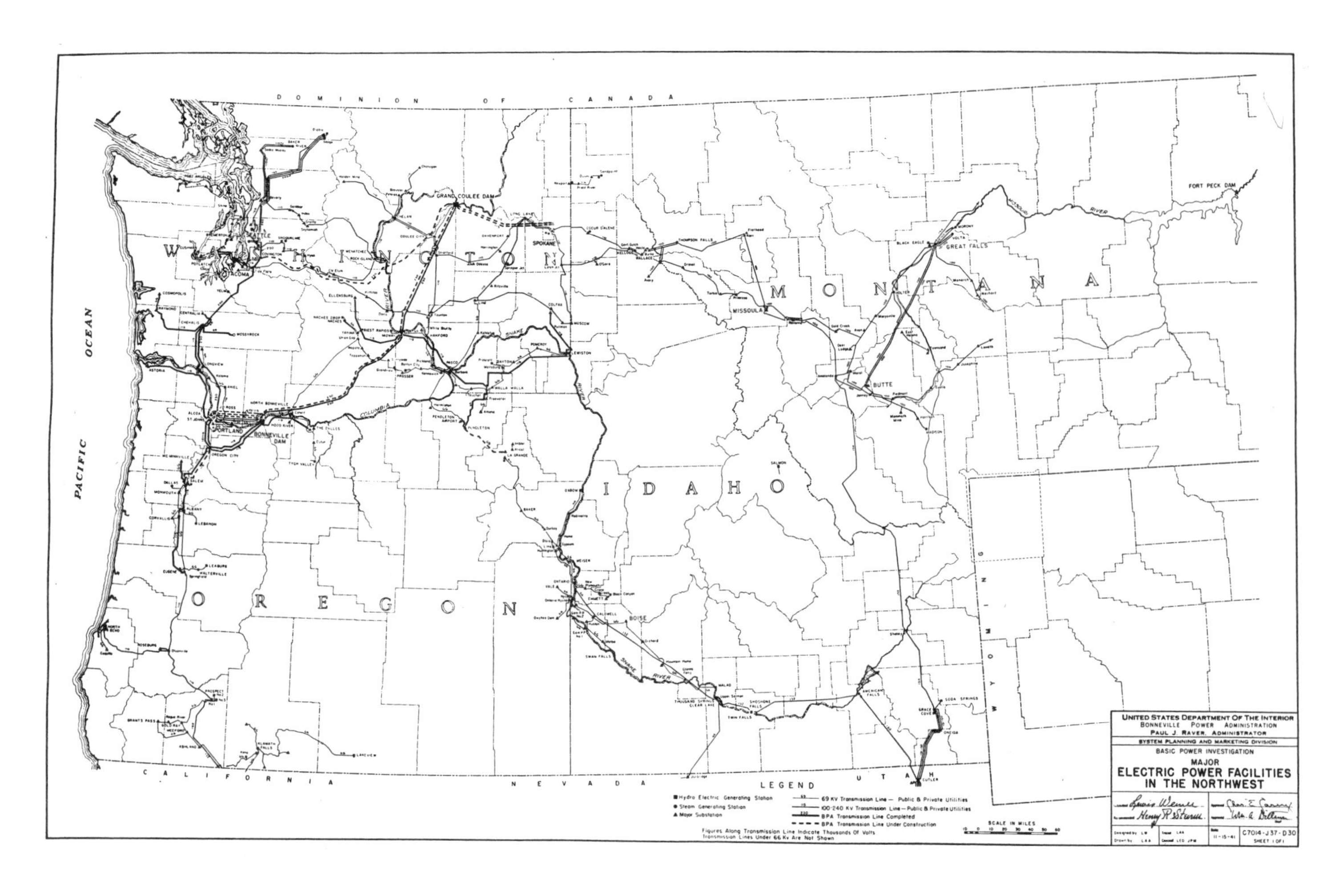

Fig. IV-7. Major Electric Power Facilities in the Northwest, 1941, from *Economic Atlas of the Pacific Northwest.*

were for 10 dams utilizing all but 93 feet of this fall for power development. The slope of the river (five times that of Ohio and Tennessee rivers) which had proved such a handicap for navigation was to be turned to advantage.

In 1941 the first power was generated at Grand Coulee Dam, the electricity to be used, in part, to pump irrigation water. With its reservoir and pumping system this dam alone was designed to provide irrigation for 1,200,000 acres of land. It was 1952, however, before the first irrigation water was delivered, long after other smaller projects in the Northwest had reached completion.

The sudden abundance of power created by the new dams was expected by many to transform the Northwest from an area whose economy depended heavily on the exportation of natural resources to one with a strong industrial base. A power grid, with uniform rates throughout the region, was adopted in order to make location of industries independent of the source of electricity. Lewis Mumford, in a report written following a 1939 visit to the Northwest, discussed the possibility

Fig. IV–8. Obviously posed publicity photograph taken in a Columbia Basin reclamation project, 1948.

of developing "greenbelt towns with low cost housing"[6] around these new dispersed industries.

For most industries power consumption represented a small fraction of total operating costs. Location near large markets and labor pools was of much more importance than location near sources of cheap power. The Northwest, separated by a great expanse from the heavily populated East Coast, was not, in spite of its cheap power, immediately attractive to any but the electro-process industries (aluminum industries in particular). And, because employment for these industries is always relatively small, they did not become a factor in new town development.

Throughout the Motor Age logging and the related wood processing industries along with agriculture and food processing remained the mainstay of the Northwest economy. Improved motor transport made possible logging of areas not accessible by either water or rail, as well as small isolated areas left behind in logged-off areas. Truck farming, as the name implies, was also well served by the newly developed highway system, as was the rapidly developing tourist industry.

In spite of the new highway system, large-scale irrigation projects, mammoth dams and the influx of population, the overall aspect of the Northwest changed less during the war and depression years than it did during the building of the railroads. It is the dream of safe, healthful, and efficiently planned cities surrounded by classified, conserved, and above all, *productive* land, and not the reality which remains the most vivid impression of the Motor Age.

---

6. Lewis Mumford, "Regional Planning in the Pacific Northwest, a Memorandum, 1939," publication of Northwest Regional Council (Portland, Ore.).

Cities and Towns

Steven Dotterrer

Portland

As new agricultural activities and an expanding lumber industry increased population throughout the Northwest, Portland became a larger and more economically stable metropolis. New technology (the interurban and the automobile) and increasing population changed the city dramatically. Efforts to control and direct city growth and make wise investments in public facilities were suggested and sometimes undertaken. Private individuals had always "planned," in the sense that they made decisions as to what would be done with their own property, but after the turn of the century it was felt a public consensus should be reached about the city's development. This new attitude led to E. H. Bennett's *Greater Portland Plan* (1912), as well as to zoning laws, neighborhood parks and housing codes.

Transportation underwent great changes during the period just before and after World War I. The streetcar system reached its peak patronage in 1919 (100,301,800 pass./year) though it remained important until after World War II. The interurbans which offered limited stop service to nearby villages, extended the range of the commuter greatly and made Lake Oswego and Oregon City suburbs of Portland. The interurbans were never firmly established, however, and patronage decreased during the 1920s. River steamer service came to a complete halt by 1920. The cause of these declines in public transportation was increased use of automobiles which permitted easier personal mobility and thus greater freedom of spatial location. Such freedom and the desire for larger homesites encouraged rapid spatial expansion.

The continued expansion of Portland took several forms. First in importance was simple outward growth—the replacement of orchards and farmland by subdivisions. The majority of these developments had grid street layouts, though the 200′ x 200′ block was practically abandoned for longer blocks, which meant less street area per lot. The curvilinear street pattern was used in a few cases, however. In the West Hills it was a necessity, and in more level areas it was used to achieve a picturesque variety. Besides outward growth, areas bypassed earlier because of steepness or marshiness were remolded for urban use. The marshy

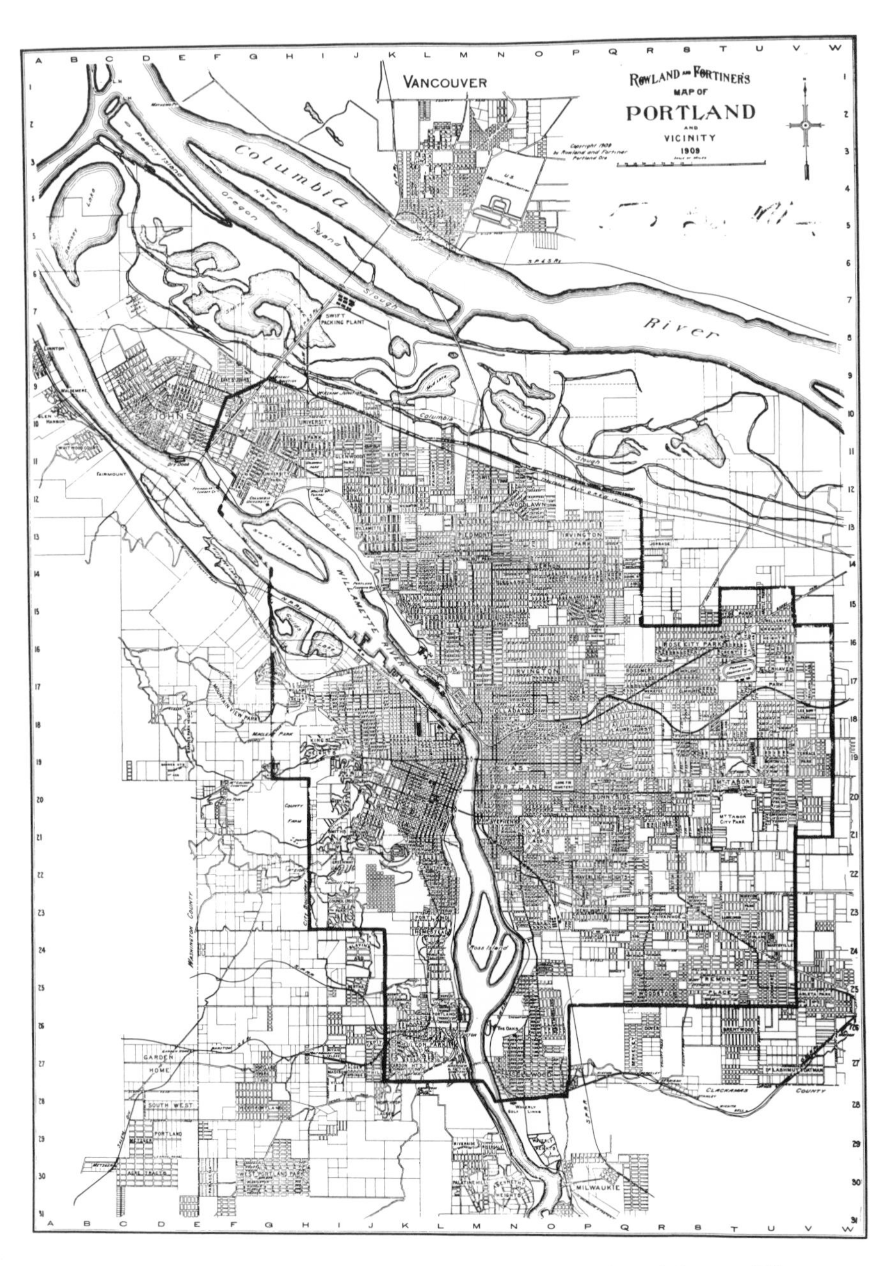

Fig. IV–9. Portland and vicinity, 1909. While downtown remained on the west side of the Willamette, the majority of the people lived on the east side. Streetcar lines are shown as dark lines in the streets. Portland's population in 1910 was 207,214.

areas of the east side riverfront were filled for industrial use. The most dramatic example of these topographic changes was the filling in of Guild's Lake (site of the 1905 Lewis and Clark Exposition) for industrial use with material obtained in cutting down Westover Heights for residential development.

Portland's parks were significantly enlarged and developed for the Lewis and Clark fair. The Olmsted Brothers of New York were hired to develop a park and parkway system for the city in 1903. Terwilliger Boulevard and numerous neighborhood parks are the result of their work.

Fig. IV–10. Portland, Guild's Lake (site of the 1905 Lewis and Clark Exposition), the Willamette River and Mock's Crest seen from the west hills. From the Hendrickson panorama of 1903.

Fig. IV–11. Portland, the northwest hills being cut down for the Westover Heights residential development.

Fig. IV–12. Portland, Guild's Lake partially filled by the Westover development. River dredgings were used to complete the project. This view also shows the filling of the Willamette River itself for the continued downstream expansion of industry. Mock's Crest can be seen in the background to the right.

In 1911–12, E. H. Bennett of Chicago, a co-worker of D. H. Burnham, who had done plans for San Francisco and Chicago, was paid by the city to develop a general city plan. Bennett predicted a population of two million people. For Bennett and others the city was a set of patterns and hierarchies which could be manipulated to produce a healthy organism. Bennett used the term "organic city," calling the "congested business center . . . the '*heart*,' the streets . . . traffic '*arteries*,' the parks the breathing spaces or '*lungs*.' "[1]

In the early city development, a relatively undifferentiated grid had been used. This pattern was logical for a city of pedestrians and horsepower. In Bennett's plan, certain streets (the arterials) were more important, wider, doing more work. The streetcar, which selected certain streets over others for its routes, made this a logical pattern. The auto, which went on any street, worked against Bennett's strong hierarchy. In addition to an arterials plan, Bennett proposed a Civic Center and several monumental grand avenues, a park system, and harbor improvements. Though the Bennett plan was approved by a public vote of all Portlanders, little actual work was carried out. Nevertheless, the broad outlines of his proposals have been accepted and carried out, whether because of his work or not it is hard to say. In 1919 the City Planning Commission was established and a zoning ordinance to control land use

1. Marshall N. Dana, ed., *The Greater Portland Plan of Edward H. Bennett* (1912), 5.

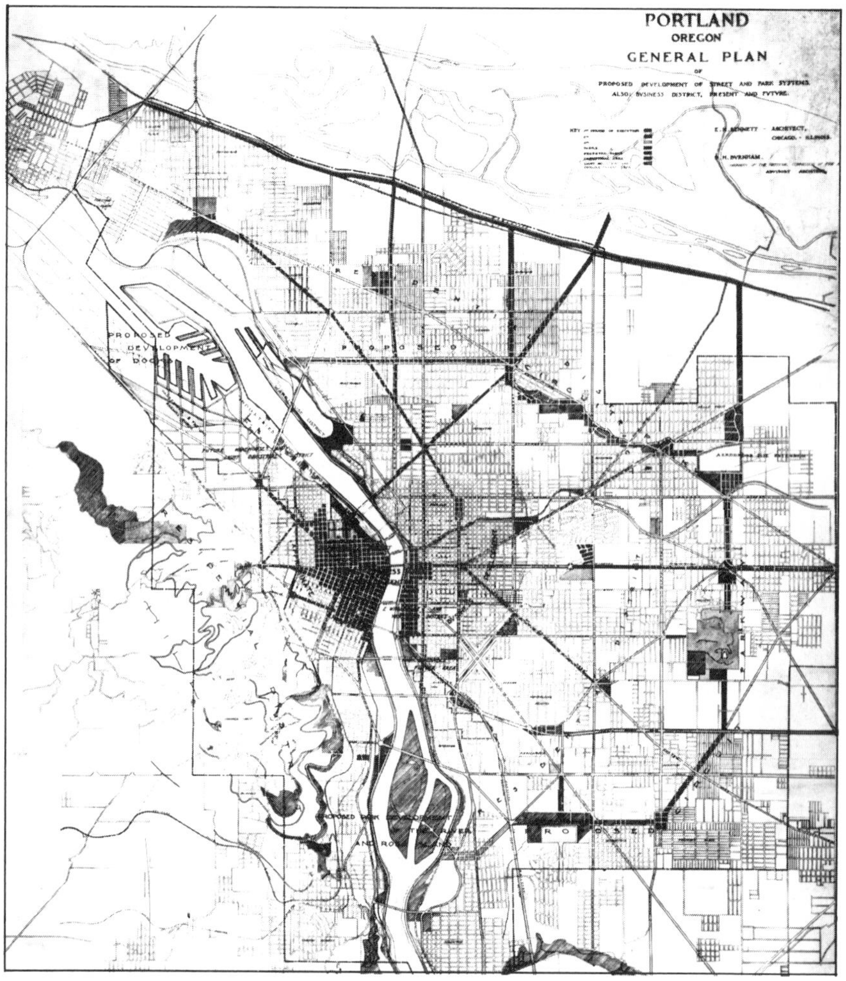

PORTLAND
OREGON
GENERAL PLAN

Fig. IV–13. The Bennett Plan for Portland, 1912, showing the proposed diagonal trafficways and circuit parkways which were to be cut through the existing street patterns.

passed. The original ordinance was designed primarily to protect areas of single family residences from intrusion by other uses, but it followed the Bennett plan proposals.

After the Lewis and Clark fair, Portland's central area enjoyed an economic boom which saw rapid increases in land value and resulting segregation of activities by their ability to pay rent. Earlier the central district had broken into broad zones such as wholesaling and retail and office. Following the fair increased land values divided the central area into ever smaller units—office and retail functions divided into subgroups. The change in architectural taste to the classical brought a strong change to the downtown skyline. In addition to increased height, a radical change in color characterized new buildings. The earlier buildings had been dark stone and brick. The favored materials of the new period were white brick and terra cotta.

The quarter block office building remained the standard office construction throughout the business area, but other forms were introduced.

Fig. IV–14. Downtown Portland from the southwest, circa 1895—the dark skyline of the brick and stone city.

Fig. IV–15. Downtown Portland from the east, circa 1930—the light skyline of the steel and glazed terra cotta city.

Several half and full block buildings were constructed, and the tall, thin slab became more common. One form of slab was the 200-foot long, tall and narrow slab two or three bays wide with a low two or three-story section behind to allow some light and air to reach the back offices. The entire office district spread rapidly westward along the streetcar lines during the 1920s, but it was not an even spread. The banks in their new "showcase" temples clustered together in a small financial district. Small speculative buildings and smaller hotels were built on the narrow Park Blocks that remained in private ownership. Doctors, dentists, and music teachers filled lower rent offices around the newly-erected public library. All of these offices maintained the ground floor store spaces typical of earlier periods.

The small store spaces were no longer sufficient for many retailers and specialized buildings like the large department stores were built.

Fig. IV–16. Portland, Alder Street with office buildings and department stores.

Broadway (formerly 7th Avenue) became the movie row and blossomed into a "white way" at night. Bulky items requiring large selling areas were forced out of the busiest section of the core by rising land costs. Auto dealers formed a west side "auto row," while the east end of the Willamette River bridges became a popular location for furniture stores as well as auto dealers because of lower land values than on the west side and good access to the downtown core.

The use of the city's streets changed considerably during the 1920s and 1930s. In the era of public transportation, there were so few vehicles that pedestrians could walk anywhere on the streets with relative freedom. Even though sidewalks were provided (mostly to keep people out of the mud) the entire street could be used for walking or even neighborhood baseball games. Movement was only one of the street's functions. The streets could be converted into exotically decorated outdoor rooms for parades, the Rose Festival, or visiting conventioneers. As automobiles grew more numerous, the smooth flow of traffic became so important that other uses of the street were severely restricted. Vehicles and pedestrians had to be separated for safety and the street was almost exclusively reserved for movement.

In the neighborhoods, some local centers like the Hollywood district on the east side offered services formerly found only downtown. The small neighborhood stores continued to spread with the neighborhoods. The emergence of the auto, plus the zoning which kept stores out of new residential areas, encouraged the creation of continuous "strips" of stores along the older trolley routes and some new streets built especially for autos. The chain store and gas station were new elements on these strips.

Industrial and wholesale activity continued to abandon the downtown waterfront. During the 1930s the downtown wharves were demol-

Fig. IV–17. Portland, Broadway at night, 1939.

Fig. IV–18. Portland, the West Burnside auto row in late 1936.

Fig. IV–19. Portland, the Hollywood district, 1939. The exclusion through zoning of stores from residential areas helped make such large commercial concentrations possible.

Fig. IV–20. Portland, seawall near the Hawthorne Bridge, 1941.

ished and replaced with a seawall. Most industry located along railroads or on the waterfront north of downtown where the river was wider. To provide expansion space for these new industries, however, large areas of the river were filled.

The greatest amount of land was taken up by residential expansion. The curvilinear street pattern was used in the more fashionable areas like the West Hills, Laurelhurst and Alameda. Laurelhurst (1909), originally gently rolling farmland on the east side, was an early private attempt to sell more than just a house lot. Emphasis was placed on the "country in the city" atmosphere provided by an aesthetically-designed neighborhood of curving paved streets, tree-lined parking strips, and a deeded neighborhood park.

The grid street pattern with bungalow houses was the more common living pattern. Following the theories of Charles M. Robinson and others, there was a shift away from the wide paved streets in residential areas. In its place appeared narrow streets with wide parking strips down each side. To accommodate the increasing number of cars, the major streets were widened. Along these major arteries apartment houses and duplexes were built.

There were also districts of denser housing. The largest and most densely populated area was northwest of downtown once a neighborhood of wealthy families. Good streetcar service made it an ideal area for apartments. The downtown area and some smaller sections of the east side also became apartment areas. Most of the apartments were small and houselike before 1910, but later large brick buildings nearly covering their small lots were more typical. Apartments rather than small single family houses were built, partially because the city had no tradition of row house development and also because the zoning code set 50 feet as the minimum lot width. In the late 1930s and 1940s the auto became common enough to create parking problems. Apartment houses required

Fig. IV–21. Portland, the Laurelhurst subdivision from the air. Shops and factories were excluded from such subdivisions by deed, and later by zoning.

Fig. IV–22. Portland, the builder's bungalows in the Irvington district.

larger lots with space for parking. Previously, most houses and apartments had no garages, although groups of wooden garages on neighborhood vacant lots or the larger concrete storage garages were fairly common.

At the outer fringes of Portland, Lake Oswego, Beaverton and Milwaukie became suburbs—accessible by frequent interurban service. The interurbans also promoted orchard or garden tracts of five to ten acres where a family could enjoy both farm and city. These outer developments rapidly became the domain of the automobile and interurban service was cut back.

The countryside became gradually less accessible and vacant areas were filled; outward expansion of the city was eliminating recreation spaces. To counteract this a program of neighborhood park development was begun. These small parks usually contained play equipment, game shelters, and sometimes a swimming pool. The Olmsted Brothers park plan (1903) encouraged continued development of the large parks acquired earlier for reservoir sites. In the 1930s an interest in natural parks led to the acquisition of large chunks of the Tualatin Mountains to form Forest Park.

During the 1920s and 1930s, Portland's central area reached its greatest concentration and the metropolitan area remained tied to this

Fig. IV–23. Portland, S. E. Belmont in 1940, before street widening.

Fig. IV–24. Portland, S. E. Belmont, after widening.

one major center, surrounded by apartment districts. At the same time, the majority of residential development was at increasingly lower densities. Rapid spatial expansion soon overtook formerly separate small towns, which then served as subcenters. The streetcar and the interurban supported the subcenter pattern, but the automobile, which was dominant by 1950, tended to stretch these subcenters into long linear strips and encouraged greater spread than was possible with public transportation.

Twin Falls, Idaho

The great arc of the Snake River between King Hill and American Falls was one of the last areas of Idaho developed for agriculture. Carey Act irrigation projects and later federal projects like Minidoka made such development possible. The Twin Falls Tract, one of the most successful Carey Act projects, was nothing less than new towns in a new or remade landscape. The dry lands along the Snake River were passed over by all the early travelers, who found the land harsh and inhospitable. In the Twin Falls area a short period of placer mining during the 1870s soon played out. Then in 1884, I. B. Perrine decided to try irrigated orchards in one of the secondary canyons of the Snake north of Twin Falls. His farm was quite successful and he became a well-known propagandist for irrigation. A survey by E. A. Jordan in 1890 showed that irrigation was feasible but not until the Carey Act of 1895 were financial arrangements possible.

Perrine redoubled his efforts to interest capitalists after the Carey Act was passed. The act provided that the state would sell land to settlers at low rates and that the Homestead Act provisions would not apply. Perrine interested the Milner family of Salt Lake City in the project, and they in turn interested Frank H. Buhl, a Pittsburgh millionaire who had originally come West to invest in iron mines. Buhl was joined by Peter Kimberly, another Pennsylvania capitalist. In 1902 a preliminary survey was completed and on January 1, 1903, the Twin Falls Land and Water Company (Milner, Buhl, Kimberly and others) and the State of Idaho signed a contract by which the state would sell land to settlers for 50 cents per acre. The Twin Falls Company agreed to build an irri-

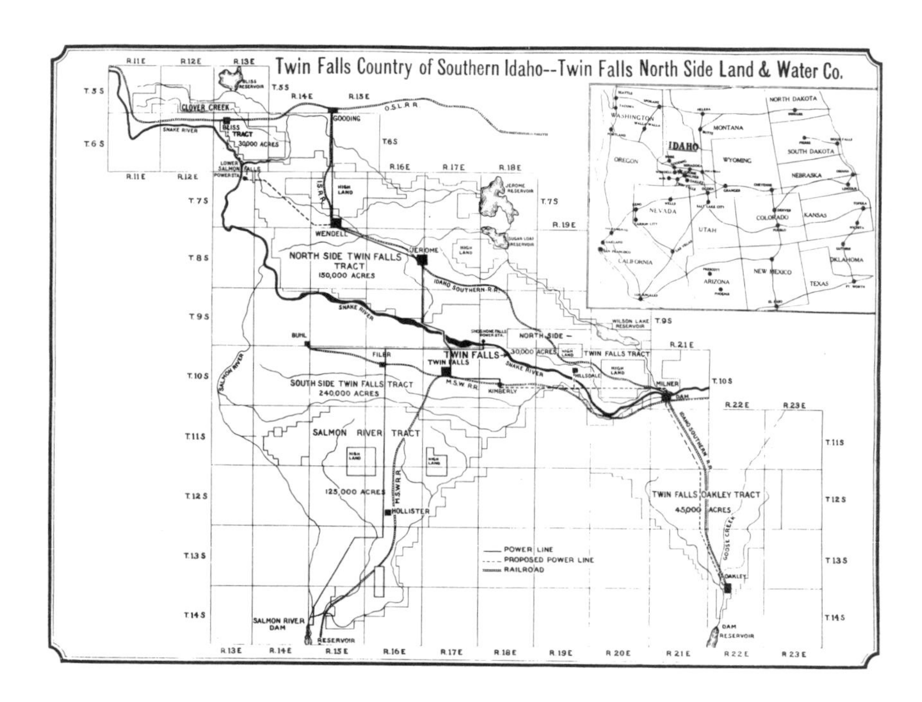

Fig. IV–25. Twin Falls country, 1909 map showing all the proposed irrigation projects, some of which were never undertaken. The first development was the South Side Twin Falls tract. From *Twin Falls Country Irrigation,* a promotional brochure.

gation dam and canals and sell water rights for $25 an acre. Purchasers of water rights were also required to buy $1.00 shares of stock in the Twin Falls Canal Company which owned and operated the canals. The original contract was for the irrigation of 276,000 acres on the south side of the Snake, known as the Twin Falls South Side Tract; 240,000 acres of this land was actually irrigated. Later a Twin Falls North Side Company with some of the same investors was formed to irrigate 150,000 additional acres around Jerome. (While additional projects were planned to bring the total area to almost 2,000,000 acres, little of this was accomplished under the Carey Act.) Soon after contracting with the state, the Twin Falls Company began building the Milner Dam and the major canals. The first rather insignificant land and water rights sales were made in July of 1903. The company persisted, however, and decided to sell more than farmland in an empty landscape.

During the summer of 1903, a surveying party under the direction of John E. Hayes, then 25 years old, surveyed the townships and sections throughout the tract and chose townsites. Twin Falls was sited near the center of the tract—on a school section, so that the company could simply purchase it from the state. The town was actually surveyed during late April, 1904. Because a rival group of townsite promoters was also promoting a town of that name, the plat, at first covering only four blocks, was rushed to the county courthouse to be recorded as the town of Twin Falls. In October of that year, a mile-square plat for Twin Falls was filed. The surveyors also laid out secondary towns including Buhl, Filer, and Kimberly.

With better advertising, the completion of the dam and canals in 1905, the promise of railroads and the layout of townsites, the sale of lands picked up. All the lots in the city of Twin Falls were sold in two-and-a-half years. Sale of town lots helped carry the irrigation company through the early years of heavy capital expenditures and little income. The town and surrounding farmlands developed rapidly after 1904. Later, development of the Twin Falls North Side Project and other irrigation projects along the Snake required more water than was available and the pace lagged from 1910 to 1914. When more water storage capacity was added in 1915, the Twin Falls Tract and its towns enjoyed another boom period which continued into the 1920s.

Though the layout of Hayes' town is the standard gridiron, variation in the width of streets and size and orientation of lots was introduced as a means of controlling land use. These simple devices were sufficient when walking, public transportation, or cumbersome or expensive individual vehicles were the only ways of getting around. Because of such restrictions different areas of activity had to be close together. The various lot and street arrangements suggested a certain use for each area. Builders followed these suggestions since they knew that two districts of department stores, for example, were not feasible. Eventually the automobile granted easy personal mobility and broke down the restrictions.

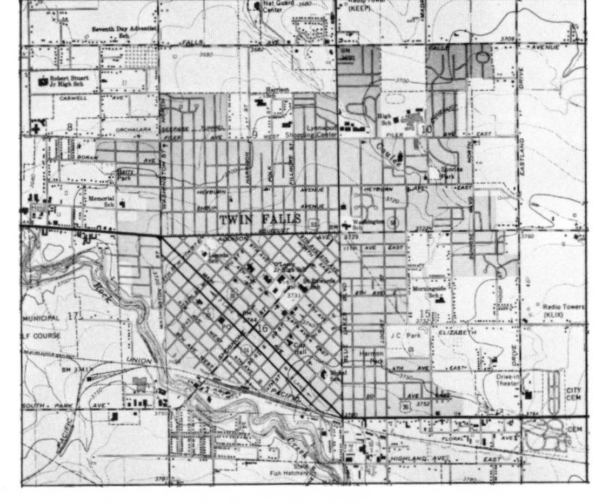

Fig. IV–26. Twin Falls, Idaho, from the 1964 USGS map. The original town is the section turned at a 45° angle. The large white area is the public square. Lincoln and Bickel schools are on the reserved school sites.

The gridiron plan of Twin Falls was turned at 45° to the compass

Fig. IV–27. Twin Falls, six months old.

Fig. IV–28. Twin Falls, two years old.

Fig. IV–29. Twin Falls, three years old.

points, so that the sun would shine in every room of the house, summer or winter, and snow would not pile up against the buildings.[2] The two streets that are diagonals of the mile square (Shoshone and Main) are wider than other streets and were intended as the main axes of the plan. Their crossing established the prime commercial location in town. In 1905 the Twin Falls investors built the Perrine Hotel at this intersection to accommodate visitors and encourage development. The bottom corner of the plan is cut off by the railroad. This eliminated Hayes' original idea of a park along Rock Creek, which roughly parallels the railroad. The railroad, which first began operations in 1905, built its station at the end of Shoshone Street, giving a terminus to this important axis. The two major streets divide the town into four quadrants, unequal in size because of the railroad. Lots along the railroad are larger than normal and were intended for industrial uses. The business area around the main intersection and on Shoshone from the railroad to the square is divided into 25′ lots. Throughout the residential sections of town the lots are 50′ wide and all face on the numbered avenues. These avenues were planted with trees by the townsite company.

Fig. IV–30. Jerome, Idaho. Irrigation company street layouts and tree planting were done well in advance of building. Tree planting was done only where the houses were expected to front on streets.

The company reserved two double-sized blocks on Shoshone Street for a public square and two others for school sites. The public square was not located at the main intersection, the prime business location, but three blocks northeast. During 1904–1905 trees were planted and a bandstand was built in the square. The two school blocks, at opposite ends of town, were placed near, but not on, Main Street.

Another investment by the town's developers was the interurban system; I. B. Perrine was president and general manager. Only about seven miles of line were built, but the projected system was 125 miles long and would have reached to Kimberly, Jerome and Buhl. To avoid the expense of installing generating stations and overhead wires, the company adopted a storage battery-powered system. Because of its unusual and difficult operation, and the increasing importance of the automobile, the system operated only from 1913–18.[3]

Due to the rapid growth of Twin Falls and the little time elapsed between planning and building, the ideas of the developers about "civic upbuilding" were closely followed. Land uses are distributed remarkably like the pattern suggested by the surveyors. Main and Shoshone streets are the major business streets. When Twin Falls County was organized in 1906, the courthouse was built on part of the public square, and in 1910–11 the high school was built next to it. The remainder became a public park, embellished with trees and monuments. The public library, a hospital, and numerous churches cluster around the public square. The initial residential zone filled up rapidly and new plats beyond the mile square were required. These new areas were platted with

2. Information supplied to author by Mrs. John B. Hayes from her husband's diary through the courtesy of Twin Falls County Historical Society.

3. OHS MSS 2099B (David L. Stearns) section of Vol. 21, on Twin Falls.

Fig. IV–31. Twin Falls, public square with courthouse, left, and high school.

Fig. IV–32. Twin Falls, aerial view, 1930s, showing extensive vacant areas near the industrial section and areas of new platting (at upper edge of photo) which did not extend original street pattern.

Fig. IV–33. Twin Falls, drinking fountain and bandstand in public square.

streets oriented to the compass points rather than in line with the 45° angle of the original plat. In contrast, large areas of the industrial sector remained vacant for many years.

Other towns in the Twin Falls tract were laid out on the same principle; none, however, were as large or grew as rapidly. Jerome (1907), the chief town of the North Side project, had the same general features, but its grid was oriented to the compass points and straddled, rather than fell within, a square mile land section. As a result, the rural grid of roads continued right into Jerome as main streets. The alley system, perfectly continuous in Twin Falls, was adjusted so that no alleys broke the commercial frontage at the major intersection. Reminiscent of the Mormon communities and New Plymouth, the outermost row of blocks, four times typical size, was divided into large "garden tracts" for home gardeners. Buhl more closely follows the pattern of Twin Falls.

The impressive aspect of Twin Falls tract towns was the speed of

Fig. IV–34. Buhl, Idaho, the railroad depot with its small manicured park facing the sagebrush desert across the tracks.

their development and the land use control achieved within a grid pattern and without zoning. The towns grew rapidly from the tent and wood shack stage to substantial settlements of business blocks and tree-lined streets that looked like those of much older towns in the Northwest. Despite leafy parks, there were constant reminders of the newness of towns and the harshness of surrounding landscape in the treelined but undeveloped streets of Jerome or the untouched sagebrush land just across the tracks from the station park. Nonetheless, to manipulate and change a landscape so completely was a remarkable achievement.

Longview, Washington

Longview resulted from the Long-Bell Lumber Company's decision to move operations from their depleted lands in the South to the Pacific Northwest. This decision was implemented in 1918 through the purchase of 70,000 acres of timber and several thousand acres for a mill site near the mouth of the Cowlitz River. Originally no town was planned, but the need to provide housing for workers (and hopefully attract a stable, non-I.W.W. work force) led to the purchase of more land and the development of a model city. R. A. Long, the head of Long-Bell, asked his Kansas City friend J. C. Nichols to act as developer. Nichols, who developed Kansas City's country club district, refused, but did agree to help get the project going. He selected Hare & Hare, Kansas City architect-planners, and George Kessler, the man responsible for Kansas City's parks and boulevards, to design the town.

While Longview and Twin Falls were both new towns built by single developers, there were several important differences. At Longview the immediate need for workers' accommodations forced Long-Bell into the role of house builder. At Twin Falls the buildings were constructed by the land purchasers. Because Long did not want a "company town," he proposed instead a "model city." His town was to represent an ideal—if not a Utopia, at least the best that could be accomplished under existing conditions. Twin Falls, while planned "on the most modern lines," was developed as a speculative town, not as an ideal. Longview benefited by following a fertile period in the development of city planning theories and practices.

Besides the City Beautiful movement, considerable interest in workers' housing had developed, especially during World War I. Men like John Nolan and Charles Robinson, early professional city planners, had written books on the planning of small towns and workers' communities. Zoning codes had been proposed or adopted in several cities. World War I and the need for war workers' housing had resulted in several sizeable projects, though none were as large as Longview. Rapid building techniques developed in some of these towns were used at Longview to get early returns on the enormous capital investment (two and a half million dollars in land alone). Twin Falls preceded all of these developments. But differences should not overshadow an important similarity. At both Longview and Twin Falls the towns were secondary. At Twin Falls irrigation agriculture was the main reason for the company; at

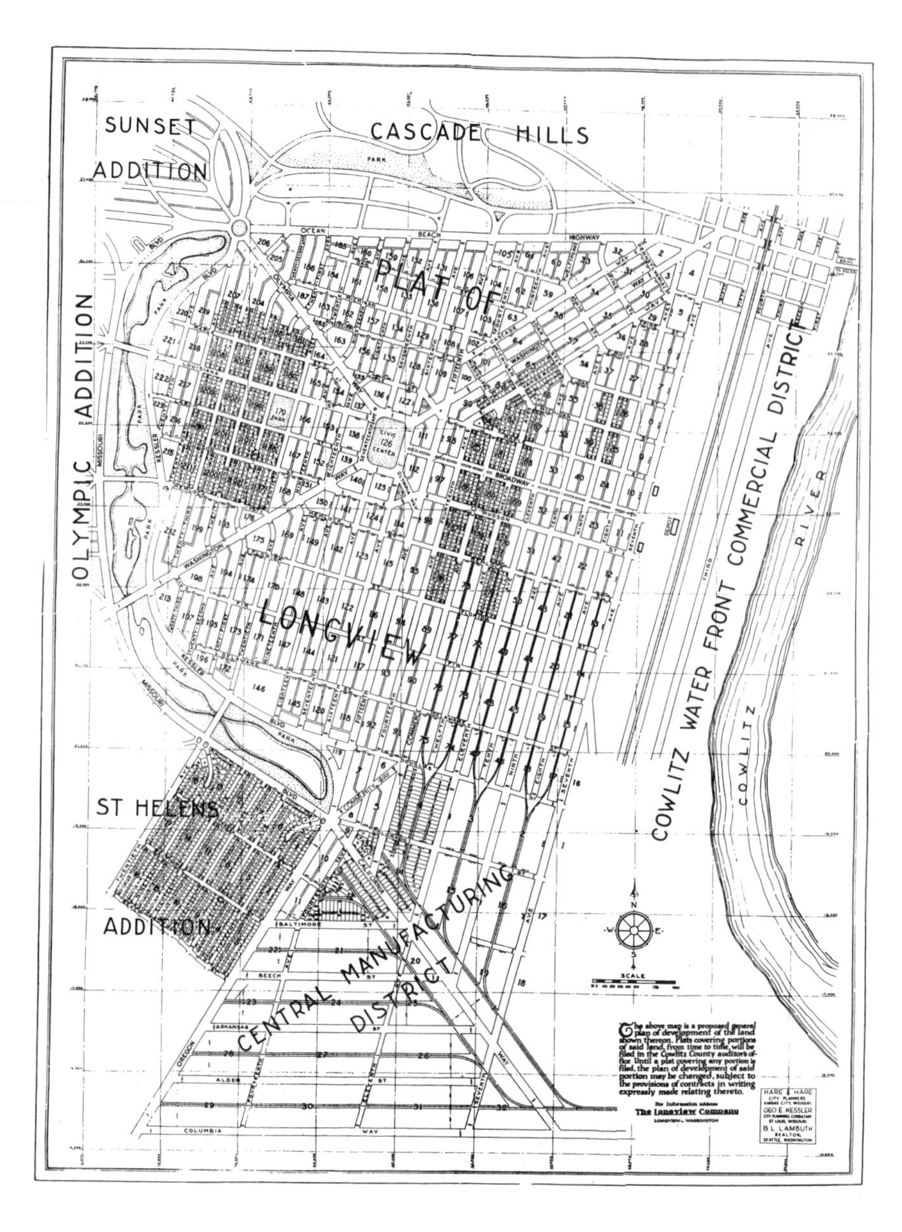

Fig. IV–35. Longview, Washington, plan of the central section. "Olympic Addition," etc. were the names of residential areas. St. Helens Addition was an early development of mill workers' housing. The width of streets was varied according to the expected amount of traffic.

Longview lumbering was the major undertaking.

The planners of Longview declared that their model city would not grow "from the inside out" like the typical American city. By "inside out" growth they meant the process of business and industrial districts expanding outward and destroying residential areas. To avoid this the planners placed each land use in its own nucleus. These nuclei were separated by expansion space and linked by broad boulevards. Public buildings were located around Jefferson (now R. A. Long) Square, with commercial uses extending toward the railroad station. Industrial plants were first located along the Columbia; different types of residential areas each had their own zone. There were separate areas for millworkers,

Fig. IV–36. Longview site circa 1923, with the mill under construction and town development just beginning.

Fig. IV–37. Longview, Broadway looking east from the Hotel Monticello to the railroad depot. The large vacant area around the cluster of commercial buildings was to provide expansion space for the growing city.

executives, apartment dwellers and home gardeners. Crescent-shaped Lake Sacajawea separated the central area from the various residential districts. As at Twin Falls, the square with public buildings was not at the major intersection so that the "100% corner" (or prime location) could remain entirely commercial.

Longview represents also an early effort to accommodate the automobile. Bypass roads were provided so that not all traffic had to drive through the center of town. The boulevards and streets were made very

Fig. IV–38. Longview, Commercial Avenue. In this street-level view of the commercial area, the town looks substantial and complete.

Fig. IV–39. Longview, Lake Sacajawea reflecting the community church. Many existing trees were preserved in the building of the town.

wide to accommodate autos, though Nichols said after a 1940s visit that he wished they were wider. No streetcars were used because of the rough surface usually associated with their rails. Instead, a Long-Bell subsidiary provided bus service.

Though planned in 1922 for a 1930 population of 50,000 people, by the 1940s there were only half this number. The Long-Bell construction had been completed by 1927 when Geddes Smith of *The Survey* magazine visited Longview. Smith commented that Longview was the "gaping skeleton of a city" where nothing was next to anything and everyone had to travel over vacant areas to reach work or shopping. Things were too far apart to walk to. He suggested that the old "inside out" way might not be good, but it was "organic" and kept things together. The weakness of the planning at Longview was that the city had to reach its planned size to work properly. As it was, only changing space requirements for each land use filled out the plan. Though the planners of Longview were able to provide the parks, boulevards, and other amenities lacking in the plans of most earlier towns, their lack of control over (or understanding of) social and economic forces kept the city from developing as they proposed.

Buildings and Gardens

A Regional Style Comes to the City

George McMath

During the two decades between 1930 and 1950 the predominant figure in Portland and Northwest architecture was Pietro Belluschi, recipient of the A.I.A.'s coveted Gold Medal in 1972. No other city has experienced such a succession of inter-related architectural firms as the Whidden & Lewis-Doyle-Belluschi triumvirate, each dominating a successive 20-year period from 1890 to 1950.

Pietro Belluschi was born in 1899, the son of an engineer, in Ancona, Italy, a small town on the Adriatic Sea near Venice. His father's work kept the family moving, and while most of his young life was spent in Rome, he also attended school in Bologna and Milan. In 1916 he volunteered in the Italian Army and served three years in the mountain artillery. After the war he returned to Rome and entered the university where he received a doctorate in architectural engineering in 1922. In the fall of the following year Belluschi came to America on an exchange scholarship to Cornell University granted by the Italy-America Society. After receiving a civil engineering degree in 1924 he traveled west and was hired as an electrical engineer by the Bunker Hill and Sullivan Company in Kellogg, Idaho.[1]

Belluschi, wishing to reach the Pacific Coast and pursue his profession, received letters of recommendation to architects in Seattle, Portland and San Francisco from Spokane architects Whitehouse and Price, who had designed a house for the mine superintendent. It was Portland's good fortune that he was also advised that A. E. Doyle was quite busy at the time. Belluschi went directly to the Doyle office and was hired in April, 1925 for the typical beginner's salary of $80 per month, less than he earned in the Idaho mines. Like any young draftsman he started out on detail drawings and worked on the Edwards and Holtz residences, the Broadway Theatre, Pacific Building and the Public Service Building, for which he designed the main lobby and much of the exterior detail. In 1927 Belluschi became Chief Designer in the firm following the

1. Jo Stubblebine, *The Northwest Architecture of Pietro Belluschi* (New York, 1953), 1, 2. Also see Portland *Oregonian,* Aug. 31, 1947.

Fig. IV–40. Lobby of the Public Service Building, one of Belluschi's earliest designs in the A. E. Doyle office.

departure of Charles Greene who had been with Doyle since 1908.

Doyle had been seriously ill for many months and in December 1927, a few weeks before he died, he reorganized the firm as A. E. Doyle & Associate, the "Associate" being William H. Crowell, the only registered architect in the group. The other partners were English-born David M. Jack, Doyle's long-time business manager, and Sid Lister, a construction supervisor. In 1933 Belluschi and engineer William Kemery became partners. Lister left the firm soon after due to failing eyesight, and Kemery passed away in 1938.[2]

Two of Belluschi's earliest designs portend the directions of much of his later work. The first, designed in 1927, but never built, was an addition to Cloud Cap Inn, the log and shingle structure on the east side of Mt. Hood that had been one of the first buildings designed by William M. Whidden. Though more sophisticated, Belluschi's proposed addition of shingled gable forms shows a respect for the original design, and for the setting, that would characterize his later work.

Fig. IV–41. Proposed addition to Cloud Cap Inn on Mt. Hood, 1927, never built. Design and drawing done by Pietro Belluschi in the A. E. Doyle office.

Fig. IV–42. Eastside office of the Pacific Telephone and Telegraph Co., 1928, designed by Pietro Belluschi in the A. E. Doyle office.

A year later he designed the Eastside Office of the Pacific Telephone & Telegraph Company. The design, a conventional but tasteful version of the "English Renaissance" in split brick and Siena travertine, anticipates the early schemes for the Portland Art Museum. Also in 1928 Belluschi redesigned the main concourse at Union Station, and began his first residential project, a grand mansion for Hamilton Corbett on Palatine Hill, a finely proportioned, simplified Georgian design.

Belluschi first achieved national recognition with the design of the Portland Art Museum, begun in 1930. That year Winslow B. Ayer

2. Letter from Pietro Belluschi to the author, February 1, 1974.

Fig. IV–43. Hamilton Corbett residence, 1928, designed by Pietro Belluschi in the A. E. Doyle office.

donated $100,000 for construction of a new building on the old Ladd School site. The school district bought the old Whidden and Lewis-designed museum at 5th and Taylor (now the "modernized" Chamber of Commerce Building).

The early design studies were Georgian or Renaissance. Gradually during the process, historical elements were eliminated and the design simplified to the present form. Noted historian Henry-Russell Hitchcock in 1940 said: "it was one of the best works of semi-modern character in the country and that it has as yet, I believe, no rival as regards to exterior."[3]

The Ayer wing, facing the Park Blocks, opened in 1932 with an exhibit of Japanese prints from the Ladd collection. The handsome facade, executed in Belluschi's favorite Willamina brick and travertine, clearly demonstrates one of the enduring qualities of his work, the concern for the setting, evidenced by the harmonious relationship to Fritsch's Masonic Temple to the north.

Six years later Belluschi designed the museum's Hirsch wing, departing from the symmetry of the original "master plan," but continuing the materials and character of the Ayer wing. Most significant was the interior, particularly the Sculpture Court, and a small open court, unfortunately covered over in later years for a members' room. These spaces were thoroughly modern as Hitchcock noted: "The great skylighted court is both ingenious and splendid, from the travertine slabs which flank the ground story supports to the skillful combination of symmetrical structure with asymmetrical lighting in the roof; while the little external court with its cantilevered travertine slab roof around the edge recalls the purity and richness of Mies van de Rohe's finest work." In

3. Russell Hitchcock, "An Eastern Critic Looks at Western Architecture," *California Arts and Architecture* (December, 1940), 21.

Fig. IV–44. Portland Art Museum, Ayer wing, 1932, designed by Pietro Belluschi in the A. E. Doyle office.

Fig. IV–45. Portland Art Museum, 1938, sculpture court in the Hirsch wing.

Fig. IV–46. Portland Art Museum, 1967 addition

1967, Belluschi in association with Wolff, Zimmer, Gunsul & Frasca prepared plans for a new wing to complete the block. It is a testament to the quality of the original design, as historian Marion Ross points out, that a contemporary addition could fit so well with the earlier building.[4]

Continuing the approach developed in the Art Museum, Belluschi designed Finley's Mortuary in 1937. Both buildings were honored by the A.I.A. by being included among the "100 Best Designs, 1920–40."

The 1930s were lean years for most architects. There was virtually no major private construction in Portland. The only significant building in the downtown area was the U.S. Courthouse by Morris H. Whitehouse & Associates, built in 1931–33. However, there was one project that attracted community-wide interest, the Public Market completed in 1933 after great controversy. About 1910 John F. Carroll, editor of the Portland *Telegram,* started a campaign to centralize the city's grocery area for the public's convenience. Finally in 1914, the City Council passed an ordinance establishing the "Carroll Public Market" along Yamhill from 5th to Front Street. The City built covered stalls on the sidewalk and rented the space to farmers and vendors for 15 cents a day.

For the first decade the Market was a huge success and it achieved national recognition. But by the late Twenties complaints about the unsanitary conditions, price fixing, and traffic congestion were frequently heard. Responding, the City Council in 1930 appointed a special commission to investigate the matter. Their report confirmed the complaints and recommended the mess be cleaned up.

At this point the City Engineer, with some Council support, proposed a public market building be erected on the east side of Front Street, between the Morrison and Hawthorne bridges. The idea did not receive universal support and factions soon developed. Some proposed alternate sites, the most prominent being the two-block area bounded by 4th, 5th, Yamhill and Salmon. Other factions were concerned about financing, and still others were flatly opposed to the project. The farmers who would be the tenants were united against the Front Street site, claiming that it was too far away from the retail area. Another group, including several architects, was opposed to any major structure along the river which might stand in the way of a waterfront "esplanade," even then being talked about.

After two years of wheeling and dealing and public hearings, the City Council approved the Front Street project, which was to be built by the private Public Market Company, with an agreement that the City would purchase the finished building. The architectural firm of Lawrence, Holford and Allyn accepted the design commission, perhaps rationalizing that if they didn't do it some other firm would. The building, a monstrous concrete warehouse over 600 feet long, was an archi-

4. Marion Dean Ross, "The Museum Building As a Work of Art," *Notes on the Collections, Number 7* (Portland Art Museum, 1967).

Fig. IV–47. "Carroll Public Market," on the sidewalks at Fourth and Yamhill.

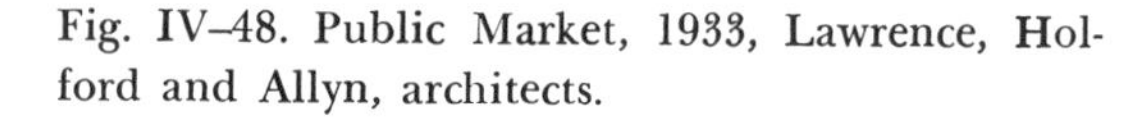

Fig. IV–48. Public Market, 1933, Lawrence, Holford and Allyn, architects.

tectural and financial disaster. All of the early objections came true. From the beginning the Market was in financial trouble. The City refused to accept the building, which resulted in 11 years of litigation and three decisions of the Oregon Supreme Court holding that the property would not go to the City but that the City must pay damages for failure to carry out their agreement.

After use by the Navy during World War II the building was purchased in 1946 by the *Oregon Journal,* which stayed for 15 years. Later it became a parking garage and for a brief period part of the structure was occupied by the Oregon Historical Society while they awaited completion of their new building. Finally in 1968 the old Public Market was acquired by the City and, ironically, razed the following year as a first step in "returning the riverfront to the people."

Ellis Lawrence seemed to have a penchant for getting involved in controversial projects. Following completion of the new U.S. Courthouse the government placed the old courthouse (now Pioneer Courthouse) on the surplus property list and made it available for private acquisition. Thus began the first skirmish in a 35-year battle to save Portland's most significant landmark. The Oregon Chapter of the A.I.A. adopted a strong resolution urging preservation. The local merchants saw it differently and there were several proposals for commercial development. One called for demolition and construction of a new office building for which Ellis Lawrence prepared design sketches. Feeling betrayed, the Oregon Chapter suspended Lawrence from membership. It was especially galling to the Portland architects as Lawrence occupied the prestigious position of Dean of the School of Architecture and Allied Arts at the University

Fig. IV–49. Pioneer Courthouse, 1869–75, A. B. Mullett, architect; west wings added 1904–1905, J. K. Taylor, architect; building restored in 1972, Allen, McMath, Hawkins, architects.

Fig. IV–50. Pietro Belluschi's own house on Portland's Council Crest, 1936.

of Oregon.

Fortunately the controversy continued until the war when the old structure again became useful to the government. After the war the battle resumed and there were several close calls during the 1950s and 1960s. Finally, in 1969, after urging by the U.S. Court of Appeals led by Judge John F. Kilkenny, and a change in government policy, the General Services Administration began planning for major restoration and reuse by the U.S. courts. Architects Allen, McMath, Hawkins prepared the restoration plans which retained and restored the essential 19th century elements while providing space and services to modern standards. In the spring of 1973 the restored building was rededicated with a ceremony in the grand courtroom, scene of much of Oregon's legal history.

The Depression had other effects on architectural practice, some for the good. The Doyle office, as with most whose practice is mainly concerned with commercial and institutional buildings, had not been involved with residential designs during the Twenties except for clients who had, or might be, parties to larger projects. Whether by necessity or desire, probably both, the firm turned to domestic architecture, and in the years 1936 to 1950 a new regional style emerged.

For Belluschi the transition from Rome to the rugged environment of western Oregon was a shock to the senses, but a shock that allowed him to see and feel, more clearly than others, the qualities and characteristics of the landscape and its vernacular buildings. He spent much time traveling and sketching along the Oregon coast, alone, and with John Yeon and Harry Wentz, painter and regional philosopher who greatly influenced both young designers.

Belluschi's first effort toward a regional approach was the design for his own house on Council Crest in 1936. In spite of the split red tile base at the front, the informal plan, with hipped and gable roof forms and natural spruce siding, expresses rural feeling not previously seen in the city. The design also shows the influence of the Doyle cottages at Neahkahnie. In the *Architectural Record* the owner (Belluschi) is quoted as saying that he desired that it be "clean and simple but not modernistic—above all that it be in harmony with the hills and Oregon firs."

The same year lumberman Aubrey Watzek commissioned the Doyle office to design his house. He also requested that John Yeon be in charge of the project. For Yeon, a 26-year-old self-trained designer, this would be his first house design, and ultimately his most well-known. There has been speculation through the years as to what extent Belluschi was involved in the project. According to persons present at the time, the design was entirely Yeon's, though he did from time to time consult with his good friend.

In spite of his inexperience Yeon knew exactly what he wanted. Employing Oregon vernacular forms and materials he showed an awareness of the spatial concepts of the International Style which he would develop more fully in later projects. The interrelated sequence of spaces, with changing vistas, each flowing one to the other, is a delight to ex-

Fig. IV–51. Watzek house, entry drive, 1937; A. E. Doyle and Associate, John Yeon, designer. Mt. Hood in background.

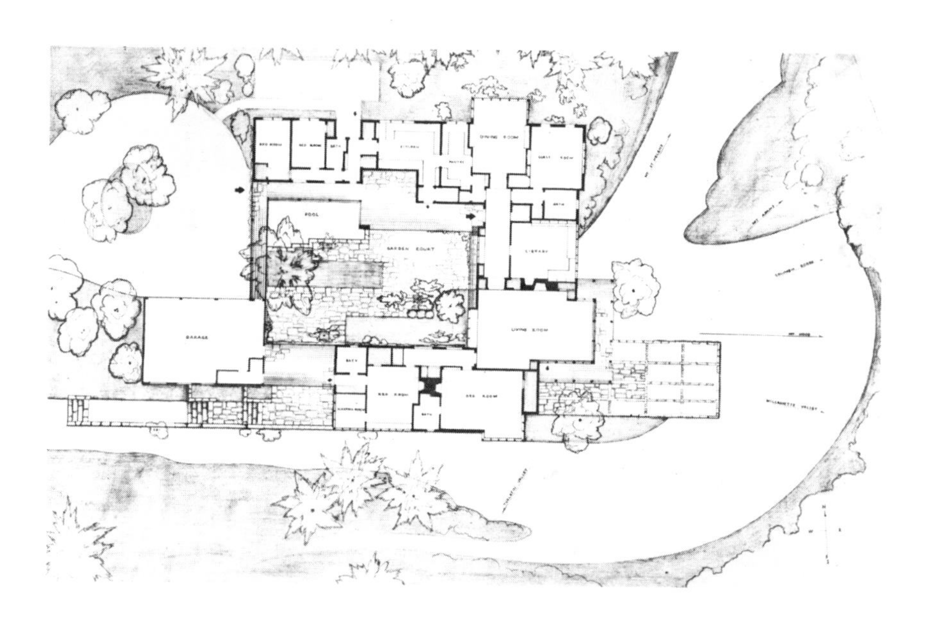

Fig. IV–52. Watzek house, plan.

perience—from the solid wall of the entry to the nearly enclosed courtyard, to the living room with its expansive view of Mt. Hood, and back to the dining room projecting into a close native landscape.

Yeon, with his concern for the totality of the project, designed the landscaping and much of the furniture, a practice he insisted on in most of his later work. A jarring note to contemporary eyes is the contrast between interior and exterior finish materials. It is somewhat startling to proceed past rough sawn fir siding and structure into elegantly detailed paneling done in a variety of species.

Fig. IV–53. Watzek house, courtyard.

Fig. IV–54. Watzek house, covered portico off living room facing east.

Yeon was adamant about details and the imagination of the draftsmen were stretched to the limit developing new construction techniques to achieve the clean profiles Yeon demanded. The apparent simplicity of detail is simple in the manner of Mies van der Rohe or Philip Johnson. Casement windows look like fixed glass. The narrow mullion is ingeniously divided, one side fixed, the other swinging. The living room windows offer another example. Double glazed, before "Thermopane," each pane and its frame had to swing out to allow cleaning, and the minimal frames had to also accommodate recessed rollscreens and venetian blinds. This attention to detail, which was typical throughout the house, required 75 sheets of full-size detail drawings, nearly the same as needed for the Public Service Building.[5]

Completed in 1937, the Watzek house was widely published and has become one of the "monuments" of the Northwest Style. Watzek occupied and cared for the house until his death in 1973. Hearing that a prospective buyer wanted to add a bedroom and install a swimming pool in the courtyard, Yeon bought it.

After the Watzek house Yeon left the Doyle office to practice on his own. The only other project he worked on in the office was a collaboration with Belluschi on some promotional sketches for Timberline Lodge. Yeon was a member of the committee that helped lobby the Timberline project through the Congress.

While the Watzek house was under construction Belluschi began

5. Interview with architect Frank C. Allen, who worked on the Watzek drawings while a draftsman in the Doyle office.

the design for the Jennings Sutor house, another "monument" of the regional style, on a site just across the road to the west. More modest than the Watzek house, some consider it superior for its simplicity and restraint, and its consistent design. All of the characteristics of the "Northwest Style" are here: concern for the setting and integration of landscaping, the open functional plan, the broad sheltering pitched roof, and the use of naturally finished native woods. Hitchcock in his 1940 review of western architecture said: "Of Belluschi's houses, that for the Sutors must easily stand among the very finest in this country." He further noted that it was "a surprisingly apt prototype of the best regional modern work in this area."

Fig. IV–55. Jennings Sutor house, 1938; A. E. Doyle and Associate, Pietro Belluschi, architect.

Fig. IV–56. Joss house, 1940; A. E. Doyle and Associate, Pietro Belluschi, architect.

During the next few years before World War II Belluschi designed several residences and a church, continuing and refining the regional expression developed with the Sutor house. The economical Joss House in suburban Portland with a view of the Tualatin Valley and Cascade Range was built in 1940. The simple gable roof, exposed trusses and decking, unfinished cedar paneling and the spruce clapboard siding provide a warm unified design that fits well with the natural landscape.

In 1939 Belluschi began the design for St. Thomas More Chapel, the first of several religious structures that would bring him national recognition. It is traditional in plan except for the unusual corner entry with its almost Oriental assemblage of posts and beams. Native materials are again honestly and naturally treated. Fir beams, scissor trusses and columns form the basic structure, while unfinished cedar walls, fir flooring and roof decking make up the interior surfaces. The exterior is covered with knotty pine lap siding and cedar roof shingles. The windows in the square base of the shingled octagonal spire provide dramatic clerestory lighting for the sanctuary.

Fig. IV–57. St. Thomas More Chapel, 1941; A. E. Doyle and Associate, Pietro Belluschi, architect.

Fig. IV–58. Nave and sanctuary, St. Thomas More Chapel.

When this mission chapel was completed in 1941 the area surrounding the west hills site was sparsely settled. After the war subdivisions developed in the area, causing St. Thomas More to become a full size parish and that brought construction of a school and parish hall. These large additions built in the 1950s tend to overwhelm the original chapel and have diminished the once rural charm of the setting.

Three houses were completed in 1941. The Myers house in Seattle was built on a narrow hilltop site with a panoramic view of Puget Sound. The house surrounds a large open courtyard which offers outdoor privacy and protection from the cool breezes off the Sound. Again, in the living room, is seen the "Studio" window of the Wentz cottage, here wrapping around a corner.

The commission for the Platt house came as a result of the client's

Fig. IV–59. Myers house, 1941, Seattle; A. E. Doyle and Associate, Pietro Belluschi, architect.

Figs. IV–60, 61. Platt house, 1941; A. E. Doyle and Associate, Pietro Belluschi, architect.

admiration of Belluschi's St. Thomas More Chapel, which the Platts frequently passed on the way to their home just below the site of their new house. It is situated high in the west hills where north summer winds can drive one indoors on the warmest summer evenings. To provide protection for the broad terrace off the living and dining rooms Belluschi stepped the plan along the west side. The L-shape of the plan forms the entrance court, an element seen in many Belluschi houses. The usual native materials are present though more "finished" on the interior than in some other houses. The vertical shiplap siding is pine rather than the favored spruce, which was unavailable at the time.

A favorite of Belluschi's, as well as many others, is the Kerr house in Gearhart sited on a grassy ridge overlooking the Pacific Ocean. The broad overhanging gable roof falling with the slope of the site provides a sense of shelter that is especially fitting for the harsh climate of the Oregon coast, and with the board and batten siding the "Oregon barn" influence is here most apparent. The log column at the entry porch is a daring yet successful touch that recalls a similar detail in the Wentz studio.

The last pre-war residential design, built in 1942, was the Coats house on Netarts Bay near Tillamook. The U-shaped plan with the entrance through a courtyard, and the multi-gabled roof forms closely resembles Yeon's Watzek house. As in the Sutor house, Belluschi again uses a combination of vertical and horizontal siding.

Along with Yeon's work, these early structures formed the basis of the regional style that would reach maturity following the war. Belluschi in a 1941 lecture sums up his thoughts on regionalism:

Fig. IV–62. Kerr house, Gearhart, 1941; A. E. Doyle and Associate, Pietro Belluschi, architect.

Fig. IV–63. Kerr house, view from ocean side.

Fig. IV–64. Coats house on Netarts Bay near Tillamook, 1942; A. E. Doyle and Associate, Pietro Belluschi, architect.

This concept of modern, therefore, will not lead us to expect it to be just another style. It cannot be labeled international style, although certain characteristics are universal; not modernistic. It should not even be called modern, because it goes back to fundamentals. It goes back to nature, if the owner's life is one of response to it. Therefore, we may deduce that a region with similar natural and human attributes may have an architecture harmonious to them. The people are neighbors, their interests are alike, they respond the same way to life, they have the same materials at hand, they have similar landscape, the same climate. So "regionalism" really has a meaning, which internationalism does not quite have.[6]

6. Stubblebine, *Belluschi,* 29.

During the same prewar period Yeon was pursuing a slightly different direction, more influenced by the International Style. Following completion of the Watzek house the general contractor, Burt Smith, was so impressed with the project that he asked Yeon to design a series of nine small houses to be built for sale. The resulting structures, built in 1938–39, show Yeon at his most creative, and perhaps for the first time, a "systems approach" was used in the design of a single family house.

Fig. IV–65. Two houses in North Portland designed by John Yeon for builder Burt Smith, 1938.

The system evolved out of a new material, exterior fir plywood, which today is the siding material most used in the home building industry. Plywood, or veneered wood, is an ancient process, known in China a thousand years ago and used throughout the centuries for paneling and furniture. However, structural fir plywood as we know it today is relatively new and followed the invention of the mechanical veneer slicer in the 19th century. Plywood received its biggest boost at the Lewis and Clark Exposition with sample panels in a variety of Oregon woods fabricated by the Portland Manufacturing Company. General manufacture followed and fir plywood was soon widely used for door panels and other similar applications.

The early animal and vegetable glues used in plywood production were water solvent, so use of the new material was restricted to indoors. In 1934 after many years of research, a waterproof glue suitable for fir plywood was developed, and a year later commercial production began at the Harbor Plywood Company in Grays Harbor, Washington.

Yeon took this new and economical material, manufactured in 4′ x 8′ sheets, and developed a building system that was eminently practical and elegantly beautiful. Using a 2′ module which established a scale appropriate to the small house, he designed a series of related wall panels that met the fundamental requirements of privacy and protection from the elements, light and viewing, and ventilation. (The 2′ module worked well for all conditions except exterior doors.) Two by four studs were set 2 feet on center and covered on the inside with plaster or wood paneling, and on the outside with conventional board sheathing, building paper and the outer layer of $\frac{1}{4}$-inch waterproof plywood. Fir battens or vertical moldings were applied at each stud, expressing the modular construction.

The most ingenious element of the system was the separation of the light and ventilation functions. Since Roman times the common window had been used for both light and air, and whether casement, awning, or double hung, an open window always impeded viewing. In Yeon's panel design the glass was always fixed, thereby eliminating expensive and complicated frames. The glass was set between the studs and "stopped in" by the plywood at the head, and by the battens along the sides. The ventilating element, placed above or below the glass, consisted of fixed exterior louvers, insect screen, and a hinged panel on the interior which could be set for any degree of air movement. The development of this simple, rational system was undoubtedly influenced, at least in part, by the complexity and difficulty encountered in the Watzek house in achieving the desired esthetic result through conventional construction techniques. With Yeon's panel system, "art" fostered a significant technical advance.

Fig. IV–66. Victor Jorgensen house, 1939; John Yeon, designer.

The last and largest of this modular series was a house built for Victor Jorgensen in 1939, later to become Yeon's own home. Always sensitive to the site, Yeon set the house well back among the existing evergreens and located the garage close to the road with a covered walkway connecting to the house. Here, Yeon varied the rhythm by using the 2′ module in the bedrooms and the service areas, and a 4′ module in the living-dining area.

Color was an important element in these houses, as it was in all his work. Some featured an accent color on the battens emphasizing the modular quality. In the Jorgensen house was first seen the dark blue-green that he used so often and which later became known as "Yeon blue."

While the prewar residential designs of Belluschi and Yeon have received the most attention through the years, others were also exploring new directions, and adapting their designs to changing social and economic conditions. Among the more notable were architects Herman Brookman, Van Evera Bailey, and Harold Doty.

Brookman, born and raised in New York, received his early training in the office of Harry T. Lindeberg, renowned for his designs of grand mansions on Long Island. In 1924 Brookman visited Portland, where he stayed and practiced architecture for 40 years. Though best known for his contribution to the design of Temple Beth Israel in 1927, the bulk of Brookman's work was in the residential field. His first commission was the grand estate of Lloyd Frank on Palatine Hill, now the campus of Lewis and Clark College. Another of Brookman's grand designs was the house at Menucha, Julius Meier's estate overlooking the Columbia Gorge. Built in the early 1930s, it replaced the earlier log structure designed by A. E. Doyle.

Fig. IV–67. Interior of Menucha, Julius Meier's estate overlooking the Columbia River; Herman Brookman, architect.

Fig. IV–68. Lee S. Elliot house, 1934, by Herman Brookman.

Brookman was a "great eclectic" in the very best sense of the word. He worked in a variety of historical styles, most often in English forms as in the Frank house, but he was equally at home with French, German, and Moorish styles which he often combined and adapted in his own unique manner. Brookman's buildings were not only beautifully designed, they were beautifully built. His supervision of the construction was thorough and demanding, and his concern for the smallest detail was legendary.

Many of Brookman's houses built during the 1930s, while based on historical styles, showed an evolving simplicity and an awareness of contemporary trends. An interesting and unusual example is the Portland Heights residence designed for Lee S. Elliot in 1934—basically English with a Modernistic treatment of the wood siding in the gables and in other details. Two years later Brookman designed the elegantly simple split tile house presently owned by Milton Zell. Following World War II Brookman joined the growing number of architects practicing in the "Northwest Style." Though he adopted the basic forms of the idiom, Brookman's personal touch was always evident.

Van Evera Bailey's career spans a period similar to that of Brookman and has been almost exclusively devoted to residential projects. After graduating from high school in Portland, Bailey trained for his profession in various engineering and architectural firms including the offices of William Gray Purcell and Tourtellotte and Hummell in Boise. During the early 1930s he moved to California where he designed and built his own houses.

Bailey returned to Portland in 1937 where one of his first projects

Fig. IV–69. Milton Zell house, 1936, by Herman Brookman.

Fig. IV–70. Ben Freedman residence, 1947, by Herman Brookman.

Fig. IV–71. Jan deGraaf house, 1940; Richard Neutra, architect, Van Evera Bailey, supervising architect.

Fig. IV–72. L. H. Hoffman house, 1947, by Van Evera Bailey.

was the alteration of the old Ladd Carriage House for the Hoffman Construction Company offices. Bailey maintained his own office in the landmark building for several years. Following the war he designed houses for two members of the Hoffman family on the wooded hills of northwest Portland.

In 1939 Bailey had the unique opportunity of working on the house for Jan de Graaf designed by Richard Neutra. Bailey supervised the construction and functioned as a "silent critic" during the design stage. When Neutra submitted sketches from his Los Angeles office, de Graaf had Bailey review the designs and recommend changes which were then returned to Neutra. The most significant of these design changes was in the exterior covering which Neutra proposed to be stucco and Bailey changed to cedar flooring boards. Bailey also made changes during construction as many of Neutra's details were foreign to local building tradition.[7]

Bailey's own designs contributed much to the development of a regional style and they were widely published during the forties and fifties. His engineering training and the experience building his own houses is reflected in his work, and he is as much, if not more, concerned with the quality and economy of wood construction as he is with style.

One Bailey development was the cone-shaped stilt foundation which addressed the problem of designing a single level house (very popular during the early postwar years) on a steep site. Conventional wisdom recognized the need to minimize the number of footings on Portland's

---

7. Interview with Van Evera Bailey.

Fig. IV–73. David Eyre house, 1948, by Van Evera Bailey.

Fig. IV–74. Van Evera Bailey house, 1959.

Fig. IV–75. D. J. McLaughlin house, 1939, by Harold Doty.

unstable hillsides which usually resulted in widely spaced posts and long beam spans requiring large floor beams. Such beams were difficult and expensive to handle during construction, and they inevitably twisted within a short period of time which caused irregular floors and other problems throughout the structure. Bailey's use of 4 x 4 posts fanning out from a few foundation points substantially reduced the beam spans, allowing the use of light framing lumber, easily handled by small construction crews. Bailey designed ten of these "stilt houses" including his own home/office completed in 1959. In addition to supporting the house, the stilt foundation carries the 10-car parking deck.

As in the case of Van Evera Bailey the work of Harold Doty was almost entirely in the field of domestic architecture. But unlike Bailey, Doty's designs evolved out of conventional historic sources. A native of Spokane, Doty also received his training in architect's offices. Following World War I army service in Europe, Doty returned to New York where he entered the office of Lucas and Caughey. Later he worked with Pierpoint and Walter Davis in Los Angeles, and in the early 1920s he came to Portland and joined the Whitehouse firm for a brief period.[8]

The architect who had the greatest influence on Doty's work was Wade Pipes, with whom he shared office space from 1925 when he started his own practice until his untimely death in 1941. Like Pipes, Doty's early houses had a consistent livable quality and reflected the influence of English residential work. By the late thirties most historical aspects had been shed and his work could be described as modern, though not to the extent of Belluschi's and Yeon's prewar designs.

The war years were busy ones for most architects and the Belluschi office was no exception. However, the nature of architectural practice was necessarily altered as there was virtually no construction that was not related to national defense. The shortage of many standard building materials, particularly steel, presented additional problems which tested the creative abilities of designers and builders alike.

An early wartime project was the alteration of an old building for the Boilermakers Union, whose membership had been greatly increased by the vast shipbuilding industry that became Portland's major contribution to the war effort. Belluschi's design called for a new marble facing, which required the installation of small steel support angles. None were available so an alternate was needed. The builder scrounged the local junkyards and finally found some old steel bedframes which met the specifications. Such resourcefulness was usually necessary to get a project completed.

Housing for shipyard, aluminum and other war plant workers was a critical problem in 1942. Vanport, a contraction of Vancouver and Portland, was built on the flood plain north of the city and contained a large share of the 17,000 war housing units built in Portland.

8. Glenn Stanton, "Harold Doty—A Tribute," *Architect and Engineer*, Vol. 146 (July, 1941), 55.

Another large temporary housing project was built on McLoughlin Heights, overlooking the Columbia River east of Vancouver. Rather than having a single master plan of the site, the Vancouver Housing Authority parcelled the area into five segments, each to be laid out by a different architect. Using several standard housing types the architects, including Belluschi, Glenn Stanton, Donald Stewart and Hollis Johnson, planned their respective areas and hoped the streets and utilities would line up. With some coordinating adjustments the final "plan by committee" was resolved, and the result, as might be expected, was a somewhat curious combination of grid and curvilinear schemes. Belluschi also designed two temporary shopping centers to serve the McLoughlin Heights project which became prototypes for centers designed after the war.

In 1942 A. E. Doyle & Associate moved from the Pacific Building to new offices in an old garage structure that had been redesigned by the firm. The following year Belluschi acquired the interests of the remaining partners, D. M. Jack and W. H. Crowell, and continued the office under his own name. Jack retired while Crowell stayed on as a part-time draftsman for several years.

Many months prior to war's end clients were anticipating their postwar needs and Belluschi was awarded commissions for two major downtown structures, the Oregonian and Equitable buildings, both completed in 1948. The Equitable (now Commonwealth Building) was the first skycraper built in Portland in 20 years, and the first of its kind to be built anywhere in the world. It was a master achievement both technically and esthetically, and it brought Belluschi international recognition. The clear, logical expression of the concrete frame represents, as noted historian Talbot Hamlin wrote, "The almost ultimate development in the field."[9] The "firsts" for office buildings were many and significant. It was the first to have an aluminum skin, the first to be completely sealed and fully air conditioned, the first to use double glazed window units, the first to employ a traveling crane for window cleaning, and the first to use a heat pump for heating and cooling.[10]

As early as 1941 Belluschi was considering the possible uses for alumninum in buildings. The idea took form in a hypothetical design for an office building done in 1943. Belluschi, along with Mies van der Rohe, Louis Kahn and 20 other nationally prominent architects, was invited by the *Architectural Forum* to submit designs for a wide variety of building types which they published under the title, "New Buildings for 194X."

Belluschi's office building proposal contained several innovations that were later developed in the Equitable, including the double glazed windows and the aluminum covered structural frame. In describing the

9. Talbot Hamlin, *Architecture Through the Ages* (New York, 1953), 651.

10. Walter L. Creese, "The Equitable Revisited," *Architectural Forum*, Vol. 128 (June, 1968), 40–45.

Fig. IV–76. Belluschi's office, a garage building remodeled in 1942 with a studio addition in 1947. Wood sculpture by Frederic Littman.

proposal, Belluschi wrote: "Our assumptions were affected by the peculiar circumstances found in our northwest region—cheap power and a tremendously expanded production of light metals for war use, which will beg for utilization after the emergency." He went on, somewhat rashly, to say: "Cumbersome, inflexible materials would be discouraged, and fire resistant aluminum alloys will do away with concrete fireproofing as now used in steel structures."[11]

11. "New Buildings for 194X," *Architectural Forum* (May, 1943), 108–12.

Fig. IV–77. Equitable Building (now Commonwealth Building), 1948 by Pietro Belluschi; A. E. Doyle's United States National Bank Building on right.

Use aluminum he did, in natural sheet form on the concrete frame, cast and anodized in the spandrels, and extruded for the mullions. When completed, the shimmering walls of aluminum and green glass were startling to most Portlanders who wondered, "When are they going to finish it?"

During the 26 years of its life the Equitable has been fairly well treated, particularly during the years it was owned by Equitable Savings & Loan. With the traditional retail shops on the ground floor there has always been pressure from tenants who want to "do their own thing." This has been allowed, providing that such tenant "improvements" stay within the structural frame, a policy that would well serve other buildings. It is a tribute to the strength of the ground floor design with its marble faced columns and recessed glass line, that a variety of store fronts can be accommodated without disturbing the basic integrity. Two additions have been made, including a 13th story in 1958. Neither departed from the original concept. While Belluschi's "monument" to modern office design may lack the warm sheltering character of his houses and churches, the fundamental qualities of organic simplicity, restraint, and taste are as evident in the Equitable as in his domestic work.

The Oregonian Building, though not as dramatic as the Equitable, still had many of the features that characterized Belluschi's postwar commercial structures: the polished stone base, green insulating glass, and the flat wall surfaces, here sheathed in limestone rather than aluminum. The problem of designing what is essentially an industrial building in an urban setting was considerably more difficult than that of an office building. But Belluschi did not forget the pedestrian. On the east side along 6th Avenue, large windows allowed the passersby a full view of the pressroom, a truly fascinating sight. Unfortunately, the violence which accompanied the 1959 newspaper strike made it necessary to board up these windows. The boarding stayed up even after settlement of the strike in 1965.

Fig. IV–78. Oregonian Building, 1948, Broadway view; Pietro Belluschi, architect.

While busy with major commercial projects, Belluschi, unlike some others in similar situations, maintained his interest in domestic architecture. His first postwar residential project was the Menefee "ranch house" completed in 1948. Continuing the regional approach developed before the war the Menefee house with its broad overhangs, exposed structure and random width board and batten siding reflects the "Oregon

Fig. IV–79. Menefee "Ranch House," 1948, by Pietro Belluschi.

Barn" influence which is most suitable for the rural setting in the Yamhill Valley. The free open plan designed around a large enclosed courtyard is a self-contained unit with living area, office, carport, and guest house all sheltered by the same roof. A focal point of the living room is a magnificent copper hooded fireplace with relief work by Portland sculptor Frederic Littman.

The same year Belluschi designed two companion houses for the Wilson family in the arid region east of the Warm Springs Indian Reservation. Here again, concern for the locale is evident. The native stone, flat roofs, and wood siding stained to blend with the native sagebrush are quite different from his houses west of the Cascades, yet they have the same functional planning, restraint, and harmony with the landscape.

The Burkes residence, finished in 1949, is Belluschi's only flat roof house design in the western part of Oregon, and the only one that might be considered to have some influence from the International Style. The plan, with closed masses defining the open living and dining area, takes full advantage of a unique wooded site located at the end of a street in Portland's northwest hills. The views constantly change, from the sweeping panorama of Mt. Hood, to the local natural landscape, to the designed space of the main yard defined by stone walls and trellis. Every room has access to it own outdoor space. At the entry Belluschi cleverly uses water with an indoor and outdoor fishpond divided only by glass. Belluschi must have been pleased with his design for the Burke house as he bought it for his own use when he returned to Portland in 1973.

Fig. IV–80. Burkes residence, 1949, by Pietro Belluschi.

During this prolific period Belluschi designed several churches that have had a profound influence on religious architecture throughout the country. For the first time a regional style is seen in non-residential buildings. Here Belluschi synthesized the characteristic elements of his houses and commercial structure: logical planning with clear structural expression, flat textured wall surfaces, native materials simply used but rich in effect, and harmony with the setting.

Two were Portland churches, both Lutheran and both completed in 1950. With Zion Lutheran, located on a cramped sloping site at the base of the west hills, Belluschi employed the familiar L-plan to form an entrance court which led to the broad porch and handsome copper-clad doors with reliefs of ascending angels by sculptor Frederic Littman. As in St. Thomas More, the basic wood structure forms the space of the sanctuary, here with pointed arches, purlins and decking. The glue-laminated arch, which later became a cliché of church architecture, was among the earliest if not the first used in a church.

Soft light enters the nave through the random pattern of individual glass blocks set flush in the brick street wall. The chancel and copper-sheathed altar are warmly illuminated by the large east window of rose and amber glass. Spruce boards and redwood battens provide a rich texture to the chancel wall. Another innovation was the saw-kerfed "acoustical" fir boards applied to the north wall. After the design was

Fig. IV–81. Zion Lutheran Church, 1950, by Pietro Belluschi.

Fig. IV–82. Sanctuary, Zion Lutheran Church.

fairly well along a check of the acoustics indicated the nave would be much too "live." Not wanting to introduce acoustic tile, draftsman Frank Allen came up with the idea of saw-kerfing the boards to increase the sound absorbing characteristics. The idea proved successful and soon after several major wood products firms were marketing the boards.

At Central Lutheran the same wood and Willamina brick are evident, though detailed in a somewhat different manner. Larger than Zion, Belluschi framed the nave with a flat Tudor arch and flat roof, possibly to minimize the bulk in the residentially scaled neighborhood. The sanctuary is formed by an unusual half-circle apse, wider and higher than the nave, and sheathed in brick with a subtle cross pattern to relieve the large mass.

The lighting technique is similar to that in Zion but more dramatic.

Fig. IV–83. Central Lutheran Church, 1950, by Pietro Belluschi.

Above the brick street wall is a lattice of stained wood mullions with red and blue glass, which provides subdued but rich lighting to the nave. Light to the chancel comes from unseen windows in the space between the nave and apse, which form an inverted U-shaped clerestory. The bright but diffused light falling on the curved sky-blue surface creates an illusion of infinite space. The exterior wood detailing, particularly the double curved entrance canopy, displays more Oriental influence than other Belluschi designs. This detailing also shows the hand of K. E. Richardson, Belluschi's chief designer.

Considered by many to be his most successful church design, and certainly the most "modern" to that time, was the First Presbyterian Church in Cottage Grove, completed in 1951. Here Belluschi was blessed with a sensitive congregation and an enthusiastic and creative pastor, Hugh Peniston, who carved the bell supports in the courtyard. The low profile, fenced courtyard, and board and batten siding are at ease with the private homes surrounding the site in this small lumber town. Unlike earlier churches, Belluschi opened up the nave to the outdoors, incorporating the Japanese-like garden into the religious experience.

Looking back on these early postwar churches, one admires their

Fig. IV–84. First Presbyterian Church, Cottage Grove, Oregon, 1951, by Pietro Belluschi.

beauty but tends to forget how pioneering they were. A review of the literature on church architecture of the period with its Gothic and Georgian examples will emphasize the point. It also emphasizes another of Belluschi's great assets—his ability to convince his clients of the rightness of his proposals. Always sensitive to people, he seemed instinctively to understand the necessity of involving and educating his clients in the design process. He said it best himself: "You can't live in an ivory tower and be successful in this modern world. You have to go with the people—ahead of them, perhaps—but along a path which they can understand."[12]

The Cottage Grove church was to be one of Belluschi's last projects before leaving Portland. In 1950, MIT, in recognition of his distinguished career, offered him the position of Dean of the School of Architecture and Planning. Belluschi accepted and assumed the post the following year. He remained there until 1965.

As A. E. Doyle had done before, Belluschi offered to sell the practice to the senior employees of the firm, K. E. Richardson, F. C. Allen, Irving G. Smith and George Kotchik. However, agreement on terms of the sale could not be reached and the firm was acquired by Skidmore, Owings and Merrill and renamed Belluschi and Skidmore, Owings and Merrill. In accord with their agreement Belluschi's name was dropped in 1955.

While Dean at MIT Belluschi continued to practice his profession, usually in a consultant role. Though his projects ranged around the world (he was sometimes referred to as "the peripatetic Belluschi"), his ties with the Northwest remained. Over the years he has designed and

12. "Architecture of the Northwest," *Architectural Record,* Vol. 113 (April, 1953), 140–46.

Fig. IV–85. First Presbyterian Church, Cottage Grove, Oregon. Its nave opened to an enclosed garden.

consulted on several major projects in Portland where he now makes his home.

Following the war John Yeon also continued to explore the modern approaches developed in his prewar houses, and in 1947 he began the design for the Visitors Information Center in association with Wick, Hilgers and Scott. To date it is Yeon's only non-residential building.

The idea for a visitors center emerged right after the war with a tourist promotion fund started by the Portland Chamber of Commerce. A building committee was formed and Yeon was asked to prepare a design for a log structure to symbolize Oregon's great timber industry. Yeon, ignoring the committee's request, went his own way, and after some struggle the design was accepted. The only vestige of the log idea

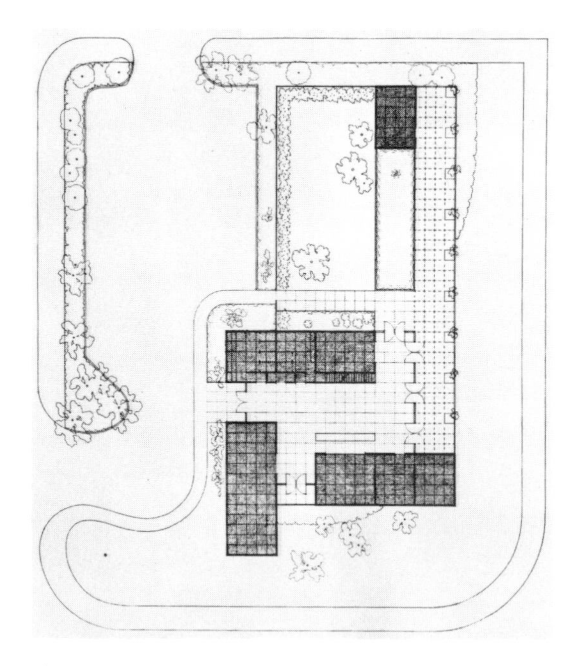

Fig. IV–86. Site plan, Visitors' Information Center, 1948; John Yeon designer; Wick, Hilgers and Scott, associated architects.

Fig. IV–87. Visitors' Information Center, drawing by John Yeon.

Fig. IV–88. Visitors' Information Center, view from northwest.

was a cutting from a 16-foot diameter Sitka spruce displayed on the grounds. At the time the site for the Visitors Information Center was most appropriate. Overlooking the Willamette River on Harbor Drive, then the main highway through the city, the building was highly visible and readily accessible to the motoring tourist.

Yeon's design, which shows a strong International Style influence, is as close to pure abstraction as a functioning building can get. There was some criticism on this point but it couldn't hold up in the face of a plan that eminently suited the intended use. Employing a 3′ module throughout, even to the toilet stalls, the glass enclosed public space is formed by three solid units of the same width but of modularly varying length and height. The solid elements contain offices, exhibit rooms and restrooms. The integral outdoor space is defined by a fourth modular unit, and a connecting fence and pergola.

The wall panels with fixed glass, plywood spandrels and louvered vents, are essentially the same as those used in his prewar houses except the module has been increased by half, which establishes a scale more appropriate to a larger public building. The panel system was skillfully articulated by color; the dark Yeon blue on the panels, wood trim in light sea-green, blue black on the exposed ends of the modular studs, and, to focus attention, wine red on the doors.

On the interior Yeon used native woods in a variety of ways. The panel system used on the exterior is continued on the interior walls of the public area, minimizing the difference between indoors and outdoors, thereby extending the space. The ceilings are vertical grain hemlock boards laid checkerboard fashion on a 6′ module. The same material was used on the exhibit room walls but in a vertical pattern, while striated plywood covered the office walls.

The Visitors Information Center was widely published and received national acclaim. Before completion in 1948 it was awarded a "Mention" in *Progressive Architecture's* Annual Design Awards. Along with Belluschi's Equitable Building, Yeon's design was among the 43 buildings (the only ones from the Northwest) selected by Henry-Russell Hitchcock for the Museum of Modern Art's prestigious 1953 exhibit: "Built in U.S.A.: Post-war Architecture."

For nearly 20 years the Information Center nobly served its purpose. Over two million tourist inquiries were recorded. But the great "changer" of postwar life, the interstate freeway system, eliminated the building's reason for existence. By 1965 few tourists entered the city on Harbor Drive, so the Chamber of Commerce moved out. They donated the building to the City, which shared land ownership with the State Highway Department, with the understanding that the structure would be rehabilitated and used. City and State, however, had other plans, and in 1967 it was announced that the building would be razed along with the old Public Market structure to allow realignment of Harbor Drive. Fortunately the cries of architects and others aware of the building's architectural significance, particularly County Commissioner David Eccles, put a stop to that plan. Soon after, the City, somewhat reluctantly,

Fig. IV–89. Visitors' Information Center, view of entry.

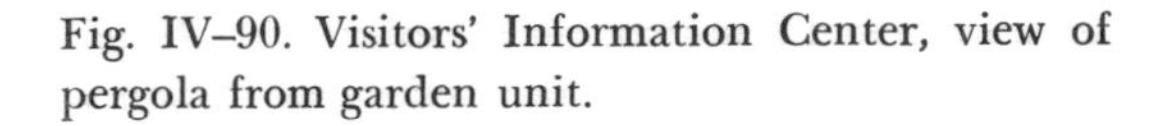

Fig. IV–90. Visitors' Information Center, view of pergola from garden unit.

began long neglected repairs and maintenance, and installed a most appropriate tenant—the Bureau of Architectural Planning. Though far from being restored to original condition, Yeon's elegant structure is now stabilized and improvements are continuing in the right direction.

Yeon's first postwar house was built in 1949 for E. W. Van Buren on a typical neighborhood lot in Portland's west hills. The setting is more urban in character than other Yeon house sites, and this is reflected in the use of brick and the more traditional roof forms—used however, in a very contemporary way. Yeon's floor plan, following the theme of earlier designs, which with the paneled wall system became his trademark, employed solid elements to define the open living and dining area. Here Yeon uses the garage as he used the garden equipment unit at the Information Center; as a terminal element for a fence enclosing the outdoor space. The panel system on a 3′ module is used where light and ventilation are needed, and the Yeon blue color provides a lively and handsome contrast with the red brick. Brick and paneled walls are continued on the interior and combine with brown flagstone flooring and his favorite hemlock board ceilings to make warm and richly colored spaces.

1950 was a prolific year for Yeon, as he completed designs for three houses. Across the road from the earlier Watzek house, Yeon designed a home for George Cottrell on a large sloping site, dense with fir trees and other native plants. Yeon's typical plan approach takes full advantage of the site. With surprise light sources and changing vistas the magnificent variety of the natural landscape is made an integral part of the indoor experience. As in the Van Buren house Yeon employs a combination of solid masses, here sheathed in flush board siding, and

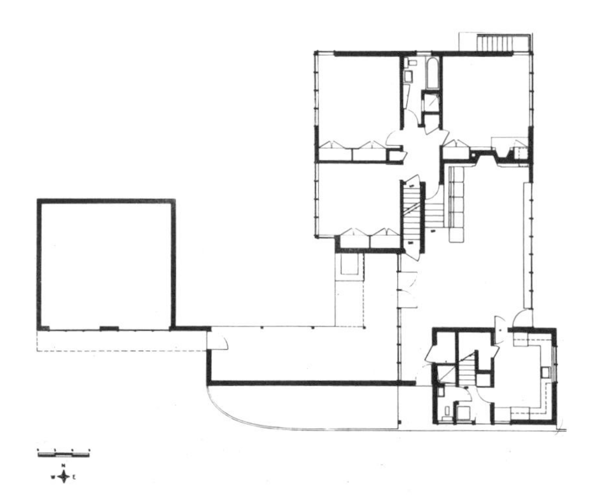

Fig. IV–91. Floor plan, E. W. Van Buren house, 1949; John Yeon, designer.

Fig. IV–92. E. W. Van Buren house, front view.

Fig. IV–93. E. W. Van Buren house, view from living room toward enclosed garden.

open elements articulated by the panel system, again in a 3′ module.

On another sloping and wooded site Yeon designed the Swan house, which on the exterior shows more influence of the rural vernacular than his previous designs. Starting with a simple board and batten wall on a 12″ module, Yeon develops it into a complex system of multiples providing strong unity, and variety where it serves a purpose. The smaller spaces have windows one or two feet wide while the windows of the larger living and dining areas are on a 3′ module.

Yeon's "palace," as he called it, was the supremely elegant house for Lawrence Shaw near Oswego. The site was formidable and presented the designer with a challenging problem: how to design a relatively small house and place it on an open, gently sloping, eight-acre site barren of trees. Yeon's solution was boldly formal at a time when any hint of formalism in design was considered treason. The main pavilion encircled by the low flat-roofed element is almost classical, as is the outrageous cornice which, though classically inspired, is a Yeon original.

Unlike most other Yeon houses, which flowed and melded with the land, the Shaw house appears as a ship at sea. Situated at the top of the slope on a low podium, the grand design is a counterpoint to the surrounding acres of grass. This approach shows Yeon's great sensitivity to the landscape. If in the Shaw design he had employed the techniques used in the other houses where the sites were quite different, there would have been a curious scale relationship with the land, and the building, very likely, would have given the appearance of a dollhouse.

As with his plywood houses of the late 1930s Yeon again uses the paneled wall system throughout, here on the 3′ module, and painted light blue with white trim. The interior, expressing the typical Yeon

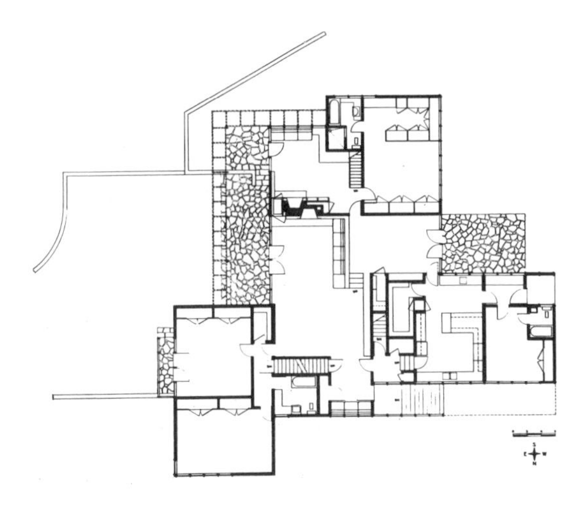

Fig. IV–94. Floor plan, house for George Cottrell, 1950; John Yeon, designer.

Fig. IV–95. Cottrell house, view from northeast.

Fig. IV–96. Cottrell house, view of entry.

Fig. IV–97. Kenneth Swan house, 1950; John Yeon, designer.

Fig. IV–98. Lawrence Shaw house, 1950; John Yeon, designer.

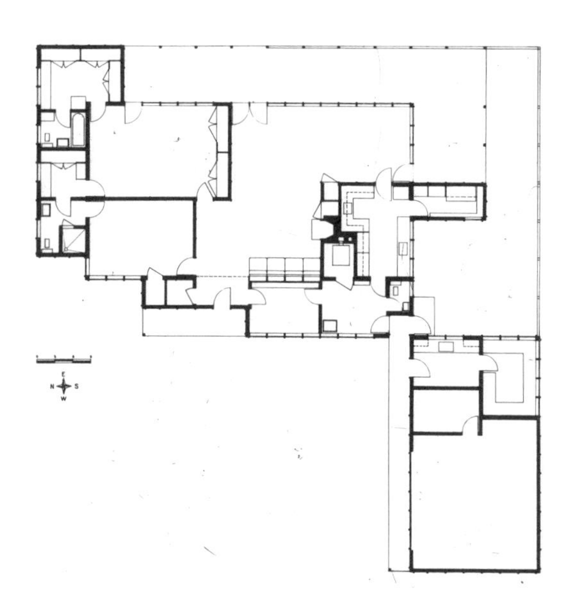

Fig. IV–99. Shaw house, floor plan.

Fig. IV–100. Shaw house, view from northeast.

planning elements, is less formal than the exterior, and is richly finished with the panel system in the living and dining areas, hemlock boards on the ceilings and some walls, and oak parquet flooring.

1950 marked the end of an era. The work of Belluschi, Yeon and a few others like Van Evera Bailey, had firmly established the "Northwest Style." Excepting Belluschi's work, the regional style had been almost entirely limited to domestic architecture, and it was perhaps Belluschi's most significant achievement that he brought what started as an approach to designing a seashore cottage to a fully developed "style"

Fig. IV–101. Shaw house, view from entry through the living room.

applicable to any building type where wood construction is allowed.

Some will undoubtedly quarrel with the formal notion of a "Northwest Style." The question has been debated from time to time though not with much zeal.[13] After all "Style" as applied to the era following the period revivals of the early 20th century is an after the fact matter, and a semantic convenience for writers and historians.

But the case for a regional style, or at least a regional design approach, developing from the mid 1930s to the early 1950s seems strong. Webster defines style as a "Distinctive or characteristic mode of presentation, construction, or execution of any art . . . " Certainly the work of Belluschi and Yeon during the Thirties and Forties was distinctive and characteristic of the climate, the terrain, and the history and attitudes of the regional populace. Hitchcock recognized this in his 1940 review of western architecture when he spoke of the emerging "regional native schools," and Belluschi, as previously noted, clearly differentiated his approach from the dogmatic universality of the International Style.

However, it is also apparent that the regional outlook began to fade in the early 1950s as the influence of Mies van der Rohe, Corbusier, and their followers grew to nearly complete dominance. During recent years regionalism, while still practiced by some, has been submerged by the search for universal design determinants. But there are increasing signs that the idea of regionalism is once again emerging as a dominant force, and with perhaps even more validity than the regionalism of the early postwar years. The new and heightened concerns about energy and the ecology are already influencing design, and as *Progressive Architecture* noted in a March, 1974 editorial, "Responsible architecture in areas such as the Southwest, the Pacific Northwest, and the Gulf Coast simply must accommodate to local climate and local expectations."

---

13. *Oregonian*, Aug. 13, 1947, magazine section, p. 5.

Everyday Architecture in the Puget Sound Area

Victor Steinbrueck

Following World War I and during the 1920s, a period held to be the "most banal . . . of American architecture," possibly related to unstable moral and social forces, residential building in Puget Sound went into the phony guise or appearance of Spanish Colonial, or California Pueblo, or a pseudo-Colonial style of some sort. There was an affected mannerism displayed which often did not get past the front door. Of course, the colonial or Eastern derivation was more popular because it was simpler and less pretentious, and more fitting to the climate. It represented a conscious turning back to early American times with hopes of security and well-being associated with the past. The California mannerisms appear inspired by the romantic American dream of future prosperity, sunshine and sun-ripened oranges that had something to do with the heyday of the movie industry and the westward flow of population to that state. California and Spanish building does not look well in the rain nor in the overcast gray light which is not unusual in the Puget Sound region.

Commercial and institutional architecture following World War I and through the 1920s until the Great Depression was mainly eclectic and mainly uncreative and lacking in originality. Architects dipped freely and unimaginatively into the past to reproduce some particular style of building which was intended to be appropriate for a particular contemporary use. Or, at least, they sought to decorate a facade with brick, stone, or especially terra cotta elements carefully copied from a European style. The lack of availability of good local building stone led to the very common use of terra cotta which has weathered very well through the years. Seattle's Smith Tower built in 1914 is a terra cotta skyscraper with incredible Renaissance Revival details where ornament occurs. Much of downtown Seattle and Tacoma (and many of the main buildings in smaller towns) is in terra cotta—most often white and either a Pseudo-Renaissance or Pseudo-Gothic Revival. This was the great period of growth and it shows in the number of commercial buildings. It was not until thirty years later (1960s) that the business districts began to experience another time of growth and change in construction. The appearances of the established retail business and commercial districts

Fig. IV–102. California Pueblo Style house, 1921.

Fig. IV–103. Colonial Revival Style house, 1918.

have changed considerably with the constant elimination of older buildings to provide parking lots, or inhumane parking structures, or an occasional severe high-rise building with its empty plaza.

In the late 1920s, an unusual sort of contemporary design, inspired but not stifled by tradition, was being created by a young and talented architect from California, Lionel H. Pries. He soon joined the faculty at the University of Washington, where he remained the most influential and inspirational member of the architecture department for more than thirty years. His concept of architectural design has a special romantic quality which combined a love of the best of the past with ability to culturally and technically relate to the present. Some of his best known students who went elsewhere to become successful and perform excellent

Fig. IV–104. Smith Tower, Gaggin and Gaggin, architects, 1914.

quality architecture are: Pete Wimberly of Honolulu; A. Quincy Jones of Los Angeles; Minoru Yamasaki of Detroit. Locally, architect Roland Terry's work shows Pries's special influence. Almost every architectural student during Pries's years was inspired by his talent and insight into the wonders and delights of architecture. He is easily the most talented architect in this region that I have known, and I hope that a worthy

Fig. IV–105. Lionel H. Pries residence, Lionel H. Pries, architect, 1950.

architectural historian will someday record his contribution to architecture both in this region and nationally. There are examples of his work in several locations which should be recorded—for instance, the Wilcox residence at Holly, Washington, and the home of Mr. and Mrs. Richard Lea in Seattle.

During the depression years of the early 1930s there was very little building; however, a few excellent and outstanding projects were accomplished. In 1931, architect R. C. Reamer built the prototype exposed concrete Meany Hotel tower in Seattle's University district. The best and most sophisticated urban buildings in downtown Seattle such as the Skinner, Stimson and 1411 4th Avenue had come from his office during

Fig. IV–106. Northern Life (now Seattle) Tower. Albertson, Wilson and Richardson, architects; Joseph Wilson, designer, 1928.

Fig. IV–107. Exchange Building. John Graham, Sr., architect; Henry Bergseth, designer, 1930.

Fig. IV–108. Depression era house, 1936.

the building period of the late 1920s. At about the same time Joseph Wilson designed two interesting and innovative structures—another exposed concrete edifice, St. Joseph's Catholic Church, and the handsome Northern Life Tower (now Seattle Tower) brick skyscraper which was one of the last (1923) commercial structures built before the bursting of the bubble of the prosperity of the Twenties. The Exchange Building, a modernistic office structure of reinforced concrete clad in yellow cast stone, was designed by Henry Bergseth for the architectural firm of John Graham, Sr.

A few other Modernistic and Art Deco structures were built after 1935 as the nation slowly began to find its way out of the slump of the depression. The frugality of depression years during the decade of the 1930s showed in compact residential forms with low-pitched roofs, close-cropped eaves and the elimination of gable overhangs and in the use of smaller windows. Porches were eliminated or reduced to a small shelter or lid. There was a continuing clinging to visual vestiges of traditional national styles such as "Colonial" which might be Georgian or Cape Cod in manner, or California Ranch House which was a kind of western colonial and thought of as being particularly free and bold, and "English" which might have touches of Elizabethan or Tudor. (I have placed the styles in quotes because there was little authenticity to their sources.)

The involvement of the federal government through the Federal Housing Authority (FHA), with financial encouragement and a myriad of controls for both building and planning, changed the quality and appearance of all private housing. Minimum standards established maximum sizes and relationships. Planning brought about the hallmark of FHA housing tracts—the curved street.

Architects were involved in the design of much of the residential building including speculative developments, due to the serious shortage of building work, so the quality of small residential work was relatively high. This held true for a few years after World War II into the 1950s. Other more creative and original work was being done in a Puget Sound version of the International Style by architect Paul Thiry (influenced by Le Corbusier), and in a Scandinavian Style, which appears more related to a Puget Sound quality, by architect John T. Jacobsen. Some young architects were struggling for the right to do what they considered original work which usually meant that it might have a flat roof. They were influenced by the California work of Richard Neutra and the New England work of Marcel Breuer of the Bauhaus. Residential planning was skillfully but not innovatively handled for family living with style mainly achieved as a selective additive decoration to the exterior and to the fireplace and interior moldings.

This all came together in the public low-income and war housing of the 1940s. The Yesler Terrace (low-income) Housing Project collectively involved five residential architects (Aitken, Bain, Jacobsen, Holmes, and Stoddard) with John T. Jacobsen, who had studied housing in Scandinavia, exercising the controlling influence in the design of the individual row house units and the overall cul-de-sac layout. Another project

Fig. IV–109. Paul Thiry residence; Paul Thiry, architect, 1936.

Fig. IV–110. Yesler Terrace public housing project. Aitken, Bain, Jacobsen, Holmes and Stoddard, architects, 1940.

was the wartime Holly Park Housing Project with the individual units largely designed by John R. Sproule working for Paul Thiry, who was a principal architect along with Frederick T. Ahlson (who did the site planning) and John Paul Jones. Both of these projects have stood the test of time for quality of design and neighborhood planning. Wartime growth to serve the booming aircraft industry and other commercial activities in the 1940s brought about the building of a number of communities usually in the tradition of single family homes, at Port Orchard near the Bremerton Navy Yard, at Salishan in Tacoma, at the Renton Highlands and other locations. A few of these projects remain. Many were built to be temporary and have been removed. Very often there was a lack of total community facilities because of a general policy of avoiding conflicts with private business and local institutions. Still they

Fig. IV–111. Speculative housing tract, 1940s.

came the closest to being total planned communities than anything else that has happened.

While these are interesting expressions of their times, the most revealing building developments of the 1940s and 1950s are the endless tracts of speculative houses of suburbia winding over hill and dale outside of every city and town. The design quality of these individual homes is high in comparison to that of older parts of the nation. There is an almost intangible Puget Sound or Northwest style expressed through the characteristic use of earth-tone stained siding, wide-overhanging low-pitched roofs, orientation to topography and views, and incorporation of existing foliage and second-growth trees as part of the landscape. The houses are regional descendants of the California Ranch House popular in the 1930s. The success of these tracts is largely due to ease of financing through FHA, along with the attraction of everyman's dream of combining the pleasures of the countryside with the convenience of the city. As suburbia has grown and grown, the realization that these hopes have not been achieved has come through total dependence upon the motor car, lack of community facilities and relationships, and isolation from urban amenities. The lessons become quite clear if the "building watcher" attempts to walk through these tracts. It can hardly be done since there are no sidewalks and every pedestrian is perceived as an interloper and consequently a danger. There is a disturbing homogeneity because each tract drew people of a similar economic and social status, and very often of the same employer. There is no urban mixture of peoples from varying ethnic, economic, educational, and cultural backgrounds. There is no identity of home or place.

The Post-World War II era brought a flurry of building construction to accommodate the increased population of the area and to make up for the lost building years of wartime. School building went on at

Fig. IV–112. Speculative housing tract, 1950s.

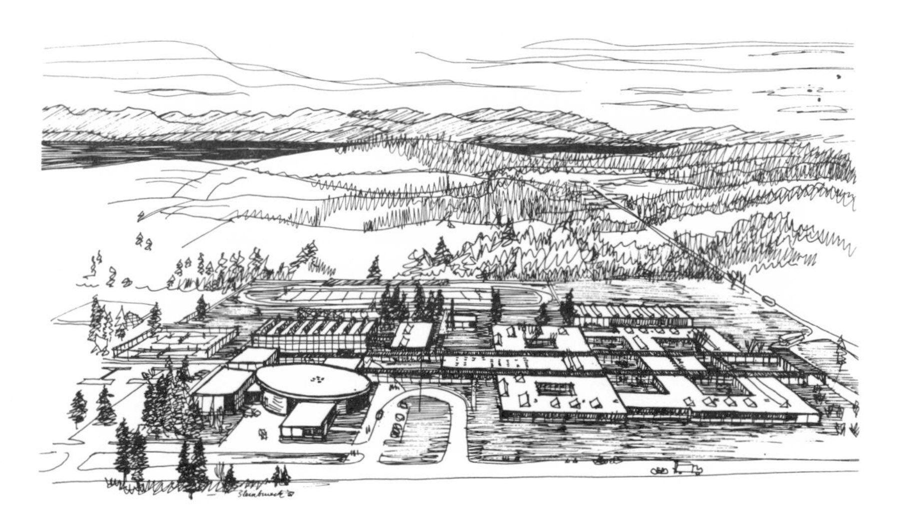

Fig. IV–113. Edmonds Senior High School. Waldron and Dietz, architects, Dan Miller, associate, 1958.

great pace with varied types of construction and plans of one-storied complexes set in vast areas of playfields. The high quality of these projects, which are often the most important elements in a town or neighborhood, indicates the esteem held for public education. Often these schools have provided the only neighborhood or community facilities for public use. The architecture is mainly in a style which might simply be called Modern (not Moderne or Modernistic) or perhaps National in contrast with International Style and in recognition of allegiance to both national and international sources. In wooded settings, architects occasionally sought to bring in a Puget Sound quality through the application of wooden board or shingle side wall surfaces and pitched shingle roofs.

I believe that some of the best quality architecture in the region is in these excellent schools. Some of the responsible architects are: Waldron and Dietz, now Waldron and Pomeroy, Ralph Burkhard; Naramore, Bain, Brady and Johanson; Robert B. Price; Dan Miller; Young, Richardson & Carleton, now the Richardson Associates; Bassetti and Morse; Harris and Reed; Sullam and Aehle; Donald Burr; Anderson, Steinhart and Theriault; and perhaps a few others.

Throughout the involvement with national styles there have existed some characteristics which may be uniquely associated with Puget Sound building. These are: (1) freedom of expression encouraged by newness of country and remoteness from stylistic sources; (2) design for mild and temperate climate, with many overcast days and soft rainfall; (3) varied and skillful use of wood; (4) adaptation to hilly topography; (5) orientation to views; (6) involvement with luxuriant plant growth, or with growing landscape; and (7) special interest in natural amenities.

Perhaps the reliance upon the abundant natural attributes of the Puget Sound country has allowed people to be satisfied with less than the most wonderful in their architecture and towns. Because of an unusual and particular combination of favorable conditions, this region is believed to be one of the special unique places of the world. Those favorable circumstances are its unsurpassed natural setting of a vast inland body of saltwater closely combined with greenery, hills, mountains, flatlands, and waterways and lakes; the pleasant or at least temperate changing climate; and the adventurous, freedom-loving (recreation) friendly people who live here. Planners call this an "amenities" area, in other words it is a good place to live, work, and play.

The Mission Style and Eclecticism in Idaho

Arthur A. Hart

Architecture in Idaho in the 1920s continued to be eclectic, as it had been from the first days of settlement. Although a ride down the residential streets of any town in the state revealed a similar mixture of Colonial, English half-timbered, Bungalow, and earlier styles, some notable larger buildings were built which underscored a taste for the Spanish Mission Style which had been prevalent in Idaho since the first decade of the century.

Certainly the 1925 Union Pacific Station in Boise, designed by New York architects Carrère and Hastings, was a dramatic reaffirmation of the felicity with which the Mission Style fitted into the landscape of southern Idaho. Blue skies, clear desert air, and sunshine set off the white stucco of the graceful bell tower, and the mild winters thereafter would deal gently with the tile roofs and stucco surfaces. The climate of colder and wetter parts of the country doomed much Mission achitecture to failure by underlining the inappropriate materials and connotations of the style.

The dramatic site of the station, on a low bluff across the valley from the state capitol, gives it a distinction equalled by few other depots in the country. The grand sweep of Capitol Boulevard and its Memorial Bridge ties the two axial buildings together—all a part of the Carrère and Hastings "city beautiful" concept to give the Idaho capital an imperial scale and orientation it had never had before.[1] Unfortunately, the grand plan of Capitol Boulevard was not protected by setback or height restrictions, and the 1964 Bank of Idaho Building and the 1952 Telephone Building have overlapped the capitol, dwarfing the view of its dome still left between them.

As striking and important a building as the depot is, it hardly represents a regional style, or even a regional choice. The New York architects worked through Union Pacific's main office in Omaha to develop a train station in a proven style, for both the Santa Fe and Southern

1. Union Pacific Railroad, *Boise, Idaho, Yesterday and Today* (Omaha, 1925), 7–9.

Fig. IV–114. Union Pacific Station, Boise, 1925; Carrere and Hastings, architects.

Pacific railroads had used Mission Style for depots for a decade by 1925.

In Boise, two other important Mission buildings were produced in the mid-Twenties: the Women's Columbian Club erected a handsome clubhouse in 1925, featuring tile, stucco, and wrought iron. C. A. Anderson completed a large downtown department store in 1927 with the familiar round-arched openings and red tile roofs of Mission fronting Idaho Street.

In domestic architecture, the large number of Mission Style houses is explained in part by the state's traditional orientation toward California. Since 1860, when the discovery of gold in Idaho brought the first large numbers of people into the area, the state has continued to attract many settlers from the land of the missions. At first they were prospectors and miners who had joined the California gold rush in 1849 and then moved on to other rushes as they developed. Many who eventually got to Idaho, for example, had first gone to Jacksonville, Oregon, after gold was discovered there in 1851.

Arch-fronted brick commercial buildings in Jacksonville look very

Fig. IV–115. House in Boise.

Fig. IV–116. Wrought iron gate.

much like their contemporaries in San Francisco. The type would be repeated a few years later in Idaho City and Boise. The huge iron doors on these buildings still bear the name plates of the San Francisco foundries which produced them. Mining and milling machinery were also being hauled into the Idaho mountains from California, so it is not surprising that architectural iron came too.

A further link to California was the fact that so many Idahoans vacationed there regularly from the beginning, and that so many merchants took annual buying trips there. By 1920, many wealthy Idahoans, the taste-makers in their communities, were visiting California every year, often staying in second homes in the winter months. Those who admired the Mission Style as it was practiced from San Francisco southward, returned to ask local architects to design similar houses and commercial structures in Idaho.[2]

That this practice preceded the Twenties, however, is clearly shown from a number of earlier buildings in Mission Style in southern Idaho. Generally speaking, these earlier examples are more Baroque in feeling than those built later, often favoring the tortured, curving false gables and irregular window shapes of the plateresque. The Boise Automobile Company of 1908 by J. E. Tourtellotte had this character, and a number of hotels built at the same time in south central Idaho in the newly opened irrigation districts are similarly picturesque.

The Northside Inn at Jerome, begun in September, 1908, by the Kuhn Brothers of Pittsburgh who developed the area, was an exotic fantasy in concrete with twin domed towers, a dramatic three-dimen-

2. Frederick C. Hummel, F.A.I.A., unpublished interview with the author, Boise, May 4, 1974.

Fig. IV–117. Northside Inn, Jerome, Idaho, one of the first buildings in the new town.

Fig. IV–118. Justamere Inn, Twin Falls, with Lincoln School in the background.

sional interplay of forms and spaces, and a cloister-like round-arched porch running across the entire facade.

At Twin Falls, the Justamere Inn had four Baroque false gables imposed upon a rectangular box form, a bracketed tile roof, and an arched main entrance flanked with massive stuccoed columns reminiscent of Mission Dolores in San Francisco. (The Lincoln School, a few blocks away, built in brick at the same time, has much the same ornamental Mission clothing.)

The Lincoln Inn at Gooding and the smaller Wendell Inn at Wendell are less obviously Mission in style, but used materials and forms in the same spirit. All of these hotels were built by the promoters of the new towns in the sagebrush soon after the irrigation canals were dug and the lands opened to settlers. Promotion often included free train tickets from the East and Midwest to would-be purchasers of farm land and town lots. The hotels were needed to accommodate the influx, attracted by ads in Eastern newspapers and colorful brochures printed by the railroads and land companies. In Chicago and other cities store windows were rented for displays of potatoes, apples, and other produce from the new Edens of the Snake River country.

Masonry construction, using native stone and locally fired brick had long been used more extensively than wood in this treeless country, and by the time the Mission Style reached Idaho, concrete was also widely used, both in poured walls and in block form.

The Mission Style was undoubtedly a popular success in Idaho for a generation. Even today, many years since the last buildings in the style were put up, the remaining ones are pleasing to the eye, have weathered well, and still seem at home in this landscape. If they are examples of "the most banal period in American architecture," as has been claimed, they have nevertheless fared better in Idaho than the English half-timbered cottages and Colonials have. Neither of the latter have ever seemed quite at home on the desert.

A building which did seem to fit in was architect Frederick C. Hummel's 1927 Egyptian Theater. The tile roofs and stuccoed surfaces had the character of Mission, even though the forms were authentic echoes of Eighteenth Dynasty Egypt. The construction was concrete, richly decorated with polychrome sculpture on a beige ground which harmonized well with the arid hills behind the city. The exotic interior, with glowing colors and gold leaf, is virtually unchanged today. Its great columns, modeled after those at the temple of Amon at Karnak, flank the only theater organ left in the state, and recall the splendor of a vanished era of movie palaces.

In Idaho in about 1930 another style became popular which added to the stucco and masonry wall tradition carried on by the Mission Style. Moderne architecture, called "modernistic" by its builders, began to appear in large structures like the Hotel Boise, 1930, with ornament derived from the Paris Exposition of 1925. Concrete was the favorite material for the rash of new schools, courthouses, and other public buildings built just before World War II, many of them as WPA proj-

Fig. IV–119. Egyptian Theater, Boise, 1926, by Fritz Hummel. Later renamed the Ada, it was the first movie palace in the state.

Fig. IV–120. Egyptian Theater, detail.

Fig. IV–121. Egyptian Theater, interior.

ects. The hallmarks of the style, no doubt spread to Idaho by the mass media as others had been before, were either a strongly emphasized verticality with fin-like finials and stylized plant-form or geometric ornament, or a streamlined horizontality with many parallel lines culminating in corner windows. Glass brick, chrome, and painted iron railings like those of a ocean liner were often coupled with porthole windows.

The failure of a regional style to emerge in Idaho must be viewed in part within the context of the rapid communications available over the past 80 years. Since the first professional architect came to the state (in 1889) there has been no isolation from the mainstream of architectural ideas in the rest of the country. Throughout the Nineties the *Idaho Statesman*, the state's leading newspaper, published plans daily for houses, churches, and other kinds of buildings in the latest styles, syndi-

Fig. IV–122. Hotel Boise, 1930.

Fig. IV–123. Cassia County Courthouse, Burley, 1939.

cated from New York and Chicago. Idaho achitectural offices in these years (and ever since) have subscribed to every periodical in the field, and most of the chief designers have traveled regularly and extensively. The young architects of Idaho sought training in the best Eastern schools, sharing in the mainstream of ideas being circulated at the time, for better or worse.[3] To speak of a cultural lag in this context is to ignore the reality of a pervasive eclecticism and exchange of ideas that was continuous from the Nineties on.

If one further considers that perhaps four out of five buildings in the state were built without the aid of an architect at all, other leveling and standardizing forces must be sought. The Radford Architectural Company of Chicago, for example, advertised itself as the largest architectural firm in the world. Its illustrated plan books could be consulted in any lumberyard or contractor's office, and complete blueprints for a house in the latest style ordered for from eight to fifteen dollars. The 1908 edition offered wash drawings of more than 300 houses, cannily

3. Hummel, interview with the author, Boise, May 11, 1974.

Fig. IV–124. "The House of Today," Twin Falls Power Plant, Twin Falls.

adapted to the popular taste of the day.[4] These houses were built, and can still be seen by the thousand, even in relatively remote Idaho, and Radford plans were sold in every state in the Union. (Incidentally, of the some 300 plans available in 1908, only one is strongly Mission in style, with three others offering a taste of the mode, which seems to underline a more direct influence from California.)

Popular magazines were another source of standardization in taste in the various eclectic styles, in the 20th century as they had been in the 19th. Many Idahoans who read *Sunset* magazine no doubt learned first about the Mission and other California styles in its pages, but *House Beautiful* and other periodicals also contributed their influences toward a homogeneous national taste for styles like Bungalow and English.

Another factor in this process of standardizing American building, as important in Idaho as elsewhere, was the widespread availability of catalog ornament and other mass-produced components for buildings. Colonial, Mission, and craftsman style doors, windows, cornices, fireplaces and staircases could be ordered by number. Architects frequently noted on blueprints the appropriate catalog numbers for their ornamental details, without bothering to sketch them in more than in a cursory fashion.[5] Whole streets were lined with houses whose common denominator was identical sashes and doors, moldings, brackets, and porch columns.

That a regional style could develop for the majority of new construction in Idaho or anywhere else under these conditions is highly

4. William A. Radford, *Radford's Portfolio of Plans* (Chicago and New York, 1908).

5. Idaho Historical Society, archive of architectural drawings.

unlikely, and to discern a regional style anywhere in the United States in the first half of the 20th century is, I believe, a highly selective enterprise for scholars who choose to ignore as insignificant the vast majority of what has been built (presumably by not recognizing it as architecture at all). Certainly the obvious fact is that "styles" in American architecture have been spread about as evenly across the country as can be imagined, and that although Spanish derivatives are more common in the Southwest than elsewhere, they do exist in New England, just as Cape Cod houses exist in California. Idaho, like the rest of the Northwest, has these and many more.

Auto Accomodations

Elisabeth Walton

The development of statewide and interstate road systems for automobile traffic and the improvement of road-building technology in the 1920s ushered in an era of unprecedented public mobility across the country. Whether in the pursuit of pleasure or business, American motorists traveled well-armed with road maps and pamphlets—modern-day versions of emigrant guidebooks, which listed reliable hotels and the location of auto camps and roadside rest areas. Few scenic and wilderness attractions were out of reach, and in the Pacific Northwest a major industry evolved to cultivate the motoring trade. "Good roads everywhere" was a slogan of the times which equated hard-surfaced avenues of transit with social and economic progress.

It was natural that one of the early and important hotels in the region specifically designed with the motorist in mind should have been sponsored by a preeminent advocate of good roads. The Columbia Gorge Hotel was completed in 1921 for Simon Benson, promoter of the Columbia River Highway, donor of related park areas, and former chairman of the Oregon State Highway Commission. A 24-acre site on a high bluff overlooking the river at the outlet of Phelps Creek a mile west of the city limits of Hood River was acquired for the development. In connection with the grand opening in June, Mr. Benson remarked: "We have built good roads, and have invited the world to come and view our beauty spots, but until now we have done nothing toward taking care of them after they arrived. With our new hotel we will, in a measure, take care of this. We are just pointing the way for others to follow in the business of entertaining tourists."[1] Benson's earlier project, the Benson Hotel in Portland, completed in the Baroque Revival Style in 1912, is still among the top-ranked hotels in the Northwest. It was Benson who backed the $400,000 project on the state's best-known scenic highway on the basis that tourist hotels were a vital supplement to the huge investment in road building, but the specific concept was attributed

---

1. *The Columbia Gorge Hotel on the Scenic Columbia River Highway, Oregon* (Portland, 1921), 18.

to Henry Thiele, formerly master chef of the Hotel Benson.[2] Under Thiele's management, the Columbia Gorge Hotel was to serve as a mid-Columbia base for motor parties spending several days sightseeing in the district.

The design was provided by prominent Portland architect Morris H. Whitehouse, who had been schooled in Portland and in the East at the Massachusetts Institute of Technology. After launching his practice in Portland in 1908, Whitehouse worked in association with others from time to time. Among his well-known commissions under various firm names were the University Club, Multnomah Amateur Athletic Club, the old Lincoln High School, and a succession of clubhouses, including those for the Waverly, Oswego, and Eastmoreland Country Clubs. While

Fig. IV–125. Columbia Gorge Hotel, Hood River, Oregon, 1921.

at MIT, where he completed his studies in 1906, Whitehouse was awarded one of the early traveling scholarships in architecture. The scholarship enabled him to spend a year at the American Academy in Rome, Italy, prior to returning to Portland.[3] Whitehouse's scheme for the hotel was Mediterranean in spirit, with white stuccoed walls, red tiled roof, and a loggia across the south end of the dining room. The plan took the form of an elongated H with a frontage of 185 feet. Owing to the manner in which the building was settled into its cliff-side site, it was four stories in height on the river side, and three stories above grade on the south, or highway side. The core of the ground story was a dining room measuring 40 by 76 feet. The kitchen wing was to the east, and the lobby, lounging room and sun porch made up the west wing, which was entered from a porte-cochere. Marking this wing also was an Italianate observa-

2. *The Columbia Gorge Hotel . . .* , 17, 21.

3. Winfield Scott Downs, ed., *Encyclopedia of Northwest Biography* (New York, 1943), 121.

tion tower 100 feet above the ground. The tower had an outside walkway which provided a prospect of the Washington shore and a sweeping view up and down the river for 25 miles. The basement contained a ballroom, bowling alley, laundry and shops. The top two floors were taken up by 48 guest rooms, each equipped with bath and telephone. The interior was consistent with the notion of Mediterranean airiness. Its boxed beamed ceiling and paneled woodwork were light-painted, and an abundance of transomed French doors opened onto various porches. The decor by Lipman, Wolfe & Company featured over-stuffed furniture with bird and floral printed upholstery and linen window draperies lined with cream sateen. The prevailing color schemes were ivory and blue or ivory and salmon pink.[4]

The hotel was not only fitted with the most modern kitchen equipment, but, as it was beyond reach of the City of Hood River water supply, it also had its own water system by which springs on a high plateau to the south were tapped by six-inch wood pipe into a 5,000-gallon steel pressurized storage tank. It was expected that when connections for electric service for an elaborate lighting system and elevator were complete, the new hotel would be the largest individual user of electricity in the county.

Landscaping planned under the supervision of E. E. Newell, Hood River City Engineer, called for driveways, walks, lawns, and a veranda and balustrade for viewing the falls of Phelps Creek. Because a section of the Union Pacific Railroad ran past at the base of the cliff below, it was planned that the railroad company would build a station at the foot of Wa Gwin Gwin Falls and an elevator would carry passengers to the hotel level.[5] A nine-hole golf course was later developed on the site as planned. Now a retirement home, the hotel is well-maintained by its present proprietors, the Neighbors of Woodcraft.

It had been the policy of the Columbia Gorge Hotel to cater to families and to people as a whole, rather than a particular class, and an attempt was made to scale rates to suit the average traveler. Nevertheless, the costs involved in operating a large hotel demanded comparatively substantial rates. The economy-minded and those in a hurry preferred making use of a growing number of auto camps.

In 1921 the numerous resorts on North Beach in Washington at the mouth of the Columbia River prepared for a banner season. Sea fishing from the rocks, surf bathing, clam digging, picnicking and horseback riding were among favorite pastimes of the locale. Long a popular summer vacation district, North Beach anticipated record crowds with completion of the Ocean Beach Highway from Chehalis. Moreover, ferries were put into use in that year between Astoria and Ilwaco, and the Columbia was no longer a bar to motor travel. An automobile boat named *The Tourist* operated by the Astoria–North Beach Ferry Com-

4. *The Columbia Gorge Hotel* . . . , 29, 31, 33.

5. *The Columbia Gorge Hotel* . . . , 27.

Fig. IV–126. Harrison's Auto Camp, Columbia River Highway.

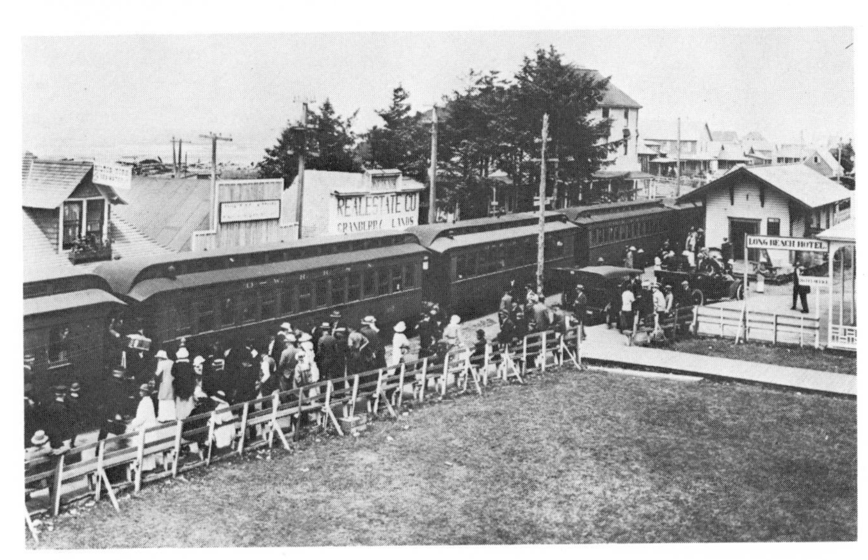

Fig. IV–127. Oregon-Washington Railroad and Navigation Company train and automobiles in front of the Long Beach Hotel, Long Beach, Washington.

pany was to make six round trips a day at the height of the season. It could accommodate 16 "machines." Fares were based upon the weight of the autos and upon the number of passengers other than the driver.[6] The new service was expected to popularize the loop trip by automobile between Portland and Puget Sound.

Free auto camps were established at Chinook, Ilwaco, Seaview, Long Beach and Ocean Park, and several tourist associations were formed.

6. Fred Lockley, "Resorts Prepare for Big Season on North Beach," *Oregon Journal,* May 29, 1921. Clipping in Oregon Historical Society Scrapbook 79, p. 64.

The free auto park early in this period was approached by the community as a public service, for it was often hoped that those who made use of the facilities would be so pleased with the comforts and conveniences they would look around with the idea of settling. At Long Beach an area of five acres was cleared in a grove near the railroad track "within sight and sound of the sea." In it, the auto park was equipped with tables and benches, comfort stations, and five brick ovens with steel cooking plates constructed by local citizens. Free fire wood was also provided.[7]

Auto camps were to be found everywhere along major highways, and nowhere was the evolution from camps to contiguous motel units more fluid than it was along the coast. Typical rental facilities for tenters, which amounted to wooden platforms, plank walls, and pitched canvas roofs, were those at Barview and Lake Lytle, north of Tillamook Bay on the Oregon coast. Garages, restaurants and grocery stores were frequently operated in conjunction with the commercial parks. Patrons often could rent stoves, dishes, linen, beds and bedding. At Lake Lytle, the use of a boat was complimentary.

At Oceanside, the Dixon Cottage Apartments were single-story frame

Fig. IV–128. Tent City, Barview, Tillamook County, Oregon.

cabins detached but huddled on pilings in terraced rows to take advantage of a short crescent of beach between two headlands. The White Cottages at Ocean Lake, built later in the period on a narrow lot running perpendicular to the sea, were smaller yet in scale and formed a contiguous row conforming to the site. Each unit had a private porch

7. Lockley, "Resorts Prepare for Big Season on North Beach," OHS Scrapbook 79, p. 64.

Fig. IV–129. Tent City, Lake Lytle, Tillamook County, Oregon.

Fig. IV–130. Dixon Cottages, Oceanside, Tillamook County.

Fig. IV–131. White Cottages, Ocean Lake, Lincoln County, Oregon.

giving access to a path to the beach below.

The phenomenon of camps and cabins notwithstanding, demand for large resort hotels continued. One of the sizeable structures of the type on the Oregon coast was the third hotel at Gearhart Park, opened for use in 1923, and boldly sited on the foredune in immediate view of the ocean. A golf course was laid out to the east. Designed by Portland architect Morris H. Whitehouse in the rambling, asymmetrical tradition

Fig. IV–132. Gearhart Hotel, Gearhart, Oregon, 1923.

Fig. IV–133. Dorchester House, Ocean Lake, 1935.

of the Shingle Style, the three-story Gearhart Hotel had a variety of hipped gables and a continuous shed-roofed dormer which contained openings of the third story. Unusually wide window openings were glazed with double-hung sash with as many as eight and ten lights in the upper sash. Uprights and railings of porches were shingled in the same fashion as the exterior wall cover. After a long career, the hotel was torn down in 1972 to make way for new development.

The Dorchester House at Ocean Lake is another of the well-known seaside inns of Oregon. It complemented the reputation for good food and hospitality of the Agate Beach Inn (1912) some 25 miles to the south. Construction of the Dorchester House was begun shortly before the Depression, lapsed, and was completed in 1935. The result was a crisp, symmetrical white frame building with a broad expanse of dark shingled roof broken by triangular and paired dormers. Two small louvered ventilators surmounted by weather vanes straddled the ridge of the roof. The chief interest of the facade was created by two large gables containing in the ground story bay windows with transoms and side lights formed of multiple small panes. The effect of these gables, of coupled double-hung sash windows with many small panes at the second story, and miniscule circular windows in the peaks of the gables, was to give pictorial relief to the light surface plane. From the west side of the inn guests viewed the Pacific beyond the stylized beds of a flower garden. Annual statewide Republican conferences were inaugurated at Dorchester House in recent years. Portland developers plan to remodel the inn and expand its capacity for convention use.

The late 1920s introduced a taste for storybook themes and novelties. In developments oriented to the roadway, such as motels, businesses, restaurants and gasoline filling stations, the mock windmills, gigantic milk bottles and pseudo lighthouses were a whimsical hybridization of architecture and outdoor advertising. An interesting filling station in Portland was designed by leading architect A. E. Doyle. A simple, electrically-lighted conical roof on a stem, it was a self-made logogram sheltering General Petroleum gasoline pumps. No longer extant, it was

Fig. IV–134. Natureland Home Auto Park, Bandon Beach, Oregon.

curiously reminiscent of a Japanese umbrella, or perhaps a miniature Clatsop Beach Chautauqua pavilion.

Among the first of a lengthy list of drive-in services to be developed for American motorists was the drive-in cafe. The form, which evolved in the early 1940s, required minimal building space but adequate pavement for automobiles which parked in well-regulated rows while the

Fig. IV–135. Dutch Village, Terwilliger Boulevard near Bertha station, Portland.

Fig. IV–136. Steigerwald Dairy, Orange Blossom Jug Restaurant, Alcazar Service Station, Sandy Boulevard, Portland.

Fig. IV–137. Lighthouse Super Service Station, S.W. Tenth and Stark Street, Portland.

bill of fare was rushed to the car door. At Waddle's Coffee Shop in Portland, the intersecting planes of the flat rain canopy and the broad vertical which carried the restaurant's graphic identification were sleekly reminiscent of the current International Style. The ultimate in efficiency for travelers en route to other destinations was the cafe which incorporated a filling station. The Rex Valley Junction Cafe on the Salmon River Highway, a main-traveled route between the mid-Willamette Valley and the coast, was a deluxe version of the concentrated conveniences offered by earlier auto parks.

Other resorts typical of the period were dude ranches and spas. However, the popularity of certain of the mineral springs resorts gradually waned as improved roads made long distance touring more attractive. Foley Springs on Horse Creek, a feeder stream of the McKenzie River on the west slope of the Cascades in Lane County, Oregon, was a select resort still much in demand in the 1920s. With hot mineral baths, a variety of hiking trails, and a comfortable lodge with capacity for 15 to 20 guests, it was ideal for family outings. An automobile was dispatched from Foley Springs to meet guests arriving in Eugene by train.[8] At Breitenbush Springs on the Breitenbush River, a tributary of the Santiam, popular facilities operated by Merle D. Bruckman from 1922 through 1955 included a large outdoor swimming tank and bath house, a lodge and dining room, store, 35 tent houses, and 62 housekeeping cottages which were available in a furnished or partially furnished state. Between June 1 and September 30, regular auto stage service from Salem was provided. Activities included fishing, hiking, horseback riding, bonfires, and dancing twice weekly.[9]

8. Information supplied by Quinland Daniels Porter, 1974, based upon family album of Foley Springs vacation, August, 1923.

9. *Oregon Resorts* (Advertising and Travel Department, Portland Chamber of Commerce, 1939), 11.

Fig. IV–138. General Petroleum Filling Station, Portland.

At Lava Hot Springs in the southeast corner of Idaho, development was influenced by the availability of strong, but comparatively lightweight building stone. Situated on the Portneuf River at the base of great stony cliffs, the town in its heyday was a well-equipped resort featuring springs of unusually high mineral content. In the State-sponsored Mud Baths, swimmers enjoyed the effect of varying degrees of cold and warmth in an outdoor pool fed from 30 springs of varying temperatures. Two large indoor pools or natatoriums were among other attractions.[10] The Whitestone Hotel, combining lobby, cafe and theatre functions on the ground floor, is typical of much masonry construction of the period east of the Cascades. In a style that is essentially Italianate, the two-story hotel is faced with rough-dressed stone on the ground story, where round-arched openings are used on the principal facade and the diagonal corner entry. The second story is faced with smooth-dressed sandstone. The roof line is simply detailed, with rudimentary stone brackets giving the impression of a dentil course from a classical entablature, and small stone blocks forming a decorative crenellated parapet.

During this period, the taste for "theme" architecture and the chalet mode associated with mountain and lakeside resorts merged in a spate of Swiss alpine buildings with elaborately bracketed overhanging eaves and rustic details. The type was especially appropriate in rugged central Idaho, where a well-known example was the Challenger Inn of the Swiss Village at Sun Valley in the Sawtooth Range. Others were the St. Georg Hotel at Ketchum and the Payette Lake Inn at McCall.

In Oregon, examples of the Swiss chalet mode are the Grand Ronde Hotel in the lumber company town of Grand Ronde on the east slope

Fig. IV–139. Waddle's Coffee Shop, Portland. Pietro Belluschi, architect, 1945.

Fig. IV–140. Rex Valley Junction Cafe, Valley Junction, Polk County, Oregon.

Fig. IV–141. Interior view, Rex Valley Junction Cafe.

10. *Idaho, A Guide in Word and Picture* (Caldwell, Idaho, 1937), 226–27.

Fig. IV–142. Bath houses, Foley Springs, Oregon, 1923.

of the Coast Range and Battle Axe Inn at Government Camp on Mt. Hood. The latter may have been influenced as much by the Forestry Building of the Lewis and Clark Centennial Exposition of 1905 in Portland in its hipped gable roof and the half-rounds of logs applied horizontally to the surface in imitation of massive log joinery.

Among the more individual treatments of the chalet mode are those at Oregon Caves National Monument in the Siskiyou Mountains in southern Josephine County. The limestone caves discovered by Elijah Davidson in 1874 were visited by a succession of conservation-minded and nature-loving tourists, including William Gladstone Steel and poet Joaquin Miller. However, it was the monograph of C. B. Watson which was instrumental in achieving government protection of the "marble halls of Oregon."[11] Under authority of the Act for Preservation of American Antiquities, President William Howard Taft proclaimed the caves a national monument in 1909 to be maintained by the U.S. Forest

Fig. IV–143. Bath house, Bruckman's Breitenbush Springs, Breitenbush, Oregon.

Fig. IV–144. Mud baths, Lava Hot Springs, Idaho.

Service. A gravel road known as the Caves Highway was opened from Cave Junction in 1922, and the Oregon Caves Company was organized a year later to commence construction of accommodations near the cave entrance. Before it was remodeled in the 1940s, the Chalet was a long, rectangular building one-and-a-half stories in height, with vertical plank siding, unpeeled bark to the weather. Overhanging eaves of the steeply-pitched shingled roof were supported by exposed rafters and out-sized ogee brackets. The building was lighted by casement windows and shed-roofed dormers. A walk-through area between the souvenir shop and the admissions office was marked by a large transverse gable with latticed tympanae.

In 1933, following steady improvements to the underground tunnels

11. C. B. Watson, *Prehistoric Siskiyou Island and Marble Halls of Oregon* (1909), 132–41.

Fig. IV–145. Whitestone Hotel, Lava Hot Springs.

Fig. IV–146. The Ram Bar, Challenger Inn, Sun Valley, Idaho.

Fig. IV–147. St. Georg Hotel, Ketchum, Idaho.

and chambers, the monument was transferred along with all other national monuments to the jurisdiction of the National Park Service. A year later, the six-story Chateau designed and built by Grants Pass contractor G. A. Lium was opened for use.[12] The new resort presented a similarly rustic exterior of unpeeled bark and a steep roof with overhanging eaves appropriate for heavy snow country. The H-shaped building was compactly settled over a narrow stream bed in a site offering limited level terrain. The Caves Highway encompasses the Chateau on three sides, terminating on the far side of the mountain stream which cascades through the basement dining room in its downhill course to the Illinois Valley.

A building widely regarded as the ultimate example of regional mountain architecture produced during this period is Timberline Lodge on the south slope of Mt. Hood. Before completion of the million dollar project in 1937, there was no large scale center of year-round recreational activity on the mountain. The development was proposed by E. J. Griffith, Director of the Federal Works Progress Administration in the State of Oregon, and construction was initially underwritten by the Mt. Hood Development Association, a Portland-based organization, and the WPA. The project was designed and supervised by personnel of the U.S. Forest Service Regional Engineer's office. The five principally credited were: W. I. Turner, Supervising Architect; Howard Griffin, Dean Wright, Linn A. Forrest, and Ward Ganno.[13] Gilbert Stanley

12. Frank K. Walsh and William R. Halliday, *Discovery and Exploration of the Oregon Caves* (Grants Pass, 1971), 25.

13. Information supplied Feb. 22, 1974, by Mr. Jack Culbreath, Special Projects

Fig. IV–148. Payette Lake Inn, McCall, Idaho.

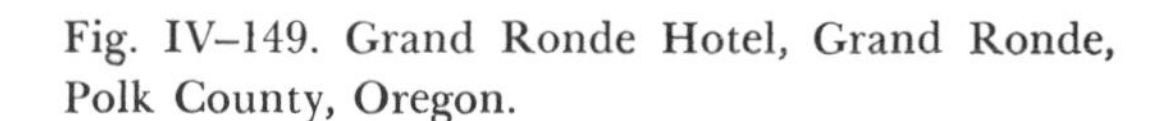

Fig. IV–149. Grand Ronde Hotel, Grand Ronde, Polk County, Oregon.

Fig. IV–150. Battle Axe Inn, Government Camp, Mt. Hood, 1934.

Underwood, architectural advisor to the U.S. Treasury Department, was designated consulting architect; A. D. Taylor was consulting landscape architect; and Lorenz Brothers of Portland were general contractors. The general superintendent of construction was William Wechner. Margery Hoffman Smith, Supervisor of the Oregon Art Project, directed decoration of the interior. Ray Neufer was in charge of wood carving

---

Officer, USFS Region 10 Office, based upon recent interview with Linn A. Forrest of Linn A. Forrest and Associates, Architects, Juneau, Alaska.

Fig. IV–151. Chalet, Oregon Caves National Monument, 1920s.

Fig. IV–152. Chateau, Oregon Caves National Monument, 1934.

and furniture construction, and O. B. Dawson supervised metalcraft and smithing.[14]

At about the time skiing became a fast-rising winter sport, and the number of visitors to Mt. Hood National Forest annually approached the 200,000 mark, the lodge at timberline took shape with the notion of federal sponsorship and control, and private management for public use. Because of the unprecedented scope and variety of work offered Oregon artists and craftsmen in a public commission, and because of the recreational need it fulfilled, the project was considered a model of social usefulness as well as distinctive design.

The site is at the foot of Palmer Glacier on the Timberline Trail which circumscribes the mountain at an elevation of approximately 6,000 feet. A system of radiating trails converge at the lodge, resume in the summit trail and culminate at 11,245 feet. To avoid the hazard of building near the edge of a deep canyon, construction was commenced at a point approximately a quarter of a mile north and up the slope from the site originally under consideration.[15]

The lodge was oriented to command a view of not only the summit, but other major peaks of the Cascade Range to the south, including Mt. Jefferson, Three Fingered Jack, and Mt. Washington. Considerable grading was required to adapt the structure to existing contours. Consulting landscape architect A. D. Taylor pointed out as a consequence of inspection trips in the early phases of construction the fragile nature of the surface soil, which is predominantly volcanic ash, and that the alpine vegetation could be easily disturbed. To minimize long-term effects of disturbing the natural ground, Taylor stressed attention to root structures of existing groups of trees, the width and alignment of the final section of approach road, the placement of footpaths, disposition of excavation materials, and provision of outlets for surface drainage from natural gullies upslope from the site. He recommended that building plans which had been drawn for the location earlier selected be modified slightly to better conform to the site under preparation. He suggested changes in the grade line of the west wing, and he felt terrace areas which were designed for summer use should be carefully related through steps and contour to the natural topography "rather than to assume a definite semi-circular form," which he thought would create a barrier between the building and the landscape.[16]

In Taylor's view, the logical space for parking was to the northwest

---

14. List of supervisory personnel, Timberline Lodge Development, interleaved with cover letter in Claire Warner Churchill, *Mt. Hood Timberline Lodge, the Realization of a Community Vision made possible by the Works Progress Administration* (Portland, 1936).

15. A. D. Taylor, "Mt. Hood Timber Line Lodge, Mt. Hood, Oregon. Report on Inspection Trip July 3, 4 and 5, 1936" (July 7, 1936), p. 1, USFS Region 6 Office, Portland.

16. Taylor, "Mt. Hood Timber Line Lodge . . . ," pp. 7–8.

on ground not slated for recreational development, where it would be screened from view of the west wing by trees. In practice, parking was developed in front of the south entrance. Several secondary facilities for seasonal use, such as tennis courts, were proposed. Among these were a limited number of cabins planned for the west side of the site. Although the cabins were acceptable to him, Taylor advised against the introduction of artificial features in the landscape such as a reflecting pool which had been contemplated for the area north of the lodge.

Preliminary drawings and sketches for the project suggest a somewhat freely interpreted dependence upon the chalet style. In one scheme

Fig. IV–153. South elevation, Timberline Lodge, Mount Hood National Forest, Mt. Hood, 1937.

Fig. IV–154. Ornamental iron workshop, Timberline Lodge.

titled "Mount Hood Timberline Ski Chalet," a wide gable offset to one end of the south elevation was the focal point of the facade.[17] It contained a two-story bank of windows several bays wide. Treatment of a frontal gable as a key element in a long facade dominated by lateral roof lines had been employed effectively in Mt. Baker Lodge (1925–26) on the shore of Sunrise Lake in Mount Baker National Forest in the Cascades immediately south of the Canadian border. Other elements used more or less consistently in the early schemes for Timberline Lodge were dormer windows, masonry ground stories, parabolic arches with radiating voussoirs, and prominent masonry chimney stacks. Several of the schemes showed conscious effort to achieve a picturesque asymmetry. The internal organization ultimately used was first developed in one preliminary scheme which included a central multi-storied lobby space and wings turned off axis.[18] Historical surface detail, such as medieval half-timbering in gables and leaded window panes in diaper patterns were used only sparingly,[19] and there were no suggestions of the half rounds of timbers applied to siding to mark off stories and bays, a treatment which was used on Paradise Inn at Mt. Rainier, and Mt. Baker Lodge.

A rendering of the executed scheme, signed by Linn A. Forrest and dated 1936, was a quantum jump from the conventional preliminary concepts. Yet, it incorporated some of the more successful features of the early designs. The focus of the building and the dominant element of the exterior is a three-story hexagon with pyramidal roof which houses ambulatory space around a colossal stone chimney. The massive core is said to have been intended to echo the conformation of the mountain summit. Although the handling of this feature was completely individual, the form was not without precedent. A colossal chimney was used in the Old Faithful Inn at Yellowstone National Park. The large pavilion is reminiscent of the multi-storied, conical-roofed, ballroom section of the opulent Hotel Del Coronado (1887) in San Diego, California.

The hinge-like plan of Timberline Lodge, as executed, consists of two wings extending from the central pavilion to the southwest and to the southeast. The ground story of rubble masonry is surmounted by two stories with a variety of wall cover, including shingle, board and batten, and clapboard siding. The attic story is lighted by hip-roofed dormer windows. Tall stone chimneys with vaulted caps project above the roofline of the wings. At the end of either wing, the shake roof is hipped and extends nearly to the ground line with a slight up-turn at the base in a manner which suggests efficiency in handling snow run-off and which anchors the building, visually, to its site. Other features which also appear to have a dual purpose of this sort are projections on north and south elevations of the west wing which slope to the ground

17. Drawing for "Mount Hood Timberline Ski Chalet," unsigned. Oregon Historical Society.

18. Drawing for "Scheme C," Mount Hood Timberline Lodge, unsigned. OHS.

19. Drawing for "Scheme D," Mount Hood Timberline Lodge, unsigned. OHS.

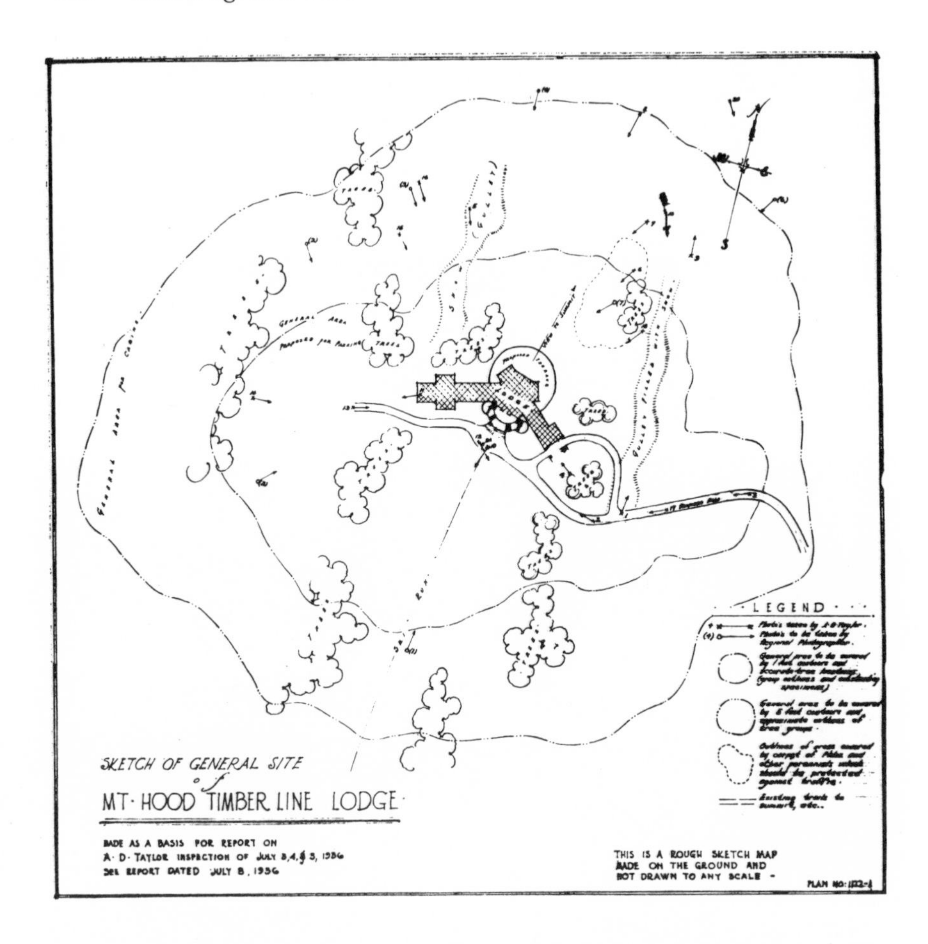

Fig. IV–155. Sketch of general site of Timberline Lodge, accompanying inspection trip report of A. D. Taylor, consulting landscape architect, July 8, 1936.

Fig. IV–156. Rendering of north elevation, Timberline Lodge, by Linn A. Forrest, 1936.

from gable-roofed dormers bisected by chimneys. Tiers of shed-roofed dormers are placed in front of the chimneys, and masonry walls terminate as buttresses at the ground line.

The average level of snowfall at Timberline is 20 feet. As prevailing winds are from the west, deposition tends to build up on the lee side, or, in effect, in the entry area inside the west wing. Skiers are provided access to the lodge by a portable tunnel which is put up each winter to shelter the ground level entrance.

Internal organization logically contains activities related to skiing in the ground floor, where the ski lounge, first aid and storage areas

Fig. IV–157. South elevation, Timberline Lodge.

make up the core. The ski grille and utility area are located in the east wing, which is serviced by a drive-through entrance at the end. The ski concession, gift shop and dormitory make up the west wing. At the first floor, or formal level, terraces on the north and south sides of the central pavilion are accessible from the main lounge. The dining room and kitchen are located in the east wing, and guest and economy rooms take up the first, second, and attic stories in the west wing.

Despite development of ski facilities on the opposite slope of the mountain in recent years, the demand for additional chair lifts and overnight housing at Timberline is pressing. Forest Service officials have

Fig. IV–158. Main lounge, Timberline Lodge.

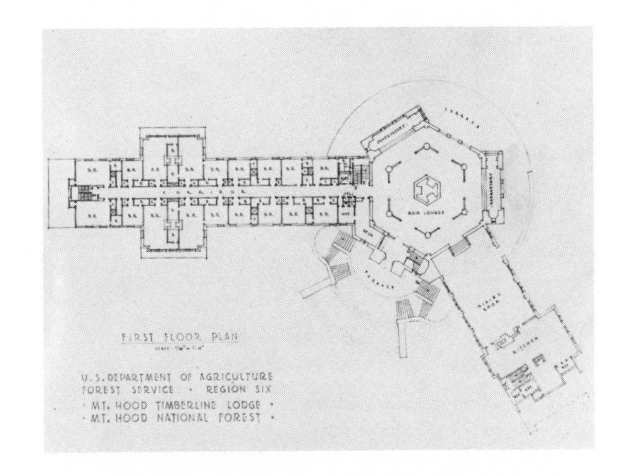

Fig. IV–159. First floor plan, Timberline Lodge.

begun to implement a plan to relieve the Lodge of its intensive use by skiers and, in the interest of economical management, to extend the capacity of the Lodge for full year-round use. A new convention wing is under construction on the northeast in a sympathetic but straightforward contemporary style consistent with qualities of the original structure. The interior, which has undergone minor remodeling over the years, will be returned to its original organization, with slight revision of use of certain of the public spaces of the ground level. Fittings and furniture are to be scrupulously preserved. Under careful consideration are certain separate ski facilities including a new lodge and hotel to be discreetly sited without intruding upon the aura of Timberline Lodge.

Natural wood finish of the interior, including pine, fir, and cedar, is a suitable foil for furnishings and decorative art which were intended to epitomize the forested region of the Northwest, its history and traditions. Newel posts formed of discarded cedar telephone poles were carved

Fig. IV–160. Guest bedroom, Timberline Lodge.

Fig. IV–161. "Eleanor Room," deluxe parlor bedroom with fireplace, Timberline Lodge.

Fig. IV–162. Amphitheatre, looking south, Timberline Lodge.

with likenesses of squirrels, coyotes, bears, badgers, and other forest animals and birds. Flagstone for the hearths of fireplaces at two levels in the six-sided chimney and for the exterior terraces was obtained from quarries near Stayton. Roughhewn pine and oak furniture was ornamented with wrought iron and rawhide. Lighting fixtures evocative of the Oregon Trail migration were formed of singletrees, wagon wheels, and ox yokes. Paintings and murals by noted Oregon artists decorated public spaces. Color schemes of the guest rooms were inspired by natural colors of meadows and forests. Each guest room had a distinct decorative scheme, and in several were displayed watercolor renderings of the wildflowers which inspired the particular scheme. Hand woven upholstery and bedspread textiles fashioned with Oregon flax and wool, and hand-appliqued cotton or linen draperies and hooked rugs were made of scraps and cuttings salvaged from WPA sewing units and discarded uniforms and blankets from camps of the Civilian Conservation Corps.[20]

The decorative scheme of Room 107 was based upon solomon seal. Draperies were decorated with solomon seal pattern on a dark brown ground. Colors of rugs, upholstery, and bedspreads were various combinations of salmon or pale brick color, brown and beige. The choice parlor bedroom was quickly titled the Eleanor Roosevelt Room after it was occupied by Mrs. Roosevelt during ceremonies on September 28, 1937, when President Franklin D. Roosevelt dedicated the Lodge as a "monument to the skill and faithful performance of workers on the rolls of the Works Progress Administration."

The importance of Timberline Lodge as a collaboration of creative arts activity in Oregon under WPA auspices scarcely can be overdrawn. Even performing arts were brought into play. The Federal Theatre produced a series of dances in connection with formal dedication of the Lodge in September, 1937. Against the backdrop of Mt. Hood were performed "Indian Celebration Dance," "Dance of the Flax Scutching Machine," and "Dance of the WPA Workers."[21] In 1939 plans for a Paul Bunyan summer festival at Timberline were laid in which Portland and Seattle Federal Theatre companies were to join forces in a production of E. P. Conkle's "Paul Bunyan and the Blue Ox" on the open stage of the amphitheatre.

Another of the significant recreational developments carried out in Oregon under federal sponsorship during this period was Silver Falls State Park. Acquisitions had begun in 1931 to preserve the canyons of the north and south forks of Silver Creek in the Cascade Range east of Salem. The park area contains a grouping of nine scenic waterfalls connected by forest trails.

A Civilian Conservation Corps camp was established at Silver Falls

20. U.S. Work Projects Administration, *Oregon: Color Schemes of the Bedrooms at Timberline Lodge* (ca. 1942).

21. Hallie Flanagan, *Arena: The History of the Federal Theatre* (New York, 1965), 298.

Fig. IV–163. Silver Falls State Park, Oregon.

Fig. IV–164. Civilian Conservation Corps enrollees disembarking from convoy trucks, Silver Falls State Park.

Fig. IV–165. Stove shelter, Silver Falls State Park.

in 1934. One of 17 such camps set up in Oregon State Parks under federal auspices during the Depression, and the longest-lived, the CCC camp at Silver Falls was intended, typically, to provide employment and boost construction of roads, parking areas, stone curbings, trails, footbridges, camp area buildings, and water systems to meet the anticipated future demand for recreational facilities. The organization of each camp included 200 enrollees, a supervisor, eight foremen, an Army captain assisted by enlisted personnel, a physician, education director, landscape architect, engineer and 15 skilled workers in forestry and other trades who instructed the enrollees. The National Park Service and the local park administrators cooperated in providing the technical supervision. Under normal procedure, plans and specifications for projects were furnished by the General Design Section of the CCC and approved by the National Park Service. Materials as well as sites were furnished by the local parks agency.[22]

In the tradition of the National Park Service, construction materials were purposefully selected to integrate with the park setting. Consistent use was made of locally quarried stone, logs, and shakes. So closely did the improvements hew to the ideal of rustic continuity with the surrounding landscape that polygonal triple unit stove shelters were constructed of logs with shake roofs, and water faucets and drinking fountains were installed in tree stumps.

The major structural project undertaken by the CCC at Silver Falls was the long, rectangular concession building measuring 112 by 65 feet, which is still in use today. It is a more developed variation of the conventional type of building erected by the CCC elsewhere. The traditional craftsmanship in these buildings makes them unusual and pleasing at a time in which lavish hand labor is economically infeasible. The ground story and large inside chimneys of the one-and-a-half-story building were constructed of random ashlar masonry. End walls of the short transverse wings at either end of the lodge were battered in a manner suggesting buttresses. The gable roof was carried on a system of dressed log plates and rafters. The loft was enclosed with vertical boards and battens. Supported by log posts, the roof extended over a veranda on one end, while the uncovered flagstone terrace was encompassed by log posts and rails. A solidly constructed suite of myrtlewood furniture for the lodge was commissioned under auspices of the Works Progress Administration. The logs were specially selected from a myrtle grove on the Chetco River in Curry County, and the lumber was kiln-dried by the Oregon State College Forestry Department.[23] In April, 1942, following completion of a substantial number of improvements during seven years of operation, the CCC camp at Silver Falls was closed and the buildings transferred

22. Chester H. Armstrong, *History of the Oregon State Parks 1917–1963* (Salem, 1965), 24–25.

23. W. A. Langille, "Silver Falls: Oregon's Premier State Park" (copy at OHS). Typescript (ca. 1946), p. 19.

Fig. IV–166. Drinking fountain, Silver Falls State Park.

Fig. IV–167. Silver Falls Lodge, Silver Falls State Park, circa 1942.

Fig. IV–168. Silver Falls Lodge under construction.

to the State.

The decades between 1920 and 1950 brought an unprecedented demand for recreation resorts throughout the region and, inevitably, a demand for improved roads to the more remote among them. The automobile and seemingly boundless fuel supplies made leisure travel possible for nearly everyone. Proliferation of auto camps and cabins gave motorists a choice between deluxe hotels and the most economical facilities. New types, such as motels and drive-in cafes, evolved to accommodate the motor car. In the Northwest, as elsewhere, construction of

Fig. IV–169. Interior, Silver Falls Lodge.

lodges and resort hotels in public holdings during the Depression provided an outlet for thousands of skilled and unskilled laborers, and craftsmen. The result was a number of distinctive buildings which draw our admiration because the quality of their craftsmanship is out of reach today in economic terms. The best resort architecture of the period was designed with a scientific as well as esthetic approach to site planning in the natural setting, which helped point the way to broader environmental awareness of the future.

Industrial Building

Lewis L. McArthur

Many changes in materials and methods of industrial construction occurred near the turn of the century. Steel shapes and sheets became commonplace in the 1890s and fire codes began to affect building prior to World War I. Kalamein doors were made locally by forming galvanized steel sheet to fit around wood door stiles and rails and then pulling the combination through a die on a draw bench. This made an airtight steel-to-wood bond and the door members were assembled with glue, pins and final soldering of the metal joint. Windows were made in the same manner and today both may still be seen, 60 years or older and still in good operating order. Sliding and swinging firedoors were made with three-ply tongue-and-groove wood cores nailed with cut nails and covered with terne plate[1] seamed from the traditional 14″ x 20″ sheet. These massive doors with their heavy track and self-closing hardware are frequently seen covering openings in masonry or concrete firewalls. Metal-clad doors were also used to provide protection against the elements or intruders. If paint were ignored too long, the coating and then the steel would succumb to rust, leaving the bare wood as sole guardian.

The most significant industrial building material was the ubiquitous galvanized corrugated sheet. While this had been made in the East and in Europe since before 1890, it had come to the Pacific Northwest prior to World War I for use in then modern mine and mill buildings. About 1920 manufacture began on the Pacific Coast and this, coupled with the rising cost of lumber and labor, caused a dramatic surge in the use of this mundane but efficient roofing and siding material. What it lacked in beauty, it made up in economy and utility. As coiled steel and continuous galvanizing lines were still decades away sheets were available only in commonly used cut lengths. The picture of the drying plant at Dundee shows a typical installation where these sheets were bevel-cut and spliced to provide exterior covering for an irregular structure. The Morrow County elevator utilizes a corrugated metal roof above a wall

1. Steel plate coated with an alloy containing up to 10% tin, the remainder being lead.

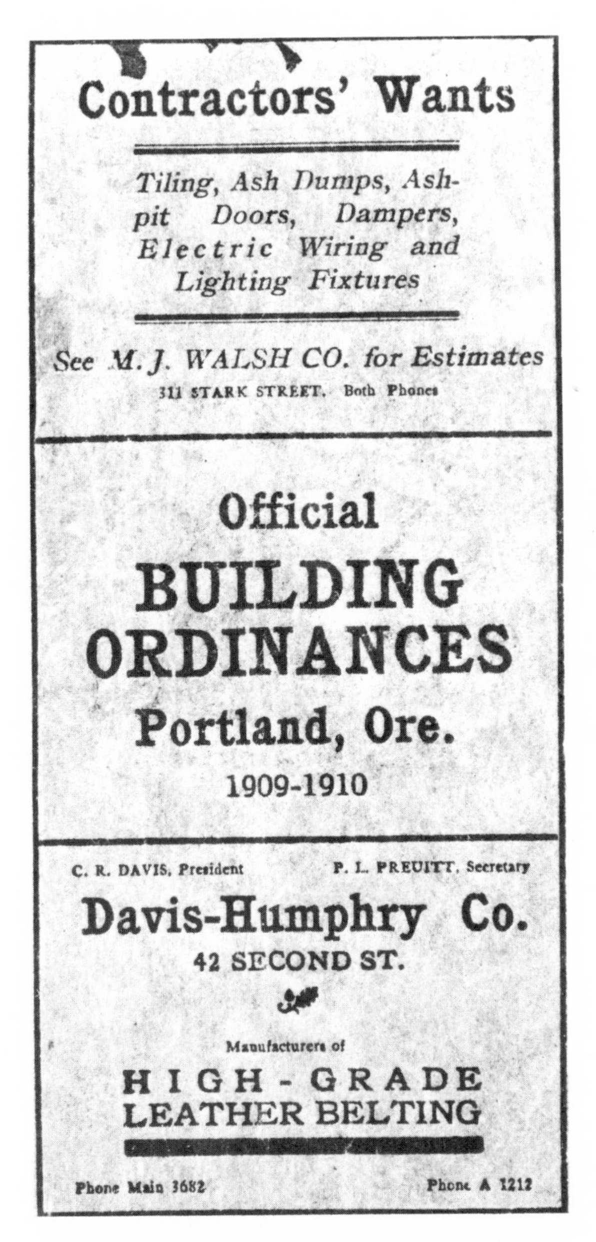

Contractors' Wants

Tiling, Ash Dumps, Ash-pit Doors, Dampers, Electric Wiring and Lighting Fixtures

See M. J. WALSH CO. for Estimates

311 STARK STREET. Both Phones

Official

BUILDING ORDINANCES

Portland, Ore.

1909-1910

C. R. DAVIS, President P. L. PREUITT, Secretary

Davis-Humphry Co.

42 SECOND ST.

Manufacturers of

HIGH-GRADE LEATHER BELTING

Phone Main 3682 Phone A 1212

Fig. IV–170. Cover of Portland Code, 1909–10. This was the personal copy of Ben F. Smith, Jr., who was with the Building Department for almost 40 years. Of the book's 156 pages, 50 plus the covers are filled all or in part with advertising. The remainder contains the building, plumbing, heating and electrical codes along with the piping regulations of the Portland Gas Company.

system of flat, stacked wood planks strong enough to resist the substantial interior lateral load.

The Edward Hines Lumber Company mill was built in Burns, Oregon in 1929. The two illustrations show an outstanding example of high-grade heavy timber construction, including wooden crane rail beams, covered with acres of galvanized corrugated steel sheets. Apparently the only steel in the framework, other than bolts and fasteners, were the vertical tension rods in the roof trusses. Lumber mills of today find their own product far too valuable to use for their own construction. As the output was shipped to Midwestern markets, the Hines mill was located at the railhead of the Union Pacific. Logs were brought from southern Grant County by a private rail line.

The advent of the motor car affected industrial construction in two entirely different ways. The mass production methods of Henry Ford drew upon the combined knowledge of raw material processing, manufacturing and component assembly techniques. The concurrent development of electric power and the internal combustion engine reduced the dependence upon water power sites or locations convenient to substantial coal or wood fuel sources. Mechanical material handling equipment moved rapidly and mills, no longer designed around a central "line shaft," found it more efficient to bring a power source to the machine rather than the other way around. Simultaneously, these same mass production methods were placing manufactured goods within the price range of an increasingly large market. This resulted in expansion of facilities to bring production closer to these new markets and the demand for larger industrial sites spread construction over large areas of agricultural land adjacent to the cities. While the basis for this lateral expansion was laid shortly after World War I, its architectural significance was not important until after World War II and it will be discussed later.

The most important construction innovation in the age of the motor car was transit or ready-mixed concrete. In Portland, Swigert, Hart and Yett made primitive mixer trucks to provide concrete for a paving job in the early 1920s. After the job was completed (about 1924) James A.C. Tait bought the 1½ and 2-yard truck-mounted mixers to supplement his sand and gravel business. Similar action was taking place all over the country and by the end of the decade site-mixed concrete was only being used on the largest jobs. The availability of transit-mixed concrete had a profound effect on industrial construction as pours could be made simultaneously over a wide area. Plant batching usually produced concrete superior to and more uniform than what normally resulted from the small, loosely supervised site mixer, but sometimes the reverse was true when poorly organized transit-mixed concrete replaced a large, well-controlled job site plant. While considerable masonry was used immediately prior to World War I, the developments in concrete exerted noticeable effects during the 1920s.

Concurrently, steel rolling mills were going into production in Seattle and reinforcing bar to complement the concrete in reinforced,

SPECIFY

ASPHALT FELT
ASPHALT PITCH } For your Felt and Gravel Roofs
DEADENING FELT
BUILDING PAPER } Costs very little more than Inferior Imitations

We carry a complete line of the above goods. Also rosin-sized Sheathing
Agents for P. & F. Corbin's High-Grade Finishing Hardware

HONEYMAN HARDWARE COMPANY
Corner Fifth and Alder Streets, Portland, Oregon

Copy No. 2

SPECIFICATIONS

of Material and Labor to be used in the erection of a

Four story and basement building for the
ST. FRANCIS INVESTMENT COMPANY

To be erected at Twenty-First and Hoyt Streets Portland, Oregon

W. L. MORGAN, Architect
322 Failing Building, Portland, Oregon

Plans and Specifications are the property of the Architect and must be returned when building is completed.

PORTLAND LUMBER COMPANY
MANUFACTURERS OF
Oregon Fir Lumber and Laths
Daily capacity 400,000. Special attention given local orders. Car and cargo shipments
Phones: Private Exchange 57; A 6035 Mills and General Offices: FOOT OF LINCOLN STREET

Telephone Main 5881 Residence Woodlawn 562
W. L. BUCKNER
Carpenter and Builder
Office and Store Fittings a Specialty—General Jobbing Promptly Attended to
No. 8 Eighth St. North, Near Ankeny, Facing Park Block PORTLAND, OREGON

N. P. SORENSEN, President L. B. MENEFEE, Vice President G. M. STANDIFER, Secretary-Treasurer F. C. YOUNG, Manager
West Side Lumber & Shingle Co.
Manufacturers of All Kinds of Fir, Spruce, Cedar Lumber and Shingles
Car and Cargo Shipments Special Attention given to Local Orders Prompt Delivery
Phones: A 3551, Main 5981 Mills and Office, FOOT OF MONTGOMERY STREET

M. J. WALSH CO.
Wiring and Lighting Fixtures
Tiling in all its Branches
311 STARK STREET, PORTLAND, OREGON
BOTH PHONES

Boynton Furnaces
Metal Frames and Sash, Metal Skylights, Cornices
Agents for Gladdin, McBean Co. Architectural Terra Cotta
Steel Ceiling Roofing of All Kinds
J. C. BAYER 204 MARKET STREET CORNER FRONT
Telephones: Main 461; A 4461

C. K. CLAGGETT
ELECTRICAL CONTRACTOR ELECTRICAL SUPPLIES
Phones: A 3395, Main 7811 NO. 74 SIXTH STREET, PORTLAND, OREGON

PORTLAND WIRE & IRON WORKS
Portland, Oregon

Portland Sheet Metal Works
CONTRACTORS FOR
Tin, Slate, Tile and Composition Roofing
Fire Proof Sheet Metal Windows
METAL DOORS METAL SKYLIGHTS
Architectural and Ornamental Sheet Metal Work
Factory, E. 7th and East Madison, Portland, Oregon

PROSPECT PARK THE CREAM OF IRVINGTON
Close in, with Fine Street Car Service, Sewers, Gas and Bull Run Water
Parked Streets, Asphalt Pavements, Cement Walks, Building Restrictions
MODEST PRICES EASY TERMS
ROUNTREE & DIAMOND
241 STARK STREET, CORNER SECOND

"IF YOU ARE BUILDING YOU NEED US"
POVEY BROS. GLASS COMPANY
Manufacturers of ART STAINED GLASS AND MIRRORS
Designs on Application
Phone Main 1521 FIFTH AND FLANDERS STREETS, PORTLAND, ORE.

H. REIMERS, CONTRACTOR BRICK AND CONCRETE WORK
Phone East 5452. Residence 515 Tillamook St.

Fig. IV–171. Front and back views of "Specification Binder." The promoter of this type of advertising does not identify himself, but he apparently supplied these in bulk, imprinted with architects' names and addresses. The faint pencil notation gives the street number as 526 NW 21st Ave. and adds, "also built at 742 SW Vista Ave."

Fig. IV–172. Sliding metal-clad fire door on masonry opening. A 1973 picture of a typical installation of 60 years ago.

poured-in-place buildings was available from local sources. Concrete buildings appeared in increasing numbers in the larger population centers to handle a variety of light manufacturing, distribution and storage tasks. They did not require the massive walls needed for solid masonry and were completely fireproof, as concrete columns and floors replaced the timber and plank normally used with brick construction. This method of building not only gave more usable floor space but also simplified fenestration and allowed for more flexible interior arrangements.

Fig. IV–173. Warehouse door, originally metal-clad. This is on the east wall of the Portland Bolt and Manufacturing Company building, NW 13th Ave. between Lovejoy and Kearney, Portland.

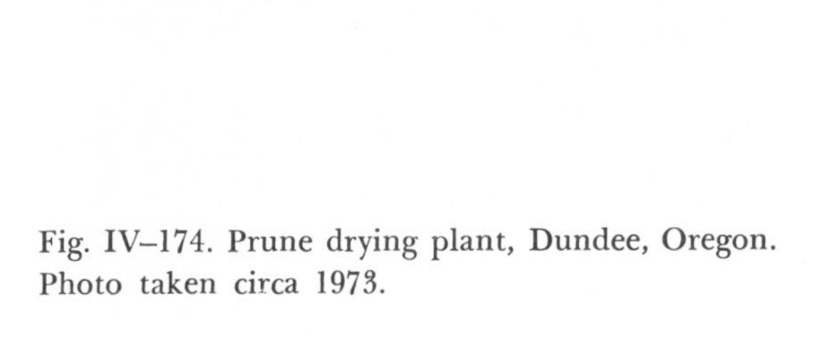

Fig. IV–174. Prune drying plant, Dundee, Oregon. Photo taken circa 1973.

Architect A. E. Doyle did early work in this field in the Portland area prior to World War I when he designed both the Ford Motor Company assembly building and the Meier and Frank Company warehouse. The former building, now occupied by the Metropolitan Printing Company, was completed in 1914 at a reported cost of $780,000. It is roughly rectangular, three stories and a basement, and structurally consists of reinforced concrete posts and floors. The interior columns are octagonal with substantial capitals to reinforce the floor-post connections. The floor forms were constructed of 12″ wide boards and, while the workmanship was neat, the lines are plainly visible. Exterior walls between the posts, stairwell walls, and certain other interior partitions are of four-inch hollow clay tile 12 inches square. Clay brick veneer marked by feature lines and minor ornamentation of terra cotta, along with

Fig. IV–175. Stacked plank grain elevator with galvanized corrugated roof, Morrow County, Oregon.

Fig. IV–176. Timber frame of Edward Hines Lumber Company mill, Burns, Oregon. Compare this with the wood framing in the Tillamook County blimp hangar (Fig. IV–185). Photo, 1929.

Fig. IV–177. Panorama of Edward Hines Lumber Company, Burns, Oregon.

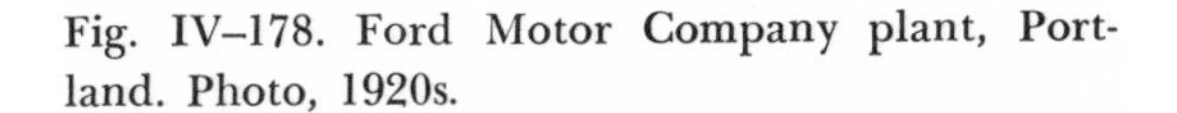

Fig. IV–178. Ford Motor Company plant, Portland. Photo, 1920s.

Fig. IV–179. Montgomery Ward Company plant, Portland. The integral corbels are designed for a still further addition. Photo, 1974.

substantial areas of large steel sash, complete the exterior. The roof deck is concrete. Originally it had a tile surface, for the plant was used to assemble automobiles which were taken by elevator to the roof for storage.

The Montgomery Ward Company warehouse and store in Portland is similar to the Ford building. It was originally built in 1922 as a 300-foot by 280-foot ell shaped building; a 120-foot by 180-foot wing was added in the 1930s to make the present "U". Round columns are used, and again, they have the large capitals for load distribution. The exterior walls between the posts have low clay brick panels surmounted by large steel sash units that completely fill the openings. It is interesting to note the integral corbels on the west wall designed to accommodate future additions. The building plans were prepared by Montgomery Ward Company under the direction of their engineer, W. H. McCaully.

At the same time, The American Can Company was building its complex on the property immediately to the east. The company prepared plans under the direction of G. G. Preis, Chief Engineer, 120 Broadway, New York City. The main factory is a four-story, 330-foot by 445-foot reinforced concrete post and floor building with large steel sash incorporating some steel filler panels. Considerable brick veneer is used for exposed walls. These three examples have a common denominator in the embryonic form of today's frame and curtain wall system.

In all these buildings, efficient design was obviously the paramount consideration. Evidently appearance was not entirely disregarded as architects of Doyle's calibre were commissioned to do purely industrial structures and engineers such as McCaully and Preis obviously were concerned with general configuration and continuity of form. One must remember, however, that 50 years ago visual excellence in reference to factories and warehouses usually meant a conformal building completely

Fig. IV–180. United States Steel Company office building, Portland. The larger trees and additional original planting are out of the picture to the right.

filling the allocated land area, hopefully with some minor ornamentation and without objectional excrescences.

The great majority of this 1920 and early 1930 construction adhered to practical engineering concepts, simple and repetitious construction, low maintenance materials, maximum land utilization and compactness by today's standards. One of the deviants appears to be the United States Steel Company's office and warehouse in Northwest Portland where a pleasant brick office complex is located amid a large, tree-studded lawn, all adjoining and contrasting with a massive five-bay steel frame and corrugated sheet warehouse. This well kept open space is the only such pre-World War II improvement the writer can recall in the area. It should be noted that the open space is confined to the point of a large gore corner, but the results are equally pleasant regardless of underlying cause.

Along with industrial building, the development of docks and terminals in Seattle, Tacoma and Portland must be examined. In the 1920s there was a common pattern including an extensive use of wood piles and heavy timber frame, all covered with corrugated sheets and divided by an occasional concrete through fire wall. Building monitors were usual for light and ventilation and large sliding or roll-up doors provided side access to the dock itself where railroad spurs held cars to handle inland shipments and receipts when ships were not actually

Fig. IV–181. Port of Portland, Terminal Number 2. This operated for many years as the Oceanic Terminal and is one of the older docks in Portland still in use. Notice the firewall through the roof at the base of the "U", and the rail spurs and loading platforms on the warehouse sides away from the water.

Fig. IV–182. Port of Portland, Berth 5, Portland. This 1973 picture shows the modern container handling facility.

loading and unloading. These terminals were primarily large on-dock warehouses for temporary storage of merchandise during transshipping. In the 1960s cargo containers were to require an entirely different terminal with large open space areas for trucks as well as rail spurs and the towering container cranes that are now so visible on the waterfront.

Besides waterfront terminals, special buildings appeared for grain elevators, food processing and cold storage plants. These often had one thing in common that added to the importance of their appearance—they tended to be isolated from other construction.

Jantzen Inc. presents an interesting history of operation and construction in the Pacific Northwest. The company was founded in 1910 as the Portland Knitting Company and in 1915 purchased and occupied the wood building which still stands at 4312 SE Stark Street. By 1920 they had run out of space and moved into the first of several buildings that were to occupy an area north of Sandy Boulevard near NE 20th Avenue. Starting in 1930 they developed the block bounded by NE 19th and 20th avenues and NE Glisan and Irving streets. Richard Sundeleaf

Fig. IV–183. Aerial view of four unit Jantzen Inc. building at NE 20th and Irving, Portland. The sawtooth skylights and bow string truss roof contrast with the conventional beam and purlin construction of the other two segments. The dyeing room in the right front corner has the same cast-in-place ornamentation but different fenestration to suit the full height, single story.

Fig. IV–184. First unit of Jantzen Inc. building, Portland. This picture taken in the late 1920s shows the details of the cast-in-place ornamentation. Molds, taken from a master, were placed within the forms.

was architect for this project which consisted of four entirely different buildings with a common exterior construction and detail.

The first unit in the southwest corner was reinforced poured-in-place concrete including interior columns, beams, floors and the distinctive sawtooth skylights. Bays varied, with a maximum span of 40 feet. Steel sash were used throughout, including the sawteeth. Next to be built was the southeast corner. This section was originally designed as a warehouse area. The exterior walls were matching poured-in-place concrete but the interior framing was wood post and beam, including the roof framing. The third unit was the north half which comprised two separate structures housing the spinning and dyeing operations. Again

Fig. IV–185. Interior of blimp hangar built for U.S. Naval Air Station, Tillamook, Oregon. This wood framed hangar was put in service in the late fall of 1942. Since the war, it has been used for various enterprises including lumber storage. To appreciate the scale, note the rail spur and four boxcars.

Fig. IV–186. Trentwood plant, Kaiser Aluminum & Chemical Corporation, Spokane. This aluminum rolling mill was built by the Defense Plant Corporation in 1942 and was operated by ALCOA during World War II. When built, it was the largest rolling mill west of the Mississippi River and had 53 acres under one roof. Construction was typical of many large war plants with concrete walls, steel roof framing with wood deck, and built-up roof.

the matching exterior wall construction was used with the typical steel sash. The northwest part housing the spinning department is two stories and the second floor area has a nominal 100-foot clear span, using bow string trusses with arched top chords cut from heavy timbers and spliced at third points, which gives a completely clear floor for the spinning machines. This second floor is reinforced concrete supported on concrete columns, round like all the other columns but lacking the identical precision of those cast in today's sonotubes. The final quarter is the same height as the other portions but all one story to accommodate the dyeing room. Here we have a fourth type of roof construction: glue-laminated beams, timber joists and heavy plank decking. The beams were the longest "glu-lams" that had been produced up to that time and Mr. Sundeleaf was the first to specify waterproof glue (because of concern over the possible effects of moisture from the dyeing operation). The entire structure is an instructive example of maintaining design integrity while varying construction to suit manufacturing requirements and changing relative costs.

Much of the industrial expansion from 1939 until the end of the war was accompanied by such a sense of urgency that speed and availability of materials precluded much attention to esthetics. Many buildings of this period still are in use today. While some remain unchanged, others have been improved by means often as simple as paint in an appropriate color scheme.

World War II does not make a clean division point; the pent-up building demand after the war carried mobilization and wartime prac-

Fig. IV–187. Swan Island, Portland. This picture, taken in 1948, shows the north end of the island with considerable ship building debris still visible. The buildings are inexpensive wood frame, built during the war when speed of construction and economy of steel were paramount considerations.

Fig. IV–188. Swan Island, Portland. A 1974 picture of the same area. New, permanent buildings now occupy the middle ground. The area is still heavily built for industrial occupancies but most buildings have grass and plantings and a green strip with trees is appearing along both main access roads.

tices well through the balance of the 1940s. Some wartime plants shifted easily to peacetime production and discovered that additional facilities were required immediately. These often were merely extensions of inexpensive wartime construction, although Boeing in Seattle did develop some distinctive structures. In other cases, new industry moved in alongside wartime activity and created extensions of the prosaic commonplace.

A great deal of wartime construction was of timber frame with corrugated sheet or wood siding. Buildings thus utilized locally available materials of relatively low cost. Some larger plants required steel crane runways but even in these cases the building frame often was of timber. The aerial view of Swan Island in Portland taken in the late 1940s shows the remnants of the once large shipyard replete with woodframe structures. The open space was paved with asphalt or gravel and plantings were non-existent. A recent photograph of the same spot shows the changes wrought by 25 years. This comparison emphasizes the fundamental difference between pre- and post-World War II industrial building and the emerging concept of buildings designed as part of an area complex with open space, public areas and visual appeal.

Parks and Gardens of Western Oregon

Wallace Kay Huntington

The transformation of the Northwest landscape from natural to man-made began when trapping ceased to be the main industry and agriculture supplanted it. Western Oregon and Washington in their primeval state were covered with a growth of Douglas fir, cedar, and hemlock so suffocating that vast areas were populated by nothing except rodents and birds. Browsing animals were thus confined to grassland perpetuated by river flood plains and indigenous man, dependent upon fish and game, did not—as is generally believed—wander through trackless sylvan glades stocked with abundant game, but instead scrounged for food along shorelines hemmed in by inhospitable forests.

Today the valleys and plains of the Northwest are comprised almost exclusively of man-made landscape; even the colors and textures of the fields are dictated by the economic potential of the soil. These changes occurred with incredible rapidity during the last decades of the 19th century. Though definitive, the change in appearance was largely superficial and due to the imposition of a different botanical selection on the land. Although usually done to increase the productivity of the soil, esthetic considerations were often a determining factor in botanical selection. The view down the main street of Antelope, flanked by Lombardy poplars that dramatize the distant treeless plains (as well as serving as a wind screen) is only one instance of the impact of an alien species on the character of the landscape. The elms that were the dominant street tree in Portland in the 19th century determined the scale and character of that city's boulevards just as the grove of sequoias at Brevoort or the plantings of Monterey cypress at Oysterville gave distinction to those municipalities.

It was the 20th century however that would make the more substantive changes to the land, climaxing in the construction of the great dams which involved the reshaping of mountains and the manipulation of rivers with a consequent transformation of thousands of acres of the landscape. The process of resculpturing the land to enhance its worth was undertaken early in the century in both Portland and in Seattle, where whole hills were sluiced down.

If property speculation accounted for a warping of the landscape

Fig. IV–189. Antelope, Oregon, 1962. The introduction of alien plants such as the Lombardy poplar alter the character of the landscape.

for man's use, highway construction to an even greater extent would change the face of the earth. A Good Roads movement had begun in the Northwest by the late 19th century and in the first decades of the 20th century, Oregon had ardent supporters of the movement. Especially influential was Sam Hill, wealthy railroad attorney, who having failed to stimulate Washington interests in a Columbia River highway along the north shore, turned his attention to Oregon. Following a visit of the entire Oregon legislature to Hill's estate at Maryhill in 1913, a State Highway Department was established. Hill had powerful support in Multnomah County as well: Simon Benson, John B. Yeon, and the publishers of both the *Oregonian* and *Oregon Journal*, Henry L. Pittock and C. S. Jackson. Since highway construction would be financed by county funds at the time, such local support was critical.

Though the benefits of a scenic highway through the Gorge was not in dispute, there was considerable opposition to the appointment of S. C. Lancaster as consultant and engineer. Lancaster, advocating a generous 24-foot roadway and maximum grades of 5%, was progressive indeed when comparing his specifications to an earlier proposal calling for a 16-foot roadbed and grades up to 17%.

Lancaster was well-known to Sam Hill and had in fact accompanied him to Europe on a previous occasion involving road construction in Seattle. Together they had studied alignment and construction of renowned roads in Europe, including the Rhine highway and the Grande Corniche along the Cote d'Azure.

Both Hill and Lancaster were pragmatists in developing scenic areas:

> From the perspective of the 1970s and our increasing concern with ecology, wilderness preservation, and esthetic harmony, the glaring mistakes and neglect of the past rise up to haunt us. It has become commonplace among environmentalists to think of technology as an enemy and to speak of engineers as agents of destruction. The cliche is apt and the opprobrium they receive is deserved in many instances, but it is only fair to acknowledge that some pioneering highway engineers were guided by sound conservation principles and even wove some artistry into their road work. Foremost among these in the Pacific Northwest was Samuel Christopher Lancaster.[1]

Actually Lancaster occupied a middle ground in conservation at a time when the lines were drawn rather sharply between the extremes of those advocating exploitation of nature and those like John Muir, opposed to any manipulation of the wilderness. In fact it was remarkable at the time that such a consensus was reached on the necessity of preserving the scenic grandeur of the Columbia Gorge. Hill envisaged the highway as the American equivalent of the Rhine and Lancaster held an almost mystical reverence for the scenery. Commencing in October, 1913 with the enlightened support of County Roadmaster John B. Yeon, serving without pay, work progressed in spite of criticism, shortage of funds and harassment by the county surveyor, and the highway was opened to traffic on schedule in 1915, though the decision to surface it with bituminous paving delayed the dedication until 1916.

Any history of engineering in America would obviously take note of Lancaster's achievement; not only was it the first paved highway in the Northwest, it established precedents in alignment and construction that would be emulated for decades throughout the region. But the engineering aspects were no more impressive than the epic sensitivity to the landscape. Using skilled Italian masons to set the dry-wall construction and face the bridges with indigenous stone, Lancaster blended the roadway into the natural terrain with consummate skill. What could have been the most devastating engineering project in the state was an enlightened exercise in taste that enhanced the view. Even the "beautification" efforts of Portland citizens who planted rose gardens and exotic

1. Ronald J. Fahl, "S. C. Lancaster and the Columbia River Highway: Engineer as Conservationist," *Oregon Historical Quarterly* (June, 1973), 102.

Fig. IV–190. Columbia River Highway by S. C. Lancaster, circa 1916. The first paved highway in the Northwest, conceived as a scenic route, preserved native vegetation and topographic features of the Gorge.

Fig. IV–191. Columbia River Highway. Native stone, used sympathetically, blended the construction into the landscape and featured innovative craft techniques.

Fig. IV–192. Columbia River Highway. Stone facing and organic forms softened the impact of construction and set a precedent of excellence for "Good Roads" advocates.

plants along the right-of-way failed to detract seriously from the integrity of the highway. It set precedents other than engineering in being the first Oregon highway where roadside parks were established, and it stimulated as well the first successful battle against billboard blight. To appreciate Lancaster's benign touch one has only to witness the contrasting Forest Service road on the Rogue River below Agness. It shows what total and irremedial devastation of the natural beauty of a river can be accomplished by thoughtless stewards of the land.

With such a precedent, the Oregon Highway Commission might have been expected to thereafter emulate Lancaster's skills, and to some extent it did. Chief among the later employees of the Highway Commission was C. B. McCullough, who joined the staff in 1919 and

Fig. IV–193. Columbia River freeway I 80 N. Expediency dominates the alignment and destruction is thoughtless and indiscriminate.

served for 16 years as planner and supervisor of construction. The notable steel bridge over Yaquina Bay at Newport, the Rogue River Bridge at Gold Beach, and the Coos Bay Bridge at North Bend are but a small sampling of his innovative designs and light touch on the landscape.

Following World War II, in a period of crucial activity, designs by the Highway Commission showed a marked deterioration in esthetic awareness; The new Columbia River Highway, I-80 N, cut an uncompromisingly destructive swath along the river that destroyed important topographic features and counted expediency as the total criterion for alignment. Overpass and bridge designs suffered as well, accounting for such clumsy engineering exercises as the Marquam Bridge in Portland but reaching a nadir at Astoria, where an incredibly ill-conceived bridge of monumentally awkward proportions did everything conceivable to debase the site. This was, perhaps, the turning point, for by the late 1960s overpass and bridge design out of Salem experienced a renaissance (responding, too, to informed "outside" professional suggestions) that produced the handsome Fremont Bridge in Portland and a series of overpass designs on I-5 that again bear witness that engineering can be an art form—an asset to the landscape.

The architectural profession proliferated after World War I and though architectural education continued to stress Beaux Arts designs for great country houses and civic centers, in actuality more and more architects found their practice entailing designs for relatively modest houses and commercial "street" architecture. Though architecture evolved along more egalitarian principles, landscape architecture continued as an elitist service—the prerogative of the wealthy—and the fashionably

Fig. IV–194. Yaquina Bay Bridge, Newport, 1936, by C. B. McCullough. Engineering as a work of art, as practiced by a worthy successor but not an emulator of Lancaster.

Fig. IV–195. Yaquina Bay Bridge, Newport. Tensile strength of steel juxtaposed against massive "exclamation marks" of concrete shows contrasting empathy for engineering materials.

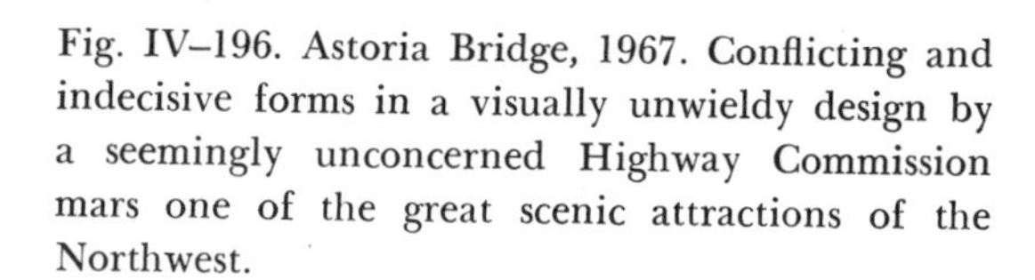

Fig. IV–196. Astoria Bridge, 1967. Conflicting and indecisive forms in a visually unwieldy design by a seemingly unconcerned Highway Commission mars one of the great scenic attractions of the Northwest.

clumsy houses of the prosperous middle class, though architecturally designed, were generally landscaped by their owners and quite often shared the ingenuous garden conceits of more modest homes. A middle class city garden in the 1920s was, by mutual consent, expected to contribute to the ambience of the street. Since front porches were an essential part of the architecture and served the outdoor living space requirement, the front yard was the primary landscape concern. The back yard, with its clothes lines fenced or screened, was often a utilitarian space for multiple use. Though Portland, with its small

Fig. IV–197. Portland, S. W. King Street, circa 1920. Power poles begin to disfigure the gracious proportions of an affluent neighborhood that has coordinated its street tree plantings.

Fig. IV–198. Portland, N. W. 25th Street, circa 1925. Ingenuous but enthusiastic home landscaping stressed decorative improvements to the street when front porches were still outdoor living areas.

blocks, generally ignored service alleys, many cities provided access to the rear for deliveries and pick-ups that otherwise might mar the gentility of the neighborhood. The cosmetic landscape of the front was therefore *de rigeur* and in addition to the entrance walk, and perhaps the driveway, of necessity it displayed beds of flowering shrubs, a foundation planting of evergreens that skirted the house with greenery that "softened" the architectural lines and prudently hid the concrete foundation (and incidentally blocked any light into the basement). Existing trees were often saved on larger lots, but they were soon supplemented by currently fashionable flowering trees—weeping cherries and dogwoods. Often, if a steep bank resulted from the siting, it was adorned with a rockery—a most fashionable adornment in the 1920s—where displays of trailing shrubs and rock plants contributed a flamboyant spring display of undisciplined color. The spirit of co-operation in beautifying the neighborhood resulted in considerable continuity in residential streets; shade trees of a single species stretched for blocks and roses were planted by the thousands in front yard displays.

The contrast between the city house and the country estate was vast and the splendid Lloyd Frank estate of Portland illustrates the difference in scale, style, and sophistication of gardens created by amateurs and those created by professionals; it also illustrates that the desire for privacy varied according to social condition. The front porch and street-oriented house of the middle income city dweller was unacceptably public to the wealthy. Herman Brookman, the architect and garden designer of the Frank estate, was trained in the New York office of Harry T. Lindeberg, where he learned the art of catering to the taste of wealthy Long Island property owners. The 60-acre estate was Brookman's first Oregon project, commenced in 1924, and is of

Fig. IV–199. Lloyd Frank estate, Portland, 1924, by Herman Brookman. Eclecticism in the 1920s, so often drained of inspiration, becomes vital and innovative in the hands of a fine architect and garden designer.

Fig. IV–200. Lloyd Frank estate. Geometric clarity and a grand scale manipulated by a master designer turn a sloping hillside into a work of art.

incomparable quality in its sensitivity to site, quality of workmanship, and free adaptation of eclectic forms.

Choosing a socially acceptable French style of architecture, he enlivened it with skillfully detailed brickwork and sculpture, imaginative window treatment, and dramatic roof forms. Discarding the static symmetry of houses that are usually designed to dominate a central garden axis, Brookman boldly extended terraces and balustrades into a natural stand of second-growth Douglas fir and capitalized on the tension that is created between a formal garden and an asymmetrical house. The axis from the house leads ultimately to Mount Hood but incorporates on consecutive stepped terraces a waterfall, reflecting pool, matching gazebos, arbors, and monumental stairs. Manipulating land forms on such a scale involved a munificent client—which Brookman had—but avoiding an ostentatious vulgarity involved a sense of taste that was too often lacking in pre-depression estates.

Employing the finest craftsmen available and supplementing the masterful plan with intricate details, the house and garden represent the best of the age and invite close examination of such imaginative incidentals as the wrought iron "Monkey Gate" leading to the conservatory, or the stylized eagle, with its "art deco" styling silhouetted against the sky. Using local brick and stone, the garden easily complements the natural colors of the landscape and seems less alien than

Fig. IV–201. Lloyd Frank estate. Cross axis below the twin gazebos carries native stone into native planting.

Fig. IV–202. Lloyd Frank estate. The glass house, as a functional accoutrement of a great estate, escapes the eclecticism of the formal architecture.

Fig. IV–203. Lloyd Frank Estate. "Monkey Gate" on the conservatory shows Brookman's infinite attention to details of craftsmanship that gave depth to Oregon's grandest garden.

the architectural style would seem to imply. Like many newcomers to the West, Brookman must have found the "shaggy" quality of the Douglas fir disappointing. This would account for the use of a "facer" planting of tidier or more romantic evergreens such as Colorado spruce and deodar cedar along the axis. Ironically, though the house is in a secure and traditional style, the conservatory was evidentally deemed a functional necessity and is so free of encumbering academic details that it appears surprisingly "modern" in its context.

In the 1920s, landscape architecture in the Northwest began to evolve from an elitist state and, as architecture had done earlier, became

Fig. IV–204. Keith Powell garden, Salem, 1929–40, by Lord and Schryver. Subtle spatial relationships and a relaxed formality give spirit to a 20th century garden surrounding a Victorian house.

Fig. IV–205. Sir James and Lady McDonald garden, Portland, by Lord and Schryver. An intimate relationship between house and garden, an invention of the middle decades of the century, effectively utilized by a skilled design team.

concerned with more modestly scaled domestic architecture. The Portland directory listed six landscape architects in 1920, and though the title could be adopted by anyone wishing to use it, some were qualified professionals and there is a notable trend toward greater sophistication of design and a closing of the time lag between East and West during the decade.

One of the milestones in the history of the Northwest garden design was the 1929 founding of the office of Lord and Schryver in Salem. Both Elizabeth Lord and Edith Schryver had been educated in New England; Edith Schryver had worked for the prestigious firm of Ellen Shipman in New York City and together (with Schryver concentrating on design and construction and Lord specializing in plant composition) they brought to Oregon an intellectual Eastern command of craft and style combined with an instinctive sense of taste. For the next four decades the office designed and supervised work in Seattle, Tacoma, Portland and Salem. Though the volume of work was comparatively small, the quality was consistently high. The recognition that their work so richly merited was never properly awarded; eschewing the cliches of shifting fashion and having for clients a monied aristocracy both conservative and publicity-shy, the gardens remained largely unpublished—too remote from public view and too subtle for popular taste. Their reputation was with the cognoscenti.

Eclecticism was the prevailing mode for architecture in the 1930s and 1940s, and the Lord and Schryver gardens were largely formal designs adapted to demanding sites where sloping property and existing trees precluded the standard formal plans used in Colonial Revival schemes. Though using axial relationships and compartmented spatial divisions, their designs could never be anticipated for there was ever an element of surprise.

The Powell garden in Salem, added to the late 19th century Dr. Luke Port house, was commenced in 1929 and added to for over a decade. The garden has gone through serious vicissitudes and changes. Its original conception was an ingenious series of related spaces surrounded by woodland and contained by a variety of framing devices that formed a structural skeleton: boxwood and holly hedges, fences, iron railings and shrubbery borders. Spatially one of the most interesting gardens in Oregon, it also had the highest quality of accessories: the Oriental jar featured in the "Scroll" garden was purchased in the Philippines by Lord and Schryver for their client; the decorative wrought iron gazebo from the rose garden at the Lewis and Clark Exposition was used as the terminus of the main north-south axis. Few gardens in the Northwest at the time had other than the standard urns and bird baths of commercial quality.

The accomodation of the landscape to outdoor living was of special concern to Lord and Schryver; the porch, an architectural transition to the outdoors, was often remote from the garden and ineffective in its relationship; the terrace of Sir James and Lady McDonald's garden shows a landscape architect's solution to relating

Fig. IV–206. Elizabeth Lord garden, Salem, 1930–40, by Lord and Schryver. Infinite variations in color and texture of plant material displayed against a sophisticated arbor and trellis background raise plant composition to an art form.

Fig. IV–207. Elizabeth Lord garden. A compartmentalized scheme of spatial organization that avoids static relationships despite a Beaux Art design discipline.

house and garden in a more intimate fashion.

Though the Powell and McDonald gardens were comparatively large, Lord and Schryver's meticulous detailing was available to clients developing no more than a city lot, and the structural clarity of formal walks, panels of lawn, boxwood edging and allees of flowering shrubs were utilized to dignify Georgian, French Provincial or Tudor town houses. Plant composition with them was an art form—albeit fragile and transient—and in the Salem garden of Elizabeth Lord we have, still surviving into the 1970s, a lost art. So subtle are the foliage colors and textures and so skillfully arranged is the succession of bloom that, like an impressionist painting, it may at first seem deceptively simple but upon closer examination the incredible command and knowledge of their media—plants instead of paint—is truly stunning. Here the geometry of the compartmented scheme is at its most effective and the quality of design in arbors and fences at its classic finest. Anyone who conceives of a formal garden as being static has only to study the calculated interplay of spatial relationships in this tour de force of garden design.

The gardens of Lord and Schryver were demanding of the client; they imposed a program of maintenance and implied a knowledge of plants on the part of the client that might well intimidate more casual gardeners, or those unwilling to pay for professional maintenance. The extensive work of Florence and Walter Gerke served a wider clientel. Though dealing with a similar program, sloping sites, existing trees, and often dramatic views, the Gerke designs, when occasion or client demanded, were less architectural and less often compartmented.

Though similarly rich in plant material, lawns less often appear as geometric shapes, but are used rather for continuity and movement. Florence Holmes Gerke was the first woman in Oregon to practice landscape architecture; the long practice of the husband and wife team bridged the era of evolving styles. Now, for the first time, "contemporary" architecture imposed new demands on landscape architects trained in the Beaux Arts tradition, and the Gerkes, using free lawn forms and asymmetrical plant groupings, handled traditional and contemporary styles with equanimity.

Fig. IV–208. Knute Qvale garden, Portland, 1959, by Florence and Walter Gerke. Contemporary architecture demanded informal paved areas and asymmetrical forms free of traditional association.

Fig. IV–209. Glenn Duncan garden, Portland, 1959, by Florence and Walter Gerke. The abstract form of the raised pool coping serves as a sitting ledge for casual entertaining.

Fig. IV–210. Lambert Gardens, Portland, by Tommy Thompson. A sumptuous commercial garden of the mid-depression years that appealed to an audience hungering for vicarious extravagance.

Fig. IV–211. Henry Cabell garden, Portland, circa 1935, by Tommy Thompson. Formal in its plan and conservative in its details, the botanically rich series of terraces indicate an impatience with academic solutions to design.

Though his Oregon career was brief, the work of Tommy Thompson in southern California has been well-known almost from his debut as the designer of the Santa Anita racetrack gardens. Though best known in Portland for his design of Lambert Gardens, a commercial nursery that supported a spectacularly colorful formal garden, his best work was the more sedate but more adventurous design for the Henry Cabell garden done in the 1930s. Angling the axis of the design so that it meets the deck of the house in a diagonal relationship, he utilizes traditional forms and materials to turn a steeply sloping site into an alluring series of formal elements so visually compelling and botanically interesting as to almost negate the disadvantages of the contours.

The career of John Yeon, which begins in the 1930s, was like a pyrotechnic display; unlike his contemporary Pietro Belluschi, whose architectural career shone as a continual illumination, Yeon's diversified achievements burst individually as against a night sky, isolated in time and space. Nothing in the Northwest tradition of architecture or man-made landscape prepares us for the mid-1930s garden designed for Mrs. John B. Yeon. Its audacious geometric form is as formal as any element conceived by Le Notre, but there the comparison ends. One seeks for prototypes: the use of bold outcroppings of skillfully arranged rocks suggests momentarily the Japanese garden but the absence of

Fig. IV–212. Henry Cabell garden. Intimate spaces and a relaxed formality give continental flair to a terraced hillside.

Fig. IV–213. Mrs. John B. Yeon garden, Portland, 1935, by John Yeon. A garden design without precedent in the Northwest, the independence from Beaux Arts tradition and mastery of form result in a major work of American garden design.

Fig. IV–214. Mrs. John B. Yeon garden. Though suggestive of Frank Lloyd Wright and having elements of the Japanese garden, the stunning originality of the conception is both underivative and unhistorical.

contrived supporting planting precludes the Orient as an elemental source of inspiration. Perhaps the early work of Frank Lloyd Wright is suggested, for the broadly horizontal wall forms with their grillwork of Roman brick enhance the site with Wright's assurance of form, so ably demonstrated in his Prairie School houses; but Yeon's forms, though similarly sculptural, pre-date Wright's more plastic experiments such as the Johnson Wax Company office and the V. C. Morris store in San Francisco.

The Yeon garden as a work of landscape art was unique in its separation from any related structure. Unlike any previous Northwest garden, it can be evaluated as an independent art form; as such it would seem to be historically the first instance where the artist's major concern was in exploring original landscape forms. Such a break with the Beaux Arts tradition was innovative indeed in the 1930s and the more remarkable for being a mature work of art rather than a tentative evolutionary step in a new direction. In Oregon it was the beginning of contemporary landscape design, but its impact was broader: published widely, it was an early indication of a viable regional architecture that surpassed in originality meretricious eclectic work then currently illustrated in Eastern publications.

Next to Timberline Lodge, the Watzek house is possibly Oregon's most famous structure. Though continually a private residence and seen by relatively few people, its publication throughout North America and Europe made it, within the decade, a classic of contemporary design. In one respect the Watzek house is the ultimate 20th century anachronism; the exigencies of a technocratic society had accounted for an inevitable specialization in architecture and related fields; the architect, engineer, landscape architect, and interior designer—all with overlapping areas of concern—had already formed a "design team," a de-personalized committee of specialists working toward a compromised solution to the problem. In contrast, the 1937 Watzek house was a Renaissance design with Yeon functioning as architect, landscape architect, interior designer, furniture designer, even to the ultimate participation—personally helping to lay the stone masonry in the courtyard. It is consequently difficult to discuss the garden of the Watzek house as though it were a separate entity from the architecture; no previous Oregon house and garden had ever been conceived with such mutual interdependence and for that reason it was the most harmonious and intellectual synthesis of disparate arts that had been achieved in so-called "contemporary" American design.

The automobile in the 1930s could hardly have been considered as the potential menace that it would later become; the incompatibility of the automobile *esthetic* versus the *esthetic* of house and garden must certainly have been apparent to any sensitive person, but any solution to the friction between conflicting elements had been largely ignored. The circular drive, the turn-around, and the forecourt had all functioned in the accommodation of the carriage, but the same solutions to circulation were less satisfactory when applied to the disruptive and alien form of the automobile.

In one of the first instances where the automobile was completely relegated to an area of its own, Yeon turned the house away from the

Fig. IV–215. Aubrey Watzek residence and garden, Portland, 1937, by John Yeon. Oregon's most famous residence employs an atrium to control space and climate and to isolate the automobile from its pervasive corruption of gracious living.

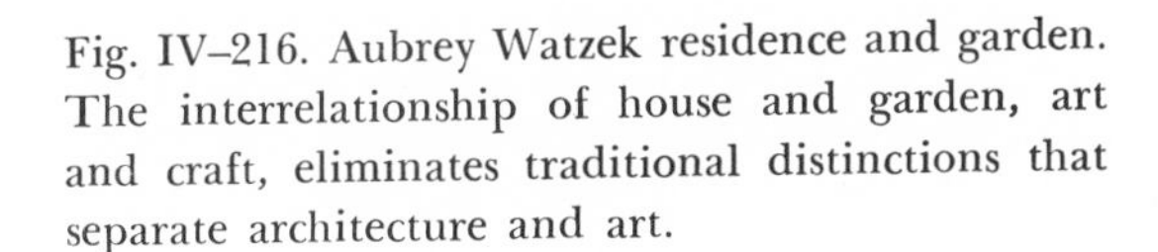

Fig. IV–216. Aubrey Watzek residence and garden. The interrelationship of house and garden, art and craft, eliminates traditional distinctions that separate architecture and art.

vehicular approach. Passing through the single door that connects the garage and parking area with the atrium, one leaves the machine world contained and subservient. Despite its logic, the house built around an atrium was an innovative introduction to the Northwest; it had functioned extremely well for the Romans, who also faced many urban problems; the domus, which evolved to minimize social, esthetic, and climatic problems, was a happy instance of form following function, and resulted in serene, self-contained, protected interior space. Though physical security could hardly have been a consideration in the choice of an atrium design for the Watzek house, esthetic and climatic considerations were as pertinent in the 1930s in the Northwest as they had been in the first centuries of the Roman Empire; the facility of the atrium in trapping winter sun and deflecting wind is obvious; privacy and control of the view from the inner windows are extra dividends, but in the design of the Watzek house the psychological impact of the spatial sequences was also a major consideration. Although it has an unparalleled view of Mt. Hood centered in the living room window, no indication of this ultimate reward is initially suggested. Passing from parking court, to atrium, to foyer and along a corridor that faces into the atrium, the view is saved as the *pièce de resistance.* The contrast between the enclosed spaces of the court and the compression of the lowered hallway ceiling contributes to the stunning impact of a magnificent room that belongs to the mountain. No panorama could be as satisfying as the contrived view that actually screens out what could have been an expansive view of the city and the Cascade Range. A projecting terrace with a modular design in grass and stone carries the eye through the window; the landscape directly in the foreground of the mountain is otherwise without incident—alpine in the reticence of its exclusively native plant material.

The garden of the atrium has an ineffable quality that escapes analysis by historic precedent; though partaking of both Roman and Japanese concepts, it is not vaguely eclectic. Only the stress on horizontal line suggests an affinity with the style of Frank Lloyd Wright, but the weight and eccentricities of Wright's domestic architecture are notably lacking.

The contrast between closed space and infinite expanse that works so effectively in the west-east progression from entrance to living room is again employed in the contrasting views to the north and south. The dining room, with its north exposure looking into deep woods, is a closed view. The floor-to-ceiling glass presses against branches of vine maple, fern fronds, and trilliums so two-dimensionally displayed that the scene seems as unreal and as graphic as a landscape depicted on a Japanese screen. From the rooms facing south, or from the open passage connecting the atrium to the outer garden, one's eye is led into the landscape, one's attention is directed by a formal axis of lawn, actually linking the formal elements of the architecture to the progressively relaxed forms of the garden—a subtle transition from man-made to natural forms.

The Victor Jorgenson house of 1939 anticipates the weightless quality and pavilion-like forms of the Portland Visitors' Information Center. Like the Watzek house, it also has the persistent concern for making a psychological break with the street, the automobile and their attendant incongruities. Here, however, the transition is accomplished by a dramatic covered passageway that leads to a house insulated from the world in an oasis of rain forest. Like the corridor in a cloister, with a wall on one side and an architectural framework on the other, the views are so harmoniously framed and so dramatically altered by the transcendant quality of light filtered through the foliage that the passage is less like a walk through the woods than like the approach to the final station in a pilgrimage.

Here again, nature is deceptively "improved" and the seemingly natural forms and textures have been manipulated—the vine maple wired to accentuate horizontal planes, the coarser native weeds eliminated, the dead fronds cut annually from the ferns, etc. Though basically a green world, the intense orange trumpets of the tiger lily seasonally highlight the monochromatic scheme. Traditionally Western man has been obsessed with a passion to dominate nature; Christianity, placing man at the apex of a hierarchy, never left any doubt that the world was at his disposal. By comparison, the Jorgenson garden is Eastern in its concept; only a mind imbued with a sense of the harmony between man and nature could have created it, and though with none of the cliches that have come to represent the Japanese garden to Western eyes, it has, in fact, distilled the essence of a philosophy evolving from Taoism and flowering in the Zen temples of Japan.

The Portland Visitors' Information Center was the one public building designed by Yeon. Given such a chaotic environment to surmount, the screened garden with its view of the waterfront framed by an arbor above and flanking pavilions was a triumph of urbanity. In 1948 at the time of its construction, the retail nurseries in the Northwest carried few, if any, native plants and Yeon's choice of vine maple, madrone, salal and Oregon grape was an innovative planting scheme—the first public use of such materials in Oregon. Faced with such a heretical urban landscape, volunteers from the Men's Garden Club were unanimous in their displeasure over the dearth of plants that they felt better represented Portland, and quickly relandscaped the building, substituting roses for the native plants. The wonderfully subtle and restrained color schemes of the structures by Yeon—blues and greens on the Jorgenson house and Visitors' Information Center, greys and greens on the Watzek house—seem to have been specifically chosen for their harmony with the landscape and serve as a background for the foliage colors of the plantings.

No Oregon architect had such an interest or knowledge of plants as did Yeon; none had ever treated landscape design as inseparable from architecture. In a fervor of creative energy, leaving nothing to chance, he agonized over subtleties of color, texture, line and form. The resulting intellect of his creations, tempered by a rare concern for "taste" in

Fig. IV–217. Edmund Hayes garden, Portland, 1940s, by John Grant. A classic informal garden that uses plant forms and textures rather than architectural devices to organize space.

an age when the concept of taste was considered antithetical to inspiration, resulted in an idiom of indigenous expression appropriate, original, and timeless.

The reaction against the academic style that had prevailed through the first decades of the century came not only from modernists who wished to abandon the Beaux Arts forms completely, but also from traditionalists who reacted against the architectural shapes and spaces of the neo-classic garden. John Grant, a Seattle landscape architect, was responsible for some of the major private gardens in Portland during the 1940s. Grant, a dedicated plantsman, believed in the romantic tradition and strove for pictorial effects. With both talent and common sense, he achieved these effects almost totally by skillful plant composition and sensitive grading of sloping lawns. Eschewing any topiary accents and minimizing the use of straight lines, he juxtaposed natural forms of trees, shrubs, and rocks with the result of a seemingly artless landscape that belies the careful calculation behind the creative effort. The Edmund Hayes garden shows a Grant garden at its finest; the large scale of the lawn and the backdrop of Douglas fir give a setting to the elegantly understated house by Jamieson Parker that makes it a classic. The unpainted exterior of the house and the large-scaled foundation planting that obscures the architectural geometry at eye level, seem to imply that the house was created for the garden rather than the garden for the house.

Fig. IV–218. David Lloyd Davies garden, Portland, 1940s, by John Grant. A rich selection of specimen plants in a setting of fine lawn suggests 18th century English prototypes.

The David Lloyd Davies garden shows plant composition as an abstract art form. In working for such clients, Grant was one of the last practitioners who could assume that the effectiveness of the garden need not be predicated on a principal of fast maturity; such gardens were

planted for a lifetime of enjoyment and as a consequence one finds such trees as oaks and beech slowly maturing into magnificent form at the same time that they are being eliminated from the landscape repertoire of the increasingly transient American society.

The garden as a lifetime project can be seen in its most civilized state in the J. W. S. Platt residence, a Belluschi design of 1941. A hill-side property without a distant view, it creates its own "inner views." One of the finest private botanical collections in the state (oftentimes a ruinous impediment to garden design), the Platt garden is not only richly rewarding in its plant material but also maintains a sense of spatial coherence. In order to accommodate and display the widest possible selection of plants in appropriate settings, the garden synthesizes climatic conditions of widely divergent types—suggesting in its loosely compartmented areas a microcosm of desert and rain forest, woodland and meadow. The gazebo at the highest point of the garden looks over a gravel garden refreshingly free of cliche—a study in abstract forms and textures that serves as a proscenium for the botanical performance beyond. Basically a naturalistic garden however, and one that demands a lifetime of dedication, it is the apogee of a type of landscape that is almost too fragile to survive the 20th century demands on human time and energy; already it suggests a more serene and gracious era that has passed.

Fig. IV–219. J. W. S. Platt garden, Portland, 1950s. Pictorial effects and botanical rarities give infinite variety to a garden that results from a lifetime dedication to gardening.

Fig. IV–220. J. W. S. Platt garden, by Richard Painter. A geometrically disciplined space serves as a foil for plant forms and textures grouped in ecological association.

Parks and Gardens in the Puget Sound Area

Thomas Allsopp*

Gardens of the Puget Sound area received national recognition when, in 1930, the annual meeting of the Garden Club of America in Seattle prompted a flurry of articles on Northwest gardens in women's magazines as well as in the more scientific magazine, *Horticulture*. By this time when there was a variety of garden styles to be displayed. Mrs. Robert P. Greer's garden was on the Garden Club tour. It was large (and still is for a city garden), and it seemed even larger because it backed on a cemetery. Neither the cemetery nor the garden had retained much natural plant material. Garden architect Carl Gould and landscape designer Otto Holmdahl attempted to create a semi-natural scene in the Japanese motif, complete with a spring-fed waterfall and stream and lush plantings of moisture-loving foliage plants. Mrs. Greer's garden reflected the trend toward the more informal garden design.

On Three Tree Point, in the city of Burien, the concept of a natural landscape had been carried even further in the large estate of G. L. Duffy. The garden was named Kewn after a sculpture by Dudley Pratt which was used as a focal point. The name means "quiet place in the woods." The landscape designer was F. J. Cole, who played a major role as designer and contractor in bringing about a respect and appreciation for natural vegetation and landforms. Much of the existing plant material was not only retained but incorporated into new plantings as an integral part of the design. This was a new concept. Gardens like Thornewood had been cut out of the woods which then became a backdrop, not an integrated part of the design.

Another garden which shows this early respect for the environment

---

*The author would like to acknowledge the assistance of the following people in researching his essay: Roberta Wightman, Landscape Architect; Don Sherwood, Seattle Park Historian; David Streatfield, Professor of Landscape Architecture, University of Washington; Norman Johnston, Professor of Architectural and Landscape Architectural History, U. of W.; Mrs. John Baxter, Historian for Seattle Garden Club; Philip Padelford; Mrs. John Hauberg; Mrs. Philip W. Cartwright; Mrs. Robert O. Phillips; Mrs. David L. Stone.

is Madiera on Gravelly Lake. Here magnificent Douglas firs, native oaks and Pacific dogwoods have been allowed to mature in a well-maintained setting of beautifully contoured lawns and ornamental plantings. The James Clapp garden and the James G. Eddy garden were both located in Medina on the east shores of Lake Washington. Garden Club members were barged from Madison Park to these gardens on a floating formal garden. The barge was moored at the dance pavilion on the end of Clapp's dock and visitors climbed up to either of the two houses through their gardens which were located in ravines. Otto Holmdahl had been the landscape designer for both of these estates. The Clapp ravine had been newly plantly with ornamental shrubs. A man-made brook, fed by a large pond near the top of the

Fig. IV–221. Gardens at Kewn, the G. L. Duffy estate in Burien, display an early trend towards an informal style of landscape gardening.

Fig. IV–222. Madiera on Gravelly Lake. The formal garden elements have been carefully blended into existing vegetation.

ravine, threaded its way down to the lake. Following the new trend, some old trees were retained and blended into the scene. Mrs. Eddy's garden had respected the natural scene even more and was described as a beautiful, woodsy glen that was "eerie and ghost-like in its charm." The owner had been content to concentrate her flower growing near the house at the top of the garden.

In 1909 wealthy Seattleite R. D. Merrill commissioned Charles Adam Platt to design his house on Capitol Hill. Platt, who designed one other

Fig. IV–223. Madiera, an early effort at preservation, has matured into a magnificent garden.

Fig. IV–224. The R. D. Merrill residence, Seattle, the entrance garden.

house in Seattle, was one of the foremost landscape architects in the country in the early years of the century. He had received most of his schooling as a painter and during his travels with his brother. He had always shown an interest in landscape gardening and when his brother, who had been working in the office of Frederick Law Olmsted, suggested that the two of them might benefit from a tour of European gardens, Platt agreed. They painted, sketched, measured and photographed the gardens they saw, and in 1894 Platt published a book titled *Italian Gardens* with "an accumulation of data richer than anything of the sort previously made known in this country."[1] The influence of his travels on his philosophy of design is seen in both his architecture and his gardens. Much of his work contains the same elements as the Merrill residence; however, in each there is a sense of individuality.

The predominant architectural styles in the Seattle area are the Colonial and the Tudor. Usually, especially with the Tudor houses, the colors are somber and the feeling is heavy. The Merrill house is different. The lines are clean and uncluttered by unnecessary detail. The color is light and the mood is Italian. It sits forward of its Tudor and Colonial neighbors on the same block. Platt had the foresight to realize that this shallow setback would allow for a more generous garden to the west—that exposure being the most desirable for entertaining and flower displays. A small brick semicircular drive encloses an area of lawn just inside the elegant wrought iron fencing on the east side facing the street. There are no shrubs. The feeling is completely open

1. *The Works of Charles Adam Platt* (New York, 1913), 4–5.

and cordial in a very small space. Two paths on either side of the drive which lead to the West Garden use the same paving pattern. Both paths pass through magnificent old rhododendrons which have grown into small trees. The effect of their strong trunks is heightened by the fact that there is no ground cover; the ground beneath them is raked and swept clean. Earlier photos show these rhododendrons much smaller, and one wonders if Platt had such a jungle in mind.

The path on the north side of the house is mainly utilitarian. On the south side, however, the house opens onto a small grass-covered terrace. Before the shrubs grew tall, this was a sunny private retreat, cooled with the sound of water from a fountain hung on the wall. A short flight of steps leads to the West Garden. Immediately at the bottom of these steps there is a cross axis at either end of which stand large statues. The West Garden is perfectly flat except for the shallow terrace directly off the back of the house. It is easy to see by the natural contour of the surrounding land that this flat shelf had to be created out of what was a sloping site. On the lower street, at the extreme west end of the garden, Platt designed a carriage house—a tasteful piece of architecture with graceful fenestration and detail. It acts as a bulkhead and is topped, level with the garden, with a pergola. The pergola is an often repeated element in Platt's gardens. Its paired columns, continuous overhanging arbor, and seats flanked with large shrubs, give the garden a sense of intimacy and enclosure and at the same time provide a focus for the vista from the house. The sense of enclosure is augmented by low walls which border the garden along the north and south.

The plant material is small and controlled by pruning. The side walls are adorned with espaliered flowering fruit trees. The espaliered pear trees predate the garden by at least 50 years. They were bought during the Alaska-Yukon Pacific Exposition and are said to have come from Belgium. The beds in front of these walls were long and narrow and held a collection of perennials which kept the garden in color all summer long. Later these beds were divided and annuals were massed to make a brilliant display. The character of the garden changed. The list of perennials had included standard varieties which had muted, pastel hues. The new varieties of annuals were bright colors. There was a central panel of lawn with a pond in the middle. Photographs from the 1930s don't show the fountain which is in this pond today; however, the Platt drawings for the garden do suggest a fountain. At each path intersection an oleander tree was placed in a white Versailles style tub to add a vertical element to the garden.

One of the members of the Garden Club of America wrote in 1930:

"Just as Whistler signed his etchings with a butterfly, so Charles Platt signs his gardens by cutting a piece out of a corner and setting a huge grey pot of flowering plants or a bay tree on the spot."[2]

---

2. *The Garden Club of America Yearbook,* 1930.

Fig. IV–225. The D. E. Frederick estate, Seattle, the entrance court with the altered mansion in the background.

Though the Merrill garden still has Platt's signature, it has changed. The perennials are gone, as are the annuals which followed them. Colored gravels in a pattern mix with clipped boxwood, and two beds of roses have replaced earlier displays. The Merrill Foundation preserves the house and gardens, using them for various social gatherings.

One of the last grand formal gardens was done in the early thirties on D. E. Frederick's estate in the Highlands of Seattle. When asked why he didn't choose a site with a view of Puget Sound and the Olympic Mountains, Frederick is said to have replied that he saw these views all the way home on his drive from downtown Seattle and had no desire to see them again when he arrived home.

Frederick chose instead to live in the woods. He purchased his estate in the Highlands community north of Seattle well back from the water. Here, surrounded by existing Douglas firs, Pacific dogwoods, bigleaf and vine maples, he built what many consider to be Seattle's finest mansion. The house is a replica of a French chateau with very steep pitched roofs, towering chimneys, and warm yellow stone. In 1934 the Olmsted Brothers were commissioned to design the garden. Out of the woodlands they carved the formal gardens as a series of green rooms as André Le Nôtre had done.

This beautiful community with its curving drives and carefully preserved natural vegetation had been laid out by the Olmsteds some years earlier. Because Frederick had built rather close to the lane passing in front of his property, the usual long entrance drive had to be omitted. Nevertheless there is a sense of arrival. The entrance court is defined by a natural arch of trees and shrubs and in the center of the court is a round pond with a towering cherub fountain continually splashing down on darting goldfish. To the west an eight-foot wall

Fig. IV–226. Frederick estate, view from cypress allee to the mansion.

conceals the service drive and a small breakfast garden. On the east the chateau forms another wall. Huge pink pearl rhododendrons are covered with full trusses of flowers in the late spring.

Directly off the library at the south end of the house there is a small terrace and pool. Beyond is one of Frederick's created views. Lawson cypress trees line either side of a central lawn panel which is bordered with all white azaleas. The Blue Pool and Tea House terminate this vista. The hedge was tenderly cared for by a European gardener who feathered the 24-foot-tall natural wall. Mrs. Frederick specified that the hedge was never to have a clipped look, so, on a specially built ladder, the gardener would work his painstaking magic. Pots of flowers placed around the pool complement those placed on the terraces around the house.

Two-thirds of the way down this vista, a cross axis cuts into it from the east. On this axis is the rectangular flower garden which has its longest dimension parallel to the allee of the cypress trees. It is sunken a few feet below the level of the surrounding garden. Flowering cherries accent the points of entry to the garden and lawn, and boxwood gives it structure throughout the year, filled out in the summer with colorful phlox.

East of the garden, a winding path leads down to the terrace and grotto which is the headwater for the series of seven pump-fed ponds which gradually step down to the north. Though overgrown and natural looking today, this was originally laid out as the Japanese Garden. One bridge which crosses the ponds leads back to the house past a small garden temple, the Temple of Love. A very popular garden feature in older gardens, this temple is sited in an expanse of lawn and consists of light colored columns supporting a delicate tracery of wrought iron.

Fig. IV–227. Frederick estate, ornamental pool from which the Spanish well could be viewed.

Carved stone balustrades line the terraces which lead along the east front of the house to the small Dining Room Garden. The paved terrace gives way to lawn in this garden. However, the balustrade continues around the lawn and eventually steps down to an ornamental pool just off the terrace to the north. On axis with this pool is a Spanish well which terminates another created vista. Existing trees form the walls of this vista and bordering the central lawn are plantings of one color of astilbe and the delicate foliage of thalictrum. The estate also included another less formal sunken flower garden and tennis courts to the west of the house.

When it became necessary to sell the estate, the University of Washington decided to buy it and preserve it as a seminar center. Complications arose however, and the Highlands bought it back from the University. Because of community restrictions, other possible buyers were turned down. Finally a contractor bought it. He employed a local landscape architect to divide the property into saleable parcels. Two were sold and built upon, a third parcel included the carriage house and the fourth included the Frederick mansion. Unable to sell the house because of its size, the owner removed over 6,000 square feet of it, including the main entrance and library wing. This left a rather awkward terrace which can't be planted because of the basement below. The stone from this demolition was used to build a new house on one of the pieces of property. Still unable to sell the reduced mansion, and unable to continue payments, the owner reverted the property to the Highlands which eventually sold it.

The Fredericks' estate was once the greatest house and garden combination in Seattle. Now, though one can still sense its past beauty and changes have spared the surrounding woodlands, the garden has lost its intended elegance.

V Freeway Forms

WESTERN STATES

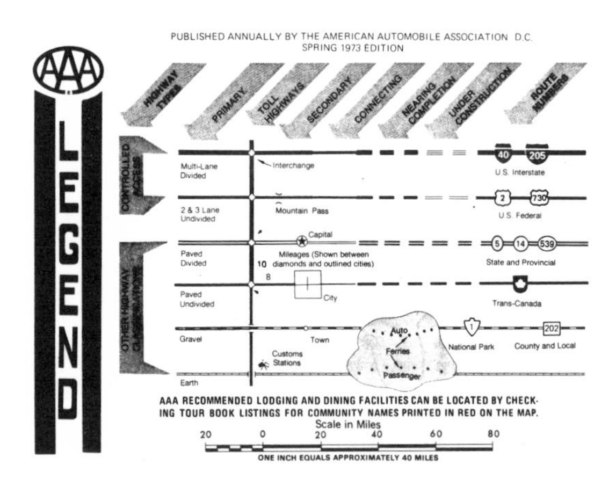

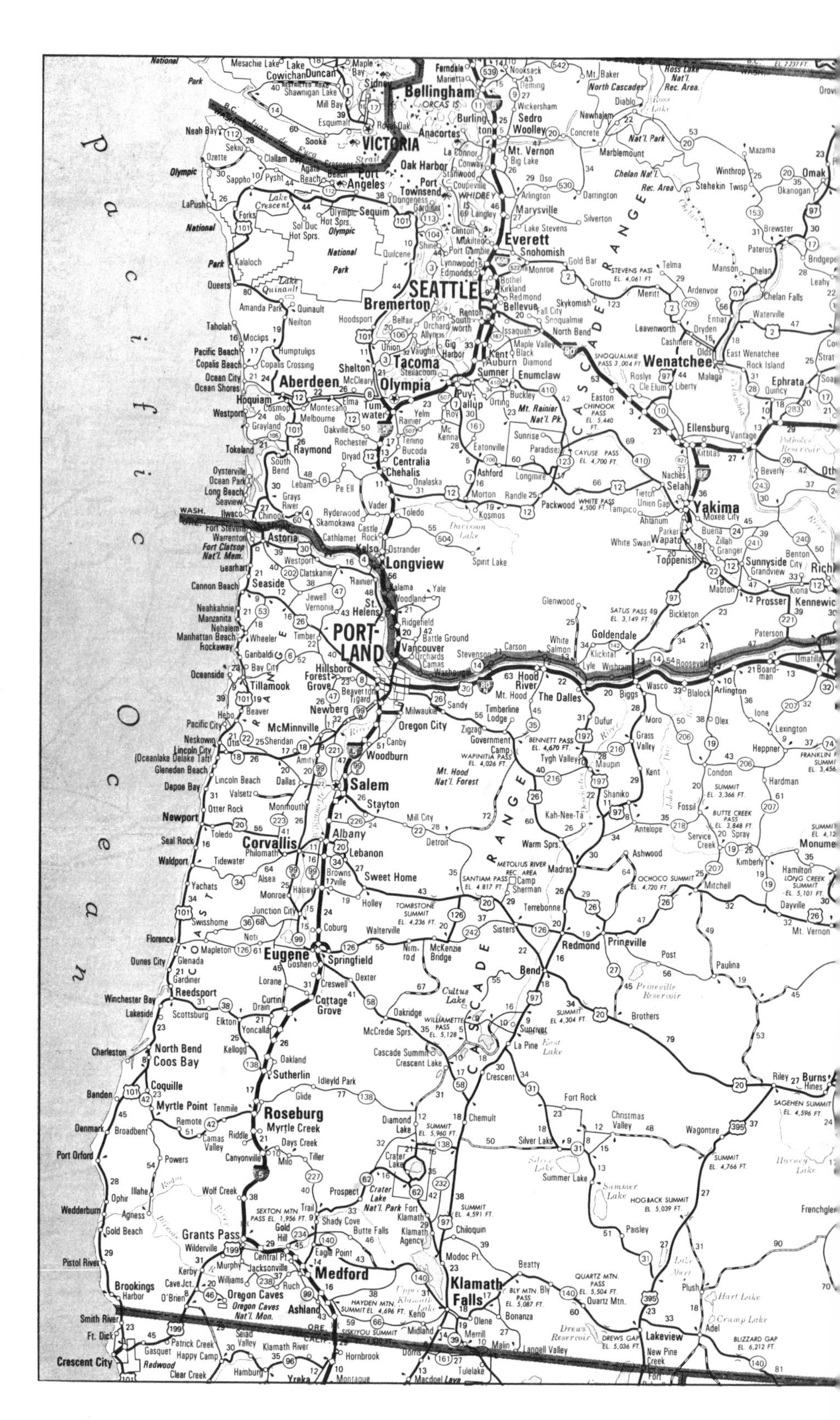

Fig. V–1. Portion of 1973 American Automobile Association map of the Western States. Although close in size to the Wilkes map, the Bancroft map, the railway guide map, and the 1936 AAA map, the 1973 version is much more abstract. Rivers are barely visible and mountains appear as nameless blobs of gray. Highways, cities and National Parks stand out.

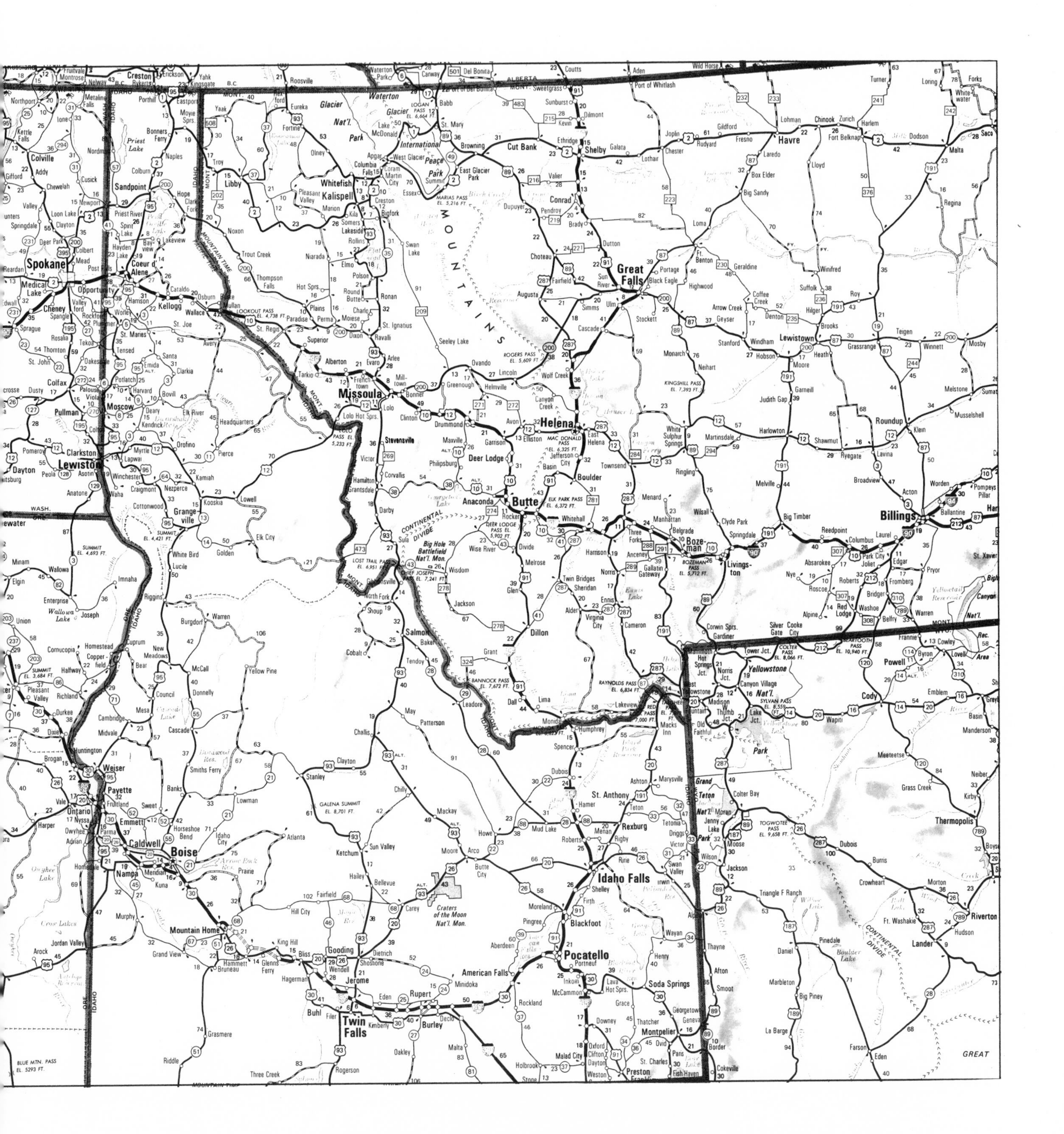

Creston
Yahk
Kingsgate
B.C.
Roosville
Waterton Park
Carway
Del Bonita
ALBERTA
Coutts
Aden
Wild Horse
Sweetgrass
Port of Whitlash
MONT.
IDAHO
WASH.
ORE.
Northport
Metaline Falls
Porthill
Eastport
Moyie Sprs.
Eureka
Glacier Nat'l. Park
Waterton Glacier International Peace Park
LOGAN PASS EL. 6,664 FT.
Babb
St. Mary
Sunburst
Kevin
Whitlash
Lohman
Chinook
Zurich
Harlem
Turner
Loring
Forks
Whitewater
Kettle Falls
Colville
Priest Lake
Bonners Ferry
Naples
Troy
Libby
Yaak
Fortine
Olney
Lake McDonald
Apgar
West Glacier
Browning
Cut Bank
Ethridge
Shelby
Galata
Lothair
Chester
Joplin
Rudyard
Gildford
Fresno
Havre
Fort Belknap
Dodson
Malta
Saco
Addy
Chewelah
Cusick
Colburn
Sandpoint
Hope
Clark Fork
Columbia Falls
Coram
Martin City
Essex
East Glacier Park
Valier
Dupuyer
Conrad
Laredo
Box Elder
Big Sandy
Lloyd
Regina
Loon Lake
Newport
Priest River
Springdale
Clayton
Deer Park
Spirit Lake
Hayden Lake
Bayview
Whitefish
Kalispell
Pleasant Valley
Marion
Creston
Bigfork
Somers
Lakeside
Rollins
MARIAS PASS EL. 5,216 FT.
MOUNTAINS
Pendroy
Brady
Dutton
Loma
Spokane
Reardan
Mead
Colbert
Post Falls
Coeur d'Alene
Medical Lake
Opportunity
Cheney
Spangle
Valleyford
Rockford
Plummer
Worley
Harrison
Cataldo
Kellogg
Wallace
Osburn
Mullan
LOOKOUT PASS EL. 4,738 FT.
Noxon
Trout Creek
Thompson Falls
Niarada
Elmo
Polson
Hot Sprs.
Plains
Paradise
Perma
Round Butte
Charlo
Moiese
Ronan
Dixon
St. Ignatius
Ravalli
Swan Lake
Choteau
Fairfield
Augusta
Sun River
Great Falls
Black Eagle
Portage
Ft. Benton
Geraldine
Highwood
Winifred
Suffolk
Roy
Sprague
Rosalia
Tekoa
St. Maries
St. Joe
Avery
St. Regis
Superior
Alberton
Tensed
Santa
Clarkia
Emida
Potlatch
Thornton
St. John
Oakesdale
Colfax
Palouse
Viola
Pullman
Moscow
Harvard
Deary
Bovill
Elk River
Kendrick
Juliaetta
Headquarters
Pierce
Orofino
Myrtle
Lapwai
Clarkston
Lewiston
Asotin
Pomeroy
Dayton
Peola
Anatone
Waha
Winchester
Craigmont
Nezperce
Kamiah
Kooskia
Lowell
Cottonwood
Grangeville
Elk City
Golden
White Bird
Lucile
Tarkio
Missoula
Frenchtown
Lolo
Lolo Hot Sprs.
LOLO PASS EL. 5,233 FT.
Clinton
Bonner
Milltown
Arlee
Evaro
Seeley Lake
Ovando
Lincoln
Helmville
Greenough
Drummond
Avon
Elliston
Helena
East Helena
Garrison
Deer Lodge
Maxville
Philipsburg
Stevensville
Victor
Corvallis
Hamilton
Grantsdale
Darby
Sula
Anaconda
Butte
Rocker
Whitehall
Basin
Boulder
Jefferson City
Townsend
Canyon Creek
Wolf Creek
Cascade
Ulm
Simms
Vaughn
Stockett
Belt
Armington
Arrow Creek
Geyser
Coffee Creek
Denton
Stanford
Windham
Hobson
Lewistown
Moore
Heath
Grassrange
Winnett
Mosby
Neihart
Monarch
ROGERS PASS EL. 5,609 FT.
MAC DONALD PASS EL. 6,325 FT.
KINGSHILL PASS EL. 7,393 FT.
ELK PARK PASS EL. 6,372 FT.
White Sulphur Springs
Martinsdale
Ringling
Judith Gap
Harlowton
Shawmut
Ryegate
Lavina
Roundup
Klein
Musselshell
Melstone
Garneill
Wilsall
Clyde Park
Big Timber
Melville
Broadview
Acton
Worden
Pompeys Pillar
Ballantine
Billings
Laurel
Columbus
Reedpoint
Springdale
Livingston
Bozeman
Belgrade
Manhattan
Menard
Three Forks
Harrison
Anceney
Gallatin Gateway
BOZEMAN PASS EL. 5,712 FT.
Park City
Joliet
Edgar
Fromberg
Bridger
Pryor
Absarokee
Nye
Roscoe
Roberts
Red Lodge
Washoe
Belfry
Warren
Bighorn
Yellowtail Reservoir
Alpine
Silver Gate
Cooke City
Corwin Sprs.
Gardiner
Wilsall
Twin Bridges
Sheridan
Norris
Ennis
Alder
Virginia City
Cameron
Wisdom
Wise River
Divide
Melrose
Glen
Jackson
Dillon
Big Hole Battlefield Nat'l. Mon.
DEER LODGE PASS EL. 5,902 FT.
CONTINENTAL DIVIDE
LOST TRAIL PASS EL. 6,951 FT.
CHIEF JOSEPH PASS EL. 7,241 FT.
Gibbonsville
North Fork
Shoup
Salmon
Baker
Cobalt
Tendoy
Leadore
Grant
Dell
Lima
Monida
BANNOCK PASS EL. 7,672 FT.
RAYNOLDS PASS EL. 6,834 FT.
Lakeview
RED ROCK PASS EL. 7,000 FT.
Mack's Inn
Humphrey
Spencer
Island Park Reservoir
West Yellowstone
Mammoth Hot Springs
Tower Jct.
Norris Jct.
Madison Jct.
Old Faithful
Grant Village
West Thumb Jct.
Lake Jct.
Canyon Village
Yellowstone Nat'l. Park
COLTER PASS EL. 8,066 FT.
BEARTOOTH PASS EL. 10,940 FT.
SYLVAN PASS EL. 8,559 FT.
Frannie
Cowley
Lovell
Byron
Powell
Cody
Wapiti
Emblem
Greybull
Basin
Manderson
Meeteetse
Neiber
Kirby
Grass Creek
Thermopolis
Union
Imnaha
Joseph
Enterprise
Wallowa
Wallowa Lake
Minam
Elgin
Riggins
Burgdorf
Warren
New Meadows
Council
McCall
Donnelly
Yellow Pine
Cascade
Cambridge
Midvale
Mesa
Copperfield
Homestead
Cornucopia
Halfway
Richland
Pleasant Valley
Durkee
Huntington
Brogan
Weiser
Payette
Fruitland
Ontario
Vale
Nyssa
Harper
Parma
Owyhee
Adrian
Emmett
Sweet
Horseshoe Bend
Banks
Smiths Ferry
Lowman
Idaho City
Caldwell
Nampa
Meridian
Kuna
Boise
Arrow Rock Res.
Prairie
Atlanta
Stanley
Clayton
Challis
May
Patterson
GALENA SUMMIT EL. 8,701 FT.
Chilly
Mackay
Ketchum
Sun Valley
Hailey
Bellevue
Carey
Fairfield
Hill City
Moore
Arco
Butte City
Howe
Craters of the Moon Nat'l. Mon.
Mud Lake
Dubois
Hamer
St. Anthony
Ashton
Marysville
Teton
Rexburg
Roberts
Menan
Rigby
Driggs
Tetonia
Victor
Swan Valley
Ririe
Idaho Falls
Shelley
Firth
Blackfoot
Moreland
Pingree
Aberdeen
American Falls
Pocatello
Portneuf
Inkom
McCammon
Lava Hot Sprs.
Soda Springs
Grace
Henry
Wayan
Georgetown
Montpelier
Geneva
Thatcher
Downey
Oxford
Clifton
Dayton
Preston
Weston
Malad City
Holbrook
Stone
St. Charles
Paris
Bear Lake
Fish Haven
Dingle
Border
Cokeville
Grand Teton Nat'l. Park
Colter Bay
Moran
Jenny Lake
Moose
Wilson
Jackson
TOGWOTEE PASS EL. 9,658 FT.
Dubois
Burris
Crowheart
Triangle F Ranch
Alpine
Thayne
Afton
Smoot
Daniel
Pinedale
Boulder Lake
Marbleton
Big Piney
La Barge
Farson
Eden
Ft. Washakie
Lander
Hudson
Riverton
Morton
Boysen
Mountain Home
Murphy
Grand View
Bruneau
Hammett
Glenns Ferry
King Hill
Bliss
Gooding
Wendell
Shoshone
Dietrich
Hagerman
Jerome
Buhl
Filer
Twin Falls
Kimberly
Eden
Rupert
Minidoka
Burley
Declo
Oakley
Malta
Rockland
Rogerson
Three Creek
Grasmere
Riddle
Jordan Valley
Arock
Crow Lakes
Owyhee Lake
Homedale
BLUE MTN. PASS EL. 5293 FT.
SUMMIT EL. 4,693 FT.
SUMMIT EL. 4,421 FT.
SUMMIT EL. 3,684 FT.
MOUNTAIN TIME
PACIFIC TIME
GREAT
Rec. Area

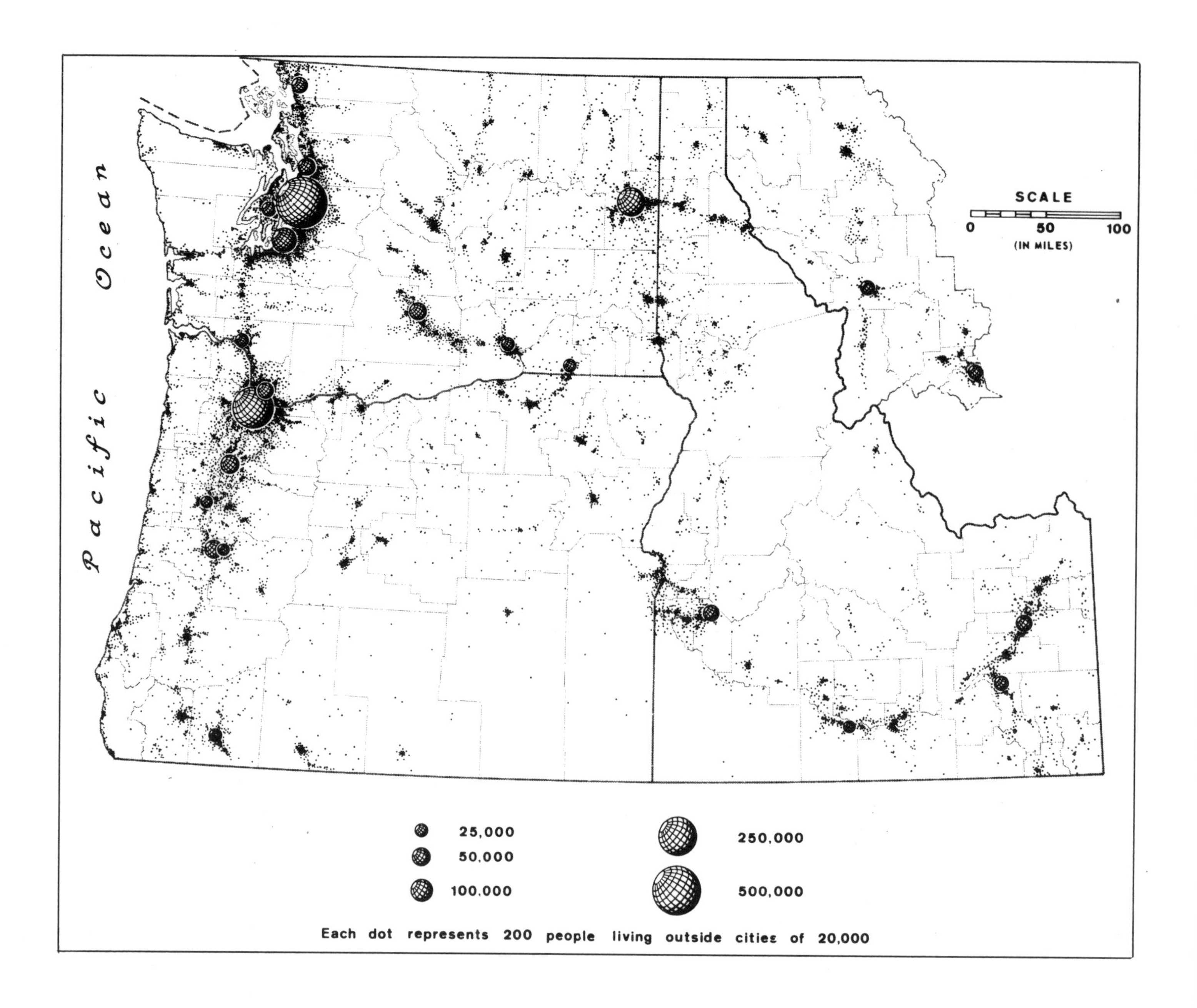

Fig. V–2. Population distribution map from *The Pacific Northwest,* published by the Batelle Memorial Institute in 1967. Concentrations in urban areas require a separate symbol.

Population Pacific Northwest 1960

Idaho	671,000
Oregon	1,773,000
Washington	2,860,000
	5,304,000

Regional Setting

Virginia Guest Ferriday

Although the Interstate freeway system is only one aspect of the postwar technological explosion its impact on regional development has been the most visible. Its construction is closely related to the accelerated growth of our cities and to the accompanying changes in land use and attitudes toward our natural environment.

Histories of the Interstate system almost invariably include variations of the following statement: "In September of 1956 . . . Congress passed a bill to construct 41,000 miles of Interstate highways that will make it possible to travel from coast to coast without a stop for traffic signals."[1] This statement imples that the system was designed primarily for transcontinental travel, but this was not the case. The Interstate freeway system had its genesis in efforts to solve traffic problems in and around urban areas, and it is there that it has had its greatest impact.

By the late 1930s traffic problems in the environs of the large cities of the Northwest were already acute. A report on freeways for the Oregon State Planning Board's Advisory Committee on Roadside Protection outlined the problem clearly:

> Often the approaches to cities are reconstructed in order to eliminate the slow and dangerous entry formerly afforded by crowded busy streets. The intention of the new road is to provide an entrance penetrating the city's outlying districts which will be free from intersections and local traffic of the former route. This objective is repeatedly defeated as the conditions of the former route are reproduced along the new. A road intended to usher the traveler rapidly into a city becomes another street, reaching far out into the country, with urban impediments along its borders even though fields of woodlands may exist beyond.

Proposed solution for this dilemma was a new type of highway, one "being built in advanced states in the East, and in modern countries in Europe," a "freeway." The secret of its success was the provision of limited access: there were no intersections except where the freeway crossed or joined another public road. Private property owners along the

---

1. *Twenty-eighth Biennial Report of the Oregon State Highway Commission* (1968), 10.

freeway were not allowed access; they were served by lesser roads. Junctions with public roads became "scientific intersections." The motorist on the freeway would be "assured a fast route, free from the interruptions of numerous grade crossings, free from chaotic sights of private developments which line the borders of ordinary roads." The freeway would "produce for motor vehicles routes comparable in efficiency to the fast routes of limited trains."[2]

The Interstate system of freeways was set up as a separate network by the 1944 Highway Act. The act defined a national network of highways so located as "to connect with routes as direct as possible the principal metropolitan areas, cities and industrial centers, to serve the National Defense, and to connect at suitable border points with routes

Fig. V–3. Seattle: the new entrance to the city, "fast moving and free of roadside clutter."

of continental importance . . ." Federal funds for freeway construction were not provided until 1965, however, and then only as the result of a massive campaign by highway-users and allied groups. Under this act states eventually receive 92% financing for portions of the interstate system as compared to 60% for the Federal Aid Primary System. It also included establishment of the highway trust fund. Previously, income

2. John Yeon (Chairman of Sub-committee on Freeways of the Advisory Committee on Roadside Protection, Oregon State Planning Board), *Freeways for Oregon; the Advantages of Freeways in Increasing Safety and Efficiency in Highway Travel* (1938), 4–6.

from highway-user taxes had been siphoned off for other governmental purposes.

Support for freeways was great enough in the Northwest for construction to begin prior to passage of the 1956 bill. The Portland-Salem Expressway (another term for freeway), financed through sale of general revenue bonds, was opened in 1952. It was later given Interstate designation.

Through the stipulation that the Interstate system was to connect the principal metropolitan areas, the 1944 and 1956 acts insured that cities received a sizeable share of the highway funds and thus narrowed appreciably the gap between rural and urban aid for road building. Because of their disproportionate representation in state legislatures, rural interests had held the advantage in obtaining financing.

Typically, a city of over 200,000 population is provided not only with radials connecting its center with other cities, but also with a central downtown loop and outer bypasses. Seattle and Portland each have three radials. Portland has a complete downtown loop and a partially complete outer bypass. Seattle, because of her restricted site, has no inner loop and only one bypass to the east, though other segments are proposed. Freeways passing through Tacoma and Spokane give them two radials each. Freeways serving other cities of the Northwest can properly be considered bypasses.

That attempting to solve local urban traffic problems with an interstate system was illogical, if expedient, is revealed in the placement of radials and bypasses where they provide optimum inter-city linkages rather than where concentrations of intra-city traffic occurs. The tendency of freeways to generate automobile traffic and thus aggravate rather than solve urban traffic problems has been generally accepted. That confusion exists as to what a freeway's proper function was, is, or should be, has been obvious in a recent dispute over construction of portions of a bypass in the Portland metropolitan area. County commissioners have requested that the freeway be made four lanes wide rather than eight and that the distance between interchanges be increased so that the freeway can serve the "purpose for which it was intended" (to carry through traffic). Others argue that it should be built as designed so that it can be used by local residents who may not be able to find jobs in their immediate neighborhoods and need a freeway in order to commute. In settling questions such as this the Northwest has for the first time been unable to look to the East Coast or European cities for experience, as in undertakings of this sort the cultural lag has been reduced to practically nothing.

Because the Interstate freeway system links major metropolitan areas, and because these areas are much the same as they were during the era of the railroad, freeways of the Northwest follow closely the pattern of railway trunk lines. The effect on regional development has not, however, been the same as that of the railroad.

Transportation of passengers and freight beyond the railroad station required transfer to another less efficient vehicle. Development was there-

Fig. V–4. Looking east up the Columbia River at the mouth of the John Day River: the old Union Pacific railroad bridge, the old Columbia River Highway bridge, and the new I-80N bridge.

fore tied closely to these discrete points along the lines. Because construction of the freeway system has been accompanied by improvements to the primary and secondary road system and because cars and trucks can so easily make the transition from one system to another, development in broad bands along both sides of freeways has been possible. The question in the last two decades has been not whether one particular site or another would be built up, but rather which geographic areas would be the next to develop. Studies of the effects of freeways in the Northwest done in the 1950s concentrated on what happened to commerce in small towns which were bypassed or on what type of building occurred in the immediate vincinity of interchanges. Soon it became apparent that such localized efforts were of relatively minor importance and recent studies have encompassed much larger areas.

Development along freeways could theoretically take place around

Fig. V–5. The Lower Tualatin Valley south of Portland, scene of intense controversy over future land use following construction of the freeway.

any city of the Northwest. But because of their natural advantages in relation to ocean shipping (Portland and Seattle) or to large areas of productive land (Spokane), and because of the agglomeration phenomenon (or in the vernacular, "people make jobs; jobs make people"), the areas around the larger cities have experienced the greatest growth. From 1950 to 1957 the three metropolitan Washington counties of King (Seattle), Pierce (Tacoma), and Spokane experienced 20 times the population increase of the other 36 Washington counties. Portland's share of Oregon's population increased from 12% in 1880 to 38% in 1965.

As the larger cities have increased in population and the unincorporated areas around them have become urbanized, land use controls, which were introduced in Northwest cities during the 1920s in the form of zoning, have been adopted by many counties. The State of Oregon requires counties to zone and to draw up comprehensive plans on which to base their zoning. Idaho and Washington both have legislation enabling counties to zone, although it is not required. Such county zoning has not been used in the same way as land classification of the 1930s was, as a means of encouraging the best possible use of farm land, but rather as a means of controlling and even limiting urbanization. Predominantly rural counties, particularly those east of the Cascades, have therefore found the zoning and planning procedures an irrelevant bureaucratic nuisance and have not cooperated in efforts to strengthen controls. (There are, of course, many rural residents who intend to develop their land for profit and who oppose land use legislation as an "infringement on their rights.") In spite of this resistance, Oregon in 1973 passed legislation setting up a state Land Conservation and Development Commission. Oregon also has a Coastal Conservation and Development Commission and Washington in 1971 passed legislation directing its Department of Ecology to protect the public's interest in its shorelines.

The question of how much control the state or county should exert over land use is part of a larger disagreement relating to the use of natural resources. Emigrants to the Northwest from the earliest days to the present have exhibited a keen appreciation of the region's natural environment. The dramatic contrasts in terrain, climate and vegetation undoubtedly stimulate awareness. Letters from pioneers contain descriptions of minutest detail of the various geographic areas. Planners of the 1930s mapped the region in every conceivable aspect. Both groups were primarily interested in what use could be made of the land. In contrast the typical urban dweller of the past two decades has had little, if any, contact with rural land on a day-to-day basis. His only direct experience with a natural environment has occurred during a weekend outing or vacation. He has thus tended to see the region less as an economic resource and more as a giant playground. This has led to strong citizens' efforts to preserve scenic areas in a nearly natural state and to a reaction by those segments of the population whose livelihood depends directly on utilization of natural resources. The conflict has been aggravated by competition for resources resulting from increased population. Acquisition of land along the Willamette River for a greenway is resisted by those who farm it; limitations on cutting timber are opposed by the lumber industry; and the suggested moratorium on dam building is fought by the power industries. These conflicts have resulted in many lawsuits and, through insistence on environmental impact studies, to use of the planning process for an end to which it is perhaps ideally suited—the indefinite delay of any concrete action. One of the most startling of these efforts was blockage by residents on the opposite shore of the Portland International Airport's runway expansion into the Columbia River. That action represented a major departure for a region which has always welcomed capital improvements of almost any kind.

Preservation of the natural environment, if accompanied by expanded facilities for tourists, has been generally accepted as good policy.

Fig. V–6. Early morning gathering at Hot Springs campground at East Lake in central Oregon, May 25, 1958. Police were pressed into service to untangle the jams on nearby roads where an estimated 6,000 anglers merged.

Tourism is usually reported by the *Oregon Blue Book* as the third or fourth largest "industry" in the Pacific Northwest. Factors limiting its growth have been shortness of season (except for skiing) and the predominance of automobile tourists, who typically don't linger long in one place; factors favoring its development have been the region's relatively unspoiled condition and the proximity of large centers of population in California. (In 1967 approximately 50% of Oregon's tourists were Californian.[3]) While many travelers to the Northwest have managed low-cost vacations by using the region's more than 300 state parks, development of second home communities which double as convention centers has increased the Northwest's share of the more lucrative segment of the tourist trade.

These second home communities, new towns planned around golf courses rather than factories, are, after the greatly enlarged metropolitan areas, the most characteristic land use phenomenon of the freeway era. Although federal tax laws and continued inflation have certainly encouraged investment in such real estate, it is doubtful that such development would have been successful without the accessibility provided by the present highway system. These new communities are a good example of the increasingly specialized use of land made possible by a highly developed regional transportation system. During the days of the early

3. Battelle Memorial Institute, *The Pacific Northwest; Economic Growth in a Quality Environment* (Columbus, Ohio, 1967), 370.

settlers each small community was very nearly self-sufficient; now the region is being knit into one interdependent whole with cultural activities, administrative functions, professional services, and industry concentrated in the two or three large urban areas, food production in the valleys and plains, and recreation along the coast and near the mountains.

Accompanying the expansion of the economic unit has been a geometric increase in the size of the components of the man-made environment. A comparison of the scale of cities and buildings appearing on the following pages with those built by the pioneers will reveal clearly the extent to which technology has altered the environment of inhabitants of the Northwest since the establishment of agriculture and shipping some 135 years ago.

Cities and Towns

Steve Dotterrer

Portland

The greatly increased wealth and population of the Northwest since World War II has had an enormous impact on Portland's recent development. Probably the greatest single influence has been the automobile. While spatial expansion has been characteristic of Portland's growth at all times, the automobile and truck have increased the potential for expansion and have eliminated most of the concentrations essential in earlier periods. Major changes in real estate practice (such as the FHA and VA loan programs) and developments in building technology and construction have generally aided this spatial expansion.

By the early 1940s the car had become the major means of transportation as the numerous street widenings and complaints about bumpy streetcar tracks reveal. Both cars and trucks gained a great advantage when Harbor Drive was constructed in the late 1940s. The Bennett plan of 1912 had included a riverside drive elevated above rebuilt wharves and warehouses and in the 1930s when the seawall replaced the wharves, a bypass roadway, a public market, and a plaza at the Jefferson Street railroad station were proposed. Only the plaza and the market were built. Near the end of World War II Robert Moses, a New York planner, suggested a six-lane limited access road along the waterfront connected to a city system of thruways and bypasses. Unlike earlier waterfront schemes, the overriding environmental goal of the Moses plan was traffic improvement. (The chief purpose, however—to provide work for war veterans[1]—was not environmental at all.) Moses' scheme, which required demolition of all the warehouses east of Front Street, was completed in 1950. Harbor Drive and the freeways which followed gave the truck and car the high speed capabilities of the railroad. Because cars and trucks are more flexible than railroads this new long distance capability insured auto-truck dominance in transportation.

1. Robert Moses, *Portland Improvement* (New York, 1943), 7–16.

Fig. V–7. Portland, Harbor Drive and the Willamette River seawall, early 1974. Since this photo was taken Harbor Drive has been closed and the pavement removed.

The Portland freeway system originally consisted of both radial and bypass freeways organized around a central downtown loop. Unlike many other cities Portland's important radials and downtown loop were built before any bypass was begun. While this freeway system has encouraged increased spatial expansion, it has not detracted as much from the central core's dominant position as freeways have in some other cities. However, recent construction of parts of the bypass has lessened the core area's importance, especially in retailing and entertainment, but also for some office activities.

The growth in service industries, with their demand for office space, has created a large market for office buildings. In fact, the downtown's continued growth has been almost entirely dependent on office space expansion. Technological developments such as air conditioning, the high speed elevator, and more highly industrialized building techniques plus increased labor costs, have encouraged the construction of large office buildings with simple, regular shapes. In addition, the concern for the corporate image has resulted in use of the highly visible building as an important part of the company's marketing program. All of these, of course, represent national trends. Squeezing all these national trends onto Portland's small 200′ x 200′ blocks, has been difficult, however. Lacking sufficient space to make the transition from the giant-scaled buildings to the man-scaled sidewalks, recent projects often appear overbearing and aloof. The architectural cliche of the "clean form" has made this transition even more difficult.

Roughly equal access to all points within the freeway loop and the drive toward separate, full-block projects has resulted in a skyline

Fig. V–8. Portland, the inner loop of the freeway system, completed late 1973. Compare the large areas of parking lots along the river with the same area in Fig. V–9.

of widely-spaced towers rather than the clustered skyline of the older, mass-transit-dependent business area. This wide-spaced pattern of towers is also caused by the difficulty of assembling the numerous small parcels on one block under a single ownership. The large developments are often built where the property is easiest to assemble rather than where car or transit access is best or according to some general city plan.

Recent real estate developments are typically separate and independent. Since there is little confidence that the city environment can provide essential services each contains as many elements necessary to its success as possible. Stores which were previously located on the sidewalk are now placed within the towers, which usually also contain a cafeteria. Retaining walls, plazas and hard edges segregate the project from its surroundings. This isolation compliments the clients' (and usually the architect's) desire to create a strong image for the project. Air conditioning and access by private automobile strengthen the closed-off feeling. The result of the separateness or isolation of projects is a new definition of downtown. No developer or architect seems willing to do a piece of the downtown, and downtown as a physical entity is being replaced by a series of individual projects. Developers and architects often claim that their projects "reach out into" or "connect with the community." The very choice of words suggests that their projects are not parts of the community. The isolation of new projects from their surroundings is increased because all older buildings are normally removed from the site when construction is begun. This is made necessary by the large volumes of office space and parking required in the new developments, but it is made possible by the modern economy

Fig. V–9. Portland, Downtown near the waterfront in the 1920s, before demolition of many riverfront structures for parking lots.

with its ability to assemble large amounts of capital for physical developments.

To provide parking space for office workers in new developments and for those changing from transit to auto, large areas have been cleared of older buildings for surface parking lots. The waterfront area near Harbor Drive, which previously consisted of two to five-story buildings, has been the most altered by this need for parking.

Manufacturing plants and wholesale houses have often located along a freeway or major arterial in the suburbs where they can be easily reached by trucks. The suburban site also offers the advantage of more land area and allows for one-story industrial plants. Offices have been slower in moving outside the downtown, but the new bypass routes

Fig. V–10. Portland, the new skyline of widely spaced towers, July, 1974.

Fig. V–11. Beaverton, a suburb of Portland, in 1964 showing the mixed strip development of commercial and industrial uses.

Fig. V–12. Portland, driver's eye view of the commercial strip.

Fig. V–13. Somerset West, a suburban development west of Portland on opening day in 1963. The cul-de-sac and the curving street are typical of residential development since World War II.

have encouraged their construction. To date most of the new suburban office construction has been built for workers serving people in the immediate area—doctors, real estate and insurance agents. The recent freeway developments, however, have encouraged regional offices of national corporations and other large office space users to move to the suburbs.

Residential development has continued to spread further into the countryside, encouraged by the highway system and the favorable mortgage market created by FHA and VA loans. Standards set by these programs have largely determined recent patterns of residential development. The original 200′ x 200′ block has almost disappeared from new subdivisions, replaced by curvilinear streets and cul-de-sacs. The average lot size has increased from the earlier 50′ x 100′. The typical new subdivision is considerably larger and the developer not only subdivides the land but also builds the houses. Often subdivisions include greenways, parks, recreation centers, and sometimes even school sites. In addition to these single family house subdivisions, numerous garden apartments have been built, frequently along heavily traveled arterials. Zoning codes have encouraged these locations so that the apartments will act as buffers between highway noise and single family homes. The hope is that the heavy traffic generated by apartments will stay off neighborhood streets. The unfortunate result is often that apartment dwellers are excluded from any sense of neighborhood and must put up with all the traffic noise. The other new form of housing is the trailer

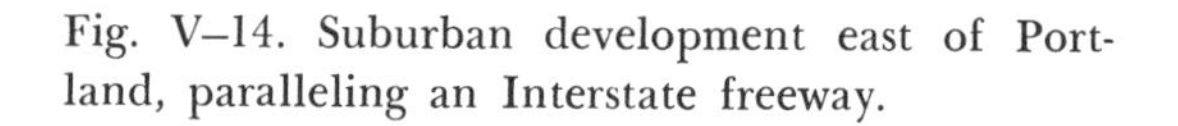

Fig. V–14. Suburban development east of Portland, paralleling an Interstate freeway.

Fig. V–15. The Brightwood apartment complex west of Portland. The garden apartment and townhouse complex are recent additions to the suburbs in the Pacific Northwest.

Fig. V–16. Portland, a recent apartment development in the southeast section.

Fig. V–17. Portland, N.W. Thurman Street, 1972. The inner city neighborhoods fight freeway construction.

court. Originally relegated to industrial areas or along major arterials, it has recently emerged as the mobile home park with many of the amenities of the typical subdivision at a price more people can afford.

In the area immediately around the downtown, highrise apartments have been introduced. Immediately after World War II, a large cluster developed at the base of Portland's west hills. More recently, others have been added in other sections through urban renewal. In the old streetcar neighborhoods two opposing trends have developed. One is the replacement of older housing by small apartment projects and commercial and industrial development. The other trend has been rehabilitation of houses for private use. These efforts have occurred both spontaneously and with city-sponsored planning, and sometimes with construction, to help the process along.

Shopping activity has undergone great changes as a result of the highway system and residential out-migration. Instead of one major center for department stores and specialty shops, Portland now has several major centers. In 1960 Lloyd Center was built, near two freeways and close to downtown. Office buildings, hotels, and some housing now surround it. In the 1960s continued residential expansion and the building of bypass freeways encouraged major centers on both east and west sides of town.

Smaller centers and commercial strips exist throughout the metropolitan area to meet local demand. The new automobile-oriented strips and centers are replacing the older streetcar centers, which are often simply abandoned or altered for light industrial or wholesaling uses. The recent buildings are larger than stores in earlier neighborhood centers. Display windows have been given up in favor of completely enclosed

Fig. V–18. Portland, Lloyd Center shopping mall —at one time the largest in the country. Downtown Portland is visible across the river.

buildings. Set back behind large parking lots, display windows served no purpose and have been replaced by signs to communicate to passersby. This continues the trend toward enclosure seen earlier in buildings on the highways. In the 1940s and 1950s restaurants were often bright and shiny and machine-like. In the 1960s the low, warm and inward-looking building became the standard.

Before the advent of the automobile and good highways, only the relatively wealthy were able to get away regularly to the mountains or the beaches. The automobile plus increased income have made these places available to many for weekend or even day trips. As a result, the pressure for local recreation facilities has lessened, particularly in the outer suburbs where residents are most likely to be able to afford the weekend trip. On the other hand, interest in preserving natural areas has increased and undeveloped hills and some of the Willamette River's banks have been purchased for, or proposed as, regional parks.

The downtown area has gained several public plazas or gathering places. Earlier downtown parks were intended to be quiet retreats amid the hubbub, or places for commemorative sculpture. The new parks are intended as active attractions and gathering places. The plaza, an

Fig. V–19. Portland, typical open-air Safeway store, 1936.

Fig. V–20. Portland, typical Safeway with large windows and parking lot, 1974.

Fig. V–21. Washington Square Mall (west of Portland) on a summer Sunday, 1974.

Fig. V–22. Portland, Canyon Road, circa 1890.

Fig. V–23. Portland, Canyon Road, 1934.

active, but extra or secondary function in the earlier, European city, has become a prime use of land in its own right. The most successful is the Auditorium Forecourt (1970) which draws large crowds almost in spite of its surroundings. One of the purposes of the gathering places or plazas is to bring more activity downtown. Another such effort is the redevelopment of the downtown waterfront. This project, agreed to in

Fig. V–24. Portland, Canyon Road (now Sunset Highway), 1973. The changing scale of transportation created by increased population and changing standards of comfort is clearly seen in Figs. V–22, 23, and 24.

principle in 1972, involves the closure and demolition of Harbor Drive, begun in May 1974. Though the traffic needs for Harbor Drive were still present, it was decided that a "people's waterfront" was more important.

This decision represents a new type of planning effort. Other examples are attempts to develop or redevelop public transportation systems and to preserve and renew older neighborhoods. For Bennett and other planners who struggled to demonstrate the advantages of planning, there was unplanned trend and planning for the trend. Recent efforts have been directed not only toward developing alternative public policies and choosing those that seem most likely to produce a quality environment, but also toward determination of what exactly constitutes a quality environment.

Fig. V–25. Portland, looking southwest from downtown to the suburbs and farmland beyond.

Freeway Towns

The increased scale of the new technology has had important effects on the smaller cities and towns of the Pacific Northwest. In some cases the new facilities, such as freeways, have brought enormous economic growth to small towns. Sometimes new towns such as Hanford, Washington, with its Atomic Energy Commission facilities, have been created. On the other hand, numerous small towns have been bypassed by modern technology—left off freeways and air routes and other modern developments.

The Willamette Valley between Albany and Eugene provides good examples of these effects. The early national highways through the valley paralleled the railroads, usually within several hundred yards. As a result, the roads served the same towns. Towns which had earlier been blessed with the business railroads brought, now simply transferred that business to their main streets where the highway usually ran. The interstate freeway, like the railroad, was built down the center of the valley. Because of wide right-of-way and limited access requirements the freeway was usually located some distance from the older towns. Each of these towns had its improved farm road and interchanges connecting it to the freeway. At these interchanges gas stations, motels and restaurants proliferated. They were followed by truck repair shops and highway-related industry. Besides serving the traveler these facilities have attracted local residents. The restaurants, the newest ones in the area, have become the favored places for club meetings and wedding

Fig. V–26. Coburg interchange of Interstate 5, Willamette Valley, Oregon, with commercial development, late 1960s. Since this photo was taken a truck repair facility and a commercial campground have been added.

receptions. For the smallest towns this has often meant development of two distinct business areas. One contains gas stations and restaurants—facilities both tourists and local residents use. The other, older business area contains services primarily for local residents, like grocery stores and barbershops.

While the freeway can pull towns apart, it can also provide big new bonanzas. Halsey is the site of a large paper mill even though fewer people live in the town than work at the plant. Workers commute to this plant from the cities of Albany, Corvallis, and Eugene. In effect, the automobile gives the company a larger labor pool than is available at any one of these towns. The mill is located away from these larger population centers, so fewer people complain about the odors. The same forces were at work when a shopping center developer proposed a regional center near Tangent. The freeway provided the necessary access.

In the late 1960s Linn and Benton counties formed a unified community college district. Just as in earlier times towns battled over the county seat, Albany, Corvallis and Lebanon battled over the college site. The solution was one typical of the automobile age: the college was placed in a field, away from all towns and with no supporting population.

The result of the free choice in location which the auto provides is a valley organized much like the valley of the pioneer era. Then the grist mill was at the source of water power, the grain elevator at the riverboat landing, and the store at one or the other or completely independent. Now each activity chooses its own location based on its own needs. The big difference lies in the number of times each place is visited. In the pioneer period, the grist mill and the grain elevator were visited only one or twice a year. People visited the store several times a year. Most time was spent on the farm. Today, the paper mill worker travels to the plant five days a week, the family to the shopping center only slightly less often. The result is an enormous increase in the number of trips compared to the pioneer era, and the increasing length of these trips in relation to periods when transportation systems required that people live near their work.

Some cities have attempted to counteract the effects of the auto. The new shopping and business areas have the advantages of newer and wider roads as well as ample parking space. Through federal urban renewal financing a number of cities have attempted to give their downtowns these advantages. Twin Falls undertook such a program. Main Street was given wider sidewalks, trees, and benches to make it more pleasant for shoppers. Buildings behind the shops facing on Main Street were demolished to provide ample parking space. Tacoma, Washington, and Eugene, Oregon, facing more severe competition from suburban shopping centers, closed their main shopping streets entirely to cars and built large parking garages nearby. In addition, access roads to the downtown have been improved, and in Eugene a formerly moribund bus system has been revived.

Fig. V–27. Twin Falls, the new main shopping street.

The towns which have been most affected by recent developments are those left off the new systems. Twin Falls' downtown may have been weakened by the competition of outlying areas, but it still has the advantage of being on the freeway and of being served by commercial air flights. It is still connected to the rest of the nation by the new transportation systems. Such towns have the economic resources to deal with decay in one area of town.

Towns like Montpelier in the Bear Lake Valley are not so lucky. Montpelier became important because of railroad repair shops which provided many jobs. The railroad also brought wholesaling and distribution activities. The early highway, U.S. 30, which passed along the east edge of town, continued this trend. Motels, gas stations, and restaurants serving the traveler located along this highway. Washington Street, which connects the railroad and the highway, is the major street for local needs. The new systems—the interstate highway and the airplane—do not go through the Bear Lake Valley. The high power line and the gas line, other ways of moving energy, do pass through the valley but unlike the railroad, which required 60 employees even in 1883, the gas pipeline has few employees located along the line. On the improved highways, with more powerful cars, fewer stops are required during trips. The traveler and the mover of goods and energy thus have little need for Montpelier. This and a declining farm population make Montpelier and many similar towns almost unnecessary.

Montpelier survives because we live in an environment that is not all brand new. Though the highway and the airplane are the new technologies, the railroad still remains. And even if it disappears as the riverboats did, the railroad will still leave its patterns. This is true for the entire region; many towns that are not vital to the new technology still remain. Old patterns persist in other places as well. If Portland,

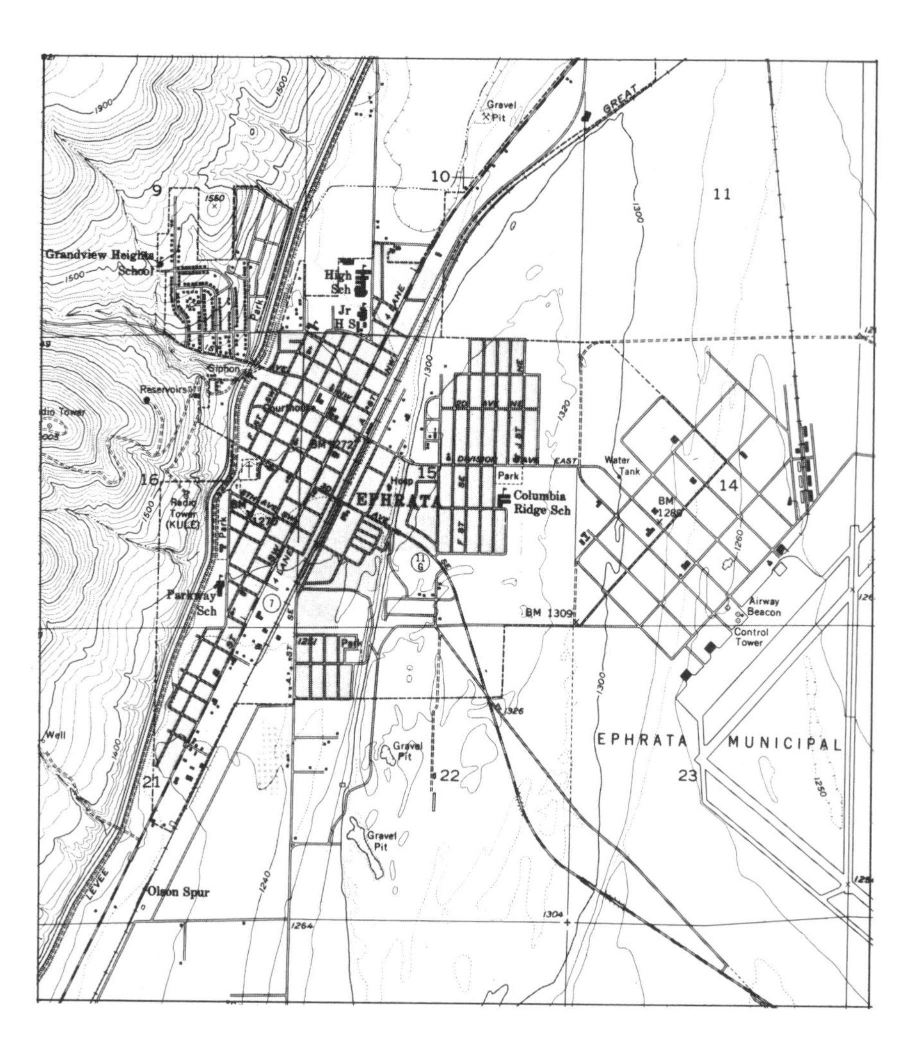

Fig. V–28. Ephrata, Washington, showing the various grid patterns developed during the town's history.

the major city in the State of Oregon, were being built today, it would not be located at the head of navigation for 1850s' ships. But inertia keeps it from moving. A narrow level area may not be an ideal downtown site, but moving a town is too costly, both socially and economically.

Ephrata, Washington, shows clearly and simply the additive effect of old and new on the total form of a town. The site had a good spring and was chosen as a roundup site in ranching times. Soon after the Great Northern Railroad was built through the valley, the town of Ephrata was platted. The original grid of nearly square blocks is aligned with the railroad, which runs roughly parallel to the hills. Later additions to the west side of town, still trapped between hills and railroad, continue this original angle, though the block size, determined by each developer, varies. The plan of the area east of the railroad and up on the 40-foot ridge is not determined by the railroad. Here the grid follows the township surveying pattern and is oriented to the compass points. Two other patterns are evident. A curvilinear pattern is used for development of a view subdivision in the hills. In the industrial area east of town the grid is aligned with the airport runways—determined by the angles needed for airplane approach. These patterns, each developed for specific purposes in their own time, together form modern Ephrata.

Such a mixture of times in one place is typical of most cities. In our daily lives we use and see places from different times. On almost any street there are buildings from several periods. When we seek recreation, we can choose from recently preserved natural areas, active recreation grounds, or the formal gardens and fountains of the 19th century. It is this choice and variety which makes the city interesting and enjoyable.

Buildings and Gardens

Portland's Towers and the 200-Foot Block

George McMath

The years since 1950 have witnessed great changes in architecture, but in a different way than the previous two decades. Belluschi, Yeon, and the others were revolutionaries, "throwing off the shackles" of historicism and seeking a new organic architecture relevant to 20th century life. That battle was over.

The significant changes over the past 25 years, especially in commercial and institutional design, have not primarily been the result of pursuing a particular architectural philosophy. Rather, these changes were mainly brought about by forces external to the traditional architectural framework; the automobile with its freeways and storage requirements, urban renewal, and the accelerating scale of economic investment, among others. Like other cities, Portland has felt (been staggered by?) the impact of these forces, and consensus has it that the impact has been detrimental to the quality of life in the city.

In suburban areas the effect of the automobile is obvious; miles of strip development with 80% or so of the land allocated to car storage. The Beaverton Highway, Canyon Road, or 82nd Avenue could be suburban "anywhere U.S.A."

In major downtown projects the parking problem was substantially different. Cars had to be stored under a building or in a separate structure. The Portland situation was made immensely more difficult by the 200-foot-square blocks laid out on sloping land with a high water table. These unusually small blocks, originally platted by Lovejoy and Pettygrove in 1845, served the city well until recent times and, along with the relatively narrow streets, provided a pleasant pedestrian scale. But times changed, and the increasing scale of development and the complexity of modern building programs presented challenging problems to Portland's architects. A variety of solutions have been tried over the years, none wholly successful, particularly if one subscribes to the Jane Jacobs view that the urban street should be a place of diversity, vitality and human activity.

The first major postwar building was Belluschi's previously noted Equitable Building of 1948, now the Commonwealth Building, but its program was essentially that of a prewar building; parking was not furnished and the ground level was allocated to shops. The next significant downtown structure was the Hilton Hotel designed by Skidmore, Owings and Merrill, who continued the preeminence established by their Portland predecessors, Belluschi and A. E. Doyle. (This position was maintained until the mid-1960s when other firms emerged to compete for major projects.)

Design of the Hilton, which would be the first new downtown hotel since the New Heathman in the late 1920s, began in 1958. Several schemes were developed in an attempt to accommodate the difficult program of a modern hotel which required underground parking, extensive convention facilities as well as the usual lobbies, restaurants, lounges and guestrooms. At the same time the designers wished to set the main

Fig. V–29. Hilton Hotel, 1963, Skidmore, Owings and Merrill.

building back from the street lines in order to provide light, air, and a public plaza. All this demanded too much of the 200-foot block. The final design had the public functions at the street level, all contained within a podium, which became the base for the tower. For economic reasons the plaza level was reserved for a private club and a very delightful convention pavilion.

The tower design is a strong expression of the reinforced concrete frame with projecting columns tapering upward as the loads are reduced. Less successful are the stick-like aluminum window mullions which encroach on the edges of the spandrel beams, diminishing the structural statement. A more practical problem of the mullions is the unsightly discoloration of the concrete caused by the drip pattern. The poured concrete frame has a bush hammered finish, which exposed the warm color of the stone aggregate. It was the first use of the technique in Portland since Doyle's 1926 Motoramp Garage at 6th and Pine.

When the Hilton was finally completed in 1963 it generated strong debate among architects and citizens alike. While generally praised in narrow architectural terms, many took issue with the broader urban design aspects. Critics denounced the "fortress walls" of the podium and the "anti-pedestrian" private plaza, and they were not at all mollified by the lush landscaping with ivy dripping over the walls. Defenders cited the difficult requirements of the building and the sunshine and air that had been let in to a congested urban area. The argument has never been resolved, though at the time opponents of the design seemed to outnumber the proponents.

An interesting footnote to the argument appeared when the Hilton design was published in the October, 1964 issue of the *Architectural Record.* The site plan illustrated was not the one constructed; rather, it was an earlier plan showing a public plaza level with a grand stairway at the corner of Broadway and Salmon Streets. The *Record,* commenting on the abandoned plan, said: "In the end, however, this generous allocation of space for purely urbanistic effect did not turn out to be feasible."

The Standard Plaza, also finished in 1963 and designed by Skidmore, Owings and Merrill, was built on a sloping block similar to the Hilton site but somewhat steeper (17-foot drop in elevation from high point to low point). Here the open plaza accessible for active public use became a reality. Though under the zoning regulations the building could have been accommodated on a half-block site, the architects convinced the client, the Standard Insurance Company, to purchase the entire block. This was a most generous grant of valuable open space and the Standard Plaza became Portland's first full block office building that was not built to the property lines.

Skidmore, Owings and Merrill studied several different approaches to the site development, including a podium type plaza similar to the Hilton. Their final design was quite ingenious and resulted in an "inverse podium" just the opposite of the Hilton. The tower, set well back on all four sides, stands on a lower level plaza which extends through the block to a curving ramp and curving stairway leading up to 6th

Fig. V–30. Standard Plaza, 1963, Skidmore, Owings and Merrill, architects.

Avenue at the corners. Entrance to the building is from the plaza at the lower level and by bridge over the plaza at the upper level, leading to Hilda Morris' bronze "Ring of Time," one of the city's better urban sculptures. The "Italianate" design of the stairway, the fountains, and other plaza details was directed by senior partner Nathaniel Owings.

A primary element of the site plan was the elimination of sidewalks and parking along the sloping side streets which would have forced the pedestrian to walk through the plaza without crossing the in-and-out driveways leading to basement parking and drive-in banking. This was quite a daring scheme, and the City Council accepted the idea that the open plaza was a good "trade off" for the sidewalks, and they adopted the necessary ordinances. The plan would probably have worked as the designers intended except for the vagaries of local politics. When the building was nearly finished, Commissioner of Public Works William Bowes, then up for reelection, succumbed to the wishes of downtown merchants and ordered sidewalks and parking to be reinstalled. However, since the granite sidewalls of the plaza extended almost to the old street line a normal width sidewalk could not be built. The result is a 42-inch sidewalk, impassable when a car door is open, and parking meters curiously mounted on metal railings and on the granite wall. In spite of the meanness of the sidewalk and the possibility of bruising a shoulder on a parking meter it appears that more pedestrians still use the sidewalk rather than the plaza to get through the block. This situation supports the premise that plazas alone, no matter how accessible, will not necessarily have active public use. A plaza needs other pedestrian generating elements either within the space or on the borders. In recent months pedestrian activity substantially increased when a restaurant opened on the plaza, an element that had been suggested by the architects at the outset.

The Standard Plaza was one of the first to use high strength steel in the building frame, which combined with the central utility core of reinforced concrete, allowed column-free space from the core to the outside walls. The structural capability of the new type steel is evident in the long beam spans clearly articulated with aluminum cladding. The tapering of the spandrels expresses the distribution of stresses in the simply supported beam structure where all lateral forces are absorbed in the reinforced concrete utility core. The choice to express such an esoteric element showed the limitations of the "Meisian" approach. By this time it had all been done and the designer was hard put to create anything very original. The style had served its purpose through the Fifties and early Sixties and the Standard would be the last major building of the gender in Portland.

Future office buildings would be more sensuous and less concerned with structural expression. And it was fitting that Pietro Belluschi, in collaboration with Wolff & Zimmer Associates, would be the designer of Portland's first major structure in the new mode. Completed in 1965, the new Equitable Center was the third headquarters building Belluschi had undertaken for the savings and loan bank since their association began in 1929 with a remodeling project. Underground parking again dictated the use of a full block podium, and though the plaza is accessible to the public, the "fortress walls" along the sloping sides, and originally along 5th Avenue prompted the same kind of "anti-pedestrian" criticism as did the Hilton Hotel walls. However, it should be noted that Belluschi's original concept, turned down by the client, called for shops along 5th Avenue. This idea was finally realized in 1971 after the Equitable was acquired by the General Acceptance Corporation. The first parking level was converted to banking and office space which

Fig. V–31. Equitable Building, 1965, Pietro Belluschi with Wolff, Zimmer Associates, associated architects.

opened up the podium on 5th Avenue and to a lesser extent on the side streets.

The main structure, described by Belluschi as "a tentative return to a more romantic architecture,"[1] consists of three uniform stories supported by free standing columns rising above a peripheral stepped platform like an ancient Greek stylobate. Belluschi again shows concern for the setting by establishing proportions and a scale that relates well with the nearby City Hall, a statement that cannot be said of another neighbor, the monstrous First National Bank Tower to the east. Podium walls and the facade are sheathed in pre-cast quartz aggregate panels which, while elegantly formed, thoroughly conceal the nature of the steel frame behind, an aspect of the design that has generated criticism of the Equitable and others in the style that has become known as the "New Formalism." The surface of the grand plaza is detailed in Belluschi's old favorites, travertine and brick.

The Oregon Historical Center built in 1966 across the Park Blocks from the Art Museum was designed by Wolff & Zimmer Associates with Pietro Belluschi as consulting architect.

Car storage was not a requirement thus allowing the designers greater freedom to involve the pedestrian, and they did it well. While the pre-cast concrete walls convey a solid massive appearance, the large

1. "Concerned With Old-Fashioned Qualities," *Architectural Record* (December, 1965), 144.

Fig. V–32. Oregon Historical Center, 1966, Wolff-Zimmer Associates; Pietro Belluschi, consultant.

Fig. V–33. Oregon Historical Center, brick paved alley connecting Broadway to the Park Blocks.

glassed areas on the ground floor allow viewing into the exhibit space from the sidewalk and from the delightful brick-paved alley extending through the block, giving meaning to the motto on the dedication plaque, "open to all."

Three years later Portland's first California designed postwar office tower was completed: the Bank of California Building by San Francisco architects, Anshen and Allen, with Barnes, Hilgers and Maslen of Portland consulting.

Situated on a relatively flat block, the inevitable underground parking, and drive-in banking are accommodated by a modest raising of the first floor level allowing easy pedestrian access to the building.

The first floor banking hall occupying most of the block is straddled by the 15-story tower. Both are clad in white pre-cast concrete while the service core is covered with gray-green slate. The soaring vertical emphasis and deeply sculptured concrete panels again give a false expression to the steel frame structure, and lack the restraint that is a characteristic of most Portland buildings.

More important than the building design was its location at the north end of the downtown core. The Bank of California was the first major office building constructed in the area since Belluschi's old Equitable Building more than 20 years earlier. This investment has stimulated other improvements on nearby blocks resulting in a healthy northern "pole" to compete with Urban Renewal and other new developments at the south end of the core, a situation that can only benefit the retail area between.

Fig. V–34. Bank of California, 1969, Anshen and Allen of San Francisco, architects; Barnes, Hilgers and Maslen of Portland, consultants.

Fig. V–35. Georgia-Pacific Building, 1971, Skidmore, Owings and Merrill, architects.

Building scale took another quantum jump in 1971 with the construction of Skidmore, Owings and Merrill's 30-story Georgia-Pacific Building. It replaced the Hilton Hotel as the state's tallest structure and became the first multi-block development in the downtown area.

Original plans called for the full building program to be contained on a single block but the Georgia-Pacific Corporation wanted their finance and accounting department to be on one floor, which meant use of a sub-grade level previously allocated to parking. The addition of this office space brought the total floor area over the limits allowed by the zoning code. Rather than reducing the height of the tower, the owners acquired a half block parcel across 4th Avenue for an eight-level parking garage and persuaded the City Planning Commission to transfer the unused "air rights" to the main block.

The garage structure is a pleasant paradox, as the pedestrian is given as much attention as the automobile. A tunnel featuring art work and a historical museum of the company's activities connects with the main building while the ground level has shops and offices set back from the upper level which provides a protected walkway.

Though parking was eliminated from the tower block a podium was again employed, and while the battered granite walls along the side streets offer little to the passerby the lower level is opened up with glazed store fronts which continue to an inside shopping lobby. Pedestrian traffic through the building is quite heavy, particularly during rainy weather. From the lower level, escalators connect with the teak panelled lobby and main entry plaza on 5th Avenue.

Fig. V–36. Sculpture in Georgia-Pacific Plaza by Count Alexander Von Svoboda. Entitled "Quest," it is better known as "Family Night at the Y."

Fig. V–37. First National Center, 1972, Charles Luckman and Associates, architects.

Focal point of the granite surfaced plaza is a gross assemblage of five nude figures hacked out of a 17-ton white marble monolith by sculptor Count Alexander Von Svoboda who described his work as "one of the last modern classical pieces ever done . . ."[2] Entitled "Quest" by the sculptor, it has become better known as "Family Night at the Y."

The Georgia-Pacific Building, probably the handsomest postwar office tower, was at the time the tallest reinforced concrete structure in the country. The uniform finish on the poured concrete frame has the quality of pre-cast work and demonstrates the advances in concrete technology developed in the Sixties. Close supervision was essential to achieving optimum results with the proprietary "Arbeiton" concrete system. The core of steel reinforcing bars was wrapped with a fine wire mesh, then dry quartz aggregate was placed in the space between the mesh and the outer steel forms. Next, concrete with white sand and cement, and conventional stone aggregate was poured into the core. Mechanical vibration forced the fine elements of sand and cement through the wire mesh to bind the quartz. After removing the forms final finish was achieved by sandblasting which removed the surface cement and exposed the quartz aggregate.

As in the Hilton Hotel design the concrete structure tapers toward the top, here so subtle that it is apparent only upon close examination. During construction, sidewalk superintendents, believing they had caught the builder in a grievous error, were chagrined to learn that the taper was intentional and the building was not out of plumb.

Several important technical and design advances were developed in the Georgia-Pacific Building, among them the first use of a fire sprinkling system in a high-rise office structure. This eliminated the need for a smoke tower, loop corridors and other elements normally required in non-sprinkled buildings. The additional cost was more than offset by the increase in usable floor area.

Other "firsts" were the coffered ceilings with 2′-square light fixtures containing U shaped fluorescent lamps, and the "heat recovery" air conditioning system which reuses heat generated within the building to the extent that the electric boilers don't come on until the outside air temperature reaches 40 degrees.

The "air rights borrowing" technique was used again by the First National Bank which allowed construction of a 40-story tower and a five-story computer center each on a full block and connected by a bridge at the third level.

When completed in 1972 the First National Tower took the title of the "State's Tallest" which it will probably hold for many years, especially if the public outcry over blocked views and violence to the skyline have any impact on public policy. Los Angeles architects Charles Luckman and Associates, with apparent disdain for Portland's urbanity, have ably expressed the essence of corporate power and arrogance in the

---

2. *Oregon Journal,* June 12, 1970, Sec. 2.

Fig. V–38. Rendering of the new Federal Building to be completed in 1975, Skidmore, Owings and Merrill, architects.

marble sheathed tower with fake fins reminiscent of Detroit auto design in the Fifties. A publicist for the Luckman firm, quoted by Ada Louise Huxtable in the *New York Times,* described the design as " '40 stories into the air, a towering challenge to Mt. Hood.' " Huxtable continued: "Against the Suave Schlock of some of Portland's current California imports, Mt. Hood doesn't stand a chance."[3]

Other than access to the building the pedestrian is ignored—unless one is particularly enthralled by hundreds of feet of pink granite wall. One hopeful element was the delightful small banking museum designed by the Oregon Historical Society and located just inside the 4th Avenue entrance. Touted in the bank's opening brochure as the only one of its kind in the Northwest, it was a popular attraction, but it didn't last two years and has been replaced by a glorified newsstand. Perhaps the additional revenue was needed to defray the cost of replacing the grotesque concrete railing that originally surrounded the tower.

Since the First National Bank Building, the designs of major projects presently under construction or on the drawing boards appear to have more emphasis on urban amenities and pedestrian activity. Skidmore, Owings and Merrill's design for the Federal Office Building provides a full block plaza between the 18-story tower and City Hall which will extend the open space of the adjacent Lownsdale and Chapman squares, and will perhaps one day be a major element in a civic center that has long been a dream of many in Portland. A civic center was first proposed in the 1912 Bennett plan, and later in the Moses plan of 1943.

Over a decade ago when the new federal building was in the early planning stages the General Services Administration wanted a site out of the core area on lower priced land. But in 1963, through the efforts of Congresswoman Edith Green, the G.S.A. was pursuaded to acquire a site in the downtown area that would reinforce the civic center idea which was again in the talking stage. This decision gave impetus to serious planning which got underway in 1967 when the City and County jointly commissioned Wolff, Zimmer, Gunsul, Frasca to plan a four-block civic center east of the Chapman and Lownsdale squares. Overseeing the planning was Commissioner William Bowes for the City and David Eccles for the County. In spite of strong support from the business community the voters narrowly defeated the project in the 1968 election.

At the north end of the downtown area the new headquarters building for the U.S. National Bank will have shops and other street level facilities oriented to pedestrian use. Designed by SOM, with Pietro Belluschi consulting architect to the owners, the five-story banking unit will be finished in 1975. A future tower will rise to the north along Burnside.

This heightened concern for the urban dweller is due at least in part to the broadened scope of Portland's city planning program and the substantial involvement of citizens' groups in the decision-making

3. *New York Times,* June 19, 1970.

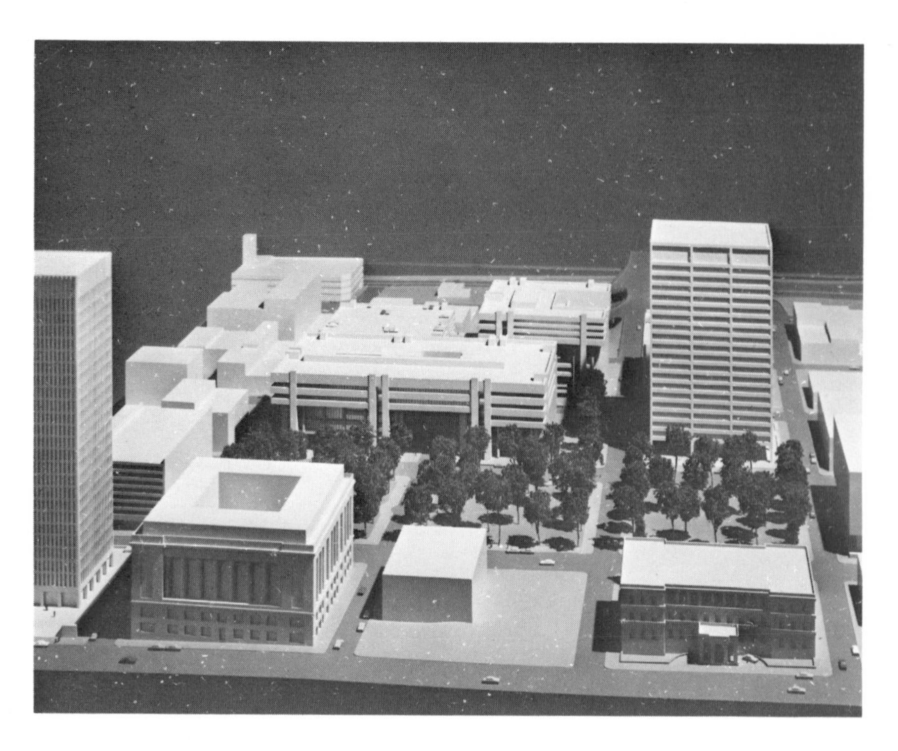

Fig. V–39. Proposed Civic Center, Wolff, Zimmer, Gunsul, Frasca, architects, looking east from 5th Avenue. Skidmore, Owings and Merrill's Federal Building is east of the City Hall seen in the right foreground. North of the Federal Building is the proposed Courts Building and to the east the Public Safety Building and a parking structure. The Civic Center was defeated by the voters in 1968.

Fig. V–40. Model of the United States National Building, 1975, Skidmore, Owings and Merrill, architects; Pietro Belluschi, consultant.

Fig. V–41. Model of proposed Portland General Electric Co. headquarters, Wolff, Zimmer, Gunsul, Frasca, architects; Pietro Belluschi, consultant.

process. Critics charge that there are too many agencies and individuals participating in design decisions and that quality will be diminished by a "design by committee" process.

Major projects presently involved in the process include the 3-block complex for Portland General Electric Company, which underwent partial redesign at a City Council meeting, and the headquarters of the Northwest Natural Gas Company which will occupy a four-block site north of Burnside. At this writing neither design is set and only time will tell if the process is valid or if "too many cooks" are involved.

Portland's designers faced a new and different challenge when the urban renewal program was established by the 81st Congress as part of the 1949 Housing Act.

Portland was among the first cities in the country to embrace urban renewal. Within a year of the federal act the Oregon Legislature adopted the necessary enabling laws which designated the Housing Authority of Portland as the local planning agency for urban renewal. After considering several possible renewal areas H.A.P. prepared plans for the Vaughn Street Project in the northwest section of the City known as "Slabtown."

Battle lines were quickly drawn between area residents and the industrial interests. Plans called for expansion of the industrial area to a buffer zone generally along Thurman Street which would have removed many blocks of "blighted housing." The plan was submitted to the voters at the 1952 general election, and with substantial help from Slabtown native Stanley Earl the measure was soundly defeated. It was also the year Fred Peterson defeated incumbent Dorothy McCulloch Lee

Fig. V–42. Model of proposed Northwest Natural Gas Co. headquarters complex, Campbell, Yost, Grube & Partners, architects.

for the mayor's office. Ironically, industrial development has occurred through the years generally in the areas proposed in the defeated plan, and district residents are still trying to hold the line.

Following the election the administration of the urban renewal program was reorganized. The State Legislature removed the planning function from H.A.P. and placed it with the City Council who were free to delegate it as they saw fit. After normal bureaucratic delays planning began again in 1957, this time under the aegis of the Portland City Planning Commission and its Director, Lloyd Keefe. The newly formed Urban Renewal Section was headed by John Kenward who would later become Director of the Portland Development Commission.

Selected for renewal planning was a 44-block section in South Portland that had been among those considered in the 1952 program. Bounded by S.W. Market Street, Harbor Drive, Arthur Street, and 4th Avenue, the area was labeled the South Auditorium Project, and generally consisted of run-down apartments, stores and modest houses of the late 19th century. The area had at one time been the center of Jewish, Italian and other ethnic communities. Planners were able to find a sufficient number of "blighted" properties to meet federal requirements and the project was put on the ballot in 1958. This time it passed. The voters approved a charter amendment that established the project boundaries, and created the Portland Development Commission to administer the program.

The first South Auditorium master plan prepared by the Planning Commission did not elicit any land sales. Consequently, Skidmore, Owings and Merrill was commissioned to redesign the plan which was approved in 1961.

While the plan established a series of superblocks, much of the 200-foot grid was retained in streets or pedestrian ways, particularly in the northerly sector, which provided an easy transition with the established city pattern, and also allowed the preservation of many fine old street trees. As with virtually all of the early renewal projects mass clearance was the order of the day. Portland was no exception. Only three structures were retained, all on the east side of First Avenue. The plan met with many objections from Commission members, real estate consultants, appraisers, etc., until the architects illustrated that the plan provided ample landscaped setbacks, tree-lined pedestrian malls, and three ample parks, and still provided a net salable land area in excess of a typical downtown block such as Meier & Frank's store block which was fully covered with building and no green areas at all. The difference was in the elimination of the vast area occupied by streets and sidewalks and replacing them with pedestrian malls and landscaping. Skidmore, Owings and Merrill was also retained as the advisors to the commission on all architectural work in the area.

When the land was once again offered for sale under the new plan, Skidmore, Owings and Merrill cancelled their contract for consultation to the commission in order to serve the developer who would be competing for the land. At this time SOM was consulted by John Kenward

Fig. V–43. Master Plan for the South Auditorium Urban Renewal Project, 1961, prepared by Skidmore, Owings and Merrill. The plan has been modified several times.

regarding replacements for consultants to the commission. Walter Gordon was leaving his position as Dean of the School of Architecture at the University of Oregon and seemed ideal for the assignment as Resident Design Consultant. The concept of a design advisory board was established and eventually, after considerable effort on the part of Kenward, Pietro Belluschi, Paul Hayden Kirk, George Rockrise and Lawrence Halprin were appointed. This group has made a significant contribution to the high standard of design.

New construction began in 1963. Most of the early buildings were low-rise office structures located on the periphery of the project. The successful developer and bidder on the land, Portland Center Development Company, and their architects, Skidmore, Owings and Merrill, broke ground in 1964 for their first phase development, by far the largest redevelopment in the project with over 24 acres of land; three apartment towers surrounded by two-story garden apartments, and an adjacent garage, retail and commercial building. The well-planned towers are flanked on the north and south by Halprin's eminently successful Lovejoy Fountain and Pettygrove Park. The fountain proved to be such a well-used "people place" that the adjacent garden apartments had to be converted to offices. The sometimes noisy activity that carried on into the night was a land use that did not mix well with normal sleeping patterns.

After completion of the apartment towers in 1966, Skidmore, Ow-

Fig. V–44. Portland Center Apartments, 1966, Skidmore, Owings and Merrill, architects.

Fig. V–45. Harrison Square, 1972, Skidmore, Owings and Merrill, architects.

Fig. V–46. American Plaza Condominiums, Travers/Johnston, architects.

ings and Merrill designed several other major structures in the renewal area, including the eight-story Boise Cascade Building (1968), the seven-story Blue Cross Building (1969), and Harrison Square (1972), an interesting design in concrete consisting of two offset rectangular structures connected by a bridge, well-concealed parking, extensive landscaping, and pedestrian arcades.

South of the Portland Center area are two projects designed by architects Travers/Johnston. The red brick design of the Ramada Inn is the result of long and difficult negotiations between the Portland Development Commission and the Ramada owners, and the Development Commission deserves high marks for resisting the standard pseudo-colonial design of the national motel chain. Immediately east of the Ramada Inn are the American Plaza condominiums which will ultimately consist of three towers and a recreation building.

Perhaps the most interesting structure in the original South Auditorium area is the recently completed 200 Market Building designed by Rudat/Boutwell & Partners. Sheathed in black glass the 18-story office structure recalls the mysterious monolith in the classic film "2001." Almost without scale on its own, the highly reflective walls present a shimmering scene of clouds, buildings and landscape.

In 1965 the Portland City Council approved a 13-block extension of the urban renewal area at the north end of the original project. Planning in the extension area has maintained the 200-foot grid and combines new construction with rehabilitation. Notable among the new buildings are the Crown Plaza and the Evans Products Building, both designed by Wolff, Zimmer, Gunsul, Frasca. Completed in 1971 the Crown Plaza is a two-block development consisting of a seven-level parking structure with a commercial arcade at the ground level, and an 11-story office building with outdoor terraces stepping toward the river at the second and third stories. The two elements are connected by a bridge at the second level which is designed to link up with the proposed "pedestrian skyway" if and when such a system is ever realized.

Rising one block to the north, the 19-story Evans Products Building is scheduled for completion in 1975. The unusual sheathing of red Willamina brick brings a stimulating variety to the skyline, and is the first use of the material in a high-rise structure since the late 1920s. It also will be the last use of Willamina brick, favored by local architects for decades. The company is completing its final contracts before permanently shutting down the kilns after continuous operation since 1892 and the production of an estimated 280 million bricks.

The South Auditorium Project and its later extensions, at least in physical and economic terms, is considered among the best, if not the best, of its kind in the country. Part of the success is undoubtedly due to the lessons learned with the ill-fated Vaughn Street Project and from the experience of earlier projects in other cities. But much of the credit must go to Ira C. Keller, Chairman of the Portland Development Commission from its inception until his retirement in 1972. A controversial figure, Keller was a strong leader and a man of action

Fig. V–47. 200 Market Building, 1973, Rudat/ Boutwell & Partners, architects.

Fig. V–48. Crown Plaza, 1971, Wolff, Zimmer, Gunsul, Frasca & Ritter, architects.

who didn't mind stepping on a few toes. These characteristics, developed in the corporate and political jungle of Chicago where he spent his earlier years, were especially suited to the job of guiding a bold new program. Perhaps Keller's greatest attribute was his insistence on quality in design, and quality in the people he chose to advise the commission.

The urban renewal area was again expanded in the spring of 1974 when the City Council approved new boundaries extending north to the Broadway Bridge and west from the Willamette River to 5th Avenue. The main thrust of planning in the 128-block area will be preservation and rehabilitation rather than clearance and new construction.

The Wood Tradition Expands

George McMath

In the Portland area, the decade of the 1950s saw the Northwest Style reach its peak, and at the same time, begin a transformation as new influences came to bear. Prior to the Fifties the regional design approach developed by Belluschi, Yeon and others had been limited to houses and churches. While the purest regional expression continued to be seen in domestic work, the Northwest Style expanded into building types that had traditionally been designed in other materials and other forms. Stained cedar and fir, overhanging pitched roofs, simple planning and detailing, became evident in banks, offices, schools, libraries, and virtually every kind of building where wood construction was allowed. Wood was even considered for the primary structure in Skidmore, Owings and Merrill's Memorial Coliseum but steel won out due to lower cost.

It was no accident that the great majority of these wood buildings were built in the suburban areas surrounding the central city. The post-war expansion of the suburbs created a demand for relatively small buildings, often branch facilities, that were appropriate for wood construction. And the designers were not hampered by the strict requirements of urban fire zones and building codes which often dictated masonry construction.

The evolution in the design of wood buildings was inevitable. The residential vocabulary of the Northwest Style could not always be adapted to other building types, and with more practitioners of the idiom there was naturally a greater variety of personal interpretation. But more significant in the transformation was the change in architectural philosophy. The idea of regionalism was on the wane as the universal approaches of Mies van der Rohe, Corbusier, and the International Style began to dominate architectural thinking.

A fine example of the integration of the Northwest wood tradition with the tenets of the International Style is the Tucker-Maxon Oral School in southeast Portland. Built in 1954, the modular wood structure was designed by David A. Pugh of Belluschi & Skidmore, Owings and Merrill. (Pugh, a graduate of Yale, later became Resident Partner of SOM's Portland office.)

Another example in a similar vein is the elegant house for art collec-

Fig. V–49. Tucker-Maxon Oral School, Portland, 1954, Belluschi, and Skidmore, Owings, and Merrill, architects.

Fig. V–50. Caudero house, Portland, 1961, Edgar W. Smith, architect.

Fig. V–51. First Presbyterian Church, Vancouver, Washington, 1956, Stewart and Richardson, architects.

tor Ed Cauduro designed by Edgar W. Smith. In spite of the forces dictating change, a few architects have carried on the regional tradition to the present. Belluschi's influence lingered on and many of the ablest architects that have been associated with the Northwest Style during the Fifties came out of the Belluschi office. Among them: Kenneth E. Richardson, Warren Weber, and Walter Gordon.

Richardson, who had been chief designer during the last years of the Belluschi office, continued on with Belluschi, & Skidmore, Owings and Merrill after SOM acquired the firm in 1951. A year later, Richardson left B&SOM to form a partnership with Vancouver architect, Donald J. Stewart. The new firm's initial project was the First Presbyterian Church in Vancouver, completed in 1956. Many elements of Belluschi's earlier churches are evident, which is not surprising as Richardson was involved in the design of several.

Designing in wood whenever possible, Richardson was interested in exploring new ways to use our native material. One innovation was the use of solid wood decking for walls as in the Midland Branch Library designed in 1957. Located in the suburbs east of Portland, the walls of the simple post and beam structure are made up of a single thickness of 4″ x 6″ tongue and groove roof decking. Structure, insulation, and finish, both inside and out, are provided in a single material.

Of the many churches designed by Stewart & Richardson, one of the more interesting is Westminster Presbyterian on Coburg Road north of Eugene. Situated in a walnut grove, the church complex was built in stages from 1954 to completion of the sanctuary unit in 1962.

The primary structure of the Fellowship Hall, the first unit built, featured another wood innovation—HB Frames, a proprietary Swedish

Fig. V–52. Midland Branch Library, Portland, 1957, Stewart and Richardson, architects.

Fig. V–53. Westminster Presbyterian Church, Eugene, Oregon, Fellowship Hall, 1954, Stewart and Richardson, architects. Nail-laminated HB Frames support roof.

Fig. V–54. Sanctuary unit, Westminster Presbyterian Church, Eugene, Oregon, 1962.

design. The frames were made up of conventional framing lumber set in vertical laminations and gang-nailed together to form a rigid frame similar to the more common glue-laminated arch.

Strong roof forms characterize the sanctuary unit which opens to an enclosed courtyard in the manner of Belluschi's First Presbyterian Church in Cottage Grove. "French drains" around the perimeter of the buildings made it possible to eliminate the usual gutters and downspouts.

As with Stewart & Richardson, Warren Weber has made significant contributions to church design. Weber left Belluschi in the late 1940s to open his own office. His churches, often characterized by unusual and complex roof forms, and intricate detailing, have a very personal touch, and are never mistaken for the work of other designers.

Walter Gordon has had an unusual and varied career with an influence on the shape of Portland far beyond the scope of his highly competent buildings. A native of Buffalo, Gordon received his bachelor's and master's degrees in achitecture from Princeton, and did further graduate study at the University of Paris and at Yale. Young architectural graduates were not in great demand in 1936 so Gordon took a job as curator of the Buffalo Art Museum. Similar positions followed in San Francisco and with the Portland Art Museum where Belluschi was a trustee. In 1940 Gordon joined the Belluschi office.

After Navy service in World War II, Gordon returned to the Belluschi firm where he stayed until he opened his own office in 1947. During the next ten years Gordon designed many distinguished houses as well as several non-residential structures. His buildings in this period were designed in the best regional tradition, and like Belluschi he considered sculpture, painting, and the other arts to be important design elements. Gordon's work toward the integration of art in architecture was recognized by an award from Artist's Equity.

In 1958 Gordon's career took another turn when he was selected as Dean of the School of Architecture & Allied Arts at the University of Oregon, succeeding Sidney Little. While Gordon enjoyed the challenge of the position, he also missed the practice of architecture, and in 1962 he resigned and returned to Portland where he formed a partnership with architects Daniel McGoodwin and John Hinchcliff.

The same year Gordon accepted the appointment as the first Resident Design Consultant to the Portland Development Commission, a position he holds to the present. In this capacity he has had a significant impact on the high quality of design in Portland's urban renewal areas. A notable instance was the involvement of San Francisco landscape architect, Lawrence Halprin, in the design of the Auditorium Forecourt. (See "Parks and Gardens," Part V.) Largely through Gordon's effort, Halprin was brought in to consult on an early design by Skidmore, Owings and Merrill which, at the time, was causing great controversy. SOM's design was ultimately rejected and Halprin was commissioned to design the project which resulted in the world famous Forecourt Fountain.

Gordon's work with the Portland Development Commission has not gone unnoticed. In recent years he has taken on similar positions with

Fig. V–55. Wessinger residence, Portland, 1948, Walter Gordon, architect.

the Salem and Eugene urban renewal agencies. Gordon's comprehensive approach to design, his restrained and thoughtful manner, and his sense of what is important has served the community well.

The 1950s also witnessed the emergence of a new generation of Portland architects. Many of these men came to the profession with common backgrounds and attitudes—most were World War II veterans and graduates of the University of Oregon. After apprenticeship and registration exams nearly all of these young architects opted to open their own offices, either alone or in partnership with a schoolmate. Consequently their early work was primarily residential. As a group their designs of the late Fifties were in the mainstream of the Northwest Style. While a few continued designing in the regional manner, most went on to develop a personal interpretation of the wood tradition.

Among the few architects who have maintained a regional outlook is C. Gilman Davis, a steadfast practitioner of the Northwest Style, and one of its most outspoken advocates. After graduation from the University of Oregon and work in Portland firms, Davis established his practice in the early 1950s. Through the years his designs have consistently expressed a regional philosophy. Both the 1955 Carlton House and the Thomas Buell house built 12 years later exhibit the essential characteristics of the Northwest Style and show the influence of Davis' long-time love affair with the "Oregon Barn."

Davis' regional advocacy has not been limited to his own designs. Through his work as Professor of Architecture in the two-year program at Portland State University, Davis has exposed a new generation to the regional philosophy. To some of his students who go on to further study it must be something of a shock to make the transition from the romanticism of the Oregon Barn to the theoretical considerations of systems

Fig. V–56. Richard A. Carlton residence, Tigard, Oregon, 1955, C. Gilman Davis, architect.

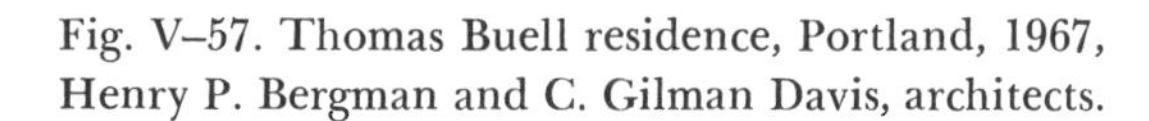

Fig. V–57. Thomas Buell residence, Portland, 1967, Henry P. Bergman and C. Gilman Davis, architects.

design and other esoteric programs seen today in most schools of architecture.

Another enduring proponent of a Northwest regional achitecture is John Storrs who, ironically, was raised in the Northeast and trained at Yale. A maverick with strong personal views, somewhat in the manner of Van Evera Bailey, Storrs wanted something different from the life style of the Northeast megalopolis. While a student at Yale he had occasion to hear Belluschi give a lecture on regional architecture. Impressed by the Northwest and Belluschi's views on regionalism, Storrs moved to Portland soon after graduation in 1950 and established his practice.

Storrs' designs have always shown a special concern and sensitivity for the setting. Simple but strong roof forms and bold expression of wood structure characterize much of Storrs' work, reflecting the rugged wooded sites he often had the good fortune to work with. The Kerr and Grieve houses are fine examples. Storrs is also able to work in a more restricted context as the design of the Portland Garden Club shows. Built in 1956, it is a thoroughly modern building that relates well to the sedate character of an older residential neighborhood.

While maintaining a small office through the years, Storrs has received many important commissions including the Salishan Lodge (see "Planned Resorts") and, appropriately, two significant projects for the forest products industry: the Forestry Pavilion at the Oregon Centennial Exposition, and the Western Forestry Center. Following the devastating fire in 1964 that consumed the log Forestry Building from the 1905 Lewis and Clark Exposition, Storrs was asked to design a new forestry exhibit

Fig. V–58. Peter Kerr house, Portland, 1959, John Storrs, architect.

Fig. V–59. James Grieve house, Portland, 1960, John Storrs, architect.

facility.

After extensive discussion and searching, a site was acquired in Portland's west hills adjacent to the Hoyt Arboretum, the Zoo, and the Oregon Museum of Science and Industry (OMSI). City-owned land was carved out of the popular Pitch and Putt golf course, a factor that drew objections from golfers and others who opposed the use of City property

Fig. V–60. Portland Garden Club, 1955, John Storrs, architect.

by the forest products industry. However, the objections were overridden when it was shown that the golf course could be redesigned, and that the educational values of the complex would be greatly enhanced by the addition of the Forestry Center.

The monument to the forest industry, finally completed in 1971, consists of two octagonal structures, an Exhibit Building, and the smaller 250-seat Theatre Building. Expansive hipped roofs covered with hand-split cedar shakes dominate the scene.

Except for the concrete foundations and the ground floor finish of both structures, wood products are used throughout, nearly all from the Northwest region. The overhanging roof of the Exhibit Building is supported by redwood posts carved by local artists. Beams are of glue-laminated Douglas fir, roof decking is ponderosa pine, and the exterior walls are covered with rough sawn cedar boards and battens.

The focus of the grand interior space is the rotunda and the "Talking Tree," framed by eight fir columns stretching 70 feet to the large central skylight. A variety of naturally finished western woods are used on the interior walls: 18″ wide white fir in the Foyer, sugar pine in Memorial Hall, ponderosa pine in the Colonial Room, and western hemlock in the Theatre Building. The well-designed exhibits, portraying all aspects of the forest industry, have proved to be a popular attraction for students and tourists.

In the late 1950s a remarkable group of young architects gathered together in an old Victorian house on the edge of downtown Portland.

Fig. V–61. Western Forestry Center, Portland, 1971, John Storrs, architect.

Fig.V–62. Western Forestry Center, redwood posts carved by local artists.

The group, all University of Oregon graduates, included Saul Zaik, William Fletcher, Donald Blair, John Reese, Frank Blachly, Alex Pierce, and designer George Schwarz. Sometimes known as the "14th Street Gang," they shared office space, ideas, and an occasional libation after work. Each had his own practice, though from time to time they collaborated on particular projects such as the two award-winning apartment houses designed by Reese, Blair, and Zaik.

After a few years the group drifted apart—Blachly and Reese and Blair and Zaik eventually formed partnerships. Most went on to distinguished careers: William Fletcher and Saul Zaik have been made Fellows in the American Institute of Architects for their design work; George Schwarz, often collaborating with his former colleagues, has done outstanding work in interior and furniture design; and Alex Pierce, in addition to designing many fine residences, has for 20 years been the most persistent and tireless voice for design quality in Portland's cityscape.

A few years later, Blair and Zaik and Alex Pierce of the 14th Street group joined with Farnham and Peck, Franks and Norman, and Stewart, Allen and McMath to form a new kind of partnership. The principals of the five firms recognized the limitations of their small offices, yet they all wanted to be involved in the design of major buildings, particularly civic projects that would have a significant impact on the community. At the same time each firm wished to maintain its own identity and the virtues of a small practice. After lengthy discussions, Architects Northwest was formed. The partnership agreement expressly stated that each firm would

Fig. V–63. Zaik residence, Portland, 1960, Saul Zaik, architect.

Fig. V–64. Colwell house, Salishan, Oregon, 1963, Fletcher and Finch, architects.

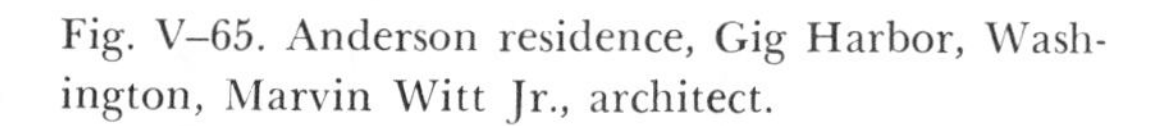

Fig. V–65. Anderson residence, Gig Harbor, Washington, Marvin Witt Jr., architect.

remain separate unless there was unanimous consent to jointly pursue a particular project. With great enthusiasm, an impressive brochure was prepared, a press party held, and several presentations were made to the

Fig. V–66. Springfield Branch, Equitable Savings and Loan Association, 1965, Wilmsen, Endicott, Unthank and Associates, architects.

building committees of major projects, including the Civic Auditorium and the proposed city-county office building. After a year and no commissions, Architects Northwest died a natural death. In retrospect it was a naive idea that probably never had a chance, but at the time it seemed to offer the best of both a small and large practice.

Many other young architects gained their early experience with the Wilmsen and Endicott office, referred to by some as the "Oregon Graduate School Annex." Robert Wilmsen and Charles Endicott, both prewar University of Oregon graduates, formed the partnership in 1948 which has evolved through the years to the present professional corporation—WEGROUP, a name that symbolizes the Wilmsen and Endicott philosophy of the group approach to architectural practice. Unlike most firms, a young architect or designer in the Wilmsen and Endicott office was exposed to every facet of architectural practice, and it is not surprising that many have gone on to establish their own successful firms. The list of talented designers who trained with Wilmsen and Endicott is unmatched in the region: Willard Martin, Gary Michael, Richard Campbell, De Norville Unthank, Otto Poticha, Donald Lutes, Ken Wallin and Robert York, to name a few.

The wide range of buildings designed in the Wilmsen and Endicott office, often in wood, have consistently been of high quality, though the design approach has varied as the group of architects in the office changed. One of WEGROUP's (then Wilmsen, Endicott and Unthank) most outstanding and widely acclaimed designs is the Central Oregon Community College in Bend, an ongoing project that has engaged the office since 1962. The C.O.C.C. has been the kind of project every architect dreams of but few get the opportunity to work on.

The college board had the rare foresight to hire the architect prior to site selection, and had the additional good judgement to accept his recommendation. The Wilmsen and Endicott office went on to prepare the campus master plan, design all of the buildings, and with other consultants, design the roads, landscaping, interiors, furniture, and virtually every physical detail of the campus.

As with most college developments the architect has been hampered by tight budgets and staged bonding which did not allow design and construction of the entire campus at one time. But this situation has perhaps been a plus—a restraint and variety have been achieved which might not have been the case if all the necessary funds had been available at the beginning.

The natural beauty of the chosen site is unequalled among college campuses in the state. The rolling virgin terrain, volcanic rock outcroppings, pine trees and a panoramic view of the snow-capped mountains of the central Cascades presented a unique challenge to the architects.

The general design concept for the campus was to blend the manmade structures into the site. The buildings, low in profile and scaled to the landscape, have been situated in an informal manner to permit the preservation of trees and other natural features, and to provide a choice of views to the magnificent scenery. Though the design of individual

Fig. V–67. Library, Central Oregon Community College, Bend, Oregon, 1966. View of Three Sisters and other Cascade peaks.

Fig. V–68. Physical Education Building, Central Oregon Community College, Bend, Oregon, 1971.

buildings is varied, reflecting the many different campus activities, great unity is achieved by a common scale and common materials—concrete and native woods.

The initial construction project consisted of four prototype classroom buildings, completed in 1963. These were followed by an administration building (1964), student center (1965), library (1966), a music-art building (1966), dormitory (1967), and most recent, the physical education and vocational-technical buildings (1971). A theatre is planned for 1975.

The campus and its buildings have received several design awards, but the most treasured accolade to the architects came from artists Carl and Hilda Morris. In a letter to Bob Wilmsen, Hilda Morris wrote:

> We tramped around up and down; saw rooflines, the outside forms that became the inside ones; the sculptural forms of the buildings, stairways (inside and outside), and recessed ground pools to catch rain drops; the purple landscaping that let, what is, be, and be better; the views of the mountains between the buildings, and more, and more. They *are* lucky to have so fine a campus.

The Wilmsen and Endicott firm was one of the prime participants in a unique building program conducted by the U. S. National Bank during the late 1950s and 1960s. Seldom has a bank, or any other large institution, insisted on such high quality design, or allowed the architects such freedom.

Guiding spirit of the program was Stuart Kidd, head of the bank's Building and Planning Department. Under Kidd's administration U. S.

Fig. V–69. Campus Branch, U. S. National Bank, Eugene, Oregon, 1965, Wilmsen, Endicott and Unthank architects.

Fig. V–70. Lebanon Branch, U. S. National Bank, 1964, Blair and Zaik, architects, interior by Lila Colwell.

National built dozens of branches throughout Oregon, nearly all of excellent design, and each the individual expression of the architect involved. Kidd championed the architect and did battle with the forces within the bank that continually argued for the economies and operational efficiencies of standard plans and details.

Whenever conditions allowed, which was usually the case, the U. S. National's branch banks were designed in wood. As a group of buildings with nearly identical programs the variety and virtuosity of wood design that was achieved is quite remarkable.

The interior design of these branches was equally distinguished, and it was all the work of Lila Colwell who had an influence on the building program far greater than her role as interior designer would normally warrant. Through her effort the bank established a policy of including works of art by the state's leading artists and craftsmen in each branch bank. Consequently, the U. S. National has the finest collection of contemporary Oregon art outside of one or two museums.

During Stuart Kidd's tenure, the local chapters of the American Institute of Architects granted ten design awards to the bank, and in 1962 the Oregon Chapter, in an unprecedented action, presented a Special Award of Commendation to the U. S. National for "good architectural design of banks througout the State."

The U. S. National Bank branches were considered choice commissions, eagerly sought after by many firms. Though the projects were parceled out to a number of talented architects around the state (all depositors of course), some would say that the Wilmsen and Endicott office got more than their fair share. Whatever, the 12 branches designed by the firm are among the best of a very good group.

A most significant event of the 1950s was the Oregon Centennial Exposition, the major activity in a statewide celebration of Oregon's 100 years of statehood. Organization for the Exposition began in 1954, and it was officially authorized by the State Legislature the following year though funds were not appropriated until the 1957 session. Many envisioned a grand "World's Fair" but a study by the Stanford Research Institute indicated that a more modest state and regional fair would be the most feasible.

Guiding the massive civic effort, which would utimately involve nearly 50,000 volunteers, was Baker lumberman Anthony (Tony) Brandenthaler, Chairman of the Oregon Centennial Commission from its inception until the accounts were closed in 1960. Serving under four governors, Brandenthaler gave firm and dynamic leadership to a project that often seemed on the verge of faltering due to lack of funds, or to the inevitable squabbling among the diverse personalities and interests involved in the planning.

After consideration of several locations, a 165-acre site along the shores of the Columbia River north of Portland was chosen. An important factor in the site selection was the presence of the 11-acre Pacific International Exposition Building (now the Multnomah County Exposition Center) which would become the main exhibit building for the Statehood Centennial.

In 1958, the Portland architectural firm of Stewart and Richardson was selected as primary architects for the Exposition. Principals, Donald J. Stewart and K. E. Richardson, both began their careers in the office of A. E. Doyle who, with Ion Lewis, had designed the Forestry Building at the 1905 Lewis and Clark Exposition. Stewart and Richardson, along with engineers Moffit, Nichol and Taylor, were responsible for the overall site layout, and the design of several exhibit structures which included major repairs and alterations to the P. I. Building. With only 14 months to plan, build and coordinate the work of private exhibitors, the architects and engineers faced a formidable task. But, with the paint still wet, the Exposition opened on schedule on June 10, 1959 and ran for 100 days.

Mainly due to modest budgets the architecture of the Exposition was somewhat less grand than many had hoped for, though there were several notable designs. The most dramatic structure was the Lumber Pavilion designed by John Storrs and engineered by James G. Pierson. Planned as a permanent exhibit building, though eventually razed, the soaring structure consisted of seven hyperbolic paraboloids, each 56 feet square, with linear skylights at the intersections. The paraboloids, then a fashionable form usually designed in concrete, were built of laminated 1″ x 4″ fir lumber.

Equally unique was the House of Religious History built in a secluded setting at the west end of the grounds. Designed by Stewart and

Fig. V–71. Forestry Pavilion, Oregon Centennial, 1959, John Storrs, architect.

Fig. V–72. House of Religious History, Oregon Centennial, 1959, Stewart and Richardson, architects.

Richardson, the dynamic effect of the flaring, glue-laminated fir arches contrasted with the quiet atmosphere of worship in the interior. Walls were constructed of four-inch thick tongue and groove cedar, naturally finished inside and out. The clerestories formed by the pagoda-like roof featured cathedral glass in an abstract pattern. The decahedron shape, articulated by the arches, accommodated the entrance and nine large wall panels, each with a painting by Carl Morris depicting religious themes.

Stewart and Richardson also designed the House of Ideas and the Northwest Natural Gas Company's "Eternal Flame," a focal point of the Exposition grounds. Also of interest was the Portland General Electric Building designed by architects Blair and Zaik.

After the close of the Centennial Exposition in September all of the structures except the P. I. Building were dismantled and removed from the site. When last seen the House of Religious History had been rebuilt as a drive-in restaurant on Highway 99 south of Tacoma.

Another Statehood Centennial event of architectural interest was the juried selection of the "10 Most Significant Designs of a Century of Oregon Architecture," published in the March 8, 1959 issue of the *Oregonian.* A wide variety of building types and ages were chosen by jury members Richard W. Norman and Robert W. Fritsch, both Portland architects, and Marion D. Ross, Professor of Architecture at the University of Oregon.

The ten designs included the Peter Britt House in Jacksonville, Timberline Lodge, and in Portland, the Jacob Kamm House, Portland

Fig. V–73. Studio-house, Eugene, Oregon, for sculptor Jan Zach, Gary Michael, architect.

Fig. V–74. Richard Campbell residence, Portland, 1965, Campbell, Yost, Grube & Partners, architects.

Fig. V–75. Charlton residence, Portland, 1962, William J. Hawkins III, architect.

Fig. V–76. Oliver residence, Portland, 1971, James C. Oliver, architect.

Fig. V–77. Oliver residence, family room with study loft.

Hotel, Oregonian Building (old), Temple Beth Israel, Central Library, the Forestry Building from the Lewis and Clark Exposition, and two post-World War II buildings, Lincoln High School and the Visitors Information Center. Five Portland buildings on the 1959 list were standing in 1919 when another jury chose the "ten most notable examples of architecture . . . in Portland." Only the Portland Hotel and the Central Library appear in both selections. (See "After the 'Fair.' ")

The 1960s saw architecture in the United States take a new direction, or more correctly, a variety of new directions. Many architects, particularly the younger ones, came to realize the ultimate sterility of the International Style—Mies van der Rohe's Seagram Building, the crowning monument to that style, had been built and there was nothing else to be done. Architects began exploring new approaches, some returning to older forms, and others breaking new ground.

But no clear direction is yet evident. Design over the past decade has tended to be less dogmatic and more personal—everyone is "doing their own thing," and given the American system, several "stars" have emerged, each with their own rather loose following.

The late Louis I. Kahn, A.I.A. Gold Medalist in 1971, was a humanist architect and teacher who had the unique talent to combine sophisticated theories of form with social purpose. During the past decade his buildings and teachings have been the most significant single influence on the course of architectural thought. On a surface level Kahn made the brick arch once again respectable, and his use of 45-degree angles, though often misunderstood, has been widely emulated.

The sculptural, and sometimes heroic designs of Paul Rudolph have received much attention and have had a substantial effect on the work of many young architects, including several in Portland who attended Yale during Rudolph's tenure as head of the Department of Architecture. Among them are William J. Hawkins III, Andrew C. Wheeler, and Gary Michael and Richard Campbell, who took graduate work at Yale. Some of their early projects show a strong Rudolph influence, occasionally combined with the regional wood tradition as in Campbell's own house built in 1965. The esthetics of Hawkins' 1962 townhouse for John Charlton, while built of wood, are based on abstract sculptural qualities rather than the articulation of materials.

A major influence on the design of wood buildings in recent years has been Sea Ranch, a second home development on the northern California coast. The group of cluster houses and condominiums was designed by Moore, Lyndon, Turnbull and Whittaker in 1964, and selected for a Progressive Architecture Design Award the following year. The "Sea Ranch Syndrome" with its integration of traditional wood structure and shed roof forms into highly complex geometric spatial organization has had a notable impact in the Northwest as well as in other regions of the country. As the Oregon Barn influenced earlier wood design, Sea Ranch has stimulated architects to explore other indigenous forms—factories, mining structures, mills and canneries have been the inspiration of many recent designs.

Fig. V–78. Old mining structure in the Silverton area. Inspiration for modern design?

A spectacular example is Portland architect James C. Oliver's six-level house built in 1971 on a lot so steep that it was considered unbuildable by conventional minds. Similar forms were used in the house for O. J. Feucht, Jr. designed by Campbell, Yost, Grube & Partners, and in the economical Boardwalk Apartments by Martin/Soderstrom/Matteson.

The renewed interest in indigenous buildings has led architects to "rediscover" the wood truss, one of man's oldest structural devices. The truss has always been recognized as an efficient and economical means to support long spans, but most earlier buildings, excepting industrial structures, would have the trusses concealed by ceilings. The more recent vogue of structural articulation brought the venerable truss out into the

Fig. V–79. Feucht residence, Portland, 1972, Campbell, Yost, Grube & Partners, architects.

open where it is especially suited to the angular geometry of many current designs. The 60-foot wood roof trusses in the Parkrose Branch of the Oregon Bank designed by Allen, McMath, and Hawkins became a major design element in addition to providing a column-free banking space. Exposed wood structure with trussed wall bracing articulate the space in Broome, Selig & Oringdulph's Mountain Park Office Building.

Industrial construction is more obviously the inspiration for the dynamic roof structure of the Tennis Court and Handball Facility at the University of Oregon. Designed by Eugene architects, Unthank, Seder, and Poticha in 1971, the sawtooth roof provides light and shelter from wind and rain with maximum economy.

Fig. V-80. Boardwalk Apartments, Portland, 1972, Martin/Soderstrom/Matteson, architects.

Fig. V–81. Interior, Parkrose Branch of the Oregon Bank, 1966, Allen, McMath, Hawkins, architects.

Fig. V–82. Interior, Mountain Park office building, Broome, Selig & Oringdulph, architects.

Fig. V–83. Tennis court and handball facility at the University of Oregon, 1971, Unthank, Seder and Poticha, architects.

A more current phenomena on the architectural scene is the philosophy and designs of Philadelphia architect Robert Venturi. His contradictory and, to many, bizarre views on architecture and cities have caused heated debate and resentment in a large segment of the architectural profession. To date Portland has not seen any "Venturi" buildings, but surely one will appear soon.

During the past 10 to 15 years architecture in the Northwest, while mildly tempered by our traditions, has followed the national trends. Except for the work of a few architects, regionalism in the Northwest is very much in abeyance. The present era seems to be one of architectural fashion—some have called it a new eclectic period as architects pick and choose among the several popular design modes. Not since the period revivals of the early 20th century has there been such a plethora of stylistic labels: Wrightian, Miesian, New Formalism, Brutalism, and Neo-Expressionism to name a few.[1] Whether this is good or bad is open to question. Certainly there is a variety on the landscape that many applaud, and the doomsayers of the 1950s who predicted that cities would become filled with aluminum curtain-wall boxes have been proven wrong.

But in reviewing the architecture of the recent era one cannot help but speculate on what designs will endure and what will be viewed as passing fashion—which buildings will soon become dated, and which will stand the test of time as Belluschi's houses and churches have. Belluschi himself recognized the trend in 1964 when he commented: "It appears to me that the great architect strives for comprehension rather than for originality for its own sake and that a thorough study of a problem, made in the freedom that knowledge provides, is always the greatest source of originality. It is the discipline of the intellect and the respect for the means at hand, therefore, that keep the architect from straying too far into the shallow waters of mere fashion."[2]

1. Marcus Whiffin, *American Architecture Since 1780, A Guide to the Styles* (Cambridge, Mass., 1969), 249–80.

2. Harry S. Ransom, editor. *The People's Architects* (Chicago, 1964), 106.

Everyday Architecture in the Puget Sound Area

Victor Steinbrueck

In the Puget Sound region, time is demonstrated from the beginnings of the white man's intrusion into the world of the native Americans, through towns which date from the earliest pioneering periods to the latest suburban residential tract development and the sophisticated inhuman urban skyscraper and central business district. The towns are microcosms of successive national trends in building styles and town growth and land use changes due to advancing technology, communication, and transportation as well as economic influences.

The automobile arrived in 1900. Dirt roads were built, then macadam, then concrete. With federal aid beginning in 1916, highways branched out to every county seat. What followed was, of course, the advent of the motor car and truck, almost replacing every other means of transportation—even for a time threatening to overcome public or mass transportation systems. The freedom of individual travel, and the ruthless transgressions of the highways and freeways, modified completely the shape and character of towns and cities and their growth pattern, as everywhere else in the United States, most particularly from the time of World War II until the present.

Air travel probably affected the Puget Sound region more because of the location, growth and economic influence of the giant industrial complex of Boeing aircraft in Seattle and its environs, than because of the changes caused by that mode of travel. That is not to deny or ignore the agricultural land use havoc created by Boeing and its industrial satellites moving into the Green River Valley commencing in 1965.

A Puget Sound building, as a cultural expression, is the product and reflection of a number of patterns of development operating simultaneously and superimposed one on the other. There have been successive stages of dominance over nature since the earliest submission to the almost overwhelming environment. However, the trend has been toward an increasing command over materials and defiance of nature or lack of general response to location and topography. Much of what has been laid out and built has been in direct violation or rejection of nature as though there was so much of it that it could never be spoiled and needed most to be controlled. Puget Sound building for most of its existence has turned its back on nature. None of the Puget Sound towns openly face the water. Every waterfront street turns its back to the open bay. For example, Port Townsend's Water Street has its buildings with their backs to the sea fronting on the street only. There has been an embryo-like recapitulation of Eastern or East Coast and Chicago developments.

There is today, however, an architectural trend which is part of the total building picture in the work of certain architects who are striving to produce pleasant functional buildings using contemporary materials and techniques, while still being responsive to traditional antecedents. For these architects there is an increasing awareness of the total scene, of the townscape, and of the role of their work in the evolving physical environment as part of the total design and identity of the place.

Fig. V–84. Pacific Builder and Engineers, Inc., 1960, A. O. Bumgardner and Partners, architects.

Small office buildings, institutions, and clinics represent some of the better postwar Puget Sound architecture produced from the designs of many capable young architects, some of whom have become the prestige firms of the region. Among these are: Terry, Tucker, and Shields, Chiarelli and Kirk, Bassetti and Morse, Waldron and Dietz, Gene Zema, Wendell H. Lovett, Robert Chervenak, Omer Mithun, Ralph Anderson, Alan Liddle, Robert Price, A. O. Bumgardner, and Ibsen Nelsen. Paul Thiry was already well established as an avant-garde designer and doing some of the finest work in this kind of building. His work continued to have an International Style character, but most work by others was in a vein that appeared more regional. Common qualities were extensive use of wood both for exterior and interior surfaces as well as for articulated structure (perhaps a contemporary Puget Sound Stick Style?). Considerable freedom of form with incorporation of exterior spaces was another aspect along with thoughtful retention of natural growth. It would seem

Fig. V–85. Bill Holm residence, 1960, Gene Zema, architect.

to be a Northwest derivative of a combination of International Style (especially the work of Gropius and Breuer), Frank Lloyd Wright, Stick Style, and Mies van der Rohe, if such a mixture is possible.

There was very little significant or large commercial building until the 1960s, when central business districts appeared to prosper with the erection of high office buildings. Progress had been exemplified more by the proliferation of parking lots through the elimination of older buildings which had become unprofitable. The new high-rise buildings emulated the styles and even unique individual characteristics of the architecture of famous Eastern firms, thus continuing in the Puget Sound tradition of looking elsewhere for security in design leadership. Examples of the 1960 Skyscraper Style are the Norton Building, the Washington Building, the IBM Building, and the Seattle-First National Bank Building.

The opportunity of the Century 21 Exposition in 1962 brought out examples of the work of most architects in the region, with much of good quality but with nothing that could be identified as significant or architecturally important except as an expression of its time. The landscaping remains the best achievement of that project.

Meanwhile a plethora of speculative apartment building had been

Fig. V–86. Norton Building, 1960, Bindon and Wright, architects; Skidmore, Owings and Merrill, associates.

Fig. V–87. "Pigeonhole" apartments, 1959.

taking place. A type of rentable, multiple-story apartment, called "pigeonhole apartments," designed to take advantage of the building codes, was being built in great numbers in the neighborhoods close to business districts. Codes allowed open balconies to be used as exit corridors to fire escapes at either end of the building. Thus, the over-economical planning forced the living rooms to face onto the public balcony thereby sacrificing all privacy. They are usually exposed concrete, or concrete block (which is cheaper), with a touch of brick or thin stone masonry as a promotional feature. They are expressive of the motivation of placing expedient development profit above human living qualities. These buildings, which are coming into disfavor, are scattered throughout the region, and are surely the permanent slums of the future.

Except for a few architects involved directly and substantially with speculative builders, there was very little or surely a decreasing involvement of architects in residential design in the 1960s continuing into the present. Wendell H. Lovett, for one, continued to do his very thoughtful and meticulously conceived and detailed residential work with a great deal more confidence and exuberance than previously. The tract developments of the 1960s differed little in character from previous decades, offering good value and design in individual homes but nothing that could seriously be identified as a neighborhood or community.

Somewhat faceless shopping centers with a pretense of accommodation to Puget Sound styling serve suburbia via the private automobile. The parent examples of super shopping centers in the Northwest and possibly America are those developed by John Graham and Company. Seattle's early (1950) Northgate and later Southcenter and the Tacoma Mall show complete subservience to the automobile and to aggressive retail trade promotion. Suburban Bellevue's central business district is a direct outgrowth of the shopping center trend and is completely a shopping center and not at all a pedestrian oriented district in the manner of older city or town centers. A unique shopping square of 1947 designed by architects Bliss Moore, Jr. and Robert Masser is the nucleus of the auto-dominated no man's land of the present town's heart.

Puget Sound, as does every other region in America, contains many supermarkets, characteristic of the present era. Older supermarket buildings have been converted to other uses or demolished as the chain stores grew to require larger stores and larger parking areas and shifted to satisfy changing customer populations. These buildings usually serve

Fig. V–88. Supermarket, 1973.

their purpose well as large commercial food warehouse stores which need not make concessions to the street nor to anything except parking and blatant signing for identification purposes. Along with gasoline service stations on every corner and a host of other drive-ins, they are part of the Puget Sound townscape not at all different from anywhere in America. They contribute to a lack of identity and the special feeling of place that is so needed and so possible here.

Recent phenomena are the many "Turnkey" housing units built under federal housing programs for aging low-income persons. These towers usually rise to 12 or 15 stories in otherwise single family neighborhoods, and are constructed of exposed concrete with a little brick masonry. While they serve an important need they are cheaply built, barely fulfilling requirements, and are turned over to the local housing authorities for use and management and maintenance. The message of these neighborhood intrusions (which do provide a decent accommodation not otherwise available to many older persons) is that private profit as a prime controlling motive is not conducive to achieving a quality living environment. The towers are a symbolic expression of the isolation of this portion of our society from the rest of the community.

Residential building has been turning toward more planned-unit developments produced and merchandized as condominiums (under cooperative ownership). Adjacent apartments or houses share integrated outdoor spaces; this is a departure from the single family lot which has been the typical Puget Sound unit. Developments catering to particular life style groups such as singles or young couples are appearing. The character of these projects has tended to be a trend toward picturesqueness with mock-mansard roofs and mock-colonial facades and melodramatic use of wood, with brick and stone enrichments of papery thin quality. There is evidence of a nostalgic nationalism—as though there could be a turning back to the "good old days."

Another direction in present-day building is in the use of exaggerated and complicated geometric forms. Some residential building and smaller structures are designed in this mode. In overall form they are reminiscent of Victorian building, without the enrichment of detail and ornament so characteristic of those styles. Buildings are aggressively assertive and individual in character although they may be pleasing in appearance when skillfully handled as in the designs of Fukui/Hobbs.

There has been an increasing willingness on the part of some architects to be involved in the renovation and reuse of good older buildings. Examples are to be found in the rehabilitated buildings of architects Ralph Anderson, the Bumgardner Partnership, Ibsen Nelsen, Arne Bystrom, Alan Liddle, and Olson/Walker Associates, to mention a few firms where there is strong personal involvement on the part of the principals.

Concern for historic preservation came late to this farthest reach of continental United States but is now significantly affecting the quality of the towns and cities. Seattle has made a strong start in the Pioneer Square and Pike Place Market Historic Districts, and now with the

Fig. V–89. Mock mansard roof, planned-unit apartments, 1970.

establishment of a comprehensive Seattle Landmarks Board to affect the entire city. Older towns led by Port Townsend—followed by La Connor, Snohomish, and Steilacoom—are establishing historic districts and designating historic buildings for preservation and continuing use. A lack of understanding that in history antiquity is relative, has been part of the problem. Even concerned historians and architects have tended to evaluate historic properties on the basis of national or European standards when there is neither the quality of architectural design nor the age of buildings to equal that of earlier settlements of the nation. However, many older residences which have survived in small towns are being restored and contributing interest to the scene while fostering local pride in the past. The Ezra Meeker house in Puyallup is a fine example of community interest and successful involvement. Ten years ago the pioneering attitude had been to knock down anything that got in the way of "progress." Clearing our way in the wilderness to build homes and farms and towns had become a tradition continued into the present day of clearing older buildings for more profitable new uses.

Establishment of protective federal and state laws for historic preservation have helped to call attention to our environmental heritage. Seattle's Pioneer Square (and Skid Road) Historic District was the first serious movement toward civic recognition of the value of older places for environmental and economic enhancement. Restoration and a new

Fig. V–90. Maynard Building entrance, 1892, A. Walkinshaw, architect.

Fig. V–91. Pike Place Public Market.

cultural life style has added considerable interest to the Seattle scene and increased property values six-fold in four years since 1970. Architect Ralph Anderson has been a leader in the architecture of restoring buildings as well as participating as an owner in several of the outstanding preservation projects. Restorations have not been completely authentic but have been adapted to present uses and tastes.

The initiative-originated ordinance for the purpose of keeping the Pike Place Farmers' Market as part of the cultural heritage of Seattle was overwhelmingly approved by the vote of the citizens in November 1972. A destructive urban renewal project was then required to be altered, and the city is now in the process of attempting to retain the kind of market that Seattleites want. As usual there are many forces seeking to exploit the situation for unharmonious private gain. A different kind of historic preservation is represented in the effort to retain Seattle's historic Market where the traditional yet changing use and entire cultural aspects of the site are the significant qualities that must not be disrupted. Here the total of social, physical and cultural qualities are interwoven and inseparable while being most vulnerable to insensitive redevelopment. The struggle to save the Market has not yet succeeded. The essence of its life is not yet understood and appreciated by the authorities involved and because its actual continuance violently contradicts the investment attitude: maximum financial exploitation of every situation. However, the Market's very existence while daily fulfilling important needs gives a strong sense of continuity and identity to Seattle. We have reached full circle in the survival of the local producing farmers at the marketplace which originally created the Market in 1907. It is once more the most important "preservation" issue.

Meanwhile, the continuing efforts for historic preservation and recognition of the uses of the past in our environment are developing general awareness of many important broad aspects of the quality of urban life. Puget Sound is a place of promises unfulfilled but with great hope for the future that man may be able to match in some measure the bountifulness of the natural setting.

Alvar Aalto in Oregon

Thomas Vaughan
and
Virginia Guest Ferriday*

Alvar Aalto, one of the six or seven internationally acknowledged masters of modern architecture, has designed only two buildings in the United States. The first, completed in 1948, is the M.I.T. Senior Dormitory at Cambridge, Massachusetts. Aalto's second American building is in a sequestered valley of Oregon, situated on a knoll which forms an acropolis for the Benedictine Monastery near the small community of Mt. Angel.

How did the world-famous architect come to design a building in a spot so many miles distant from his home in Finland—a building whose contemporary design contrasts so sharply with the pseudo-Romanesque style of the other buildings at the Abbey? Aalto was not attracted by the possibilities of financial remuneration; he had turned down commissions for buildings costing many times that of the proposed library. Father Barnabas Reasoner, one of the prime movers for the project, explains the philosophy behind the selection of Aalto as architect for the library:

> We appreciate the beauty of architecture and design on principle; it is involved with our Catholicity, with our concept of man and with our concept of the dignity of man. Monks in the Middle Ages had an appreciation of arts and crafts and were their greatest exponents. . . . They were the ones who trained our ancestors and gave them an appreciation of civilization. Man in his own way uses the talents and abilities God has given him, sees the beauty around him and makes a statement about the world around him . . . in his own age, in his own way and with his own materials.

For the monks of Mt. Angel the new library would be their statement.

The outstanding site and the desire to hire an architect who would understand their statement led the monks to Aalto, who had similarly expressed a feeling for human beings. "He didn't want his buildings to dominate his people. There was never a flaunting of technique more than a real concern for human beings. Aalto has always taken the position that buildings are for people and not the other way around."

---

*Nadine Skov Finch did the research for this chapter.

The monks' approach to persuading Aalto to design their building was disarmingly simple. They wrote to Aalto, explained "we need you. We have this magnificent monastic site, and we don't want to spoil it. We want you to improve our site and give us a building that will fill our needs in a beautiful and intelligent way."[1] That did it. Aalto responded to the request and began designing, working at first from photographs and plans of the site. In 1967 he visited Mt. Angel and moved the building ten feet to save two Douglas fir trees and to provide a view between the library and the adjacent building.

The resultant building, paid for by an anonymous donor, is unmistakably Aalto. There are recognizable trademarks: the visually simple handling of complex relationships; forms, like the fan-shaped plan of the library's reading rooms and stacks, and the curved clerestory skylight that floods the space with light; details, like the slatted natural wood screens, undulating walls, and white interior surfaces. But most characteristic of all is the complete individuality of the solution based on the uniqueness of the building's requirements and of its site.

The monastery buildings are arranged around the perimeter of the table-top site to define an open mall space. The library, perched on the north crest of the slope between two existing buildings, reinforces the sense of enclosure of the mall, its fan-shaped plan providing a graceful modulation between the older structures. This exterior shape fits the surrounding landscape of Douglas firs and pine trees, and the orientation allows the library to take advantage of the north light and a broad view of the Willamette Valley and the Coast Range and Cascade Mountains beyond. Only the library's top floor is visible from the campus; the other two floors descend the hillside to which the building adheres. This method of siting is similar to earlier projects designed by Aalto on the sloping, pine-studded hills of Finland.

The contemporary building exterior conflicts in no way with its neighbors, reflecting the color of their stone in its buff-colored brick walls. When approached from the campus, it appears as a simple and unassuming structure, giving little indication of the dramatic space of its interior. Upon entering the building at the third floor one passes through the lobby and down a few steps to the control desk. Radiating from this central control point are the stacks and reading areas which are separated from the control desk by a moat-like opening on the floor below. The curved railings of this opening are designed to serve as study counters which share the light provided by a sloping clerestory skylight at the roof. The north light from above is bounced into the space by a sculptured wall, flooding the two floors below and also providing a source of indirect light at night. The curved study counters are fitted with individual lamps, designed by the architect, which provide supplementary light only when and where needed. Beyond the balcony study counters the stacks radiate like spokes to the high-windowed outside

1. Portland *Catholic Sentinel*, Jan. 26, 1968, p. 12.

Fig. V–92. Mt. Angel Abbey Library, near Mt. Angel, Oregon, 1970, Alvar Aalto, architect.

wall which is lined with individual study carrels designed by Aalto. Windows with views over the valley are unexpectedly small and few. "It is a place to work, flooded with controlled daylight, with equally controlled glimpses of the countryside."[2]

The multi-level fan-shaped design affords maximum visual surveillance of every part of the space from the control desk, a scheme which shares design philosophy with Aalto's earlier library in Viipuri, completed in 1937 and destroyed during the war.

To the right of the lobby, which also serves as an exhibit space, is the rare book room containing a fireproof humidity-controlled vault.

2. Ada Louise Huxtable, *New York Times,* May 30, 1970, p. 50.

Fig. V–93. Mt. Angel Abbey Library, moat-like opening with curved clerestory and study counters.

The space in the lobby, which seats 100, literally flows, with an undulating rear wall covered with hemp fabric and fir slats typical of that used in other Aalto buildings. Opposite walls are of finished white concrete which bear the wood grain of the forming boards. The ceiling repeats the radiating wood slats found also over the control desk of the main library. The furniture in this room, chairs of black leather and molded birch, were, like all the other furnishings, designed by the architect.

The process of executing Aalto's design for the library was simplified somewhat by the appointment of DeMars and Wells of Berkeley, California, as on-site architects, responsible for carrying out Aalto's design through the development of working drawings. They were assisted by Erik Vartiainen, who had worked for Aalto in Finland while schematics for the project were being developed and was at that time in the United States attending professional school.

The contractors for the project were Reimers and Jolivette of Portland. Phil Loughlin of the contracting firm, who was in charge of the project, has indicated that the most interesting aspect of construction was the unusual shape of the building. Initial layout of the building was accomplished by establishing 12 work points determined by a computer. The fan shape also dictated that the structural steel beams and their angles of intersection were all different from one another.

Aalto's concern for human beings is evident in the completed building. He has created warmth and serenity through the use of muted colors and natural materials—concrete, brick, wood, and glass. His blending of natural and artificial light is masterful. In total, his building brings a sense of meaning to a religious community and provides a setting for communication between all persons.

Planned Resorts

Virginia Guest Ferriday

The second home communities built recently in the Pacific Northwest make earlier resorts seem incomplete and amateurish in comparison. Up until the early 1960s prospective vacation cottage owners were typically shown a street layout, perhaps in the vicinity of a lodge, and a choice of lots. Design, construction, landscaping and development of recreation facilities were, for better or for worse, an individual matter. In contrast, potential investors in the new, planned resorts are offered a total environment—the product of teams of site planners, architects, landscape architects, engineers, interior designers, artists, and golf course and pool design specialists. Examples of resort architecture of the 1960s and 1970s must therefore be examined as part of these total communities rather than as individual works.

Salishan, on the Oregon coast, is one of two such resorts developed by John Gray of Portland. Its 600 acres lie at the mouth of the Siletz River on Siletz Bay. The site includes a 2½-mile-long sandspit, separating the bay from the ocean, and a wooded area which extends from a cliff overlooking the ocean inland around the south end of the bay.

The name Salishan was used to designate the language group to which the Sitka Indians belonged. When purchased by Gray in 1961 the land had been little used since the days of these Indians. Portions had been logged during World War I when Sitka spruce was in demand for airplane construction and parts had been used for dairy farming.

The initial master plan was begun in 1961 by the Portland office of Skidmore, Owings and Merrill. They placed the lodge complex, with the guest room units, and a portion of the golf course east of the coast highway (which roughly bisects the property) and the rest of the golf course, the golf shop, tennis courts, swimming pool, apartments and individual house sites west of the highway in the wooded area and on the sand spit. According to Gray the inland side of the highway was chosen as the site for the lodge both to avoid the heavy maintenance associated with an ocean front site and to bar commercial traffic from the privately developed areas.

By leasing rather than selling land the developers were able to withhold streets on the ocean side from public use and thus to limit

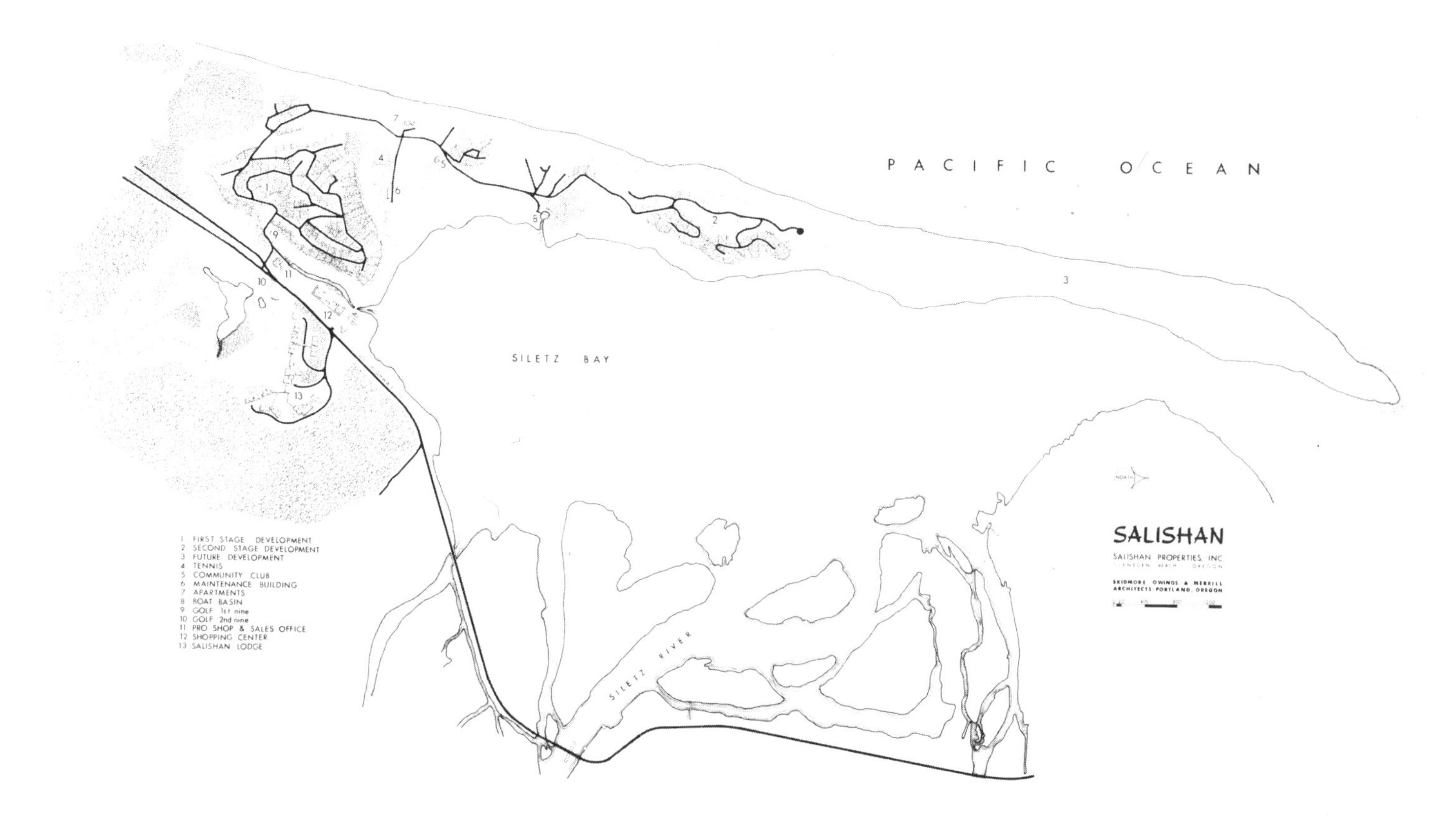

Fig. V–94. Salishan, Gleneden Beach, Oregon. Master plan by Skidmore, Owings and Merrill, 1961.

beach access to Salishan homeowners and to those entering by foot along the ocean to the south. (Oregon laws have since been changed so that it is possible to maintain public roads even when land is privately owned.)

The lodge with its convention facilities, 12 eight-unit guest room buildings and four-unit apartment building were designed by John Storrs, of Portland. The lodge building sits on a promontory some 70 feet above the highway with views over the bay to the ocean beyond. It was, Storrs said, designed to look "as if it had been dropped into the woods"[1] and it does. Its low-pitched, informally grouped roofs and extensive use of wood tie it firmly to the site. The guest room units step up and down the hillside from the lodge and are connected to it by walkways covered with board-on-board roofs similar to those used by early Oregon pioneers for simple sheds and porch roofs.

Wood was used almost exclusively inside and out: rough sawn board and batten, rough sawn plywood, hemlock columns, and cedar shakes outside; wood paneling, board and batten, tongue and groove, and a minimum of plaster inside. Two works of art are in wood: a mural screen by Eugene Bennett behind the bar and a carved wood panel by LeRoy

1. "Resort Designed to Fit a Scenic Site," *Architectural Record* (January, 1967), 145.

Fig. V–95. Salishan Lodge, 1965, by John Storrs.

Setziol in the dining room. Globes in the bar chandelier are Japanese glass floats—the frequent find of Northwest beachcombers. Furniture and textiles are in earth colors. Spaces are small scale and intimate.

Storrs, who enjoys playing the role of master builder, worked out many of the construction details with craftsmen on the site. His feeling for wood is evident in the structural connections which are as decorative as they are functional.

Following construction of the lodge a group of condominiums, called the Longhouse, designed by Blair and Zaik of Portland, was built on the sand spit where it meets the mainland. These wedge-shaped units are similar to the condominiums built at Sea Ranch, the well-publicized resort on the California coast. The shed roof form at Sea Ranch was supposedly a response to prevailing wind patterns which were studied in detail. Whether this claim is valid or not, the form in its bold simplicity is undeniably appropriate to the dramatic sites along the Pacific Coast. By staggering the Longhouse units the architects exploited the compositional possibilities of the roof form and created the necessary protected recesses for outdoor seating. The sheathing of cedar shingles provides needed textural interest.

Subsequent construction at Salishan followed the precedent set by the lodge complex and the Longhouse. A high level of architectural design has been maintained throughout the development, largely as a

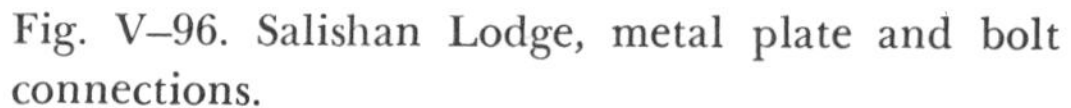
Fig. V–96. Salishan Lodge, metal plate and bolt connections.

Fig. V–97. Longhouse condominiums, Salishan, 1964, Blair and Zaik, architects, as seen from Siletz Bay.

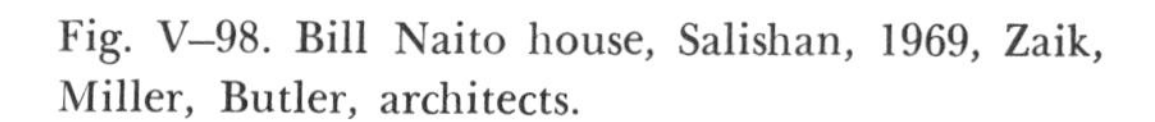
Fig. V–98. Bill Naito house, Salishan, 1969, Zaik, Miller, Butler, architects.

result of lease restrictions which require that all building plans, plot plans, landscaping, color schemes, lighting and maintenance meet with the approval of an architectural committee. Guidelines set by the committee state, among other things, that houses should be one story high, that views be safeguarded, and that materials indigenous to the Northwest be used. Some recent additions have veered toward suburban Spanish and others display a surprising degree of exhibitionism in their forms but the overall quality is far above that found in even the most expensive urban development where no such controls operate.

According to a statement by John Storrs published in an architectural magazine shortly after the lodge was completed, the goal of those working on the development was "to take this piece of ground and leave it the way it is."[2] Unfortunately, the Pacific Ocean was not a party to this agreement. Waves began eating away at the spit during the winter of 1971 and in December of 1972 the tide carried away some 20 feet of property, leaving three houses hanging over the waves. An emergency rock fill temporarily solved the problem but in January of 1973 during heavy rains and high tides, a $60,000 house under construction toppled into the sea.[3] Undaunted, property owners set about having the damaged spit repaired and during the following winter no further disasters occurred. The question of who was responsible for the loss has, however, not been settled.

The second resort with which John Gray has been involved, Sunriver, has had a much less eventful history. It is roughly ten times the size of Salishan and is located in a totally different setting—the dry, flat area east of the Cascades near Bend, Oregon. Part of its 5,500-acre site served as a training center for the Corps of Engineers during World War II. Of the remainder a portion had been logged off and some had been used for grazing. In addition to sunshine, it offers skiing at nearby Mt. Bachelor, swimming, tennis, horseback riding, golfing on an 18-hole course, and fishing in the Deschutes River, which meanders in and out of the property.

The master plan was prepared by Royston, Hanamoto, Beck and Abbey, landscape architects of San Francisco. Development began in the southern two-thirds of the property. The principal road of the development leaves the highway to the east and leads more or less directly to the lodge. Secondary roads make loops on either side of this main road. Attached to the secondary roads are more loops, which in turn have clusters of small circular roads on which the houses and condominiums are located. The overall effect in plan is of nothing so much as a large bunch of dried grapes. Each cluster is given its own identity, with names such as "Meadow Village" and "Overlook Park."

One of the most successful features of Sunriver has been the system of bicycle trails which is completely separate from the road system. Constructed at a cost of $11,000 per mile, these trails connect all the living units to each other and to the community facilities.

The lodge, designed by George T. Rockrise and Associates of San Francisco, with James T. Amis as partner in charge, J. Matthew Myers as project manager, and William F. Olin as job captain, is a massive

2. "Resort," p. 147.

3. Bert Webber, *What Happened at Bay Ocean; Is Salishan Next?* (Fairfield, Washington, 1973), 29–40, back cover.

Fig. V–99. Lodge, Sunriver, Oregon, 1969, George T. Rockrise and Associates.

Fig. V–100. Mountainview Lodges, Sunriver, 1970, Wilmsen, Endicott, Greene, Bernhard, Associates, with golf course in foreground and outdoor amphitheater in background.

Fig. V–101. Mountainview Lodges.

Fig. V–102. Keith and Vicky Adams residence, 1972, Sunriver, Oregon, Zaik, Miller, Butler, architects.

building reminiscent of the National Park hotels and is well suited to act as an anchor for this large, rambling resort. Like the lodge at Salishan it is built almost entirely of wood, but at Sunriver it is the great sweep of the laminated beams, the enormous bulk of the lava stone fireplaces and the heavy roof forms rather than the details which impress.

As at Salishan, attracting convention business was a major consideration. At Sunriver it was decided to use condominiums for accommodations rather than build special guest room units. The first condominiums, by Church and Shiels of Portland, were built near the lodge and have the same massive proportions. Subsequent condominium units, by Zaik-Miller and Wilmsen, Endicott, Greene, Bernhard and Associates, among others, are tucked away in the lodgepole and ponderosa pine and are smaller in scale and more playful in form. They and the many private houses follow closely the woodsy theme.

With a planned population of 5,000 to 5,500 families, one quarter of whom may conceivably live there the year round, Sunriver will provide many of the services of a small city. In addition to the recreational facilities there is an airport, an outdoor amphitheater and a shopping center. Much is made of art exhibits and cultural activities and through a Homeowners Association residents have some measure of self-government.

Located north of Sunriver in the Deschutes River Valley at the foot of the ridge from which it gets its name is Black Butte Ranch. Master plan for this 1,500-acre family resort was done by Robert Perron, landscape architect, and its lodge by Colburn, Sheldon and Kaji, with whom

Fig. V–103. Golf Course Condominiums, Black Butte Ranch, Oregon, 1973, Fletcher and Finch, architects.

Perron shares office space in Portland. The lodge and two groups of condominiums, one by Hal and Goodhue, of California and another by Fletcher and Finch, of Portland, in their use of lean-tos, vertical wood siding and wood shingles recall the forms and materials of outbuildings built by early Willamette Valley farmers. In the lodge the architects have emphasized vertical movement to such an extent that the interior seems to be composed almost entirely of stair landings. It is an intriguing building, one which compels exploration.

Farther north in central Oregon, taking advantage of the "340 days of sunshine and one inch of rain per year" on the Warm Springs Indian Reservation, lies Kah-Nee-Ta. This resort had its beginnings in 1963 when the Warm Springs Indian Council voted to use a portion of the $4 million compensation they received for loss through inundation of their ancestral fishing grounds at Celilo Falls on the Columbia River to repurchase and substantially expand a resort village around the hot springs located in the Warm Springs River Valley. Called Kah-Nee-Ta Village and including pools fed by the springs, guest cottages, a restaurant, a mobile home area, and some "authentic" Indian tepees available as camping units, it opened in 1964. It was an immediate success.

In 1965 the Council voted to build a convention center. Because jobs would be created by its operation they were able to obtain a grant of $2,434,000 and a loan of the same amount from the Economic Development Administration. To this the tribe added $291,000 to finance the $5 million Kah-Nee-Ta lodge. Wolff, Zimmer, Gunsel, Frasca, and Ritter were hired as architects with Brooks Gunsul as partner in charge, Joy

Fig. V–104. Black Butte Lodge, 1971, Colburn, Sheldon and Kaji, architects.

Fig. V–105. Dining room, Black Butte Lodge.

Gannett as project manager, Gary Larsen as designer, and Pietro Belluschi as architectural consultant.

Ground was broken in 1971 and the lodge opened in 1972. Located a mile downstream from the 1964 complex, the new building is strikingly sited on an almost barren hillside 200 feet above the valley floor. The architects used many of the design motifs which have become *de rigeur* for expensive, architect-designed houses in the Northeast (large, abstract masses supported on round columns, walls at 45°), but at Kah-Nee-Ta these devices have been exploited to produce an entirely relaxed and comfortable environment rather than a self-conscious show of sophistication.

The building plan is basically triangular with its base resting against the hillside and its apex jutting out over the terrain. The 90 guest rooms on the two sides overlooking the valley have individual balconies facing southeast and southwest. The dining room is in the western angle, taking advantage of the spectacular desert sunsets. The other public rooms are arranged freely on the north side. Behind them lies the terraced parking lot. In the large interior court is a swimming pool, protected from the wind and warmed in winter by the sun trapped there.

Fig. V–106. Kah-Nee-Ta Lodge, Warm Springs Indian Reservation, Oregon, 1972, Wolff, Zimmer, Gunsul, Frasca and Ritter, architects.

Fig. V–107. Kah-Nee-Ta Lodge from south.

The exterior is sheathed in rough sawn vertical siding of cedar stained an earth yellow. Columns for the walkways around the courtyard are treated peeler logs. Inside the architects have used cedar, oak and ash.

Features of the lounge are fan-shaped wooden trusses similar to those used by Alvar Aalto in his 1951 Village Hall, and a massive concrete fireplace with effective bas relief decorations designed by Harold Balazs. These he executed by carving pieces of styrofoam, gluing them to paper and placing them in the concrete forms.

Construction in this isolated area presented problems. Many of the supplies had to be brought from Portland, 114 miles away. The soil, made up of dust and ash from a volcanic eruption of some one million years ago that had weathered to clay,[4] tended to pick up moisture and swell. So a membrane about the size of a football field was laid in the excavation and covered with rock; the structure was then backfilled with non-expansive soil.

Not all recent Northwest resorts have been developed from scratch. Elkhorn in Idaho, was built to complement the 1936 resort at nearby Sun Valley. Planned by Sasaki, Walker Associates, Inc., of Sausalito, California, and Killingsworth and Brady, of Long Beach, California, it is located on 2,950 acres of almost completely treeless land. Three hundred acres of this land is slated to be covered with buildings, another 400 acres will be paved and the rest (75%) will remain as open space. Roadways are being kept to a minimum and residents encouraged to use foot and bicycle paths, ski and equestrian trails. In its early stages of development, the resort resembles a European mountain village. Condominiums are grouped around the village center, which includes shops, restaurants and an ice skating rink. Focal point of the village, and of the valley, is an enormous bell tower.

More condominiums will be built around the center but in order to keep the village visually small and compact, private residences will be located in the small finger valleys off the big valley. For each building site the planners have designated an envelope within which the house must fit.

Development of well-designed quality resorts such as Salishan, Sunriver, Black Butte, Kah-Nee-Ta, and Elkhorn has been accompanied by promotion of some which were not so professionally put together, the so-called "sagebrush subdivisions." Typical of these is one located in the high desert country in southeastern Oregon, an area unsuccessfully homesteaded around 1915. By the 1930s much of the land where this resort lies had become county property through nonpayment of taxes. In the 1940s a land and cattle company bought about 70,000 acres, most from the county at 25 cents an acre. It changed hands again in 1959 and in 1961, 70,000 acres were sold to a real estate development company for

---

4. Ralph Mason of the Oregon Dept. of Geology as quoted in an undated publicity release, Rockey/Marsh Public Relations, Inc. (Portland).

Fig. V–108. Elkhorn, Idaho, begun in 1972, Killingsworth and Brady, architects; Sasaki, Walker Associates, Inc., planners and landscape architects.

Fig. V–109. Bell tower, Elkhorn village.

$10 an acre. From 1961 to 1967 this company sold 99% of the land at prices reportedly as high as $1,100 an acre. The buyers were nearly all Californians. In the middle 1960s only about one percent of the owners were living on their land. The few buildings constructed are similar to those found along any suburban commercial strip. The area had been used for grazing prior to its promotion as a resort. As to its future a Bureau of Land Management report commented as follows: "Perhaps some day the valley will support a substantial population of retirement, recreation, and community service dwellers—then again, the cow may get it back."[5]

This project can be viewed at best as a failure, and at worst as a swindle. But with the exception of this and a few other such dubious developments, Northwest resorts of the past decade represent an impressive achievement, one which has given the region many superb buildings and an exposure to the advantages—and disadvantages—of the planned community.

5. As quoted in Dale E. Courtney, "The Oregon Desert, 1967: A Pioneer Fringe?" *Association of Pacific Coast Geographers Yearbook*, XXIX (Corvallis, Oregon, 1967), 17, from which information on this development was drawn.

Industrial Building

Lewis L. McArthur

After World War II major changes took place in construction. Industrial might was a major factor in the Allied victory and there were numerous military construction projects in front line areas as well as others derived from the vast support and supply activities. Projects such as the pre-cast harbor sections for the invasion of France in 1944 and the almost instantaneous construction of forward landing fields did not affect the Pacific Northwest directly, but they did influence many opinions as to what might or might not be feasible under ordinary conditions. The highway requirements of the hordes of automobiles that poured from the factories demanded gigantic grading capabilities and the bridge programs brought about widespread use of pre-cast prestressed concrete beams and such new innovations as reusable self-supporting steel forms. Reusable metal pan forms were used for building floors. The slip form, moved by hydraulic or screw jacks, came into use for tall structures of uniform cross section such as grain elevators. Sectional tubular scaffolding permitted high staging for large areas.

There were other new developments in concrete. Multiple slab casting made possible tilt-up construction and lift slabs jacked up floor by floor. Flat pours also simplified the finishing of concrete, with the result that surfaces such as exposed aggregate and terrazzo soon came into common use. Pre-cast beams were followed by a full range of pre-cast to order sections, both for exterior wall surfaces and for special structural applications. Flat and shaped floor and roof deck sections became available in stock sizes and on special order. Sandblasted and other special finishes followed for exposed areas.

Wood construction followed in its own style. The glue-laminated beam took every conceivable shape as tapered, curved and angular members were custom made to develop an architectural theme or fill a special structural requirement. Roof and floor joists were devised with wood chords and steel web members designed to utilize both materials to their maximum strengths. The forest industries introduced a great variety of plywood, hardboard and particle board, but with a few exceptions these have been limited in industrial and manufacturing construction to form work and underlayments for floors and roofs.

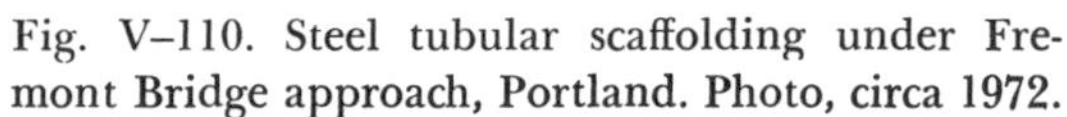

Fig. V–110. Steel tubular scaffolding under Fremont Bridge approach, Portland. Photo, circa 1972.

Fig. V–111. Fremont Bridge pier, 1972.

The continuous rolling mill produced a ribbon of plain or galvanized sheet steel from 12 to 30-gauge in thickness, up to three or four feet wide, and in a one-piece coil as heavy as one wished (up to 10 or 15 tons), all like a giant roll of adding machine tape. Development of in-line, mill-applied paint soon followed to give a full range of colors with a life expectancy far beyond anything field applied. Continuous roll formers were added which produced not only the conventional corru-

Fig. V–112. The slip form in action. Continuous cast concrete grain elevator built by Balfour Guthrie & Co. Ltd. on east bank of Willamette River in Portland in 1955.

gated sheet but a host of new profiles to serve both structural and architectural needs. These were readily available (for larger quantities) in any practical length, thereby eliminating troublesome end laps. Round and square structural tubing became commonplace and found many structural and architectural applications.

However, these changes and advances in construction materials and methods are only partially responsible for the types of industrial build-

Fig. V–113. Plant building of the Boeing Company, Seattle. Photo, circa 1960.

Fig. V–114. Benaroya Industrial Park, Portland, 1974.

ing we have seen in recent decades. The impact of the automobile, first mentioned in the preceding section, has exerted its almost overpowering force. Because much choice land close to the centers of cities was already occupied, new industry moved to the perimeters where ample space was available to build and expand horizontally instead of vertically. Edwin J. Cohn, Jr., expands upon the theories of Lewis Mumford and others writing in the 1930s and 1940s and defines this trend in *Industry in the Pacific Northwest and the Location Theory* (Columbia University, 1954):

> Dispersion of industry from the larger manufacturing centers to towns and rural areas was predicted. The automobile and truck, more flexible than railroads or waterways, were to assist in this process. With the removal of these two barriers to industrial decentralization—transportation and power—the progressive urbanization of industry which had been taking place since the Industrial Revolution was to be reversed, or at least retarded, by the movement of factories to the countryside.

Vast employee parking lots were a necessity and, as many facilities were detached from other amenities, pleasant eating areas and cafeterias were often added, at times accompanied by outdoor facilities or landscaping. The employee became more conscious of his surroundings, and concurrently the surrounding neighborhood became more conscious of the appearance of the new members of the family who arrived full grown at birth. Conspicuous examples in metropolitan Portland are the Tektronix plants (Beaverton) and Omark Industries (Milwaukie).

The term "Industrial Park" was coined to describe groupings of light commercial and industrial buildings. They first came about as land developers assembled compatible businesses which shared the costs of utilities, streets, fire protection and other general overhead associated with new development. As developers continued their search for attractive light industry, competition caused upgrading of the industrial parks. Engineers, who had traditionally designed plant buildings, found that more and more customers desired architectural excellence, so that in industrial building architecture and engineering came to have indeterminate boundaries. Engineering firms often included architects on their staffs; architects expanded their economical evaluation programs and related engineering activities. Even heavy industry and major public and private utility projects gave consideration to esthetics. While this attention may have been cursory for some large plants, a great deal of time and effort has been given to the profile of highly visible projects such as Portland's newer sewage treatment facilities and the Trojan plant of Portland General Electric Company.

Jantzen Inc. hired architects to design their Sandy Boulevard complex built in the 1930s. After World War II they continued to expand their operations outside of Portland. Their most recent addition is the plant in Hood River completed in 1972. The site was reclaimed from a slough adjacent to the Columbia River and posed considerable foundation questions. Mackenzie Engineering Incorporated was designer with Eric T. Saito as project architect. The structure is composed of exposed aggregate tilt-up panels, steel columns, glue-laminated beams, wood pur-

Fig. V–115. Tryon Creek sewage plant, Lake Oswego, Oregon, 1972.

Fig. V–116. Jantzen Inc. plant in Hood River, Oregon.

Fig. V–117. Building for Richard Abel & Company, Inc., west of Portland. Photo circa 1973.

Fig. V–118. Entrance to Richard Abel & Company, Inc. building.

lins and plank decking. Reinforced concrete spread footings develop suitable bearing pressures on the fill. The north side of the building has a steel pilaster system so that the wall panels may be relocated in the event of future expansion. The office section was originally designed to face the river but was reversed to improve the appearance from the adjoining freeway. It utilizes cedar-faced wood above, while the main entry and loading areas are topped with weathering Cor-Ten[1] steel roof panels. An outside landscaped lunch area is provided as an amenity for the numerous plant employees.

The Richard Abel and Company, Inc., building west of Portland designed by Peck/Grady meets similar needs. The tilt-up walls with exposed aggregate finish are bolted to pre-cast pilaster fin sections, permitting an ultimate fourfold expansion. There were no unusual interior clearance problems so the building has steel columns, glue-laminated beams, joists and wood decking. Colored Galbestos[2] siding provides a continuous horizontal tie around both the high and low sections of the building and the fin theme is continued through the main entry, which is surmounted by a semi-open canopy featuring exposed glue-laminated beams. The Abel Company is a major distributor of books and employs several hundred people at this facility.

---

1. A special type of steel which on exposure to the weather forms a dense oxide patina that inhibits further corrosion and thus preserves the structural integrity of the steel.

2. Corrugated steel coated with zinc, asbestos, asphalt and a waterproof finish.

The surrounding area is largely open space and the grading and planting are designed to reduce the visibility and obscure the installation as much as possible. The plant generates a large amount of waste paper, and as incineration is no longer completely feasible because of air pollution, a machine converts this to a readily disposable mulch.

While tilt-up concrete walls gave a new exterior look, warehouse and industrial building still required individually designed and engineered interior framing to suit spans and loads. To do this efficiently, the pre-engineered rigid frame steel building was introduced on a large scale in the 1950s. A certain amount of work had been done for wartime construction utilizing interchangeable sections, and this concept was furthered by several manufacturers. Most followed a set pattern of offering a number of different clear span widths in bay modules of 20 to 24 feet. The frames were made from wide flange beams or welded from strips of steel plate, usually in the form of two knees bolted together at the peaked centerline of the building. The critical point occurred where roof intersected wall; here the frames reached maximum size and strength, thus avoiding a major bending stress where the column joined the footing and simplifying foundation design. The advent of coiled steel and continuous roll forming of sheet metal shapes provided light, efficient girts and purlins. Prefinished galvanized sheet coil was rolled in several profiles and a variety of colors for both roofing and siding. New series of fasteners came on the market, including pop rivets, self-drilling sheet metal screws, and self-tapping screws with special heads for machine driving. As the demand for steel buildings grew, appearance improved

Fig. V–119. Omark Industries, Inc., Construction Tools Division plant near Milwaukie, Oregon. The basic rigid frame steel building shows on the right.

and many combinations of stock parts were assembled to meet a variety of engineering and architectural requirements.

The Omark Industries, Inc., Construction Tools Division manufacturing plant in Milwaukie is a typical example of this steel construction. The large building has a 128-foot clear span 360 feet long in 24-foot bays with a minimum interior clearance of 20 feet. The structure is insulated for both thermal and noise transmission. The 3,000-square-foot office building includes special aluminum sash wall sections and a copper fascia. Interior finishes are conventional, including acoustical ceiling.

Pope & Talbot, Inc., has progressed in the lumbering industry from the muley saw of 1853 at Port Gamble through a series of changes presently culminating in the new Oakridge mill designed by H. C. Mason and Associates and completed in 1972. This is probably the most up-to-date and automated sawmill in operation today. The aerial photograph can only show the general layout and does not do justice to the size (the building housing the barker unit shown in the detailed picture is difficult to locate at the front of the seemingly small complex at the left rear corner of the logpond). In the early days, materials at hand were used for industrial construction. This is no longer possible. At the Oakridge mill steel and concrete have been used for foundations and framework, partly because of fire and maintenance requirements, but also because much of the complex machinery must be mounted on completely rigid foundations. Accuracy affects both quality and costs (a variation of five thousandths of an inch in a saw kerf can mean 500 square feet more yield in 100,000 board feet of one-inch board). The buildings

Fig. V–120. Barker unit building at Pope & Talbot, Inc., Oakridge, Oregon.

Fig. V–121. Aerial view of Pope & Talbot, Inc. mill at Oakridge. The barker unit is near the point of the area at the left rear corner of the millpond. Photo, 1973.

themselves are all steel and mostly rigid frames with solid 4″ x 6″ girts and 3″ x 12″ wood purlins covered with a 3/4-inch medium density overlay plywood topped with a conventional built-up asphalt roof. The "knee out" style gives a pleasant appearance and also provides a vertical interior wall particularly convenient for crane runways. The large main building has only one row of center columns, giving maximum uninterrupted floor space, and supervisory personnel are located on a high mezzanine balcony situated to give an unobstructed view of the entire operation. Some of the heavier pieces of machinery, such as the main head rig, are mounted on isolated individual foundations in order to minimize vibration and movement.

The Trojan plant of Portland General Electric Company is the first privately owned nuclear generating plant in the Pacific Northwest. The company engaged Pietro Belluschi, the architectural firm of Wolff, Zimmer, Gunsul, Frasca, and landscape architects Lawrence Halprin & Associates to handle the general design of structures and grounds within the parameters imposed by physicists and engineers. While the project is still under construction in the spring of 1974, the most striking feature, the cooling tower, is finished and presently dominates the immediate scene. Research-Cottrell designed the tower, with a form calculated for optimum draft characteristics, but also falling within reasonable economic limits. The shape is an offset hyperboloid and has been used at a number of European generating stations, although the Trojan tower is the largest constructed up to this time. It is 385 feet in diameter at the base and 499 feet high. For 27 feet above the diagonal support columns the wall is 3.5 feet thick, but above this point it tapers to a minimum of 10 inches for most of the upper part. A five-foot-wide by one foot thick horizontal top ring provides lateral stiffness. Reinforcing bars are #6 and #8, placed approximately 6″ on centers. It is interesting to note that the "vertical" bars are all straight lengths so angled as to lie completely within the form. The shell was constructed by pouring a series of five-foot-high monolithic rings in adjustable slip forms raised by hydraulic jacks. After each ring had attained the necessary strength, the form was raised, adjusted and the next lift again poured.

Nuclear reactor cooling towers will probably be few enough in number that they will always attract some attention. Major dams and bridges are often visually prominent. Our rapidly developing technology undoubtedly will require other monumental structures. The problem of fitting such man-made items to the environment will require architectural ingenuity as well as engineering skill.

In concluding the chapters of this book dealing with industrial building, the author must call attention to two severe limitations. First: it has only been possible to select a few typical examples of historic highlights. The work is a broad spectrum; structures of great architectural excellence are grouped with the mundane, as well as those totally lacking in aesthetic value. This is the way history shows it in the past and the way it will in all probability continue. Second: while an effort has been made to cover the entire Pacific Northwest, practical considera-

Fig. V–122. Cooling tower, Portland General Electric Company Trojan Plant near Rainier, Oregon. Photo, 1973.

Fig. V–123. Adjustable slip forms during construction of the Trojan Plant cooling tower. Photo, 1972.

tions and available photographs and research data have resulted in inclusion of a disproportionate share of buildings in Oregon and Portland. Washington and Idaho have been slighted but certainly not for want of interesting past and present structures.

Portland, Seattle and most of the other presently important Northwest cities were located for commercial and industrial reasons, and not because the prospective inhabitants were impressed by the environment or natural beauty. A smaller number were sited for convenience to agriculture, but of these the ones that have increased in importance are the ones that also provided the complementary business to support the agrarian areas. For the first 100 years Northwest industry paid little heed to its impact upon the environment. This has been changing since World War II, and the last ten years have brought a host of new rules by government and new standards, many self-imposed, for industry. The challenge of the next decade will be how to adapt industry and industrial construction (which we must have if our population centers are to remain viable) to these new rules and standards—how to maintain our economic base and still arrest or reverse the trends that degrade our environment.

In the late 1950s the American Institute of Architects initiated a program of awards for outstanding design. Each local chapter rated projects within its area in a number of categories including industrial and warehouse construction. The winning structures in these competitions represent many of the outstanding architects of the Pacific Northwest, and their work has had a marked effect upon the appearance of better styled industrial work. Space does not permit the inclusion of even a small percentage of the winners, but they are well documented and information is available at local A.I.A. chapter offices.

Parks and Gardens of Western Oregon

Wallace Kay Huntington

The dissolution of American cities, which was already underway in the 1940s, was temporarily halted during World War II. Construction materials that formerly went into suburban housing were channeled into high priority military or defense projects; the increase in numbers of automobiles slowed and gas rationing curtailed driving during the war years. But the inexorable mark of the automobile had already been established. Though the beginnings of suburban sprawl hardly seemed threatening at the time, the development of linear commercial zones had made some impact. Zoning regulations, suspect with many Americans as infringing on basic rights, were inadequate to stem this new phenomenon of growth. The automotive and fast-food industries, chief benefactors from the strip development, spawned a new type of non-architecture that utilized building materials undisciplined by tradition: plastic, metal and glass confections prefabricated and completely oriented to an automobile esthetic. Though initially erected to take advantage of existing patterns of transportation, they soon began to generate traffic themselves. They were, moreover, totally dependent on advertising and nighttime illumination.

Outdoor advertising had a unique impact on American cities. One of the major differences between European and American cities is not so much architectural as it is in the relationship between architecture and foliage. The ambience of European cities which American tourists seek out is largely due to the novelty of tree-lined city center streets; boulevards in Paris, London, Berlin and Madrid have the additional continuity of regularly spaced trees plus changing shadows and sheltering summer coolness of overhead protection. American cities by contrast confine street trees to residential streets and parks, and the commercial areas are largely bare of foliage patterns or protection. Advertising and signboards are thus unobscured in the American business district. Competing for attention, they attempt by size, illumination and novelty to supersede each other and the resulting visual chaos is endemic to the American scene. Taking ugliness for granted, Americans in the mid-20th century equated it with prosperity and free enterprise. With the development of linear commercial developments, street trees became a liability

Fig. V–124. Canyon Road, Beaverton, 1950s. A surviving farmhouse keeps a melancholy vigil over a used car lot as suburban communities began to disintegrate visually in the postwar years.

Fig. V–125. Billboard, Portland. Presented with apologetic grandeur, a billboard of the 1930s seems less threatening than it will become in the era of freeways.

to the successful hawking of hamburgers and milkshakes.

Barbur Boulevard, Sandy and Interstate had already eroded prior to the war; it was to be expected in larger cities such as Portland. It was the smaller communities such as Salem, Eugene, and Medford that underwent such a rapid transition in the 1950s. Salem was typical; even into the 1940s the major entrances to the city were tree-lined residential streets; within 20 years Portland Road, Commercial Street and State Street had become chaotic treeless expanses of flashing signs, asphalt, and "plastic" architecture.

If advertising was without restraint, it was at most an esthetic rape of the landscape. Of seemingly greater consequence at the time was the hazard to safety and traffic movement that resulted from the unrestricted access and egress from the hundreds of parking areas essential to the function of roadside businesses. Existing arterials, strained by the growing population and new affluence engendered by the war years, ceased to function efficiently. Alleviating bypasses and new roads, such as that connecting Seattle and Tacoma, were obsolete before their completion. Thus, the federal highway system, planned in the post-war years, took into account the physical problem of controlled access but not the esthetic problem of signs and billboards. Ironically, the Federal Highway Act provided rather generously for landscaping the freeway corridors, though leaving the standards flexible and to be determined by the individual states. Oregon's initial landscape program was a model of propriety and restraint; using native plants and large massing, the freeways escaped the exotic "botanical corridor" look of the Eastern parkways. Washington, more niggardly in their expenditures and more prone to flowering trees and shrubs, achieved rather less by their residential scaled plantings. In the 1960s however, always sensitive to criticism, the Oregon Highway Commission capitulated quickly to the criticism that their plantings were "colorless" and abandoned the good taste and common sense that had prevailed; the late 1960s and 1970s saw the introduction of iris, peonies, and grave-like beds of lilies. Washington, meanwhile vastly improved and simplified its landscaped corridors.

The Shopping Center, today so essential to the suburban way of life, was a novelty in the postwar years. Though a logical outgrowth of the urban expressway, these shopping nodes developed with a spontaneity that caught city planners and zoning commissions quite unprepared to cope with such new pressures. The earliest centers were bleak indeed: clusters of unimaginative buildings surrounded by unrelieved asphalt. Salem's Capitol Shopping Center cleared a residential area and removed every existing tree without planting even token alleviating greenery. Regulations requiring screening or trees were after the fact and though the convenience of their location and availability of parking made them acceptable, their amenities were minimal.

The affluence of the new shopping districts was in inverse proportion to the viability of the "downtown" area. With unrented upper floors and dwindling profits, the merchants' reaction caused a wave of destruction of historic 19th century buildings. By reducing the taxes and overhead and at the same time profiting from the resulting low investment parking lots, property owners turned great areas of what had been cohesive office and shopping blocks into wastelands of parked cars. The pathetic code requirements that landscape screening be provided assured a burgeoning business in arborvitae hedging. The arborvitae, though requiring relatively little care, was not a panacea for a disintegrating core area. Without water or adequate soil and battered by endless bumpers and seared by exhaust fumes, the stiff peripheral rows of dying shrubs added only a further note of melancholy. Frustrated by growing desolation, many cities adopted ordinances requiring a certain percentage of area in a parking lot to be planted, but usually these well-intended rules were ineffective. Trees, that might have alleviated the sterility, were anathema to developers and sign companies, and were avoided in favor of plantings below eye level; the complying juniper and cotoneaster beds were inundated in a sea of cars.

Portland's Lloyd Center, though undistinguished architecturally, was undoubtedly the most thoroughly planned and progressive—and at the time the largest of all the Northwest shopping centers. The device of placing the majority of the parking beneath the pedestrian circulation on the upper levels, minimized the long walk through parked cars. Having reached the stairs, the shopper was divorced from asphalt and traffic. Sign control eliminated the ubiquitous chaos of clutter and lights and made possible a street tree program that lent an air of humanity to the landscaped malls which extended in four directions from the central plaza. Designed around an ice arena, and landscaped more generously than any previous commercial venture of its kind, it had an air of urbanity the others lacked. The covered pedestrian mall was hardly a new invention; the great gallerias in Italy and the arcades in London and Paris are substantially the same concept, but the Lloyd Center was a landmark in Northwest planning. Its commercial success however provided no answers to the merchants of sprawling shopping centers where land cost was comparatively low, since its location was urban rather than suburban. Its progeny were few. Throughout the 1960s and 1970s the Northgates, Southgates, Eastgates, and Westgates provided surface parking endlessly, meeting the minimal token landscape requirements of frustrated planning commissions. The arterial strip developments of the earlier decades became a reticulated pattern enmeshing all the major cities by the 1970s, with one shopping center connected to the next by continuous featureless sprawl. The great linear mega-cities of the East Coast were duplicated in the Northwest: Everett-Seattle-Tacoma was the longest of the linear developments; Vancouver-Portland-Milwaukie-Oregon City was runner-up as a planner's nightmare.

Fig. V–126. Camas Mall by Perron Partnership, 1968, one of the early Northwest efforts to reconcile the automobile and pedestrian.

The shopping mall as the answer to the malaise of "downtown" came tentatively to the Northwest. Already beyond the experimental stage in other cities in the United States, it had met with qualified success in a number of instances. Coos Bay mustered the unlikely public enthusiasm for the first pedestrian mall, followed by Camas, Washington. Avoiding major rerouting of traffic, both schemes provided a more hospitable atmosphere by means of a pedestrian boulevard graced with trees, professionally designed street furniture, and varied paving textures. The sophisticated architectural embellishments of the Coos Bay Mall perhaps point up the weakness of its architectural background, making the new work appear somewhat alien, but the provision of overhead shelter and the extra space with its plantings and benches improve the street and give a much-needed centripetal energy to the city. It was a brave and significant step for Coos Bay to take.

Camas Shopping Mall was a landscape rather than an architectural solution to the problem facing so many cities where core area vitality had waned. Perron Partnership arrived at a compromise between the automobile and pedestrian, granting the pedestrian a larger share of space but not eliminating automobiles. With a minimum disruption of the fabric of the street and at minimum cost, trees and benches were added, sidewalks expanded and street furniture coordinated. Though largely a cosmetic treatment, the commonsense solutions effectively gave character to what had been a relatively faceless community.

Eugene's Mall was a project of such magnitude as to hardly warrant comparison with previous Northwest mall projects. It not only eliminated automobiles (including cross-traffic) from a major segment of the core area and provided for off-street parking, but also necessitated a major and prolonged disruption of the economic life of the city. A collaborative design involving city planners, architects, and landscape architects, the landscape features were largely determined by Mitchell, McArthur and Gardner, who literally set about rebuilding the city. The commercial architecture along Willamette Street bears no closer scrutiny than that of Coos Bay or Camas; unsentimental about 19th century architecture, most of which has disappeared behind specious facades of indeterminate style, the city presented the challenge not of ugliness so much as of mediocrity and how to overcome its impact on the new design.

The still to be completed project as yet defies analysis as a total entity. The linear spaces once devoted to streets with flanking sidewalks are still recognizable, but rather than being occupied by automobiles,

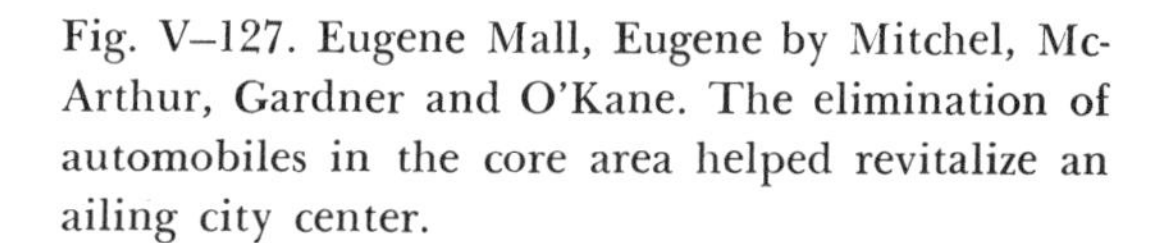
Fig. V–127. Eugene Mall, Eugene by Mitchel, McArthur, Gardner and O'Kane. The elimination of automobiles in the core area helped revitalize an ailing city center.

Fig. V–128. Eugene Mall. An architecturally controlled environment characterizes Oregon's most extensive and sophisticated urban redesign.

the spaces are filled with human-oriented furnishings: benches, arbors, fountains, etc. The paving patterns are richly and continuously varied in arbitrary materials and trees are abundantly used in groves, block formation or as single specimens. The welcome sign control, the quality of construction, and the sophistication of detailing are immediately apparent and prevent the blandness of the building facades from being assertive. Claiming that it is "over-designed," contemporary critics object to the *horror vacui* and labyrinthian circulation that precludes any continuous overhead protection from rain or sun. Indeed, the opportunity to provide an urban designed space of moderate scale at the intersection of Willamette and Broadway streets seems to have been squandered for a curiously indecisive fountain, but the ultimate success or failure of a project with such ramifications must be gauged on human terms and the activity generated by the mall would indicate that a more vital city center has resulted from the radical surgery undertaken.

The maximum utilization of urban space had, of necessity, been controlled by building codes in the 1920s and 1930s. Aerial space of proliferating skyscrapers that threatened to choke out light and air from the streets of Chicago and New York was restricted, but high land values dictated the economics of office building construction and almost without exception buildings in central Manhattan and in the Loop filled out the maximum space allowed them by fiat. The exceptional post-war Lever Brothers headquarters building in New York by Skidmore, Owings and Merrill heralded a new philosophy: it was the beginning of corporate identity with architectural excellence. With an admirable spirit of generosity, the great corporations began to succumb to a spatial charity and allow plazas, fountains and trees to occupy a portion of the astronomically valuable street-level space. Lever Brothers with its pool and courtyard, the Seagrams building with its plaza and fountains, became corporate symbols of largess and established a new and infectious "less is more" philosophy of land utilization.

Not surprisingly, Skidmore, Owings and Merrill's Hilton Hotel in Portland was one of the earliest Northwest manifestations of 20th century designed urban space as a part of the architectural package. Exclusive space to be sure, since it occurred at the second floor level and was restricted to members of the International Club located there, it nevertheless was a contribution to central open space that wouldn't have occurred two decades earlier. Though gained at the expense of a formidable street-level podium and marred by a romantically jumbled planting scheme, the space created between the Hilton tower and Public Service Building was of itself a handsome creation.

Other designed spaces followed and of these perhaps the most effective was the enclosed courtyard of the Blue Cross Building (now the Portland Water Bureau) by landscape architect Arthur Erfeldt, who used a geometric framework as spare in plan as a Mondrian painting. The reflections and counter-reflections from water and glass and the tailored plant material selection make an elegant and surprising oasis in the heart of the city.

Fig. V–129. Blue Cross Building (Portland Water Bureau) by Arthur Erfeldt. An enclosed urban space, enhanced by a skillful blend of foliage and water, maintains a geometric framework.

Whereas commercial buildings in the 1920s, 1930s and 1940s almost invariably extended to the property lines, the new designs dictated at least token landscaping. In the case of Portland's new Equitable Building, a plaza of fearful symmetry so generous in space and trees as to appear almost suburban was created by the architects. The Standard Plaza has a miniature scaled sunken garden, featured anachronistic boxwood hedging and blue pools with recirculating water. Georgia Pacific, with a street level plaza and a monumental piece of statuary, more cautiously reserved its landscape terrace to the second floor level, where a tailored urban roof garden by Michael Parker discreetly demonstrated to the Hilton Hotel the difference between an appropriate urban planting versus the Hilton's "wildwood" scheme.

The result of the new trend was invariably a greater amount of urban greenery: trees and shrubs in heretofore unexpected places. Though occasionally effective as individual beautification projects, the total impact of the lessening density of space utilization was to contribute to the decline in urban vitality; shopping streets receded and the new office complexes without street level retail outlets offered in many cases a palatable inhospitality to the pedestrian. Ada Louise Huxtable, in her *New York Times* column, noted after a visit to Portland in 1972 that the destruction of architecture to create parking lots had given Portland the familiar "bombed out" look so prevalent in American cities. Inadvertently, the new landscaping of core area buildings had also created voids and damaged the intensity of urban life in a subtle but insidious way.

The middle decades of the 20th century were quiescent years in park design in the Northwest. No national figure of the caliber of Olmsted appeared to set a design pace, and until World War II no cataclysmic event occurred to serve as a catalyst for urban improvement. What progress occurred was in the acquisition of park land along the coast and along rivers, where state parks of low intensity use were laid out for camping and picnicking. The necessity for more urban parks and parks designed for greater intensity of use became increasingly apparent in Western cities only in the postwar years. Changing social attitudes also would dictate design changes, and particularly in the disillusioning years fomented by the Korean and Viet Nam wars, the usage of public parks changed. "Keep Off the Grass" signs were generally effective until the postwar years; however by the 1960s such a dictum would invite intentional violation. Such a defiance of authority demanded a design accommodation, as did the increasing numbers of people using parks for a wider variety of uses. The passive Victorian and Edwardian park was for social congregation and strolling; benches were provided, but the use of the urban park was carefully circumscribed. The necessity for specialization was one of the results of the changing mores and life styles. New facilities had to be provided in parks: Little League and Soapbox Derby facilities, jogging trails, park structures that could accommodate indoor sports and dancing, more and larger public swimming pools—all these were imposed on a reluctant and under-financed park department. Indestructibility was another specification imposed on park designers as vandalism increased. Gone was the age when parks were a display of botanical wonders, and shrubbery became a liability that interfered with the necessary policing of urban parks. The new park was to be, therefore, a creation for mass use and it must be built of obdurate materials: stone, concrete, metal or heavy timber. It could contain trees but not flowers; it could contain lawn only if the lawn were designed to take dispersed usage rather than invite shortcuts or circulation. Given the prognosis, the outlook for park design might seem grim indeed, but it was not to be so; despite, or perhaps because of, the new exigencies Oregon passed into an era of amazingly creative urban design. In Portland not since 1914 when E. T. Mische left the park department had such innovative work been done.

Fig. V–130. County park blocks, Eugene, by Lloyd Bond, 1957. A new look in urban parks; lawns and planting areas diminish in size and romantic informality gives way to pragmatism.

Eugene, with its endemic restlessness and impatience with the outmoded, undertook in the 1950s a major reorganization of blocks adjacent to the newly designed Lane County Courthouse. In the first instance of a contemporary urban park in Oregon, local landscape architect Lloyd Bond designed a multiple level sequence of spaces with fountains, sculpture, and arched canopies—all without precedent in the state. The stress on space, form and texture rather than on botanical interest was innovative, but even more remarkable was the high quality of sculpture highlighting the design. Salem had but recently risen in righteous indignation at the prospect that a bronze Renoir sculpture of Venus might be given to the city as a feature of the new Marion County Courthouse. Eugene, more progressive in its attitudes, accepted an abstract bronze by Zack and a fine fountain by Tom Hardy.

Haussman's transformation of Paris from a medieval to a modern

Fig. V–131. County park blocks, Eugene. High quality of sculpture, paving patterns and fixed benches initiate new concepts in park design.

city was only possible because of the unquestioned dictatorial authority of Napoleon III, and American city planners, bogged down in endless compromise, might justifiably look back with envy at Haussman's effective arrogance. Similarly, one must grudgingly admire the Portland Development Commission's authoritative handling of Urban Renewal projects; though high-handed to a Second Empire degree, their accomplishments similarly seem to justify their arrogance. Lovejoy Fountain, Pettygrove Park, the Auditorium Forecourt and the Park Blocks at Portland State University were major additions to Portland, and at least the Auditorium Forecourt and Lovejoy Fountain were significant works of art. The Portland Development Commission was unhampered by skimpy funds, felt no obligation to award design commissions to socially acceptable local landscape architects, and by going directly to landscape architectural firms of such international renown as Halprin and Associates and Sasaki, Walker, they eliminated internecine squabbles among local critics who might question designs or concepts emanating from

Fig. V–132. Lovejoy Fountain, Portland, Lawrence Halprin & Associates. Unabashed use of concrete and abstract contemporary forms characterize the innovative design.

offices of unknown stature.

In San Francisco the concept of the Lovejoy Fountain might not have seemed radical, but to Portland, where a concrete esthetic had no evolutionary background, Lovejoy came as a shock to many, a surprise to everyone. Architects and site planners recognize the arbitrary angular forms of the stepped terracing as being derived from cardboard models of contoured sites, but blown to full dimensions and perpetuated in concrete the strong sense of stylization becomes the design motif itself; monumentality and accommodation to heavy usage are byproducts. The unapologetic surfaces of concrete textured by the impressions derived from the wood forming give a sense of spontaneity to the construction. Though ostensibly a waterfall, no romantic imitative effects compromise the interpretation; the sharp edge, architectural line and sculptural mass are far removed from nature's inspiration, though the noise and excitement remain to elate the observer.

The immediate popularity and use of the fountain by the younger

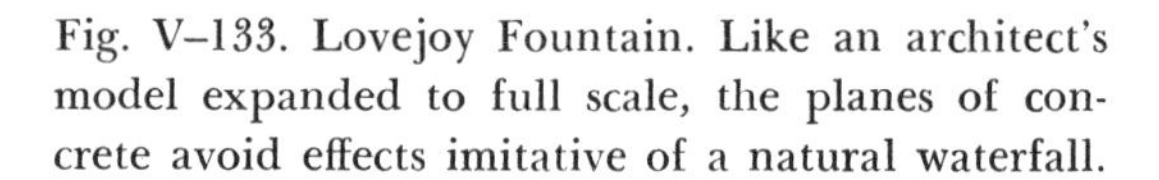

Fig. V–133. Lovejoy Fountain. Like an architect's model expanded to full scale, the planes of concrete avoid effects imitative of a natural waterfall.

Fig. V–134. Pettygrove Park, Portland, Lawrence Halprin & Associates. Sculptural mounds and organic shapes display lawn patterns as important from above as at eye level.

generation (a popularity that fostered an element of puritanical displeasure at such wanton hedonism) was symptomatic of changing attitudes. The disappointment of the older generation grown to expect soft lines, natural materials and botanical interest was to be expected; the age of the mossy rivulet was passing.

Pettygrove Park, also out of Halprin's office, was as placid and organic as Lovejoy was agitated and geometric. A microcosm of mountain landscape with precipitously contoured mounds of turf and groves of trees through which undulating ribbons of paving served the pedestrian, it was plastically conceived but still as strongly sculptural as was Lovejoy. Turf, rather than being an infinite and formless surfacing material, is used to "paint" abstract forms on the surface of the earth—less for use than for its visual impact.

The culminating masterpiece of the Portland Development Commission's enlightened autocracy was the Auditorium Forecourt. Originally conceived as an accoutrement of the remodeled auditorium, it was patently obvious that the newly unveiled architecture of the auditorium was too weak to be sustained by any satellite embellishment. The City's arbitrary and esthetically damaging decision not to allow the street closure between auditorium and forecourt definitively terminated any hope in this direction. Thus, the Forecourt was destined to stand isolated and on its own merits.

The design, by Angela Danadjieva Tzvetin in Halprin's office, on its sloping site and unassisted by its architectural surroundings, was to some extent a hybrid between the previously constructed Lovejoy Fountain and Pettygrove Park, combining the stylized earth "sculpture" and groves of trees of Pettygrove with the crisp concrete forms and textures of Lovejoy. The excitement of falling water to the human observer seems almost to stem from primordial sources and here, with sophisti-

Fig. V–135. Auditorium Forecourt, Portland, Lawrence Halprin & Associates. A lavish gesture by Portland Development Commission results in a work of major significance in American landscape design.

cated pumping equipment and an escarpment of crystalline concrete forms, a veritable Niagara of water cascades in exhilarating counterpoint rhythms into the basin. Ingeniously, the basin itself, with "floating" pads of concrete, is dropped to a lower level than the street, giving a tangibly enclosed amphitheater of space. The conception is indeed theater-like with the waterfall becoming the performance, the basin the proscenium and the steps serving as standing and seating space for the audience. But if theater inspired, it is certainly not the classic Western theater but the newly experimental "Living Theater" which demands audience participation. The participants have been, from its inauguration, infectiously involved. It was a major concession on the part of the city government to retreat from the protectionism so inherent in local government; gone are the railings and barriers; waived are the code restrictions, and on warm summer days the "theater" is filled with enthusiastic performers.

Portland's Park Blocks have achieved a special status in the community and the civic veneration of the park strip has prevented such ill-conceived "improvements" as was proposed in the 1950s of replacing the elm trees with flowering cherries. Perhaps only the Development Commission's freedom from the necessity of public participation allowed them to violate the status quo and make a major change within this hallowed territory without the expected public remonstrance. The remodeling of the Park Blocks within Portland State University's campus is again a creditable performance from the Development Commission, a model of restraint and good sense. Without the sacrifice of a single tree, the contours of the site have been subtly manipulated and major paved areas have replaced the worn turf; gratifyingly, the sense of continuous space has been preserved by keeping a low scale to all walls, benches and steps, so that the only verticals are the remaining elm trees.

Fig. V–136. Portland State Park Blocks, Portland, Sasaki, Walker and Associates. A restrained design that avoids assertive forms and accommodates heavy and varied usage.

Serving the needs of Portland State students without becoming a monument to the designers, the plan by Sasaki, Walker is an unassertive and functional solution to the problem of intensively used park space.

The street tree program initiated in the South Auditorium site by the Development Commission was another plus for the community. The dwindling number of street trees in Portland through natural attrition had begun to visually ruin a number of previously pleasant streetscapes. A concurrent trend toward planting badly out of scale flowering trees instead of shade trees had also caused a deterioration of the environment. The trend was reversed however during the 1960s when elms and scarlet oak were again introduced in continuous array by landscape architect David Thompson, giving a bigness of scale and welcome dignity to the urban renewal site.

Though the City of Portland continued to ignore the advisability of a city-wide street tree program and functioned with an archaic street tree ordinance that treated trees as a nuisance, the City of Salem undertook such an all-encompassing planting program (even including the core area) that the future of the city appeared brighter for the next half century.

Though local landscape architects had been given short shrift by the Portland Development Commission, the office of Robert Perron was functioning independently, and Unthank Park, followed by Woodlawn Park, show spirited designs, architecturally firm and rational. Play equipment for children in the 1960s and 1970s is a far cry from the ubiquitous swings and teeter-totters of the mid-century decades. Both more massive and more sculptural, the new trend indicates an awareness of child psychology, tending to encourage improvised play and more imaginative use

Fig. V–137. Unthank Park, Portland, by Perron Partnership. Imaginative forms and indestructable materials encourage children's total involvement.

Fig. V–138. Woodlawn Park, Portland, by Perron Partnership. Nineteenth century pre-conceived ideas of play equipment have given way to 20th century fantasy architecture.

of inert materials.

Though the mainstream of civic landscape improvement was channeled along the lines of rational and articulate architectural parks, a minor counterpoint occurred in the movement to construct a Japanese garden in Portland. A generation born after the bitterness of World War II was maturing and the old enmities had been replaced by a wave of enthusiasm for things Oriental. Without qualms at being eclectic in an era when other forms of eclecticism were unfashionable, the proponents transformed an appropriate site in Washington Park into a self-contained series of traditional Oriental vignettes. Oriental art forms, unlike their Western counterparts, stress historic continuity and tradition above originality, and therefore lend themselves to infinite repetition and variation. Thus, the Japanese Garden Society's intent, wisely implemented by Japanese landscape architect Dr. Tono, was a largely successful recreation of the familiar Japanese garden forms. Though the attempted duplication of the garden at Ryuanji, at a reduced scale, was an embarrassing parody of the original, the more freely interpreted scenes have a verisimilitude both highly competent as design and sentimentally appealing. The danger of an enterprise with such insidious charm was in the offspring it engendered: the "Gravel Garden" recreated as a setting for the Ranch Style house. Out of context and done with more enthusiasm than style, these largely home-designed assemblages of sprawling pine and arid bark dust had the appeal of "minimum maintenance," but so little remained alive in the plastic mulched and sun scorched plats that the effect was often more lunar than Oriental.

If the incidence of Japanese inspired garden design was an aberration in Western society, it continued with considerable persistence and

Fig. V–139. Japanese Garden, Washington Park, Portland, Dr. P. Takuma Tono. Traditional Japanese garden forms skillfully re-created in a Western context.

though the quality varied widely, at its best it seemed at least as much at home in Western America as the other eclectic garden styles. Landscape architect Arthur Erfeldt was one of the few Occidental designers sufficiently versatile to handle the traditional Oriental motifs with the same skill as the European formal tradition. In the Grossman garden, working with a sympathetic client, he created a harmonious blending of rock and foliage, water and sand, so much in the Oriental manner that one might think momentarily that the distant presence of Mt. Hood was in truth Fujiyama.

Erfeldt's training was American and Swedish and his sophisticated residential designs, tilting either to the traditional or contemporary as the occasion demanded, were invariably stylish. The pool and arbor set against a stone wall in the C. W. Morden garden was such a successful translation of contemporary Scandinavian forms into Northwest materials that it was actually published in Sweden.

Fig. V–140. Dr. Albert Grossman garden, Portland, Arthur Erfeldt. Rocks, plants and textures composed in an Oriental mode.

Decks, rather than porches, were the late 20th century answer to outdoor living space; particularly on sloping sites where they could float above the surface of undisturbed soil, but also on older houses where they could be added without compromising the architecture. The low-scaled deck and built-in benches that Erfeldt added to the Edwardian home of the Cyrus Walkers seem to float in a sea of foliage and it is such a classic of contemporary design that it would be difficult to guess that it was built as early as 1954.

The sketch for the entrance court added to the Leland residence in Longview shows a contemporary idiom conceived in traditional materials plastically treated to formalize the entrance on an awkwardly sloping site.

Two major factors account for the rapid evolution of professional garden design in the 1960s and 1970s. One, the changing nature of the profession, could be traced to educational background which produced a generation of landscape architects more closely allied to architecture than had been traditional in the Western world, where often painting or sculpture had been more directly influential. With landscape architecture as a form of specialized architecture, the garden becomes an extension of the house and often the delineation between the two ceases to exist. This trend accounts for a concurrent change in "heroes"; Thomas Church and Roberto Burle-Marx, both plant oriented and less architectural in their designs, had set the design pace in mid-century. By the Sixties, Halprin and Sasaki had usurped professional primacy in

Fig. V–141. Dr. Albert Grossman garden. A vignette of convincing authenticity suggests traditional Japanese prototypes.

Fig. V–142. C. W. Morden garden, Portland, Arthur Erfeldt. A non-historic design using traditional materials in one of Portland's earliest manifestations of contemporary Scanadinavian design.

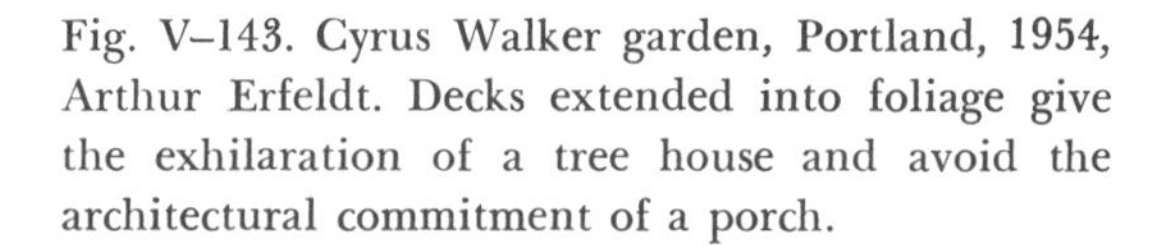

Fig. V–143. Cyrus Walker garden, Portland, 1954, Arthur Erfeldt. Decks extended into foliage give the exhilaration of a tree house and avoid the architectural commitment of a porch.

Fig. V–144. Leland residence, Longview, Washington, entrance court by Arthur Erfeldt. Sketch of a plastically conceived design in concrete and brick.

Fig. V–145. Judge Charles Crookham garden, Daryl May. Extending above a sloping site, the straightforward deck and bench serve as a foil for foliage textures and shadows.

Fig. V–146. Don G. Swink garden, Portland, Chandler Fairbank. Curving exterior forms of rail and bench are juxtaposed against angular interior forms of concrete in this richly textured deck.

the United States and their architectural affinity carried the day. The Melvin Peters residence, a sophisticated city garden by Perron Partnership, is the epitome of articulate architectural detailing. Enclosing spaces both peripherally and overhead, it creates outdoor rooms that have the exhilarating quality of a tree house suspended in a grove of Douglas fir.

The other factor contributing to changing concepts of the Western garden was the proliferation of activities making a demand on leisure time: boating, skiing, golf, tennis, swimming, even the time spent in commuting to the suburban residential communities cut into the avail-

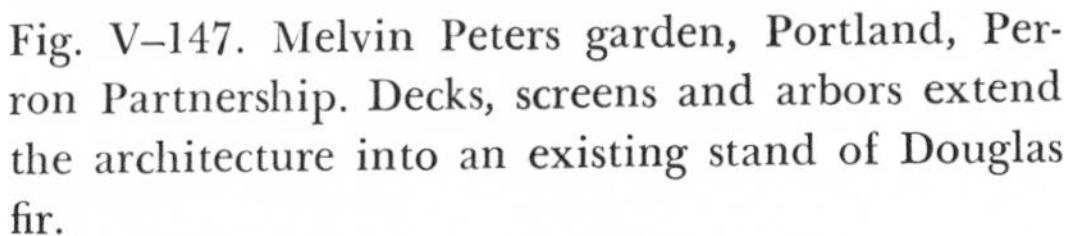

Fig. V–147. Melvin Peters garden, Portland, Perron Partnership. Decks, screens and arbors extend the architecture into an existing stand of Douglas fir.

Fig. V–148. Salishan, Barbara Fealy, landscape consultant. Oregon's first comprehensive resort that avoided slick urbanized landscape schemes in favor of conservation.

able free time. In a less hectic era, gardening had been looked upon as a pleasurable diversion; when gardening was conceived of as a chore rather than a recreational activity, the concept of the garden necessarily changed. Minimum maintenance was achieved by the elimination of lawns, the use of larger areas of paving, decking, or ground covers, the use of evergreens rather than deciduous trees and shrubs, the use of fences rather than hedges or screen plantings. Swimming pools proliferated in the gardens of the affluent and second homes in eastern Oregon or along the coast were increasingly common with city residents. The second home, serving as a contrast to urban living, fostered a new attitude toward the natural landscape; full time residents of Bend or the coast towns were usually anxious to urbanize their environment and their gardens reflected styles and attitudes imposed from without. But the weekend visitor was more apt to be sympathetic to the climatic discipline nature imposes and the development at Salishan legally restricted plantings to endemic species. Other vacation communities, Sunriver and Black Butte, followed suit. Such respect for the environment not only better preserved the natural qualities of the site but also eliminated the necessity of nurturing plants requiring artificial life-sustaining programs. Barbara Fealy was involved as the major landscape architect of Salishan and her self-effacing salvage of the natural features of the

Fig. V–149. Robert Spahr garden, Lake Oswego, William K. Roth. Classic shapes and studied restraint lend elegance to a usable waterside deck free of encumbering rails.

site made it the most sympathetic commercial venture yet undertaken along the coast.

What had once appeared to be limitless space in the West, seemed by the 1970s to have shrunk. America's agrarian dream of living on a producing plot of ground in the country led too often to sprawling suburbs, too often to exploitation by developers turning real farms into non-productive "ranch style" communities. The search for physical space became more keen as it became more elusive and the means of assuring space led to 20th century solutions. One solution for assuring space was to build on previously "unbuildable" lots, sites so precipitous that only engineered steel foundations could support a residence with a "guaranteed" view. Golf course frontage was another "guaranteed" view and coupled with the increased popularity of golf, the golf course community, often of condominiums, furnished a view of human activity and a modicum of economically viable space groomed at no direct cost to the owner. The most expensive but in some ways most satisfying way of acquiring a vested interest in space was to live on lakefront or riverfront property. The cost of such land soared astronomically in the postwar years, leading to more intensively developed land, but to those who could afford the tariff, the space and activity of waterfrontage solved the psychological needs of the era. William Roth's design for a serene and railless deck suspended over the water of Lake Oswego at the residence of Robert Spahr is characteristic of the 20th century solution for assured space. The quality of abstract sculpture characterizes the waterfront development by John Herbst, Jr. at the Lake Oswego home of Robert B. Nottingham. Compactly assembled on steeply sloping property tied together by an intricately detailed stairway are the provisions for

Fig. V–150. Robert B. Nottingham garden, Lake Oswego, John Herbst, Jr. All the accoutrements of the 20th century active and informal life adapted to a sloping lakeside property.

Fig. V–151. Reese Lamb garden, Portland, 1973, W. K. Huntington. An entry court with fountain by Merideth Apperson serves as a transition between street and house.

boating, swimming and barbecueing—the exemplification of the 20th century active and informal life.

While the general trend in the 1960s and 1970s was toward the suburbs, those reconciled to the city and rewarded by less dependence upon the automobile, made more intensive use of their available space. The Reese Lamb residence in Portland's West Hills has such an intensively developed property. The house by Harold Long projects decks and pavilions into the garden and the Matisse-like forms of lawn by Wallace K. Huntington, treating the landscape more as a painting than an extension of the architecture, are a part of the man-made view.

The relative importance of the swimming pool in the garden is magnified in the decades of spatial exploration. Having been treated as a recreational facility set apart from the landscape in early and mid-century decades, the swimming pool now becomes a dominant element in the garden. The pool at the Jack Dulong residence by Perron, designed around an existing tree, uses a combination of "hard" surfaces, wood and concrete, to lessen the maintenance that lawns had imposed on pool owners of a previous generation. Both pool and adjoining outdoor rooms, furnished and functioning much like indoor spaces but

Fig. V–152. Reese Lamb garden. Sculptured lawn forms framed by a calligraphic line contrast with the architectural enclosure.

Fig. V–153. Jack Dulong garden, Portland, Perron Partnership. The swimming pool serves a decorative function beyond its use for recreation.

Fig. V–154. Jack Dulong garden. Outdoor rooms expand the architecture into the garden without any sacrifice of privacy.

with the advantage of greenery and fresh air, are extensions of the house. The pool at the Guy Mount, Jr. residence, by John Herbst, Jr., occupies a terrace adjoining the house and intricately related to it by decks and stairs. As the pool becomes an esthetic object in the landscape, its shape is of greater significance and the simple rectangle that sufficed for swimming now is altered to provide esthetically satisfying forms coordinated with their architectural context.

Oregon has had, almost from the decades of its settlement, a strong sense of community. This has been manifest in many ways that have had an impact on the land: the generous donations of private property which became the foundations of impressive park systems and University sites; the ambitious undertaking of the Lewis and Clark Exposition which involved so much of the citizenry in a splendid celebration commemorating the past but anticipating the future; the philanthropy of patrician families that nurtured struggling institutions such as the Library, Art Museum, and Oregon Historical Society; and the public support and appreciation of painters, sculptors, architects and landscape architects who shaped materials or shaped the land in a manner that was subtly infused with regional characteristics.

Today, more than 35 million Americans move each year, one out of six in the nation. There is no denying that this is a threat to what has been a positive contribution to regionalism and sense of community.

Community is a corner of society in which the individual can feel some confidence of acceptance . . . and can maintain a continuing association with others, whose familiarity is comforting. Community provides a mooring for the spirit, for community is a restraint that liberates. It

Fig. V–155. Guy Mount, Jr. garden, Portland, John Herbst, Jr. Interrelationships of house, decks and pool are strongly coordinated to preserve existing trees on a hillside property.

relieves us of the need continually to prove our worth. It diminishes the destructive social process of judging and being judged, which cripples our capacity for thinking and acting freely and with honesty. Members of a community may not be friends, but they are not strangers. The relationships of community also provide that sense of shared purpose and shared concerns which is elemental to the concept of society itself. All the other components—culture, language, ideology, economic process, political structure—have crystallized around this nucleus.[1]

The era of the custom-designed home and the private garden may well be passing; increasing population, the social and physical services necessarily financed by taxation, the shortage of materials and the waning sources of fossil fuels, all these pressures so acutely felt in the decade of the Seventies would seem to be corrosive of our physical environment. It is ironic, however, that despite these obvious adversities, despite the declining quality of mass-produced housing and despite the continued exploitation and ill-management of land resources, there does seem to be a viable community of involved and concerned human beings. There is no doubt that we have the technology and artistry to build well, no doubt that we can shape the land wisely for our use and pleasure, no doubt that both artist and patron are still extant. The increasing concern for these matters by a wider spectrum of society and a greater number of individuals offers the hope that we might cease to treat the land as an expendable resource and learn to venerate our heritage.

1. Richard N. Goodwin, "Reflections," *The New Yorker*, Jan. 28, 1974, pp. 36, 37.

Parks and Gardens in the Puget Sound Area

Thomas Allsopp*

Social and economic forces have worked together in recent times to change garden and park designs. People are looking for new recreational experiences. Increased leisure time, mobility, and population are putting pressure on parks—particularly the larger National and State parks. Some of the larger mountain and seashore parks have had to close, take reservations, or in some cases, charge admission; these restrictions, combined with the immediate high prices of fuel, will probably restrain the urge to get away to the mountains. People will be "getting away" to the city parks.

The Seattle Park Department has begun to prepare for the growing demands. They have been aided greatly by the passage of the Forward Thrust Bond Issue which allocated monies for new neighborhood parks and playgrounds, many new swimming pools (indoor), recreational facilities in existing parks, as well as areas like the Gas Plant Park which will be partially funded by the bonds. The newly formed Fort Lawton Park, now called Discovery Park, will be Seattle's largest. Plans include some recreational facilities here but the park will serve mainly as a natural preserve with woodland and beach trails unmatched in the city. It is ironic that in 1903 the Olmsted Brothers suggested Seattle persuade the military to give them the remote fort. In 1930 the U. S. Army offered the acreage to the city for one dollar. It is only in recent years that the city has realized the value of this property.

As this new park develops so do the older ones. Old bathhouses have been converted to classrooms by the Park Department which sponsors classes in cooking, painting, yoga, dance, pottery and other arts and crafts. There has been enthusiastic response to the programs. The Park Department is also expanding its plan for "Bicycle Sundays." On specified days throughout the summer major roads through some of the parks and the arboretum are closed to all motor traffic. A further

*The author would like to acknowledge the assistance of the following people in researching his essay: William E. Talley, landscape architect; Robert Chittock, landscape architect; and Mrs. Philip W. Cartwright.

step has been taken to accommodate the increasing bicycle traffic. Special lanes have been designated for bikers on Ravenna Boulevard between the campus of the University of Washington and Greenlake Park.

The lack of space in urban areas and the demand for local recreational facilities is forcing city planners and landscape architects to look to rather unlikely and unusual sites for recreational potential. Sites which have been scarred by industrial use have been leveled and turned into open spaces and parks. In Seattle such a parcel of land—the old gas plant—was found very near the city center. The design for this park is a most interesting example of landscape rehabilitation and has gained nationwide attention.

Just north of the Seattle central business district, on the shore of Lake Union, the gas plant is located on a peninsula which projects a prominent 400 feet out into the lake. For years it was considered an eyesore. Though views to the south into the city and Mount Rainier in the distance are quite desirable, the community which located itself there when the plant was in full operation faced east and west to avoid looking at the black mess of tanks, towers, and sheds. Its reputation as blight was magnified during the early stages of the environmental movement when the site was found to be seeping oil into the lake and a major spill occurred after a freeze. It took a farsighted city councilwoman to see any potential for the site as a city park. In 1962 Mrs. Myrtle Edwards convinced the city to contact the Washington Natural Gas Company and ask them if they had any plans for abandoning the old plant. According to an article in the *Seattle Times,* this was "the beginning of the agreement through which the gas company is phasing out its operations on the north shore of Lake Union and the city is acquiring it tract by tract." Total price for the 15.8 acres: $1,336,352.[1]

Immediately, numerous groups in the city came up with suggestions for appropriate uses for the park. The Floating Homes Association put in a bid for a marine park. An article in *Argus* proposed a children's playground. Another maritime park proposal included a lighthouse. One faction decided that it would be a perfect place for another arboretum. Many of these early park-like proposals were rendered impractical when numerous test pits were dug on the site to examine the structure of the soil. Actually there *was* no soil; what was there showed up quite clearly in a range of different colored layers of waste materials. The plant had created the peninsula out of oil sludge, arsenic wastes, and other residue from different refining processes. The conclusion was that without vast sums of money being spent to import earth, the site could not support much plant growth. Richard Haag, the landscape architect for the project, sees the site accommodating a different type of park than Seattle now has. He says that "The tradi-

1. *Seattle Times,* Sept. 4, 1966.

tional escape from the city into the sylvan settings of remote areas has changed for many people into a seeking of a more active encounter."[2]

Seattle does have a tradition of parks which provide for a "more active encounter." Leschi Park has already been mentioned, as has Madison. Luna Park was developed after both of the others had been destroyed by fire. Just east of Alki Beach, the city's major bathing beach, Leschi boasted of an enclosed swimming pool with heated salt water, a giant carousel, caged animal displays, exhibits from different countries and a large roller coaster. After it burned, another park with rides, Playland, was established on Bitter Lake. Because it was

Fig. V–156. Luna Park with its roller coaster and giant covered carousel.

plagued with rumors of unsafe rides and was so far from the city, Playland was eventually dismantled and replaced with a retirement home. In 1962 Seattle hosted a World's Fair and, when it was over, the city inherited another park in which were located an arena for sports, the Science Pavilion, the Play and Opera houses, and a Fun Forest and Amusement Arcade.

Haag hopes to create a new sort of amusement park utilizing unique structures on the old gas plant site. Following the new adventure playground philosophy, Haag brought children to the site from area grade and high schools and the University of Washington where he teaches. He witnessed firsthand the fascination of various age groups for the industrial machinery which had been left at the plant. Much to the dismay of those who would have leveled the plant, in his

2. *Seattle Post Intelligencer,* Aug. 5, 1971.

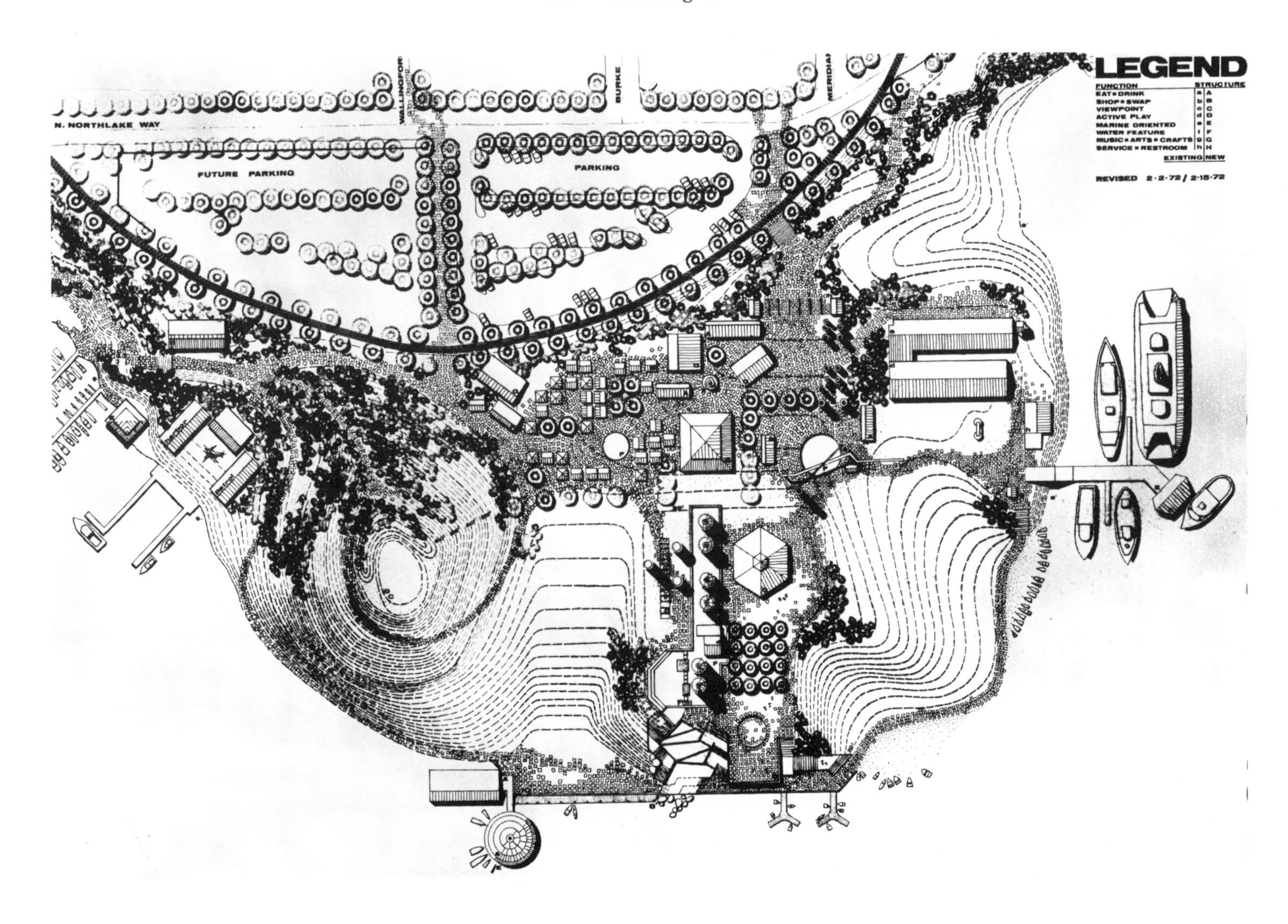

Fig. V–157. Overall master plan of the Gas Plant Park.

preliminary design schemes Haag proposed to save a majority of the structures. After many letters to the editors, public and private meetings, and revisions the city accepted the plan. Work was begun.

New obstacles are constantly appearing, including the necessity of removing over eight miles of pipe which was threaded through the site. However, work is progressing and all of the structures which were scheduled for removal have been taken off the site, leaving a few sheds and six cracking towers to become major features in later park development. The first phase is scheduled to be completed by the end of the summer of 1974. It will include picnic areas, parking facilities, a comfort station, and a children's play barn.

Already one part of the site is open, though not completed. On the west end a huge mound of dirt has appeared, compliments of a nearby highrise office tower. It will be seeded with grass and used as an observation hill with a platform at the top. Eventually there will be areas for dancing, movies, concerts, displays of all sorts, food concessions, rock festivals, and other innovative possibilities for recreation. The historic ship society will be allowed to moor its display of old ships at a special dock. They have already collected a sailing schooner and the lightship Relief. The park will be linked with other waterfront parks by a system of water taxis, and on land the Burke Gilman pedestrian trail on a nearby abandoned rail line will encourage people to walk or ride bicycles to the park. The Gas Plant will come alive at night, unlike other Seattle parks which close at dusk. So this park should provide well for those "seeking a more active encounter" within the city of Seattle.

When the Interstate highway was being planned through Seattle, the engineers encountered problems which had faced R. H. Thomson years before. A hill was in the way. Though the means by which it was accomplished were different, the solution was much the same: the hill was cut down. This brutal surgery split the city in half. Capitol and First hills, which had gradually flowed into the city before the freeway came, were now connected to it only by a series of overpasses. The natural form of the hill was erased. This scar is being healed in one small section and the connection will be restored. From the Seneca Street to the University Street Overpass, the freeway will be lidded with a park.

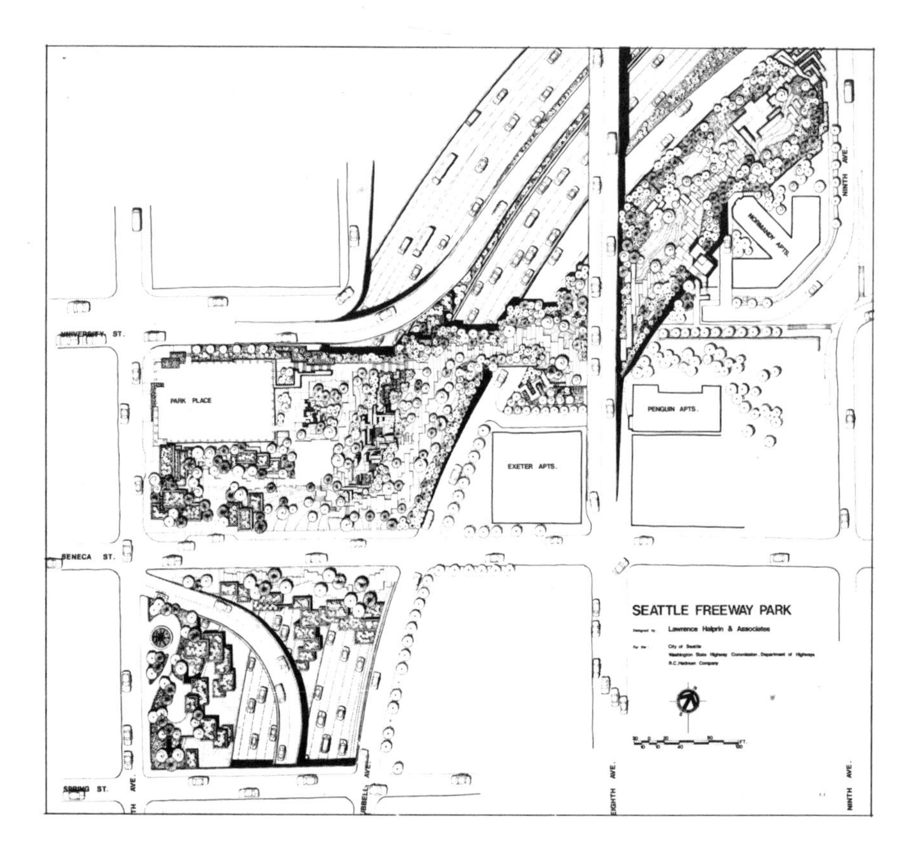

Fig. V–158. Overall plan for Seattle Freeway Park.

Fig. V–159. Central park area in Seattle Freeway Park.

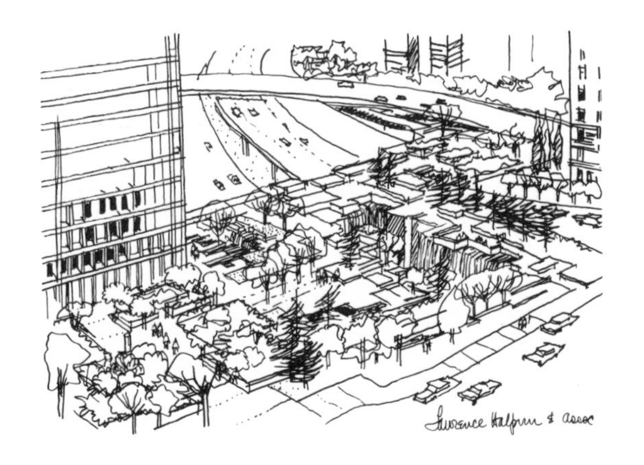

Fig. V–160. The main plaza and cascade in Seattle Freeway Park.

The idea for the freeway park arose when the State Highway Department agreed to cover the freeway there. The resulting 4.5-acre park will be the only such park in the nation. It actually is a very sophisticated roof garden; concrete I-beams will carry the park over the 120-foot wide chasm created by the freeway. Lawrence Halprin's office in San Francisco is the designer, represented in Seattle by the landscape office of Sakuma, James, Peterson. The designer in charge of the park, Angela Danadjieva Tzvetin, is also the designer of the highly successful Forecourt Fountain in Portland. Her conceptual sketches for the park indicate a continuation of the landscape theme which that office has already designed for the new executive tower located on the west end of the proposed park. Here the plaza level of the new building consists of a series of large planter boxes stacked on top of one another, creating an architectural landscape. During the summer, those boxes not filled with lawn are overflowing with colorful annuals which make a brilliant floral show.

According to the designer, she is continually changing the design of the park to include more lawn areas as she feels lawn is an important and versatile element providing year-round physical as well as visual enjoyment. Lawn adds less weight to the structure than would trees or paving. There will be plenty of trees, however, according to park plans. Water is the major feature of the park. Concrete slabs, displayed vertically, will form a canyon and, at varying heights, water will cascade over the concrete, forming thin curtains. Stairs will weave in and out of the maze of falls and short streams, and there will be opportunities for visitors to come in contact with the water. Early designs also show a window through which cars can be seen on the freeway below. A parking garage will be constructed where the lid meets the ground on the east side of the highway to help alleviate the pressure for more parking in the central business district. In this same area, along the edge of the park, there will be a small play area for children which will include a pool, benches for children-watching, as well as gardens for everyone to enjoy.

In the early development of Seattle, the opportunity for obtaining a major city park was lost. Very rarely does a city get a second chance—and never before has that chance been provided by an Interstate freeway.

Contributors

Thomas Allsopp	Landscape Architect, Seattle
C. Gilman Davis	Professor of Architecture, Portland State University
Philip Dole	Professor of Architecture, University of Oregon, Eugene
Steven Dotterrer	Architect, Portland
Virginia Guest Ferriday	Architectural Designer, Portland
Arthur A. Hart	Director, Idaho Historical Museum, Boise
Wallace Kay Huntington	Landscape Architect, Art Historian, Portland
Lewis L. McArthur	Designer and Estimator, Portland
George McMath	Architect, Portland
Thomas M. Newman	Professor of Anthropology, Portland State University
Victor Steinbrueck	Professor of Architecture, University of Washington, Seattle
Thomas Vaughan	Executive Director, Oregon Historical Society, Portland
Elisabeth Walton	Architectural Historian, Seattle
Marion Dean Ross General Consultant	Professor of Architecture, Head, Department of Art History, University of Oregon, Eugene

Illustration Credits

SYMBOLS

ISHS	Idaho State Historical Society
LC	Library of Congress
OHS	Oregon Historical Society
UW	University of Washington Libraries Special Collections
WSHS	Washington State Historical Society

I ORIGINS

I–1, I–2, OHS. I–3 National Archives. I–4 Portland Art Museum. I–5 through I–10 OHS. I–11 Portland Art Museum. I–12 Field Museum of Natural History, Chicago. I–13 American Museum of Natural History, New York. I–14 through I–16 OHS. I–17 Provincial Archives, Victoria, B.C. I–18 through I–20 OHS. I–21, I–22 LC, copies at OHS. I–23 OHS. I–24, I–25 National Park Service. I–26, I–27 LC, copies at OHS. I–28 through I–30 OHS.

II PIONEER DAYS

II–1 The Bancroft Library, University of California, Berkeley. II–2, II–3 OHS. II–4 *The American Settler's Guide,* 1882. II–5 OHS. II–6 George Hayward lithograph, photocopy at OHS. II–7 through II–9 OHS. II–10 Lt. Lorenzo Lorain photo, OHS. II–11 through II–14 OHS. II–15 A. H. Wulzen photo, OHS. II–16 through II–18 OHS. The Bancroft Library, University of California, Berkeley. II–20 Wesley Andrews photo, OHS. II–21, II–22 *Historical Atlas Map of Marion and Linn Counties, Oregon,* 1878. II–23 Fred W. Wilson Collection, OHS. II–24 OHS. II–25 Wesley Andrews photo, OHS. II–26, II–27 Polk County Historical Society. II–28 Wesley Andrews photo, OHS. II–29 through II–31 OHS. II–32 through II–34 Wesley Andrews photos, OHS. II–35 through II–43 ISHS. II–44 OHS. II–45 *Farmer's and Emigrant's Guide,* photocopy in Philip Dole collection. II–46 Philip Dole photo. II–47 HABS photo, LC, print at OHS. II–48 Philip Dole collection. II–49 Federal Writers' Project, LC, print at OHS. II–50 HABS photo, LC, print at OHS. II–51 State of Oregon Inventory of Historic Sites and Buildings. II–52 through II–55

Philip Dole photos. II–56, II–57 *History of Lane County, Oregon,* 1884. II–58 Lithograph of Joseph Sawyer farm, *Historical Atlas Map of Marion and Linn Counties, Oregon,* 1878. II–59 William Brown drawing, *Carpenter's Assistant,* 1852. II–60 *Historical Atlas Map of Marion and Linn Counties, Oregon,* 1878. II–61, II–62 Philip Dole drawings. II–63 Philip Dole photo. II–64 *Historical Atlas Map of Marion and Linn Counties, Oregon,* 1878. II–65 through II–67 Philip Dole photos. II–68 *History of Lane County, Oregon,* 1884. II–69 Philip Dole photo. II–70 Philip Dole drawing. II–71 *History of Benton County, Oregon,* 1885. II–72 OHS. II–73 Courtesy Douglas Grove. II–74 Oregon State Highway Division. II–75, II–76 Philip Dole photos. II–77 HABS photo, LC, print at OHS. II–78 Courtesy Miss Mildred Stafrin and Mrs. Andrew Irwin. II–79 Philip Dole drawing. II–80 Philip Dole collection. II–81 *Historical Atlas Map of Marion and Linn Counties, Oregon,* 1878. II–82 OHS. II–83, II–84 Sheila Finch drawings. II–85, II–86 State of Oregon Inventory of Historic Sites and Buildings. II–87 HABS photo, LC, print at OHS. II–88 State of Oregon Inventory of Historic Sites and Buildings. II–89 *Historical Atlas Map of Marion and Linn Counties, Oregon,* 1878. II–90 through II–92 Philip Dole drawings, after HABS drawings. II–93 Philip Dole photo. II–94 Courtesy Ed Johnson. II–95 State of Oregon Inventory of Historic Sites and Buildings. II–96 HABS photo, LC, print at OHS. II–97 Herb Yates photo, OHS. II–98 Photo-Art Commercial Studio photo, OHS. II–99 Philip Dole photo. II–100 Courtesy Douglas Grove. II–101 through II–105 Philip Dole drawings. II–106 John Jameson sketch, OHS. II–107 HABS photo, LC, print at OHS. II–108 Philip Dole drawing. II–109 Philip Dole photo. II–110 HABS photo, LC, print at OHS. II–111 Philip Dole collection. II–112 Philip Dole drawing. II–113 *Historical Atlas Map of Marion and Linn Counties, Oregon,* 1878. II–114 Courtesy Lyle Hadley. II–115 Philip Dole photo. II–116 *American Agriculturist.* XXIII (March, 1864), 73, Oregon State University Library. II–117, II–118 Philip Dole photos. II–119, II–120 Philip Dole drawings. II–121 Philip Dole photo. II–122, II–123 *Historical Atlas Map of Marion and Linn Counties, Oregon,* 1878. II–124 Philip Dole photo. II–125 *Historical Atlas Map of Marion and Linn Counties, Oregon,* 1878. II–126 through II–129 Philip Dole photos. II–130 Coutesy Kreta Albright. II–131 Lane County Pioneer Museum. II–132 Philip Dole collection. II–133 HABS photo, LC, print at OHS. II–134 Michael S. Thompson photo, OHS. II–135 Philip Dole drawing. II–136 Philip Dole photo. II–137 *History of Lane County, Oregon,* 1884. II–138 Philip Dole drawing. II–139 Courtesy Lena Belle Tartar. II–140 Courtesy Ruth Stoller. II–141 OHS. II–142 Lane County Pioneer Museum. II–143 Philip Dole photo. II–144 Courtesy Clyde Starr. II–145 Philip Dole photo. II–146 *History of Benton County, Oregon,* 1885. II–147 Courtesy Clyde Starr. II–148 HABS photo, LC, print at OHS. II–149 State of Oregon Inventory of Historic Sites and Buildings. II–150 Federal Writers' Project. II–151 *Historical Atlas Map of Marion and Linn Counties, Oregon,* 1878. II–152 Courtesy Mrs. Edwin Miller. II–153 HABS photo, LC, print at OHS. II–154 Federal Writers' Project. II–155 State of Oregon Inventory of Historic Sites and Buildings. II–156 *Historical Atlas Map of Marion and Linn Counties, Oregon,* 1878. II–157 OHS. II–158, II–159 State of Oregon Inventory of Historic Sites and Buildings. II–160, II–161 OHS. II–162 through II–164 Philip Dole photos. II–164 Courtesy Lester Will. II–166, II–167 HABS photos, LC, prints at OHS. II–168 Unidentified lithograph, photocopy at OHS. II–169 ISHS. II–170 OHS. II–171 Crawford photo, OHS. II–172 through II–177 OHS. II–178 Ben Maxwell Collection, Salem Public Library. II–179, II–180 OHS. II–181 Suzzallo Library, University of Washington. II–182 Photo-Art Commercial Studio photo. II–183, II–184 OHS. II–185 U. S. Forest Service photo. II–186 Lewis McArthur drawing. II–187, II–188 OHS. II–189 Alfred Edelman photo. II–190 through II–195 OHS.

III RAILROAD ERA

III–1, III–2 OHS. III–3, III–4 Virginia Guest Ferriday drawings. III–5 OHS. III–6 Virginia Guest Ferriday drawing. III–7, III–8 OHS. III–9 Suzzallo Library, University of Washington. III–10 through III–16 OHS. III–17 *Oregonian* photo, OHS. III–18 OHS. III–19 Angelus Collection, University of Oregon. III–20 through III–24 OHS. III–25 Wesley Andrews photo, OHS. III–26 *Oregon Journal* photo, OHS. III–27 Wesley Andrews photo, OHS. III–28, III–29 OHS. III–30 Wesley Andrews photo, OHS. III–31 OHS. III–32 Steven Dotterrer photo. III–33 United States Geological Survey, Montpelier Quadrangle, 1911. III–34 ISHS. III–35 through III–38 Wesley Andrews photos, OHS. III–39 Multnomah County Library. III–40 *Illustrated History of Walla Walla County,* 1901. III–41 Wesley Andrews photo, OHS. III–42 "A New Plymouth Colony," Mss 263, ISHS. III–43 "New Plymouth Colony (Ltd.)," 1896, Mss 263, ISHS. III–44 City of New Plymouth, Idaho. III–45, III–46 Wesley Andrews photos, OHS. III–47 ISHS. III–48 through III–50 OHS. III–51 through III–55 Wesley Andrews photos, OHS. III–56 *West Shore,* April 1880, OHS. III–57 *History of Lane County, Oregon,* 1884. III–58 Philip Dole drawing. III–59 Philip Dole photo. III–60 Courtesy Lena Belle Tartar. III–61 Courtesy Kreta Albright. III–62 Southern Pacific photo, OHS. III–63 Philip Dole drawing. III–64 through III–67 Philip Dole photos. III–68, III–69 Philip Dole drawings. III–70 Philip Dole photo. III–71 Southern Pacific photo, OHS. III–72 OHS. III–73 SP&S Collection, OHS. III–74 Philip Dole photo. III–75 "Halsted's Hay Fork Attachment," *American Agriculturist,* XXIV (July, 1865). III–76 Philip Dole photo. III–77, III–78 Philip Dole drawings. III–79, III–80 Philip Dole photos. III–81 Lane County Pioneer Museum. III–82 Philip Dole photo. III–83 through III–87 A. H. Gould, Specifications and drawings for A. S. Pullen, 1906, Mss 1085, OHS. III–88 *Oregon Journal* photo, OHS. III–89, III–90 Philip Dole photos. III–91 *Historical Atlas Map of Marion and Linn Counties,* 1878. III–92 through III–94 Philip Dole collection. III–95 *History of Southern Oregon . . .,* 1884. III–96 through III–101 Philip Dole photos. III–102 OHS. III–103 Courtesy Norman F. Jones. III–104 Lane County Pioneer Museum. III–105 Philip Dole photo. III–106 OHS. III–107 Southern Pacific photo, OHS. III–108

Philip Dole drawing. III–109, III–110 Philip Dole photos. III–111 M. M. Hazeltine photo, OHS. III–112 Walter Boychuk photo, OHS. III–113 OHS. III–114, III–115 Wesley Andrews photos, OHS. III–116 OHS. III–117 Francis Seufert photo, OHS. III–118 through III–121 ISHS. III–122 Francis Seufert photo, OHS. III–123, III–124 Gladys Seufert photos, OHS. III–125 Dwight Williams photo, ISHS. III–126 ISHS. III–127 Walter Boychuk photo, OHS. III–128 Alfred Edelman photo. III–129 M. M. Hazeltine photo, OHS. III–130 ISHS. III–131, III–132 Francis Seufert photos, OHS. III–133 *Oregon Journal* photo, OHS. III–134 Francis Seufert photo, OHS. III–135 C. Gilman Davis drawing. III–136 Francis Seufert photo, OHS. III–137 through III–140 John H. Lundell, Jr. photos. III–141 C. G. Davis photo. III–photo. III–142 Francis Seufert photo, OHS. III–143, III–144 *The Architecture of Country Houses,* 1851. III–145 Walter Boychuk photo, OHS. III–146 through III–148 OHS. III–149 Mirza Dickel photo. III–150 OHS. III–151 Lane County Pioneer Museum. III–152 ISHS. III–153 Mirza Dickel photo. III–154 Walter Boychuk photo, OHS. III–155 OHS. III–156 Wesley Andrews photo, OHS. III–157 OHS. III–158 Mirza Dickel photo. III–159 Seth Pope photo, OHS. III–160 Francis Lambert photo, OHS. III–161 Walter Boychuk photo, OHS. III–162 through III–168 OHS. III–169 Walter Boychuk photo. III–170 through III–175 OHS. III–176 Walter Boychuk photo, OHS. III–177 *Oregon Journal* photo, OHS. III–178 through III–181 OHS. III–182 Courtesy Douglas Grove. III–183 OHS. III–184 ISHS. III–185 Werner Lenggenhager photo, III–186 OHS. III–187 Francis Seufert photo, OHS. III–188 OHS. III–189 Minor White photo, OHS. III–190 through III–192 OHS. III–193 through III–195 Minor White photos, OHS. III–196 Walter Boychuk photo. III–197 Gladys Seufert photo, OHS. III–198 Werner Leggenhager photo. III–199 Mirza Dickel photo. III–200 OHS. III–201 Richard H. Engeman photo, OHS. III–202 Gladys Seufert photo, OHS. III–203 OHS. III–204 Gladys Seufert photo, OHS. III–205 OHS. III–206 Gladys Seufert photo, OHS. III–207 OHS. III–208 Southern Pacific photo, OHS. III–209 Francis Seufert photo, OHS. III–210, III–211 OHS. III–212 University of Oregon Library. III–213 through III–216 OHS. III–217 Robert L. Hacker photo, OHS. III–218 Mirza Dickel photo. III–219 OHS. III–220 Francis Seufert photo, OHS. III–221 OHS. III–222 Mirza Dickel photo. III–223, III–224 OHS. III–225 Gladys Seufert photo, OHS. III–226 B. A. Gifford photo, OHS. III–227 Angelus Studio photo, OHS. III–228 OHS. III–229 Edmund Y. Lee photo. III–230 through III–232 OHS. III–233 C. O. Miller photo, OHS. III–234 OHS. III–235 C. O. Miller photo, OHS. III–236 Courtesy M. D. R. III–237 Photo-Art Commercial Studio photo. III–238, III–239 OHS. III–240 B. A. Gifford photo, OHS. III–241 OHS. III–242 University of Washington. III–243 ISHS. III–244, III–245 University of Washington. III–246 Seattle Historical Society. III–247 The Bancroft Library, University of California, Berkeley. III–248 *Oregon Journal* photo. III–249 Peasley-Jourdan photo, George McMath collection. III–250 Portland Architechural Club *Yearbook,* 1910. III–251 Southern Pacific photo, OHS. III–252 George McMath collection. III–253 Angelus photo, OHS.

III–254 OHS. III–255 Angelus Collection, University of Oregon Library, Eugene. III–256 Fred De Wolfe photo. III–257, III–258 George McMath collection. III–259, III–260 OHS. III–261 Angelus photo. III–262, III–263 OHS. III–264 Angelus photo, OHS. III–265 Walter Boychuk photo, OHS. III–266, III–267 Portland Architectural Club *Yearbook,* 1910. III–268 Angelus photo, OHS. III–269 Walter Boychuk photo, OHS. III–270 Angelus photo, OHS. III–271 Alfred Monner photo, George McMath collection. III–272, III–273 OHS. III–274 B. A. Gifford photo, OHS. III–275 Portland Architectural Club catalog of 5th exhibition, 1913. III–276 through III–282 OHS. III–283 Acme photo, OHS. III–284 OHS. III–285 Wesley Andrews photo, OHS. III–286 A. M. Prentiss photo, OHS. III–287 through III–289 OHS. III–290 Southern Pacific photo, OHS. III–291 OHS. III–292 George McMath collection. III–293 through III–295 OHS. III–296 Photo-Art Commercial Studio photo, George McMath collection. III–297, III–298 OHS. III–299, III–300 George McMath photos. III–301 Angelus photo in *Pacific Architecture,* 1912. OHS. III–302 Edmund Y. Lee photo. III–303 George McMath photo. III–304 George McMath collection. III–305 OHS. III–306 Victor Steinbrueck drawing (copyrighted). III–307 UW. III–308 through III–312 Victor Steinbrueck drawings (copyrighted). III–313 Victor Steinbrueck drawing (copyrighted), UW. III–314 Victor Steinbrueck drawing (copyrighted). III–315 ISHS. III–316 Jessie Williams photo, Federal Writers' Project, OHS. III–317 Walter Boychuk photo, OHS. III–318 Alfred Monner photo, *Oregon Journal* Collection, OHS. III–319 through III–324 ISHS. III–325 through III–327 *Oregon Journal* photos, OHS. III–328 Wesley Andrews photo, OHS. III–329 *Oregon Journal* photo, OHS. III–330 through III–333 ISHS. III–334 through III–336 OHS. III–337, III–338 WSHS. III–339 ISHS. III–340 Wesley Andrews photo, OHS. III–341 through III–343 OHS. III–344 Weister photo, OHS. III–345 M. M. Hazeltine photo, OHS. III–346 OHS. III–347 through III–349 Drake photos, OHS. III–350 Kiser photo, SP&S Collection, OHS. III–351 through III–355 OHS. III–356 ISHS. III–357 Wesley Andrews photo, OHS. III–358 through III–360 OHS. III–361 National Park Service. III–362 B. A. Gifford photo, OHS. III–363 Wesley Andrews photo, OHS. III–364 WSHS. III–365 Wesley Andrews photo, OHS. III–366 through III–369 OHS. III–370, III–371 Oregon State Highway Division photos. III–372 Cronise Studio photo, Mission Mill Museum, Salem, Oregon. III–373 through III–376 OHS. III–377 Southern Pacific photo, OHS. III–378, III–379 OHS. III–380 Oregon State Highway Division photo. III–381, III–382 OHS. III–383 through III–385 Seufert photos, OHS. III–386 Wesley Andrews photo, OHS. III–387 OHS. III–388, III–389 Alfred Edelman photos. III–390 OHS. III–391 Wesley Andrews photo, OHS. III–392 through III–396 OHS. III–397 Caughey drawing, photocopy at OHS. III–398 through III–401 OHS. III–402 A. M. Prentiss photo, OHS. III–403 Herb Alden photo, *Oregon Journal* Collection, OHS. III–404 Mirza Dickel photo. III–405 OHS. III–406 *Oregon Journal* photo, OHS. III–407, III–408 OHS. III–409 Wesley Andrews photo, OHS. III–410 through III–412 OHS. III–413, III–414 Mirza Dickel photos. III–415 OHS. III–416 A. M.

Prentiss photo, OHS. III–417 OHS. III–418, III–419 UW. III–420 Seattle Park Department Photograph Collection. III–421 Thomas Allsopp drawing. III–422 OHS. III–423 *American Country Homes of Today,* 1913. III–424 Thomas Allsopp collection. III–425 Gary Savage photo. III–426 Thomas Allsopp drawing. III–427 Seattle Park Department Photograph Collection. III–428 Gary Savage photo.

IV MOTOR AGE

IV–1 American Automobile Association, 1936. IV–2 *Economic Atlas of the Pacific Northwest,* 1942. IV–3 OHS. IV–4 City of Portland photo, OHS. IV–5 Wesley Andrews photo, OHS. IV–6 *Economic Atlas of the Pacific Northwest,* 1942. IV–7 *Regional Planning, Part 1—Pacific Northwest,* 1936. IV–8 Bureau of Reclamation photo, OHS. IV–9 through IV–11 OHS. IV–12 *Oregon Journal* photo, OHS. IV–13 through IV–16 OHS. IV–17 *Oregon Journal* photo, OHS. IV–18 through IV–20 City of Portland photos, OHS. IV–21 *Oregon Journal* photo, OHS. IV–22 OHS. IV–23, IV–24 City of Portland photos, OHS. IV–25, IV–26 OHS. IV–27, IV–28 ISHS. IV–29, IV–30 OHS. IV–31 ISHS. IV–32 through IV–34 Wesley Andrews photos, OHS. IV–35, IV–36 OHS. IV–37 through IV–39 Wesley Andrews photos, OHS. IV–40 through IV–43 OHS. IV–44 Walter Boychuk photo, OHS. IV–45 Alfred Monner photo. IV–46 Hershberger photo, Portland Art Museum, IV–47, IV–48 OHS. IV–49 George McMath photo. IV–50 Walter Boychuk photo, Pietro Belluschi collection. IV–51 through IV–54 OHS. IV–55 George McMath photo. IV–56 K. E. Richardson photo. IV–57 Walter Boychuk photo, *Oregon Journal* Collection, OHS. IV–58 Erven Jourdan photo, Pietro Belluschi collection. IV–59 Dearborn-Masser photo, Pietro Belluschi collection. IV–60 Chas. R. Pearson photo, Pietro Belluschi collection. IV–61 Rondal Partridge photo, Pietro Belluschi collection. IV–62 Leonard Delano photo, OHS. IV–63 OHS. IV–64 Leonard Delano photo, Pietro Belluschi collection. IV–65 George McMath photo. IV–66, IV–67 OHS. IV–68 George McMath photo. IV–69 through IV–74 OHS. IV–75 George McMath photo. IV–76 K. E. Richardson photo. IV–77 Walter Boychuk photo, OHS. IV–78 George McMath photo. IV–79 Ezra Stoller photo, Pietro Belluschi collection. IV–80 Roger Sturtevant photo. IV–81 Roger Sturtevant photo, Pietro Belluschi collection. IV–82 G/H photo, *Oregon Journal* Collection OHS. IV–83 Roger Sturtevant photo, Pietro Belluschi collection. IV–84 K. E. Richardson photo, Pietro Belluschi collection. IV–85 Julius Shulman photo, Pietro Belluschi collection. IV–86 through IV–88 OHS. IV–89 Photo-Art Commercial Studio photo for Portland Chamber of Commerce, OHS. IV–90 through IV–101 OHS. IV–102 through IV–104 Victor Steinbrueck drawings (copyrighted). IV–105 Victor Steinbrueck drawing (copyrighted), UW. IV–106 Victor Steinbrueck drawing (copyrighted). IV–107 Victor Steinbrueck drawing (copyrighted), UW. IV–108 Victor Steinbrueck drawing (copyrighted). IV–109 through IV–113 Victor Steinbrueck drawings (copyrighted), UW. IV–114 Garrett photo, ISHS. IV–115 through IV–118 ISHS. IV–119 Wesley Andrews photo, OHS. IV–120, IV–121 Garrett photos, ISHS. IV–122 through IV–124 Wesley Andrews photos, OHS. IV–125 A. M. Prentiss photo, OHS. IV–126 B. C.

Markham photo, OHS. IV–127 OHS. IV–128 Wesley Andrews photo, OHS. IV–129 OHS. IV–130 Bell photo, OHS. IV–131 Wesley Andrews photo, OHS. IV–132 OHS. IV–133, IV–134 Wesley Andrews photos, OHS. IV–135 through IV–139 OHS. IV–140, IV–141 Wesley Andrews photos, OHS. IV–142 Courtesy Mrs. John Quincy Adams Daniels. IV–143 OHS. IV–144 through IV–148 Wesley Andrews photos, OHS. IV–149 through IV–152 OHS. IV–153 Oregon State Highway Division photo. IV–154 Federal Writers' Project photo, OHS. IV–155 United States Forest Service photo. IV–156 OHS. IV–157, IV–158 Federal Writers' Project photos, OHS. IV–159 OHS. IV–160 Sawyer's photo, OHS. IV–161, IV–162 Federal Writers' Project photos, OHS. IV–163 through IV–168 National Parks Service photos, Oregon State Highway Division. IV–169 Oregon State Highway Division photo. IV–170, IV–171 OHS. IV–172 through IV–175 Alfred Edelman photos. IV–176 through IV–178 OHS. IV–179, IV–180 Alfred Edelman photos. IV–181, IV–182 Ackroyd photos. IV–183, IV–184 Photo-Art Commercial Studio photos. IV–185 *Oregonian photo,* OHS. IV–186 Kaiser Graphic Arts photo. IV–187 Herb Alden photo, *Oregon Journal* collection, OHS. IV–188 City of Portland photo, OHS. IV–189 Seufert photo, OHS. IV–190 through IV–192 OHS. IV–193 *Oregon Journal* photo, OHS. IV–194 Walter Boychuk photo, OHS. IV–195 Federal Writers' Project photo, OHS. IV–196 Francis Seufert photo, OHS. IV–197 Angelus photo, OHS. IV–198 B. A. Gifford photo, OHS. IV–199, IV–200 OHS. IV–201 Mirza Dickel photo. IV–202 Walter Boychuk photo, OHS. IV–203 Mirza Dickel photo. IV–204 OHS. IV–205 Fred Nielsen photo. IV–206, IV–207 OHS. IV–208, IV–209 Jim Morris photos. IV–210 OHS. IV–211, IV–212 Frank I. Jones photos. IV–213, IV–214 OHS. IV–215, IV–216 Oregon State Highway Division photos. IV–217 Edmund Hayes photo. IV–218 Mirza Dickel photo. IV–219 Chas. R. Pearson photo, OHS. IV–220 Don Normark photo. IV–221 UW. IV–222, IV–223 Gary Savage photos. IV–224 Thomas Allsopp drawing. IV–225 through IV–227 Gary Savage photos.

V FREEWAY FORMS

V–1 American Automobile Association map, 1973. V–2 *The Pacific Northwest,* 1967. V–3 Richard H. Engeman photo, OHS. V–4 Francis Seufert photo, OHS. V–5 Oregon State Highway Division. V–6 *Oregon Journal* photo, OHS. V–7 Steven Dotterrer photo. V–8 Photo-Art Commercial Studio photo. V–9 OHS. V–10 Richard H. Engeman photo, OHS. V–11 *Oregon Journal* photo, OHS. V–12 OHS. V–13 *Oregon Journal* photo, OHS. V–14 Oregon State Highway Division. V–15, V–16 Steven Dotterrer photos. V–17 Richard H. Engeman photo, OHS. V–18 Portland Chamber of Commerce photo, OHS. V–19 *Oregon Journal* photo, OHS. V–20, V–21 Steven Dotterrer photos. V–22 OHS. V–23 City of Portland photo, OHS. V–24 Oregon State Highway Division photo. V–25 OHS. V–26 Oregon State Highway Division. V–27 Steven Dotterrer photo. V–28 OHS. V–29 Hershberger photo. V–30 Morley Baer photo. V–31 Ezra Stoller photo. V–32 OHS. V–33 Art Hupy photo. V–34 Putnam photo. V–35 Fred De Wolfe photo. V–36 Richard H. Engeman photo, OHS. V–37 C. Bruce Forster photo. V–38 through V–40 Photo-Art Commercial Studio photos. V–41 Wolff, Zimmer, Gunsal, Frasca. V–42, V–43 Photo-Art Commercial Studio photos. V–44 Morley Baer photo. V–45, V–46 Edmund Y. Lee photos. V–47 C. B. Harding photo. V–48 Art Hupy photo. V–49 Skidmore, Owings & Merrill. V–50 Chas. R. Pearson photo, courtesy Ed Caudero. V–51 Hugh N. Stratford photo. V–52 Allen, McMath, Hawkins. V–53, V–54 Tom Burns, Jr. photos. V–55 Dearborn-Masser photo. V–56 Courtesy C. Gilman Davis. V–57 OHS. V–58, V–59 Edmund Y. Lee photos, John Storrs collection. V–60 John Storrs collection. V–61, V–62 Western Forestry Center. V–63 OHS. V–64 Edmund Y. Lee photo. V–65 Courtesy Marvin Will, Jr. V–66, V–67 Robert Lindsay & Associates photos. V–68 Edmund Y. Lee photo. V–69 Tom Burns, Jr. photo. V–70 Edmund Y. Lee photo. V–71 Photo-Art Commercial Studio photo, OHS. V–72 Allen, McMath, Hawkins. V–73 Robert Lindsay & Associates photo. V–74 Edmund Y. Lee photo. V–75 Allen, McMath, Hawkins. V–76, V–77 Alan McCoy photos. V–78 Drake photo, OHS. V–79 Campbell, Yost, Grube & Partners. V–80 Martin, Soderstrom, Matteson. V–81 Allen, McMath, Hawkins. V–82 Alan Hicks photo. V–83 Edmund Y. Lee photo. V–84 through V–87 Victor Steinbrueck drawings (copyrighted), UW. V–88, V–89 Victor Steinbrueck drawings (copyrighted). V–90 Victor Steinbrueck drawing (copyrighted), UW. V–91 Victor Steinbrueck drawing (copyrighted). V–92, V–93 Edmund Y. Lee photos. V–94 Photo-Art Commercial Studio photo. V–95, V–96 John Storrs collection. V–97 Edmund Y. Lee photo. V–98 Art Hupy photo. V–99 Edmund Y. Lee photo. V–100 Robert Lindsay & Associates photo. V–101 Edmund Y. Lee photo. V–102 Art Hupy photo. V–103 through V–105 Edmund Y. Lee photos. V–106 Hershberger photo. V–107 Dick Farris photo. V–108, V–109 Elkhorn at Sun Valley. V–110 *Oregonian* photo, OHS. V–111 Alfred Edelman photo. V–112, V–113 *Oregonian* photos, OHS. V–114 Alfred Edelman photo. V–115 City of Portland photo. V–116 Photo-Art Commercial Studio photo. V–117, V–118 C. Bruce Forster photos. V–119 Alfred Edelman photo. V–120 Photo-Art Commercial Studio photo. V–121 Western Way Inc. V–122, V–123 Jan Fardwell photos. V–124 Alfred Monner photo for the *Oregon Journal*. V–125 OHS. V–126 C. Bruce Forster photo. V–127, V–128 Northwestern Photographics photos. V–129 Arthur Erfeldt collection. V–130, V–131 Keith Renner photos. V–132 Portland Development Commission. V–133 Edmund Y. Lee photo. V–134 Virginia Guest Ferriday photo. V–135 Portland Development Commission. V–136 Mirza Dickel photo. V–137, V–138 C. Bruce Forster photos. V–139 Fred De Wolfe photo. V–140, V–141 Jeanette Grossman photos. V–142 Arthur Erfeldt photo. V–143 Western Wood Products photo. V–144 Arthur Erfeldt drawing. V–145, V–146 Western Wood Products photos. V–147 C. Bruce Forster photo. V–148 Edmund Y. Lee photo. V–149, V–150 Western Wood Products photos. V–151, V–152 Edmund Y. Lee photos. V–153, V–154 C. Bruce Forster photos. V–155 Western Wood Products photo. V–156 UW. V–157 Richard Haag & Associates. V–158 through V–160 Lawrence Halprin & Associates.

Selected Bibliography

Additional bibliographical materials not listed here include state, county and city histories, historical atlases, promotional pamphlets, and periodicals (especially *West Shore,* published in Portland from 1875–1891).

Native Shelters

Barnett, Homer G., "The Coast Salish of British Columbia," *University of Oregon Studies in Anthropology,* No. 4. Eugene, Ore. 1955.

Cook, James, *A Voyage to the Pacific Ocean Undertaken by the Command of His Majesty for Making Discoveries in the Northern Hemisphere in the Years 1776–1780.* 3 vols., London, 1784. (Facsimile edition.)

Driver, Harold E., *Indians of North America.* Chicago, 1961.

Duff, Wilson, and H. Kew, "Anthony Island, A Home of the Haidas," *British Columbia Provincial Museum of Natural History and Anthropology Report, 1957.* Victoria, 37–64.

Kroeber, A. L., *Cultural and Natural Areas of Native North America.* Berkeley, 1953.

Lewis, M., and W. Clark, *Original Journals of the Lewis and Clark Expedition, 1804–1806,* R. G. Thwaites, ed. Vols. III and IV, Antiquarian Press, 1959. (Reprint of 1904–1905 ed., New York.)

Newman, Thomas M., *Tillamook Prehistory and Its Relation to the Northwest Coast Culture Area.* Department of Anthropology, University of Oregon, Eugene, 1959.

Olson, R. L., "Adze, Canoe and House Types of the Northwest Coast," *University of Washington Publications in Anthropology,* Vol. 4, No. 1.

Ray, Verne F. "Culture Element Distributions: The Plateau," *Anthropological Records,* Vol. 8 (1942), 99–257.

Ray, Verne F. "Lower Chinook Ethnographic Notes," *University of Washington Publications in Anthropology,* Vol. 7 (1938), 29–159.

Spencer, Robert F., Jesse D. Jennings, eds., *The Native Americans.* New York, 1965.

Steward, Julian, "Culture Element Distributions: Northern and Gosuite Shoshone," *Anthropological Records,* Vol. 8 (1943), 203–392.

Stewart, Omer C., "Culture Element Distributions: Northern Paiute," *Anthropological Records,* Vol. 4 (1939), 361–446.

Vancouver, George, *A Voyage of Discovery to the North Pacific Ocean and Round the World in which the Coast of North West America Had Been*

Carefully Examined and Accurately Surveyed. 3 vols., London, 1798. (Facsimile edition.)

Vastokas, Joan M., *Architecture of the Northwest Coast Indians of America.* Ph.D. thesis, Columbia University, 1966, reproduced by University Microfilms, Inc., Ann Arbor.

Walker, Deward E., Jr., *American Indians of Idaho.* Anthropological Monographs of the University of Idaho, No. 2, Moscow, 1971.

City and Regional Planning

For early developments the numerous city, county and state histories are valuable. Other sources include the journals of state and local historical societies, promotional pamphlets and special anniversary newspaper publications. More detailed information can be found in college theses (for which many libraries have indices) and in federal, state and local planning reports.

Battelle Memorial Institute, *The Pacific Northwest, Economic Growth in a Quality Environment.* 2 vols., Columbus, Ohio, 1967.

Budd, Ralph, "Developing the Pacific Northwest," *Civil Engineering,* Vol. 1 (September, 1931), 1071–74.

Burnham, H. J., "For the Land's Sake," *Oregon Historical Quarterly,* LIII (December, 1952), 223–34.

Butler, John S., "The Columbia River—for Irrigation and Power—Comprehensive Study by Army Engineers," *Civil Engineering,* Vol. 1 (No. 12, 1931), 1075–80.

Cohn, Edwin J., *Industry in the Pacific Northwest and the Location Theory.* New York, 1954.

Corning, Howard McKinley, *Willamette Landings: Ghost Towns of the River.* Portland, 1973.

Dick, Everett, *The Lure of the Land.* Lincoln, Neb., 1970.

Fahl, Ronald J., "S. C. Lancaster and the Columbia River Highway: Engineer as Conservationist," *Oregon Historical Quarterly,* LXXIV (June, 1973), 101–44.

Federal Writers Project, Idaho, *Idaho, A Guide in Word and Picture.* Caldwell, Idaho, 1937.

Federal Writers Project, Oregon, *Oregon, End of the Trail.* Portland, 1940, 1951.

Federal Writers Project, Washington, *The New Washington; A Guide to the Evergreen State.* Portland, 1950.

Fite, Gilbert C., *The Farmer's Frontier, 1865–1900.* New York, 1966.

Freeman, Otis W., "Human Relations to Northwest Geology," *The Scientific Monthly,* Vol. 46 (February, 1938), 150–56.

Hedges, James Blaine, *Henry Villard and the Railways of the Northwest.* New Haven, Conn., 1930.

Highsmith, Richard M., *Atlas of the Pacific Northwest.* Corvallis, Ore., 1953.

Johansen, Dorothy O. and the late Charles M. Gates, *Empire of the Columbia.* New York, 1967.

Johansen, Dorothy O., "The Role of Land Laws in the Settlement of Oregon," introduction to *Genealogical Material in Oregon Donation Land Claims,* Vol. I. Genealogical Forum of Portland, Oregon, 1957, unpaged.

McKinley, Charles, for the Northwest Regional Council, *Five Years of Planning in the Pacific Northwest.* Portland, 1939.

Meinig, Donald W., *The Great Columbia Plain; A Historical Geography, 1805–1910.* Seattle, 1968.

Meinig, Donald W., "Isaac Stevens: Practical Geographer of the Early North-

west," *Geographical Review,* Vol. 45 (November, 1955), 542–58.
Northwest Regional Council, *Economic Atlas of the Pacific Northwest,* Second Edition with Descriptive Text. Portland, 1942.
Oregonian Publishing Company, *The Oregonian's Handbook of the Pacific Northwest.* Portland, 1894.
Quiett, Glenn Chesney, *They Built the West: An Epic of Rails and Cities.* New York, London, 1934.
Russell, Pearl, "Analysis of the Pacific Railroad Reports," *Washington Historical Quarterly,* Vol. X (January, 1919), 3–16.
Scott, Harvey W., *History of the Oregon Country.* 6 vols., Cambridge, Mass., 1924.
Smalley, Eugene V., *History of the Northern Pacific Railroad.* New York, 1883.
Snyder, Eugene E., *Early Portland: Stump Town Triumphant.* Portland, 1970.
Winther, Oscar Osburn, *The Great Northwest, A History.* New York, 1947.
Wolfe, Myer R., "Urbanization in the Columbia Basin," *The Town Planning Review,* XXVIII (July, 1957), 111–30.
Wolfe, Myer R., *Towns, Time and Regionalism.* Seattle, 1963.

Buildings

Alden, C. H., "Architectural Trends in the State of Washington." *Architect and Engineer,* Vol. 132 (March, 1938), 12–31.
Alexander, Edwin P., *Down at the Depot.* New York, 1970.
American Institute of Architects, Portland, Oregon Chapter, *A Guide to Portland Architecture.* Portland, 1968.
The Architect and Engineer, Vol. LVI (March, 1919), (entire issue devoted to Portland architecture and planning).
"Architecture of the Northwest." *Architectural Record,* Vol. 113 (April, 1953), 134–46.
Barber, Joel C., "A History of the Old State Capitol Buildings of the State of Oregon." M. A. thesis, University of Oregon, June, 1960.
Barker, Burt Brown, compiler, *The Dr. John McLouglin House; A National Monument.* Oregon City, Ore., 1949.
Bean, Margaret, *Campbell House.* [Spokane?], 1965.
Cheney, Charles H., "The Work of Albert E. Doyle, Architect of Portland, Oregon." *The Architect and Engineer,* Vol. LVIII (July, 1919), 39–86.
Cook, Jimmie Jean, *"Particular Friend, Penn's Cove."* Coupeville, 1973.
Croly, Herbert D., "Portland, Oregon, the Transformation of the City from an Architectural & Social Viewpoint." *Architectural Record,* Vol. XXI (June, 1912), 591–607.
Culp, Edwin D., *Stations West.* Caldwell, Idaho, 1972.
Daughters of the American Revolution, Oregon Society of, *Oregon Historic Landmarks.* 1957.
Daughters of the American Revolution, Oregon Society of, *Oregon Historic Landmarks: Eastern Oregon.* 1959.
Daughters of the American Revolution, Oregon Society of, *Oregon Historic Landmarks: Oregon Coast.* 1966.
Daughters of the American Revolution, Oregon Society of, *Oregon Historic Landmarks: Willamette Valley.* Portland, 1963.
Daughters of the American Revolution, Susannah Lee Barlow Chapter of Clackamas County, *Historic Homes of Clackamas County, Oregon.* Oregon City, 1947.
Dole, Philip, "The Calef Farm: Region and Style in Oregon." *Journal of the*

Society of Architectural Historians, Vol. 23 (December, 1964), 200–209.

Dole, Philip, "Farmhouse and Barn in Early Lane County." *Lane County Historian,* Vol. X (August, 1965), 23–43.

Dorson, Richard M., editor, *Folklore and Folklife.* Chicago, 1972.

Duniway, David C., *Salem; State Centennial Guide, 1859–1959.* Salem, 1959.

Elliott, H. N., editor, *History of Idaho Territory.* San Francisco, 1884.

Federal Writers' Project, Oregon. *The Builders of Timberline Lodge.* Portland, 1937.

Federal Writers' Project, Oregon, *Oregon, End of the Trail.* Portland, 1940.

Federal Writers' Project, Washington, *Washington: A Guide to the Evergreen State.* Portland, 1941. Especially 154–58.

Finch, Sheila Ann, "The Bybee Houses and the Appearance of the Greek Revival in Oregon." M. A. thesis, University of Oregon, 1970.

Fowler, Constance, *The Old Days In and Near Salem.* Seattle, 1940.

Francaviglia, Richard V., "Western American Barns: Architectural Form and Climatic Considerations." Association of Pacific Coast Geographers *Yearbook,* Vol. 34, 1972.

Friedman, Ralph, *Oregon for the Curious.* Portland, 1966 (useful for directions and locations).

Garth, Thomas R., Jr., "Early Architecture in the Northwest." *Pacific Northwest Quarterly,* Vol. XXXVIII (July, 1947), Seattle, 215–32.

Grieff, Constance M., *Lost America—Mississippi to Pacific.* Vol. II, Princeton, N. J., 1972.

Hale, Richard W., Jr., "The French Side of the 'Log Cabin Myth.'" *Massachusetts Historical Society Proceedings,* Vol. LXXII (October, 1957–December, 1960), 118–25.

Hamlin, Talbot, *Greek Revival Architecture in America.* New York, 1964.

Harpham, Josephine Evans, *Doorways into History.* Eugene, 1966.

Hart, Arthur A., "Architectural Styles in Idaho: A Rich Harvest." *Idaho Yesterdays,* Vol. 16, No. 4, 2–9.

Hecker, Anne, "The Wood Tradition of the Northwest." *AIA Journal,* Vol. XLIX (June, 1968), 106–10.

Historic American Buildings Survey, ed., *Historic American Buildings Survey Catalog.* Washington, U. S. Government Printing Office, 1941. (With each completed record there is a page of data, giving the present ownership, condition, name of builder, and date of building where known. Reproductions available from the Library of Congress.)

Hitchcock, Russell, "An Eastern Critic Looks at Western Architecture." *California Arts and Architecture,* December, 1940, 21–23, 40, 41.

Hosfield, John D., "A Study of the Architecture of Pietro Belluschi: Oregon 1925–50." M. A. thesis, University of Oregon, June, 1960.

Hume, M., compiler, *Seattle Architecturally 1902.* Seattle, circa 1901.

Idaho State Historical Society, "Architecturally Significant and Historic Buildings of Boise, Idaho." *Information Sheets* Nos. 1–12, 1970–71.

Jones, Edward Gardner, editor. *The Oregonian's Handbook of the Pacific Northwest.* Portland, circa 1894.

Kalez, Jay J., *Saga of a Western Town—Spokane.* Spokane, 1972.

Knuth, Priscilla, *"Picturesque" Frontier: The Army's Fort Dalles.* Portland 1968.

Kouwenhoven, John A., *Made in America.* Newton Center, Mass., 1948.

Lassiter, D. L., "Architect E. H. Fischer." Paper, School of Architecture Library, University of Washington.

Lomax, Alfred L., *Later Woolen Mills in Oregon.* Portland, 1974.

Lomax, Alfred L. *Pioneer Woolen Mills in Oregon*. Portland, 1941.
Lynes, Russell, *The Taste Makers.* New York, 1949.
Maas, John, *The Victorian Home in America*. New York, 1972.
McDonald, Lucile, and Werner Lenggenhagger, *The Look of Old Time Washington.* Seattle, 1971.
McDonald, Lucile, *Where the Washingtonians Lived.* Seattle, 1969.
McMath, George A., "The Mess that is Man-Made Portland." *Greater Portland Commerce,* Vol. 51 (Aug. 4, 1967), 8–11, 28–30.
Marlitt, Richard, *Nineteenth Street,* Portland, 1968.
Mattila, Walter, "The Pioneer Finnish Home." *FinnAm Newsletter,* Portland, Finnish-American Society of the West, Vol. 6 (May, 1971).
Mitchell, Claire, *Walla Walla Remembers.* 1969.
"The National Register of Historic Places." *Idaho Yesterdays,* Vol. 17, No. 4, 14–21.
Nelson, Lee H., "Architects of Oregon: Piper and Williams." *The Call Number,* University of Oregon, Vol. 20 (Spring, 1959), 4–6.
Nelson, Lee H., *A Century of Oregon Covered Bridges, 1851–1952*. Portland, 1960.
Nelson, Lee H., "White, Furness, McNally and the Capitol National Bank of Salem, Oregon." *Journal of the Society of Architectural Historians,* Vol. XIXXIX (May, 1960), 57–61.
Newspaper Syndicate, *Residential Portland,* 1911. Portland, 1911.
Pevsner, Nikolaus, *Pioneers of Modern Design*. New York, 1949.
Portland Architectural Club, *Yearbook*. Portland, 1908, 1909, 1910, 1913.
Render, Lorne E., "Gothic Revival Churches on the West Coast before 1890." M. A. thesis, University of Oregon, June, 1967.
Report of the Lewis and Clark Centennial Exposition Commission. Salem, Oregon, 1906.
Robinson, Willard B., "Northwest Architecture, 1843–1893." Thesis, The Rice Institute, April, 1960. Film #117 University of Idaho Library.
Ross, Marion Dean, "The 'Attainment and Restraint' of Pietro Belluschi." *AIA Journal,* Vol. 58 (July, 1972), 17–24.
Ross, Marion Dean, "Architecture in Oregon 1845–1895." *Oregon Historical Quarterly*. Vol. LVII (March, 1956), 33–64.
Ross, Marion Dean, "Architecture in Oregon One Hundred Years Ago." *Pacific Architect and Builder*, Vol. 65 (May, 1959), 22–23, 43–45.
Ross, Marion Dean, *A Century of Architecture in Oregon, 1859–1959*. Portland, 1959.
Ross, Marion Dean, "Jacksonville, an Oregon Gold-Rush Town." *Journal of the Society of Architectural Historians*, Vol. XII (December, 1953), 19–25.
Ross, Marion Dean, "The Museum Building as a Work of Art." *Notes on the Collections*, No. 7, Portland Art Museum, Portland, Oregon, 1967.
Ross, Marion Dean, "One Hundred Twenty-Five Years of Building." *AIA Journal*, Vol. XLIX (June, 1968), 120–26, 172, 178–86.
Ross, Marion Dean and Jack E. Boucher, "Jacksonville in HABS Color." *Historic Preservation*, Vol. 24 (April–June, 1972), 26–29.
Seattle Architectural Club, *Yearbook*. Seattle, 1910.
Seattle of Today, Architecturally. Sanders and Lawton publishers, Seattle, early 1900s.
Sias, Patricia, "An Examination of Influences on Selected Tacoma Architecture 1890–1914." M. A. thesis, University of Puget Sound, 1971.
Simpson, Jerry, *Victorian Port Townsend*. 1961.
Spokane Metropolitan Area Transportation Study. Spokane, 1968.

Statewide Inventory of Historic Sites and Buildings. An Inventory of Oregon historic sites, buildings, structures, districts, and objects, which provides data essential to state land use planning and offers the citizen valuable information serving his individual interest. To be published for public use in early 1975.
Stave, Thomas and Roland Colciander, *Spokane Sketchbook. Seattle,* 1974.
Steinbrueck, Victor, *A Century of Seattle Architecture.* Seattle, 1953.
Steinbrueck, Victor, *A Guide to Seattle Architecture.* 1850–1953. Seattle, 1953.
Steinbrueck, Victor, *Market Sketchbook.* Seattle, 1968.
Steinbrueck, Victor, *Seattle Cityscape.* Seattle, 1962.
Steinbrueck, Victor, *Seattle Cityscape #2.* Seattle, 1973.
Stevenson, Jim, *Seattle Firehouses of the Horse-Drawn and Early Motor Era.* 1972.
Stubblebine, Jo, editor, *The Northwest Architecture of Pietro Belluschi.* New York, 1953.
Sweatt, Robert C., "The Architecture of the Pacific Northwest." *Architectural Record,* Vol. XXVI (September, 1909), 167–71.
The 'Uncommon' Schools, Klickitat County P. U. D. 1971–72 *Annual Report.*
Vaughan, Thomas and George McMath, *A Century of Portland Architecture.* Portland, 1969. 2nd edition.
Walton, Elisabeth, "A Note on William W. Piper and Academy Architecture in Oregon in the 19th Century." *Journal of the Society of Architectural Historians,* Vol. XXXII (October, 1973), 231–38.
Withey, Henry F. and Elsie Rathburn, *Biographical Dictionary of American Architects (Deceased).* Los Angeles, 1956.
Wolfe, Myer. *Towns, Time, and Regionalism.* [Seattle, 1963.]
Whiffen, Marcus, *American Architecture Since 1780—A Guide to the Styles.* Cambridge, Mass., 1969.

Parks and Gardens

Beaux Arts Society, *Homes and Gardens of the Pacific Northwest.*
Berral, Julia S., *The Garden.* New York, 1966.
Calvin, Brenda, *Land and Landscape.* London, 1970.
Collins, Alf., "Parks, Art of Cluttered Confusion or . . . ," *Environmental Design West,* 1970.
Downing, A. J., *A Treatise on the Theory and Practice of Landscape Architecture.* New York, 1853.
Dutton, Joan P., *Enjoying America's Gardens.* Reynal and Company Inc., 1958.
Fein, Albert, *Frederick Law Olmsted and the American Environmental Tradition.* New York, 1972.
Fitch, James M. and F. F. Rockwell, *Treasury of American Gardens.* New York, 1956.
Garden Club of America Yearbook, 1930.
Kassler, Elizabeth B., *Modern Gardens and the Landscape.* New York, 1964.
Maas, John, *The Victorian Home in America.* New York, 1972.
Ortloff, H. Stuart, *The Book of Landscape Design.* New York, 1959.
Perkins, Mrs. J. C., "Quiet Gardens in the Northwest," *House and Garden* (June, 1927), 63–67.
Pierce, I., "Three Years of Garden Making in the Northwest," *American Home* (March, 1943), 22–23.
Pratt, Mrs. Frank J. Jr., "Pioneer Gardens," *Little Gardens* (Fall, 1934).
Seattle Post-Intelligencer, "Visit These Outstanding Northwest Gardens," July 2, 1971.

Shelton, Louise, *Beautiful Gardens in America.* New York, 1916.

Sherwood, Don, "A History of Seattle Parks," continuing project sponsored by the Seattle Park Department.

Tacoma Garden Club Annual Meeting booklet published with illustrations of Tacoma's great gardens, 1930.

Tunnard, Christopher, *Gardens in the Modern Landscape.* New York, 1948.

Washington State Parks and Recreation Commission, *Statewide Plan for State Parks,* 1965.

Index